Kirklees COUNCIL

Culture & Leisure Services
Red Doles Lane
Huddersfield, West Yorks HD2 1YF

This book should be returned on or before the latest date stamped below. *Fines are charged if the item is late.*

'Some   ading
them.   ever
read.   huge
demaı   ı, this
book i   men
and w   *ınthly*

'The ı   their
loved   *graph*

'One t   rmity
of sen   ѵo of
the mı   .early
a cent   *Times*

'Captı   ;et of
soldie   *News*

'An eı   ırs to
Afgha   *Mail*

'They   :lling
insigh

You may renew this loan for a further period by phone, letter, personal visit or at www.kirklees.gov.uk/libraries, provided that the book is not required by another reader.

ₔ Post

NO MORE THAN THREE RENEWALS ARE PERMITTED

'With   s and
Afgha   three
years reading 30,000 of them.'   *The Mirror*

'A poignant and sometimes heartbreaking book.'   *The Sun*

'A touching collection.'   *Daily Mail*

'A very moving book.'   *ey Daily Telegraph*

'Book of the month.'   *Britain at War*

D1340752

'For author Siân Price this ha   ving into the lives of men who wrote these very personal goodbyes.'   *Daily Record*

'An aspect of war never fully looked at before, the farewell letter writing by troops is fascinatingly and movingly explored.'   *Northern Echo*

~ ~

If You're Reading This...

LAST LETTERS FROM THE FRONT LINE

~ ~

SIÂN PRICE

Foreword by Saul Kelly

FRONTLINE BOOKS, LONDON

FRONTLINE BOOKS, LONDON

If You're Reading This: Last Letters from the Front Line

First published in 2011 by Frontline Books, an imprint of
Pen & Sword Books Limited, 47 Church Street, Barnsley, S. Yorkshire, S70 2AS
www.frontline-books.com

This paperback edition published in 2014 by Frontline Books

ISBN: 978-1-84832-740-5

For more information on our books, please visit
www.frontline-books.com,
email info@frontline-books.com
or write to us at the above address.

Typeset by JCS Publishing Services Ltd, www.jcs-publishing.co.uk
Printed in Great Britain by CPI Group (UK) Ltd, Croydon, CR0 4YY

~ ~

CONTENTS

~ ~

To the fallen, and those left behind

~ ~

ILLUSTRATIONS

~ ~

ACKNOWLEDGEMENTS

This book has its origins in a BBC Radio 4 documentary of the same name, and I owe Siobhan McClelland a huge debt as that programme was her original idea. Due to a car accident she was unable to make the programme, which was a topic with deep significance to her. Her uncle had penned such a letter before serving in Northern Ireland. Producing that programme took me on a journey into the hearts and minds of some of the soldiers, sailors and airmen of the past three hundred years.

Farewell letters have become a subject that has consumed over three years of my life. I have scoured the world's archives in search of letters from various conflicts and different nationalities, spoken to thousands of former servicemen and women and heard the memories and stories of bereaved families. In reading whole collections of letters I have found myself becoming incredibly close to those people, privy to intensely private thoughts and emotions. I hope I have done justice to all of the men and women in this book and paid some small tribute to those who pay the ultimate sacrifice in war.

I am deeply indebted to a number of people, and thank everyone who has contributed to this book – but particularly wish to thank Gareth Glover, Don Evans, Susie Fleming, Rod Suddaby and staff at Imperial War Museums; Natalia Dannenberg, Alastair Massie at the National Army Museum; Takeshi Kawatoko, Elsie O'Dell, Sarah Holmes, David Devenny, Tristram Clarke at the National Archives of Scotland; Lisa and Robert Foster, Effie Karageorgos, Marie Perry, Annie Caitlin, BFBS Television & Radio, SSAFA, the RAF Benevolent Fund, the Royal British Legion, Jane Ellison at the BBC and Terry Lewis at Tinderbox. I would also like to thank Michael Leventhal at Frontline Books and project manager Jessica Cuthbert-Smith for their patience and encouragement throughout.

Finally, I want to thank friends, family and loved ones who have joined me on this often-emotional ride – providing support, enthusiastic encouragement and a running reminder on looming deadlines!

~ ~

AUTHOR'S NOTE

The author gratefully acknowledges the permission granted to reproduce the copyright material in this book. Every effort has been made to trace copyright holders and to obtain their permission for the use of copyright material. The author apologises for any errors or omissions and would be grateful if notified of any corrections. In a few cases it has not been possible to locate living descendants and we would welcome correspondence with information.

In quoting primary sources I have corrected some spelling and modernised punctuation in some places for ease of reading.

~   ~

FOREWORD

FOR SEVERAL YEARS AN impromptu military ceremony was held nearly every week near a busy roundabout on the A417 outside the UK Defence Academy at Shrivenham, Wiltshire, in the south-west of England. A small group of people from all backgrounds – civilians, serving military personnel and representatives from the local branch of the British Legion – gathered on a dusty verge to honour the passing of the cortèges from RAF Lyneham, near Wooton Bassett, to the Coroner's Office in Oxford. The black hearses carried the flag-mantled coffins of the young men and women who had died serving their country fighting the Taliban in Afghanistan. Such a regular sight in the English countryside, breaking the comparatively mundane routine of daily life, cannot but prompt thoughts about who these young men and women were, what they had witnessed and achieved in their short lives and how their families and the nation were coping with their loss. Sadness can be mixed with anger at the cost and reasons for the war in which they lost their lives. However, this is more likely to be a civilian than a military response, since modern British service personnel have a professional ethos and way of thinking which allows them to cope with casualties and to continue to perform what they see as their 'job'. This does not mean that they forget their fallen colleagues. On the contrary: they remember them, and their predecessors, in a series of memorial services held on campaign or in the annual Remembrance Day services held at every military establish-ment, as well as in towns and cities up and down the land. The families of the fallen also remember them in their own private ways. Central to this personal remembrance are photographs, favourite objects and letters. The last can be the most evocative since they represent the final thoughts of a lost loved one. They become treasured possessions, read and re-read as often as need be, by way of comfort but above all remembrance of the lost family members. In the internet age these memories can be shared on memorial sites, and added to. These have become the latest ways of dealing with grief but also perpetuating memory. As generations pass, memories will fade unless the fallen are immortalised.

The value of this book is that it revives the memories of past generations of young men who went to the wars, from the Napoleonic to Afghanistan, through their own words, expressed in their last letters home to their loved ones. In doing so, Siân Price seeks to pay tribute to all those who made the 'ultimate sacrifice' by laying down their lives in war. It is always the sign of a good book when the reader is prompted to reconsider previous assumptions about a subject. Siân Price's collection of last letters does that. She makes it clear that these letters were written for a variety of reasons. There was a fundamental need to say a last goodbye to family and friends, to express love and gratitude, to reassure, to reconcile, to comfort and to make practical arrangements in the event of death. But Siân Price also shows men's motivation for going to war, and how this has subtly changed over the centuries. Between the nineteenth and twenty-first centuries, the readiness to die for 'Heaven, Home and Mother' was replaced by 'mateship' and more recently by 'just doing a job'. The last is testimony to the professional nature of the modern British armed forces, as opposed to the vast conscript armies who fought the world wars, and the slum-dwellers who fought Queen Victoria's wars. There are certain constant themes: disgust and disillusionment with politicians and 'red-tabs', or the higher command; the feeling of self-sacrifice for a better future; cheerfulness in the face of adversity and possible death; above all, black humour. These last letters show that these young men wanted their families and friends to understand their personal experiences of war.

For this reader, the most poignant chapters are on Iraq and Afghanistan. Why should this be? Perhaps because I know, or have known, some of the men who have fought and are fighting these wars. I have taught them, talked with them, laughed with them and tried to help them become educated soldiers, sailors and airmen. Nor should we forget the women. Increasing numbers of young women are serving in the armed services, and their experiences of war will be chronicled in the future. Women are not bystanders in war. Surely the most vivid portraits in this book are of the ex-Empress Eugenie of France visiting the site of her son's death on active service against the Zulus in South Africa, and of Melissa, the widow of PFC Jesse Givens, killed in Iraq on 1 May 2003. The memory of Jesse's letters to his unborn son 'Bean' will stay with me for a long time.

Saul Kelly

~ ~

Introduction

Anyone who writes one of these letters is basically saying I'm very sorry I'm not there. I wish I still was.[1]

THERE WERE FOUR OF them on the train. No older than eighteen, they huddled in the passageway knocking back cans of lager and joking boisterously about what lay ahead. It transpired these boys were young soldiers heading back to barracks and facing deployment to Afghanistan. In bullish mood, they started to talk about the adrenalin-charged risks of combat. 'It's just not going to happen to me is it?' they all agreed. I hope it did not. I also hope that they followed the advice routinely given to soldiers deploying today, to write a farewell letter to their loved ones.

Military farewell letters have a long history, no doubt coinciding with the rise of literacy. Throughout history they have represented the fundamental human need to say goodbye a final time when going into a situation from which they may never return. Regardless of rank, nationality, age or sex, farewell letters have a universality that perhaps no other type of writing has. The commonality of purpose, motivation and sentiment underlines the fact that soldiers are not faceless automatons. Accidents of birth determine sides, affiliations and beliefs. The farewell letter humanises and equalises.

During the course of writing this book, I have talked to countless families and service people about the emotions of both reading and writing a farewell letter. Fundamentally they have all told me the same story. Farewell letters force us to confront what we dare not think about: death and mortality. More than that, at their heart, they contain the simplest expression of what underpins humanity: love and gratitude.

These are not easy letters to write. Some people have broken down while writing them, and others have produced copious drafts until they are satisfied with the words. The profound emotions poured forth into these letters almost seem at odds with the archetypal idea of the dispassionate, focused service-man/woman. One military chaplain explained this dichotomy with a story of the Spartans. Before combat, they would make two bracelets from green twigs.

On one they would inscribe the word 'wine', to represent their role as farmer, son, husband, lover. Inscribed on the other was the word 'blood'. The 'wine' bracelet was left in a basket and the 'blood' bracelet worn into battle. Soldiers in battle, mere men at home; this separation of worlds is achingly clear in farewell letters written by people who have to compartmentalise their emotions and keep them in check in order to be able to undertake perhaps the toughest, riskiest job in the world. 'They've all been instilled with the "it'll never happen to me" attitude. A farewell letter could be construed as a survival of the mind technique,' explained one soldier's girlfriend.

Where possible in the book I have tried to use the 'in the event of my death' letter. I have also included many that simply read as final farewells. Whether a few sentences of foreboding within a generally chirpy letter home or an annotated and personalised will, they are no less moving and treasured. Indeed, throughout history, the farewell letter has come in a variety of forms that continue to change in our multimedia world. Some have been the frontispiece to meticulous diaries of wartime service and some have been miniature, almost microscopic, words carefully written on tiny pieces of paper. One farewell from Gallipoli, discovered in an Australian archive, was even in code! Written on a card five centimetres square, it comprised a strange series of capital letters, dots and Xs that were decoded as the mournful 'If I get killed.'[2]

Some letters have been written as the person lay mortally wounded, and are chillingly stained with fragments of mud, smears of sweat and unsettling bloodstains. Many men wrote letters on the eve of a great charge or battle: a cathartic expression of impending doom. In many instances, dying men have dictated epitaphs for a colleague to transcribe and pass on, along with their deeply moving condolences. In their last breaths it was a way of, once again, being at home with loved ones. Others letters have been written with a macabre inevitability in mind: the countless soldiers who have experienced premonitions of their death, kamikaze pilots and condemned prisoners. 'I am perfectly tranquil in mind and prepared for my fate,'[3] wrote John Andre on the eve of his execution for spying during the American Revolution.

It is impossible to know for certain how long these types of letters have been written, although a formalised postal service to troops in battle has its roots in the early seventeenth century. One of the earliest examples I discovered dated from 1745, written a few hours after the Battle of Fontenoy during the War of Austrian Succession. Phil Browne confided to his brother,

> it is very uncertain whether I may live to see out the day or the sun rising tomorrow morning . . . I have a calm mind & don't fear anything from the consequences of death being perfectly resigned to the will of the great & Incomprehensible Being who . . . hath a just right to recall it when & in what manner he pleases . . .[4]

Over the centuries, farewell letters have had a poignant consistency as well as marked differences and I have tried to tease these out in each chapter. They range from the hauntingly romantic and desperately sad to the rip-roaringly comedic or angrily polemic. 'Dear Mum and Dad. You were right. I should have gone to college' was one bitter farewell from Iraq. Meanwhile many letters – particularly those of the Victorian period, the stiff upper lips resolute unto death – have been staunchly unsentimental and matter of fact. A necessary practicality in the uncertain arenas of war.

One constant theme of all letters over the centuries has been the expression of love for family. The heartfelt and heartbreaking 'I will always love you' has the power to encapsulate a lifetime of memories in one simple line. The religiosity of letters has mirrored the faith of wider societies through history, although letters from the American Civil War and the First World War stand out for their religious fervour. In their last moments, many secularists have found hope and comfort in faith: 'If we meet never again on earth, we shall meet in Heaven' has been the optimistic message of countless farewell letters.

It has not only been recent conflicts that have prompted soldiers to vent their vitriolic spleen; political views suffused farewell letters of the Napoleonic and American Civil Wars. Haunting reproaches about traitors and poor leadership reverberate loudly across the centuries. In the past, politics was bound up in the 'glory' of dying in battle – a bloodthirsty rejoicing in self-sacrifice on the altar of a country or an ideal. ''Tis glorious to die for one's country and in defence of innocent girls and women from the fangs of the lecherous Northern hirelings,'[5] wrote William Plane during the American Civil War. Today those words and language have virtually disappeared. Pride in the role and absolute patriotism are as strong as ever, but contemporary farewell letters reiterate a love for the job, rather than the fight. 'I will do what is required of me' has become a modern soldier's mantra.

Finally, farewell letters are unavoidably confessional. They represent the last message from that person, and become his or her legacy. The enduring desire to resolve issues, explain behaviours and feelings bursts through many of them. Farewell letters have been used to confess affairs, offer advice to avoid the repetition of mistakes, and to divulge long-hidden secrets. One of the most extraordinary examples came in a father's astonishingly candid farewell to his children during the Second World War. Private Frank Lee was having marital difficulties when he left for war in 1942 as a medic.

There is a war on, boats are being torpedoed, bombs etc & in addition there are all the probable dangers of war on land & from the Air. Maybe I shall never see either of you again nor hear your dear voices, but this letter, may, if I fail to return, bring us near together once again – across the seas, the years and may even be across the void of death. Yet, if & when you read this letter, which you are both too young to understand as yet, try to remember that your Daddy loves you & will love you, forever and always. You are always in my mind and I can truly say that my only real worry in this war, is that I shall never see you again, or know what you will grow up to be like . . . I married your Mother 8 years ago tomorrow . . . I believe she loved me & I did love her & in a way I still do, although I have small cause to do so now . . . She wrote, said she did not care for me & had found someone who loved her & who she loved. I came home a fortnight ago on leave. He had gone to Cheshire, but was writing to her. I found part of one of his letters. She was very cold & snappy with me, going out of her way to make me miserable . . . I threatened to buff him but she said she would go out with him in any case & shoved his photo under my nose. That's your Mother, who has ruined my home & happiness. I wish it could be different but it can't be. I pray I may get safely home to you & do for you what I know a woman who is so unfaithful to her home & husband never will or can do.[6]

Ultimately Frank survived and divorced his wife.

All farewell letters have been written at very specific times in people's lives, and are intrinsically linked to their situation at the time. This is so much so that many men have never re-read the words they wrote. One Welsh Guardsman recalled with some embarrassment how he had tucked away his farewell letter: 'To me it would be like opening a Pandora's Box to see what I wrote back then.' Many servicemen/women who have written a farewell letter and then survived have ripped it up or burned it at the end of their service. Far from false machismo, this act seems to embody the need for closure on a finely tuned chapter in their lives; a desire to never relive their darkest moments. One soldier explained, 'We all know we could pay the ultimate sacrifice, it's just what you have to do,' and burned his letter when he returned safely from Iraq. One army mother recalled her reaction when her son informed her he had written a letter and entrusted it to his godparent: 'It's just that awful mixture of being practical and accepting the risks involved, but the sentimentality that comes with it. Part of the conversation we had was spent looking one another in the eye and saying I love you. A farewell letter is the same.'

That there is an understandable unwillingness to share private farewell letters from the most current conflicts has become apparent while writing this book. Again this is in contrast with the First and Second World Wars, where mothers often published farewell letters from their sons for the world to read and learn lessons. One soldier left a note that his farewell letter should be published to 'bring home to succeeding generations the intensity of feeling engendered amongst the fighting forces when faced with an action which all realised might well result in heavy casualties. This letter may be typical of hundreds and indeed thousands left behind . . . To me this is the most sacred relic that I have of these war-torn days.'[7] For many of the bereft there is catharsis in sharing these most private documents with a wider audience. For others, just talking about the farewell letter is painful and difficult. No doubt it will take the passage of time and history before many contemporary farewell letters will be shared with the historian and wider audience. To read these letters is to peel back the layers of a person to their very core: deeply personal and intense. It is no surprise many families have no desire to share the contents.

Letters become treasured possessions, providing enduring comfort in times of loss. Their survival is testament to their importance, and many have been bequeathed as heirlooms through several generations or entrusted to archives. The legacy of such letters cannot be underestimated. They provide a snapshot, bearing witness to an individual under extreme circumstances, and offering an insight into the emotions felt when staring death squarely in the face.

The reaction of families to these priceless letters has remained unchanged throughout history. One widow of a Vietnam veteran told me how her husband's letter 'sustains those of us left behind, for through the letter, love lingers'. Contemporarily, I have talked to recipients who re-read their letter every day, those who sleep with the folded letter next to their bed, those whose letter is virtually falling apart through so much handling, and those who have tucked it away, safe in the knowledge of its presence, but not drawn to read it frequently. Moreover, it has often taken people a long time to steel themselves to open and read their letter. They represent finality as well as enduring love. When wives, mothers, children and lovers touch that letter, they are touching the page their loved one once handled. When they read the words, they can imagine their loved one speaking it out loud. Farewell letters are a last tragic link with a person and reanimate the ghosts of the fallen. Be it a letter from the eighteenth century or the twenty-first, these voices from beyond the grave still speak eloquently and forcefully of the tragedy of war.

In the pain of death, spoken words often fail.

Words written down, last forever.

~ 1 ~

AT WAR WITH FRANCE

I only send these few lines written according to your desire in hurry & confusion to assure you that in spite of your forgetfulness, my affection for you is as strong as ever, & that if a cannon ball hits me tomorrow I believe I shall die thinking of you.[1]

BETWEEN 1793 AND 1815, Britain was Napoleon's fiercest opponent on land and sea. He had declared he must 'destroy the English monarchy'[2] and claim the island nation as French territory. This was no sustained battle. The French Revolution of 1789 was the touch-paper that sparked the revolutionary wars of 1793 to 1802. Temporary peace following the Treaty of Amiens in 1802 was cause for celebration, but did not last. Between 1803 and 1805 Britain was under constant threat of French assault. The Peninsular War began with the French invasion of Spain in 1807, and lasted until 1814. There then followed the Hundred Days of 1815 when Napoleon escaped from exile in Elba. Battles such as Trafalgar, Badajoz, Vimeiro and Waterloo became – and remain – etched in the public consciousness for their immense loss of life and sheer, chaotic bloodiness. It was a period of distinctly mobile warfare as Britain and ever-changing coalitions fought to stave off Napoleon's self-proclaimed desire to 'rule the world'.[3] This was fighting on an unprecedented scale, across Europe, South America, the Caribbean and the East Indies.

France under Napoleon was in pursuit of expansion and conquest rather than peace. Achieving a French European order was seen as a progressive self-affirmation for the country and Napoleon revelled in the glory of battle to achieve what he believed to be the greater good for the world. In short, there was a culture of war running through this period, as unbridled battle bred more battles, and victory bred avarice.

In 1793, the British Army was 15,000 strong at home, with a further 30,000 troops abroad. Bills were passed to raise a further 25,000 soldiers and 19,000 militia,[4] as well as drafting in troops from Hanover. By the time of the Napoleonic wars, one in ten British men was in the army, and boys as young as eight could be found on board ships. Conscription was never introduced in this period; ordinary recruits were drawn from army and militia volunteers, and raised by navy press gangs and recruitment posters that promised that 'bringers of good recruits will receive three guineas reward'.[5] By 1811, the combined army and naval strength was in the region of 640,000 men, with almost continual recruitment due to the incredibly high death tolls.

In Britain, the upper ranks of navy and army were largely made up of upper- or middle-class men, including a large number of sons of clergymen and solicitors. Many bought their commissions into regiments and used their family connections to further their career and bolster their pay. According to the letters and accounts that survive – albeit largely from the literate officer ranks – this class difference did not make for overly soured relations. After all, they were fighting together to defeat the enemy, and skilled officers would wield a sword as quickly as the privates. The archetypal image of the drunken, ill-organised and poorly trained common soldier was certainly true to some degree, but harsh discipline kept men largely in check. Lieutenant Woodberry wrote, 'no one can detest corporal punishment more than I but – subordination must be kept up or we shall all soon go to the dogs.'[6] We should not forget, of course, that when the call came to spring into action, these men were the workhorses of the war machine. Countless gave their lives to the cause. Training and weaponry varied in quality over this long period and many men learned the art of hand-to-hand combat in the arena of real war.

In spring 1798, a French army massed on the Channel coast, sparking very real fears in Britain of an invasion. The thought of the imperial eagle decorating the spires and bastions of British identity led to a genuine 'great terror'. Histrionic posters compared the French to 'spiders' who would 'weave a web around their victim', and painted them as murderous pillagers and rapists who would stop at nothing to stake their claim. A poster in the West Wales port of Fishguard asked, 'Will you, my Countrymen, while you can draw a trigger, or handle a pike, suffer your daughters, your sisters, and wives, to fall into the power of such monsters?'[7] The menace galvanised people and Parliament into action: defensive fortresses were built along the coasts and reserve corps raised. In the event, the threatened invasion was something of a damp squib, but Britain was united in a common cause against this 'Corsican scoundrel'. He and his threat became an inspiration for caricatures, songs, plays and poetry. Anti-Napoleon ditties flooded the newspapers: 'Buonaparte, the Bully, resolves to come over . . . From a Corsican Dunghill this fungus did spring . . .'[8]

On a serious note, fear penetrated the national psyche. This was to be a war to the death against a formidable opponent. With a photographic memory and tremendous work ethic, Napoleon often worked eighteen hours a day, handling and digesting masses of complex information. He was confident, ambitious and styled himself as a conqueror complete with Romanesque laurel wreath crown.

In 1801, Britain and the Ottomans forced the French to surrender in Egypt, and the 1802 Treaty of Amiens signalled an end to hostilities between France and Britain. This short-lived peace brought temporary respite and relief to many men who had been away from home for months – even years. Rear-Admiral Collingwood wrote home, relieved that 'the hope of returning to my family, and living in quiet and comfort amongst those I love, fills my heart with gladness.'[9]

Trafalgar in 1805 was Britain's most emphatic naval victory: a demonstration of tactical splendour and derring-do. Twenty-seven ships defeated thirty-three French and Spanish ships off the coast of Spain without the loss of a single British vessel. Battles fought over the years following Trafalgar shaped the face of Europe and its constitutions for decades to come. Wellington and Nelson emerged as iconic names from battles on land and sea. Napoleon's audacious escape from imprisonment on Elba in February 1815 was a final attempt to engage in glorious war once again. It culminated in perhaps the most famous battle in European history at Waterloo. Napoleon and his desire for French imperial domination was snuffed out for good.

In more than twenty-two years of intermittent battle, over one million French people were killed, and the death toll for the rest of Europe was estimated to be as high as five million. The Marquis d'Argenson, France's foreign minister, aptly proclaimed, 'Triumph is the most beautiful thing in the world . . . but its foundation is human blood, and shreds of human flesh.'[10]

LEAVING FOR WAR: EMOTIONAL AND JOYOUS FAREWELLS

For the men leaving for war throughout this period, the overwhelming sentiment was one of excitement, patriotism and happiness, although for those left behind, wrote Lieutenant John Hildebrand, there was 'less enthusiasm in the female breast'.[11] Some wives were able to travel with their husbands, while others tearfully waved them off from ports, having given them good luck charms, locks of hair and miniatures. Many of these men would never have left Britain before and went cheerfully into the unknown. Joseph Coates wrote, 'Oh with what pleasure did I leave – little thinking or even caring what befell me, only of seeing strange places and fresh faces.'[12] Encountering new peoples, cultures and languages was an attractive by-product of far-flung conflict, as one soldier wrote about his experiences in Copenhagen: 'the lower order of people are very ugly but very clean, there is some very pretty women, they have a genteel air with them which you don't find everywhere.'[13]

There was a faint trace of nerves in some early correspondence, although men tried to dampen such thoughts in letters home. Captain John Lucie Blackman regarded his fate – whatever that might be – as 'la fortune de guerre'.[14] Gunner Andrew Philips wrote in 1804, 'Dear Father & Mother . . . I am sore afraid that we will never see one another again,'[15] and J.O. Hewes informed his father in 1807, 'We have cleared away for action and is ready at a minute's warning to put to sea. It is expected to be a very severe action.'[16] Men largely relished the opportunity to make a contribution and display their mettle: 'This, my dear parents, is the happiest day of my life; and I hope, if I come where there is an opportunity of showing courage, your son will not disgrace the name of a British soldier,'[17] wrote George Simmons. Regardless of nationality, those left behind faced an anxious wait for the fate of their loved ones. Mademoiselle de Touche wrote to Duke Fitzjames, 'Return, dearest, I beg thee. I await thee . . . Adieu my dearest, do not forsake me. I embrace thee with all my heart.'[18]

UNDIMMED PATRIOTISM: TOTAL BELIEF IN THE CAUSE

Literacy was poor among the rank and file,[19] but officers' accounts and the small number of letters surviving from the lower ranks are testament to an unabashed patriotism and belief in the cause the men were fighting, buoyed by stirring speeches from their officers – who undoubtedly believed every proclamation they made. Newspapers and bulletins whipped up a jingoistic frenzy that the campaigns were 'the cause of England – the cause of civilized Europe, and of all the World'. News of each 'glorious' victory was splashed onto posters and front pages with cries of 'Huzza my Boys' and accounts of how they 'drubb'd the enemy'. As soon as reports came in, they were hurriedly printed – emphasising the numbers killed. 'Great News in Spain,' read one, '. . . I am just from Spain. Dupont and Twenty Thousand Men ARE TAKEN.'[20]

Just as the British public lapped up news from overseas, letters home were equally brimming with patriotic conviction. Major-General Sir William Ponsonby wrote home days before Waterloo: 'There seems to be in England a decided feeling of war & perfect confidence as to the successful result . . . Bonaparte will certainly have need of all his extraordinary abilities to resist the immense force about to attack him.'[21] Years earlier, William Thornton Keep had similar convictions: 'Bonaparte is now to fall or never. The combined efforts of his enemies are destined to crush him. But if he escapes, the consequences will be dreadful to England and the other nations of Europe.'[22] Even European dignitaries were united in their anti-Napoleonic sentiment. Letters betraying any trepidation at Napoleon's force were few and far between. Francis D'Oyly admitted to his mother, 'Me and you are the only two . . . who appear to think that we shall not speedily upset Napoleon.'[23]

Patriotism was flourishing among French ranks too. One soldier wrote home, determined to fight to the death – 'it is important that military and maritime present a movement and show of infinite uniforms' – describing the battle as akin to 'la chasse' (the hunt).[24]

A Soldier's Lot: Daily Slog and Hardships

'I have been this three years at sea and 'as not 'ad my foot on shore,'[25] grumbled John Wilkinson. This period of warfare kept men away from home for months on end and it was no surprise that there was frustration with their lifestyles – particularly among the lower ranks who could not ask family at home for money to buy extra blankets, clothes and boots to replace the ones that had fallen apart.

Living conditions varied according to rank but the mobile nature of conflict meant men were often sleeping in shared beds, in sodden and muddy pitched tents or wherever they could find shelter. One soldier in Malta in 1810 described his bed as three boards on top of two trestles, with a dead cat under the overhead floorboards dropping maggots into his face during the night.[26] In the navy, lower ranks slept between the guns, in hammocks or on tables; they were, though, at least assured of regular meals (and beer), fruit, and prompt medical attention. For soldiers, food was rationed, basic and often meagre – small wonder many men turned to theft to quiet their rumbling bellies. It was a tough, unremitting way of life only made bearable by the strong camaraderie between men, forged through shared experience. The regiment became an erstwhile family.

During this period, as well as the mortal risks that came with each battle, the men faced rampant disease. Outbreaks of 'Walcheren fever'[27] in the early 1800s killed thousands of men, and plagued others for decades to come. Crowded, dirty, makeshift camps meant outbreaks of diarrhoea, and typhoid (which was sweeping Central Europe in 1813 anyway) spread easily, with devastating effect. It was estimated that for every soldier killed on the battlefield, four would die from disease.

Pay at this time would have been around two shillings and four pence per day[28] for a corporal and even lower for privates. However, it was more than many men could earn at home, and military service at least came with a pension. Wages were often in arrears, though, and many men relied on home for extra provisions. In the navy, pay was a little more regular and the capture of an enemy ship brought prize money that was shared out among the entire crew.

Men could be awake and active for days at a time. Corporal Joseph Coates wrote home after three days of non-stop fighting and marching. 'What I [would] have given for a few hours rest but in vain, no rest, but fighting. Marching and Fatigue was our lot, but in the midst of all my conflicts while soldiering I was quite resigned to my condition for this reason.'[29] One Prussian soldier wrote home to his wife in 1806: 'For five days we have had to manage with only bad bread; all the horses which remained with us fall from tiredness . . . For eighteen days we have not been paid.'[30]

Postage was problematic during this period. A letter from home had a huge impact on morale – it was a link to loved ones left behind – but the difficulties of knowing where a soldier was and so addressing letters correctly, as well as the logistical issues of finding a postal conveyor during fierce fighting or marching, meant delays were inevitable. Frustration was evident in letters home. 'I wrote two letters to my father and has not had any answer from him . . . let my father know that I do wish him to write as soon as possible,'[31] scribbled William Nelson in 1810, while sixteen-year-old Ensign Joseph St John indignantly wrote, 'I must say that you people in Wiltshire are the worst hands at writing letters that I ever saw, for to every 6 letters from me, you hardly write me one.'[32]

The Grim Reality of Battle: Muskets, Misery and Mortality

The universal sense of excitement at going into a battle was laid bare in letters home. One anonymous officer before the Battle of Vimeiro wrote, 'In our first charge, I felt my mind waver; a breathless sensation came over me, the silence was appalling. I looked along the line: it was enough to assure me, the steady determined Scowl of my companions assured my heart, and gave me determination.'[33] J.O. Hewes even found splendour in battle. 'At 6 o'clock at night saw the red hot shot and shells flying which looked beautiful flying in the air' – sentiments that were quickly sobered by 'a shell . . . [that] took of one of our lieutenants legs, broke his collar bone, cut him very bad on the head and almost knocked one of his eyes out'.[34]

Warfare at this time brought men face to face with shocking scenes that, peculiarly, were often described in letters home in an unemotional, stark tone. William Thornton Keep gave this account of his injury:

> The bullet struck me down and covered me with the crimson fluid, spurting like a fountain from my mouth, whilst I was laying on my back. The blow was severe, it was like a cart wheel passing over my head . . . I was surprised at the quantity of blood that flowed from my mouth, and it was some time before I could remove it effectually from my face and hair and eyes.[35]

Likewise, Rear Admiral William Stanhope Badcock wrote this exhilarating yet matter of fact account of his capture by the enemy in Malta in 1806:

I will now tell you the particulars of our capture . . . 4 of the Corsicans got up and asked for a drink of water which was given them, but they threw the water down and 3 of them seized me, one took me by the throat, another held my hands behind me, and the other drew my cutlass, and attempted to run me through the body, but fortunately I got my hands loose, and received the cutlass slightly in my right hand, and endeavoured with my left to get it from him, but my hat flew off, and I received a blow on the head with a stick which brought me down. One fellow then knelt upon my breast keeping fast hold of my throat, and another held my head back, and wanted the fellow with a cutlass to take it off . . .[36]

Again, the paucity of letters from men in the lower ranks generally leaves us reliant on officers' accounts, but those which do exist mirror the battle sentiments of their superiors. It was not a lack of learned vocabulary that meant that men described what they had witnessed in unsentimental terms. The unemotional tone was due in part to shock and part to becoming desensitised to the situation, and was also symptomatic of the idea that this was what military life was all about. Men became used to blood and guts as integral to war and simply had to carry on with their job. 'It was my duty and I had no choice but to resist to the death or be killed with all around me,'[37] wrote Lieutenant Hildebrand in his memoirs. The horrifying aftermath of battle, with bits of body strewn across the field and the agonising groans of men slowly dying, must have been near-impossible to face. Some letters alluded to the loss of friends – 'the Honour acquired by the Regiment is but a small consolation for the loss of such friends. It is true that the enemy suffered much more; but the sacrifice of all the Frenchmen that ever existed, would not console me for Bringhurst alone'[38] – but did not dwell on the fact and quickly changed the subject. Nobody knows how many men ended up in lunatic asylums following their experiences in the field.

As battles continued, there was a clear sense of disillusionment with the tragic consequences of war – particularly from the upper echelons, where the officers had to deal with swathes of their men being slaughtered. Major-General Robert Long reflected, 'I dislike butchery in all its shapes & forms, & of all kinds of butchery that of the human species is to me the most odious . . . A Profession that is at constant war with one's feelings cannot be an agreeable one.'[39]

Newspapers at home printed lists of the dead and injured – a gruesome weekly tally that must have been painful, anxious reading for families. Indeed, men who escaped without serious injury recognised how lucky they had been. Private James Dilly, who was shot at Badajoz, wrote,

by the blessing of God I am quite recovered . . . I thought at one time that you would never hear from me anymore for I suffered most dreadful . . . The dead covered the ground for a long way round and I now think of the old saying 'A soldier is like a game cock, if he wins one battle he is sure to be tried again'.[40]

Although it was drummed into soldiers and sailors that they must defeat the enemy, there was empathy with them and a healthy respect for the fallen on all sides. Napoleon was the object of hatred; the men were simply fellow soldiers as Rear Admiral Badcock discovered; '[one] came and sat with me and said they were quite sorry for being at war with us, but unfortunately, their country was under the thumb of Bonaparte.'[41]

It was inevitable that military life took its toll on men and all wrote about their hopes for an end to it so they could come home. William Nelson admitted, 'our officer does talk peace very much and we do live in hope that before next Spring I shall get home again for we have been 10 months from England and have not had 18 days fresh provisions in that time.'[42] Paul Phipps reassured his mother in 1813 that 'I would hope the fate of the Peninsular is at last decided & that a final peace will be the result, I certainly now entertain some ideas of seeing England before the winter, the pleasure it will give me cannot be described . . .'[43]

Despite the conditions, realities and longevity of war, there was palpable pride in military life. Captain William Warre reflected, 'thus ended this glorious day in which the valour and intrepidity of gallant fellows was most conspicuous.'[44] Pride was echoed in the flamboyant uniforms of officers with plumed hats, sashes, white breeches, sabres and swords. It was also apparent in the letters home, where the call to fight for one's country was viewed as fate, and to pay the ultimate sacrifice was to die an honourable death.

LAST LETTERS: COMMON THEMES

Nobody wanted to go to war consumed with thoughts that they might die, but the huge numbers of casualties must have forced everyone to have some dark thoughts about their fate, however fleeting. Before he left for sea, Nelson apparently went to see his own coffin while it was being built.

There are some letters surviving written by ordinary soldiers and sailors, as well as condolence letters that reported on last words and actions. As men left for the battle, their thoughts were with family. Captain Edward Kelly 'took a farewell of you and my children in my warmest imagination',[45] while Thornton Keep wrote to his brother, 'I am now about to bid perhaps a long adieu to England, and to those whose feeling hearts have beat so long in unison with my own, and whose but yours can better tell the painful import of that most distressing word farewell'.[46]

In common with descriptions of action, many farewells were unsentimental and matter of fact in tone. 'I will be very anxious to hear from you all for we don't know the day or hour that we might depart this world. I have no more at present,'[47] wrote Gunner Andrew Philips. Many men were also concerned about having made the requisite arrangements for their loved ones. Peter Sadler was a boatswain on HMS *Cumberland* who added a postscript to his 1802 letter to say, 'I am sorry to inform you that this day we are Ordered to part company . . . I mentioned to you in my last letter about a will. Desire Mr Goodon to make one leaving you whole executor and send it home and I will keep it in the house at Hull to be left to you'.[48] Similarly, Thomas Marlow wrote to his parents, 'if I should never see you any more I hope you will receive my share of money and keep the use of it while you live and then I hope you will let it be divided equally among my brother John's children.'[49]

For those who were killed without having written a farewell letter, it fell to officers and friends to break the news and pay their condolences. In lieu of a note from their loved one, the value of this type of farewell should not be underestimated for the comfort it must have given families. First Lieutenant William Hennah wrote to the widow of George Duff:

Alas! Madam, how unfortunate shall I think myself, should this be the first intimation you may have of the irreparable loss you have met with! What apology can I make for entering on a subject so tender and so fraught with sorrow, but to recommend an humble reliance on this great truth, that the ways of Providence, although sometimes inscrutable, are always for the best.[50]

Distinct themes emerge from the farewell letters of this period. First, they were almost always religious. Private James Dilley wrote, 'thanks be to God I bear it up with a good hearth and I hope by the blessing of God that I shall live to see you once more.'[51] In his diary in the early hours of 21 October 1805, Nelson scribbled a final prayer in his diary: 'I commit my life to Him who made me, and may his blessing light upon my endeavours for serving my Country faithfully. To Him I resign myself.'[52] Following fierce fighting at Castalla, Joseph Coates admitted 'fixing my eyes on the sun I thought its very likely when thou risest again I may be in another world, but through the abundant mercy of God I was preserved again.'[53]

Secondly, there was an utter fidelity to the cause, to the end. Death as a soldier was seen as the ultimate noble sacrifice one could make – a sentiment keenly felt on both sides. Waterloo was described as a 'glorious grave'[54] by Jerome Buonaparte, while Migeul de Alava remarked, 'Nothing but the importance of the triumph can compensate for a loss so dreadful.'[55] One Prussian father writing of his son, considered death 'ignoble' unless it came in battle. 'Pray to heaven that he had died for his fatherland his weapons in hand.'[56] Last commands before leading the charge were, 'Dead or alive . . . we must hold our ground,'[57] and a report had one Thomas Main singing 'Rule

Britannia' mid-operation on the surgeon's table![58] This utter dedication to making the ultimate sacrifice was summed up in a letter written by Lieutenant George Simmons, describing seeing a comrade fatally shot in the head: 'Men look at that glorious fellow, our comrade & brother soldier, he now knows the grand secret, he has died nobly for his Country & without a pang of suffering. My boys I trust he is on the high road to heaven.'[59] This letter was found in a William Darby's cap in 1815: 'Regret not . . . we must sooner or later die, console yourself in having had a son who died honourably in his place of suffering, doing his duty and soldiering his efforts towards the attainment of a public objective.'[60]

Finally, the majority of last letters were written on the eve of a battle or after having experienced a traumatic fight. Nelson famously wrote to 'dearest beloved Emma' on the eve of the Battle of Trafalgar:

> May the God of Battles crown my endeavours with success! At all events I shall take care that my name shall ever be most dear to you and Horatia, both of whom I love as much as my own life; and as my last writing before the battle will be of you, so I hope in God that I shall live to finish my letter after the battle.

When she received the letter, Lady Hamilton wrote on it: 'O miserable, wretched Emma! O glorious and happy Nelson!'[61] Captain George Duff of HMS *Mars* wrote, 'Dearest Sophia, I have just time to tell you we are going into Action with the Combined Fleet. I hope and trust in God that we shall all behave as becomes us, and that I may yet have the happiness of taking my beloved wife and children in my arms.'[62] Captain John Lucie Blackman seemed reluctant to finish a letter he wrote on the eve of Waterloo until he absolutely had to – a chink in the confident bravado he had hitherto displayed. 'I shall leave this open till the last moment, in the meantime, I beg leave to assure you and my dearest mother that I am most dutifully and affectionately yours.'[63]

Through the letters and accounts of men killed and those who survived, last thoughts can be reanimated and remembered. There may be a disconnect in time, but the emotions and sentiments have endured for centuries and give a resonant voice to the millions of men killed in over twenty years of bitter conflict with France. For those left behind, the sadness was mutual: 'my heart is broken within me'[64] were the words of just one bereaved brother.

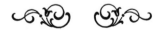

Major Arthur Rowley Heyland
Killed at Waterloo, 18 June 1815

Born on 27 September 1781 in Belfast to Rowley and Mary Heyland, Arthur enjoyed a privileged upbringing (Plate 1). Religion loomed large in his life – his mother was the great-grand-daughter of the Reverend Alexander McDonald, and his wife was the daughter of the Reverend John Kyffin in Bangor, North Wales. He married Mary in 1805 and they went on to have five sons and two daughters.

After an education at Eton and then Aberdeen, Arthur bought a commission to enter the army as an ensign in the 49th Regiment. By 1801 he had been promoted to lieutenant and was serving in the 14th Regiment of Winchester. On 7 August 1804 Heyland became captain of a company in the 40th Regiment of Foot; one of only three regiments to serve throughout the Peninsular Campaigns.

In 1808, when Napoleon declared war on Portugal after taking the Spanish Crown, Heyland fought in fierce battles at Rolica and Vimeiro under Sir Arthur Wellesley.[65] Indeed, Spain and Portugal were the main arenas where Heyland saw action. In July 1809 he was injured at the victorious Battle of Talavera, where Napoleon's army of 46,000 men inflicted heavy casualties on the British Foot Regiments during an audacious advance. Over five thousand British men were killed and wounded.

Heyland took part in the Siege of Cuidad Rodrigo where, alongside the 30th Foot, his regiment captured this frontier fortress – gateway to an advance into Spain. At the second siege of the Badajoz fortress, the company sustained massive casualties (over four hundred men killed and wounded) and Heyland himself was wounded. He was sent to Estremoz in Portugal to recover, acting as garrison commander to over ten thousand men.

By 1813 Heyland was back in action. His regiment played a central role in Wellington's efforts to drive the French out of Spain, marching hundreds of miles and engaging in the bloody battle of Vittoria. On a battlefield stretching over twelve miles, they faced an enemy army more than sixty thousand strong. The Anglo-Spanish and Portuguese force numbered 78,000, but suffered over five thousand casualties. The 40th Regiment fought so bravely that they were awarded the 'Pyrenees' honour. The battle would be the last major fight in Spain, and paved the way for Wellington to invade France.

Having survived Vittoria, little more than a month later, on 27 July 1813, Heyland was severely wounded again. Perhaps it was the last close shave he wanted to experience; he had returned to Cork by 1814 and sought permission to retire.

Napoleon's escape from Elba in February 1815 precipitated Heyland's return to active duty. He was ordered to take command of the 40th Regiment once again as part of the Sixth Division under Major-General Lambert. At first in reserve, the 40th marched for two days to within a few miles of Waterloo. They were then ordered to the centre of the allied line, near La Haye Sainte, where they were bombarded with shot and cannon but refused to retreat. Driving back Napoleon's final attack, they were ordered to advance. The bombardment Heyland and his men were under was an unimaginable hell. Heyland was no stranger to the battlefield and had evaded death on a number of previous occasions, but it is clear that the prospect of Waterloo must have been like no other to prompt Heyland's farewell letter. This was a man with supreme confidence and military skill, yet he felt the need to prepare to say goodbye. It was an ominous move. He was killed the next day.

My Dear Mary

What I recommend my love in case I fall in the ensuing contest, is that my sons be educated at the Military College, except Arthur, who is hardly strong enough: the hazards of a military life are considerable, but still it has its pleasures, and it appears to me of no consequence whether a man dies young or old, provided he be employed in fulfilling the duties of the situation he is placed in this world.

I would wish my son John, whose early disposition has made us both happy, should serve in the infantry till he is a lieutenant, and then by money or interest be removed to a regiment of light cavalry. I trust his gentlemanly manner and his gallantry in the field will make his life agreeable. Kyffin might try the artillery service and make it an object to be appointed to the horse artillery, which he can only hope for by applying himself to the duties of his profession. Alfred must get in a regiment of infantry, the 95th for instance, and my young unborn must be guided by his brother John and your wishes.

For yourself, my dearest, kindest Mary, take up your residence in Wales, or elsewhere if you prefer it, but I would advise you, my love, to choose a permanent residence. My daughters, may they cling to their mother and remember her in every particular.

My Mary, let the recollection console you that the happiest days of my life have been from your love and affection, and that I die loving only you, and with a fervent hope that our souls may be reunited hereafter and part no more.

What dear children, my Mary I leave you. My Marianna, gentlest girl, may God bless you. My Anne, my John, may heaven protect you. My children may you all be happy and may the reflection that your father never in his life swerved from the truth and always acted from the dictates of his conscience, preserve you, virtuous and happy, for without virtue there can be no happiness.

My darling Mary, I must tell you again how tranquilly I shall die, should it be my fate to fall, we cannot, my own love, die together; one or other must witness the loss of what we love most. Let my children console you, my love, my Mary. My affairs will soon improve and you will have a competency, do not let too refined scruples prevent you from taking the usual government allowance for officers' children and widows. The only regret I shall have in quitting this world will arise from the sorrow it will cause you and your children and my dear Marianne Symes. My mother will feel my loss yet she possesses a kind of resignation to these inevitable events which will soon reconcile her.

I have no desponding ideas on entering the field, but I cannot help thinking it almost impossible I should escape either wounds or death. My love, I cannot improve the will I have made, everything is left at your disposal. When you can get a sum exceeding £10,000 for my Irish property, I should recommend you to part with it and invest the money, £6000 at least, in the funds, and the rest in such security as may be unexceptionable. You must tell my dear brother that I expect he will guard and protect you, and I trust he will return safe to his home.

ARH.[66]

Heyland had – for perhaps the first time – been forced to confront his own mortality. He appeared remarkably composed and calm about the prospect of death; perhaps he had been carrying the 'what if' thoughts about his children's future and wife's financial arrangements for some time. It seemed to have taken the proposition of Waterloo to commit them to paper. Heyland's letter stands out for his absolute commitment to his military role. There were no regrets – indeed the best way his family could honour his memory would be for his sons to follow directly in his footsteps. What shone through the letter, however, was the undying love Heyland had for his wife and children. His only regret on dying would be to die without his beloved Mary.

On 18 June 1815, any sentimental thoughts would have been pushed to the back of his mind as the impending battle took precedence. Heyland led his troops into position on the battlefield. For hours they were stationary near La Haye Sainte, under constant bombardment and suffering massive losses. At seven o'clock Wellington personally delivered the orders to advance. Eye-witness accounts relate that a cheer went up as the men strode forward. Heyland was struck by a musket ball in the neck. He had no sword, no horse and no cap. He was just thirty-four – the same age as his wife. According to a memorial at St Patrick's Church in Coleraine, his body was 'instantly removed by his brother officers with affectionate zeal and regret'.

Heyland's wife was now left with Marianne, aged eleven, John, aged ten, Anne aged nine, Arthur, around eight, Kyffin, aged seven and Alfred, aged two. Mary Heyland was also pregnant with Herbert when her husband was killed, but he tragically died in May 1816, aged just eleven months. John, as his father had wished, became Captain John Rowley Heyland of the 35th Foot, although it appears that none of his other sons opted for a military career.

Mary erected a tomb for Heyland's body, in a garden at Monte St Jean, near the battlefield. It remained there for 150 years, protected by railings until the

1920s, when the monument was removed and re-erected at the Wellington Museum in Waterloo.

Ensign the Honourable Samuel S. Barrington

Killed at Quatre Bras, 16 June 1815

BORN IN 1796, SAMUEL Barrington was the third of seven sons of the Reverend Lord Viscount Barrington, of Durham Cathedral and Elizabeth Adair, daughter of Lady Caroline Keppel. Privately educated, at the age of eighteen Samuel was following his older brother George into the military and was commissioned into the 1st Foot Guards in 1814. In the latter half of 1814, Europe was in a state of armed peace, and the first few months of Barrington's duty was spent in parades and 'feu-de-joie'[67] displays on the Queen's Birthday and other auspicious occasions.

Barrington was clearly a spirited man – in a letter home he wrote of how 'there is no eloquence like force and no sauce so good for one impudent fellow as thrashing.' Such was the way of normal and accepted army discipline at the time. However, he was clearly a popular soldier among his men. Following his death there were a flood of letters of condolence that praised his 'exemplary conduct' and 'intelligent, attentive and conscientious . . . discharge of his duty. As a gentleman he was only to be known to increase the list of his numerous friends.'

Barrington wrote his farewell letter after having visited the site of the 1792 Battle of Jemappes. This had been the first major victory for the French troops of the new Republic, where they defeated Austria and captured Brussels. Although the French suffered higher casualties (over two thousand) the battle marked the birth of aggressive French warfare and signalled an intention that France would not be constrained by its borders. The significance of this was clearly not lost on Barrington, who at the end of March 1815 was facing the destructive force of a French army in the same location. Indeed, on 17 March the battalion had received orders to take to the field and march towards Enghien. Barrington wrote to his mother: 'I rode out yesterday with 2 others, to view the different positions of the French and Austrians at the famous battle. The best information that we could obtain we did upon the field and could make it all out very well.'

Barrington was in confident mood at this time, relishing the prospect of action but at the same time holding a healthy respect for Bonaparte and his tactics.

If we ever get back to England I will give you some account of it and hope also to tell you of the fine style we will knock the French about, if we can but get up our reinforcements from England before they advance against us. We are all in highest spirits here and anxious to try our strength with the first who dare oppose us. If we do but get the Duke of Wellington we are sure to lick them. Of course all sorts of reports fly about here as in other places, but nothing very certain is known or at least published. I believe Bonaparte's chief plan, will be the old one of setting the allied powers together by the ears and then coming off best of all himself. I think however, if we should have the good fortune to take him, he will not be alive many moments.

On 26 March Barrington reached Ath, twelve miles outside Enghien, where he wrote this letter. Here they reinforced the allied line in a position to resist the expected Napoleonic attack from Valenciennes. Barrington had also received two letters from his mother at this time, and it may have been that this simple reminder of home was enough to produce a momentary reflection on the worst actually happening and to prompt him to write a farewell note. The expected besiegement of Lille was now off – instead the regiment was to await the foe in the Enghien area.

I have nothing to say for myself, but that I am as well and happy as ever I was in my life and if I escape with a whole skin, shall think myself well off and be thankful. If on the contrary some unlucky ball finishes me, I trust I shall not be wholly unprepared to face danger and death.

There was no further mention of death in Barrington's letters – the farewell sentiment was succinct and curt. Barrington was only nineteen at this point, and the confidence of youth, arrogance of breeding and bravado of soldiering may explain the succinctness of his message. Nevertheless, there were hints within the letter of nerves and anticipation at the fight ahead. Eager he may have been to square up to the enemy, but the dangers of battle could not be easily suppressed.

If anything goes on here, I will take care to write in good time. I am just going to ride, if I meet with any adventure I will tell you . . . There are two reports in circulation at the moment, one that we march tomorrow, the other that Napoleon is assassinated by Marshall Mortier, neither of which do I believe, although I should not be sorry to hear both confirmed . . . I fancy that we shall

1 Part of the letter from Samuel Barrington, c. April 1815 (Staffordshire Record Office).

hear more inharmonious music soon. Give my love to all that care about me, or I about them and to my father . . . Ever your affectionate son, SSP Barrington.[68]

The run-up to Barrington's final fight was spent preparing for battle, but with a healthy dose of escapism in the form of balls and cricket matches. The men received a glowing review following inspection by the Duke of Wellington and seemed in confident mood.

Barrington's final letter home was written on the eve of the Battle of Quatre Bras – two days before Waterloo. The 1st Foot were at Enghien, around fifteen miles west of Waterloo. Surprisingly, there was a mere passing reference to the pending battle and no sign that he had any qualms about it. 'It is now said that we shall not stir a step in this business until the advance of the Prussians, when I suppose we shall come upon the French like hail.' Instead, he wrote about the weather and how he had kicked a captain down the stairs. Letters written on the eve of battle tend to fall into two categories: those soldiers who used the opportunity to say farewell and pour out their emotions lest they not return, and those – like Barrington – who made no mention of it, perhaps not wanting to tempt fate. The fact he wrote home on this date was significant; whether subconsciously or not, he had ensured there was a final communication with his mother. That night the battalion had been warned to be ready to move at a moment's notice, and every soldier would have been aware of the foreboding undertones of those instructions.

Just after one in the morning of 16 June, Barrington's battalion marched along the Nivelles road to the southern part of the Bois de Bossu, ready for battle against Ney's 24,000 French troops: a route of some twenty-six miles. They reached their position at around nine o'clock and planned to attack at two in the afternoon. The French had more infantry and cavalry and, as Barrington and his men 'advanced (with bayonets fixed and cheering)', Barrington was shot in the head with a musket ball, and died instantly. He was one of six officers from his battalion to be killed during the battle. 'Nothing could exceed the gallantry both of the officers and men,'[69] read the official regimental history. In total more than 2,500 British men were killed in that engagement.

Both sides claimed victory. It was a battle that foreshadowed and set the stage for one of the greatest showdowns in military history – Waterloo.

On 23 June 1815, news arrived of Barrington's death through a letter written by the commanding colonel, Alexander Lord Saltoun.

He fell in action, in the Bois de Bossu . . . instant in the most gallant execution of his duty and even under these melancholy circumstances, it must be some consolation to his friends to know that his death was instantaneous and not attended with the slightest suffering and that his body was the next morning buried on the field of battle. From the circumstances of the ground on which he fell being immediately afterwards in momentary possession of the enemy, I regret to say that on our regaining it, they had taken possession of his sash and sword and what other things he had about him which I should have wished to save to send them to your lordship.

A later letter revealed that his sash had been recovered and sent to his mother, along with his writing desk.

Further letters of condolence arrived, which must have provided great comfort to his family. 'Believe me my dear Lord, when the memory recurs to the events of that glorious day, the name of Barrington will long live in a corps in whose ranks he so nobly fought and fell,' wrote Major Henry Askew, while an anonymous officer's letter remarked:

> The fate of poor Barrington is very distressing and his friends feel it most acutely at least I do, for never was there a better officer, a kinder friend or a more gallant soldier. I wish his parents could have seen him at the head of his company, cheering his men forward, with his sword in the air, it would have made their hearts proud.

Barrington had taken off his tall black 'shako' hat to cheer the men forward, leaving him totally exposed to shot.

Barrington was one of 4,700 casualties that day, but surviving letters create a remarkable portrait of his final few hours. Just before he fell, he said his prayers in a corner of the field 'and then rushed on with undaunted courage to the attack'. He apparently did not pray to survive, but 'prayed to be saved after death'.[70]

The bravery of the regiment did not pass unnoticed. They went on to fight at Waterloo and at the end of the Napoleonic Wars in July 1815 the regiment was renamed 'Grenadier' by Royal decree, in honour of their role in defeating the French Grenadiers at Waterloo.

Corporal John Culley

Survived

BORN ON 6 FEBRUARY 1770 to John and Elizabeth (née Millington), Jonathan (John) Culley was baptised in the local church in the small village of Burbage, Wiltshire, which had a population of around a thousand people at that time. The Culleys had been in the village since the early 1700s, and Jonathan was the youngest of eight children born over twenty-two years. His mother died shortly after his birth, in June 1770. It was likely that the family – including his grandparents – all lived on the Marquis of Ailesbury's Savernake estate, where his father was a gardener.

John junior worked as a labourer before joining the Queen's Dragoon Guards at the age of twenty, and was clearly literate. Only two of his letters have survived, both written to his grandparents; they were saved with

Savernake estate papers, indicative of their resonance and importance over the centuries.

When Culley joined the regiment in 1790, the French Revolutionary Wars had started. Regiments were crying out for reinforcements and it was likely that he volunteered to join in response to this. When French Revolutionaries declared war on all the European monarchies, including Britain, on 1 February 1793, the Queen's Dragoons were sent to the Low Countries, and marched to Tournai, where they joined with Austrian and Prussian troops to form an observation corps during the siege of Valenciennes. After the city fell, the regiment marched towards Dunkirk, where the Duke of York ordered that the Queen's be allotted to the Hanoverian division under General Freytag. Headquarters were established at Hondschoote, and fierce fighting broke out as the French advanced. Freytag was injured and the troops forced to retreat in the face of French aggression. The terrain made it near-impossible to fight on horseback, and soldiers were ordered to fight on foot. On 8 September they were in retreat towards Furnes in Belgium.

On 25 September 1793 John Culley wrote to his grandparents with news from the front. Soldiering was proving a tough existence and he had experienced the death of a friend. This only strengthened his resolve to continue the fight and triumph.

> David is dead. He was killed with a bomb shell and we all goes through a deal of hardships for [I] have not been in one bed since we left England but we don't mind that for we fight like heroes. I have been 24 hours on horseback at a time and we are very glad to have the opportunity to lay down before our horses to get an hour sleep with the bridle hitched on our arms and . . . it makes me think of a hail storm to hear the cracks . . . about my ears. There was 6 thousand of us smacked 20 thousand of the French and we was not strong enough and we was obliged to retreat . . . we have taken valiant strides and we marched 10 thousand prisoners out of the town . . . and there was 2 thousand lain dead . . . we drew them out of the town and there was 6 hundred drowned making their escape over the river and we expect to have another attack at Dunkirk . . . Our army is about 3 hundred thousand strong and we shall be stronger yet for the French is 5 hundred thousand strong and we expect to take Dunkirk and Paris before we go . . . Flanders is a very fine country and so is France but we cannot understand their language . . . and they are very deceitful people.

Despite his confidence, and exaggerated numbers of troops, the very real experience of battle had forced Culley to face his own mortality. The siege of Dunkirk between late August and early September had been a resounding failure, demonstrating how ill equipped and poorly trained the British army was at this time. Two thousand men were killed and wounded in addition to men dying from diseases rampaging through camps. Perhaps knowing this, though not wanting to admit it, was the prompt for Culley's farewell postscript. Indeed, it was written from the Dutch border where they had been forced to retreat.

> Now grandfather and grandmother, there is the same God abroad as there is at home and I hope we shall met in another world if we don't in this but we don't expect it will be settled – not this summer – and I should be glad if you will be so kind [as to] send word to my cousins . . . that you have heard from me and give my love to them and I desire to be remembered to Gerry Hiller and John and all the family . . . I give kind love to you all so nothing more at present from your loving grandson and daughter . . . Dear Grandfather. I hope you will make yourselves happy about me for I don't think that a Frenchman is born that can kill me and I am sworn to serve my King and Country and I will fight for it as long as I have got a drop of blood in my body. But it is very shocking to see the towers burnt down and the people lying dead and the blood squashing over the horses feet as we ride along.[71]

On 26 April 1794 two French columns of around 30,000 men attacked the Allied position at Cateau, driving them back and capturing two villages. They

2 Part of the letter from John Culley, September/October 1793 (Wiltshire and Swindon Archives).

started to form up for battle below the ridge-line. The Duke of York positioned his troops out of sight of the French in order to take them by surprise when they advanced. As the trumpets sounded the charge, ferocious fighting commenced in a hail of grape and shot. The Duke of York praised the men for having 'acquired immortal honour to themselves', and awarded the regiment £500. It was during this action that Culley was injured – crushed when his horse fell on top of him (probably after being hit). He was lucky to have been removed from the battlefield and treated. There was no organised ambulance service, and surgeons were woefully overstretched. Many men were left to die in the field or perished on improvised operating tables and makeshift field hospitals, despite the many remarkable operations surgeons did carry out.

In May 1795 Culley was back with his regiment 'damme nere Osenbrock',[72] where the regimental headquarters were positioned. It was here on 10 May that he wrote once again to his grandparents, desperately hoping he would be coming home soon.

This comes with my obliging to you hoping these few lines will find you both in good health as this leaves me at present thanks be to God for it and I received your last letter the 7th of May and I hope you will excuse my not writing before, for I have been away from the Regiment this two months on duty and joined the Regiment the 6th of May and then I received 3 letters all together; one from you and two from my wife . . . She and the boy have not been very well and it gives me [a great] deal of trouble. Dear grandfather and grandmother . . . many thanks for your kindness to my wife . . . There is a talk of our coming home and I wish it may be true and there is a great many transports . . . and we expect to go aboard but whether we shall come home or whether we shall land in any other port . . . we don't know . . . There is great talk that the Prussians have had peace . . . we expect to come home to England this summer and when you write to my wife again you give my kind love to her and tell her that I am with greatest hopes on coming home . . . [I] volunteered to fight the Dutch then I could come home so bad as I want to come home for they are the worst villains upon Earth for when we went there to protect their country they turned out and joined the French . . . I have nothing more.[73]

It wasn't until the end of the year that the regiment arrived back in England, landing in South Shields in December 1795. No official figures were compiled for the losses sustained by the regiment, but Culley was one of the lucky ones who survived.

Following years of bloody fighting in the Revolutionary Wars, Culley signed his discharge papers at Canterbury on 24 May 1802, to receive all his clothing, and pay arrears from the time of 'inlisting . . . to this present day'. The standard papers confirmed that he 'hath served honestly and faithfully in the said regiment fourteen years', but added that he was being discharged due to his 'being very infirm from a hurt he received from his horse falling upon him when in action near Cateau on the 26th April 1794'.[74] It was an injury he had carried for almost a decade. He returned home to his wife and three children and eventually died in 1845, aged seventy-five.

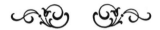

LIEUTENANT CARL THEODOR KÖRNER
Killed at Leipzig, 25 August 1813

BORN IN DRESDEN ON 23 September 1791, Körner was the son of a counsellor of appeals, an official who mixed with the intellectual elite (Plate 2). Carl's mother was the daughter of an acclaimed artist engraver called Stock. He was an active child, and became an adroit fencer and rider, and an accomplished musician. He enjoyed an eclectic education, studying mining, law, history and philosophy at a number of institutions and with private tutors before moving to Vienna and deciding to become a playwright at the age of twenty. His first work – a celebration of heroism and nationalism – was met with critical and popular acclaim, setting the tone for his work to come, in a country where anti-Napoleonic sentiment was growing.

On 5 March 1813 Prussia declared war on France, joining an Austrian, Russian, Swedish and British alliance. King Friedrich Wilhelm appealed to his people to embrace the war effort, and, swept up in this wave of patriotic emotion, Körner signed up with the Volunteer Freikorps on 19 March 1813. Armed with letters of recommendation, he soon rose to the rank of lieutenant. He wrote enthusiastically to his father that 'Germany rises! The Prussian eagle, by the beating of her mighty wings, awakes, in all true hearts, the great hope of German freedom.'[75] Military life provided inspiring and prolific fodder for his poetry, which he wrote throughout his service.

Körner wrote of war as 'not the sort of war that crowns know of / It is a crusade, a holy war.'[76] Unlike the poets of old, though, he was not afraid to air his personal feelings and experiences. It was perhaps a means of preparing himself for battle and dealing with the heady turmoil of emotions afterwards. In making himself the central character in his work, Körner could pour out his angers, frustrations and innermost thoughts. It must have been a hugely cathartic process to commit verse to paper. One minute war was a fantastic adventure, the next it was dark and desolate, yet strangely addictive. In his 1813 poem 'Horseman's Song' he wrote:

> Honour is the wedding guest
> And the Fatherland the bride
> He who lustfully embraces her
> Has been married to death.[77]

Each major battle prompted a new poem – often composed on the eve of action – and represented a farewell from the poet. On 12 May 1813, the morning of the battle of Danneburg, he composed 'War Song'. 'Brethren! This hour as it dawns on us now / Impels us to join heart and hand in the vow / To be true while we live; to be true if we die!'[78]

By mid-May 1813 Napoleon had already triumphed at Lutzen. Körner was appointed adjutant to Major von Lützow, and on 28 May accompanied him on an expedition towards Thuringia. After ten days, the troops received notice of an armistice at Plaue and decided to rejoin their infantry, confident that they would not be attacked. At Leipzig, however, they met enemy troops and Körner was struck on the head by a sword as he sought an explanation for the encounter. Fighting broke out and several men were wounded or taken prisoner. Körner managed to escape on horseback, deep into the forest. This event was the inspiration for his poem 'Farewell to Life' – a romantic paean he claimed to have composed as he lay wounded and expecting to die.

> My deep wound burns; — my pale lips quake in death, —
> I feel my fainting heart resign its strife,
> And reaching now the limit of my life,
> Lord, to thy will I yield my parting breath!
> Yet many a dream hath charm'd my youthful eye;
> And must life's fairy visions all depart;
> Oh surely no! for all that fired my heart
> To rapture here, shall live with me on high.
> And that fair form that won my earliest vow,
> That my young spirit prized all else above,
> And now adored as freedom, now as love,
> Stands in seraphic guise, before me now.
> And as my fading senses fade away,
> It beckons me, on high, to realms of endless day![79]

Rescued the next day by peasants, Körner eventually made his way back to the banks of the river Elbe, and rejoined his fellow soldiers. Mindful of having had one lucky escape, later that month, Körner ensured he composed a private farewell to his sweetheart. Suffused with dark thoughts, he wrote: 'In two days we expect our deadly nuptials.'[80] Consumed by thoughts of death as a glorious, binding contract into which he was pleased to enter, he also wrote a poem that revealed his unabashed desire to embrace death. To die in an insignificant skirmish or in an action unrelated to direct enemy attack would be to die an insignificant, meaningless death. While on guard duty he wrote this farewell poem – a dream of the perfect death for a poet.

> Shall I die in prose?
> Poetry, thou source of fire
> Break loose with shining ruin,
> Quickly![81]

On 17 August hostilities resumed, and on 28 August, Körner was mortally wounded while in pursuit of the enemy near Rosenberg. Hit in the stomach, liver and spine with musket balls, he was knocked unconscious. He died soon afterwards in a neighbouring wood.

Körner was buried under an oak tree in the small village of Wöbbelin, near Ludwigslust. Hours before his death, Körner had composed his 'Schwertlied' or 'Song of the Sword', and was reading it to a friend as the call to action came.

Korner	Thou sword upon my belted vest
	What means thy glittering, polished crest?
	Thou seem'st within my glowing breast
	To raise a flame – hurrah!
Sword	A horseman brave supports my blade;
	The weapon for a freeman made,
	For him I'll move, for him I'll wade
	Thro' blood and death – hurrah! . . .
	I hold myself in dread reserve,
Sword	Fierce, fond in battle field to serve,
	The cause of freedom to preserve,
	For this I wait – hurrah! . . .
Körner	Let joy act in those polished eyes:
	While radiant sparkles, flashing rise;
	Our marriage-day dawns in the skies
	My bride of steel – hurrah![82]

It was a fitting last testament for this idealistic and supremely talented poet. Körner's death at just twenty-two granted him posthumous esteem as the ultimate fallen hero. His father published his poetry in 1814 to widespread – and enduring – popularity. His poems came to embody the German celebration of glorious death in warfare, up to and including the Second World War, when Josef Goebbels, among others, quoted from his work.

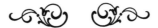

PRIVATE CHARLES STANLEY
Killed at Waterloo, 18 June 1815

CHARLES STANLEY WAS BORN to parents John and Mary on 13 March 1792 and grew up in Edwinstowe, a small village in the heart of Sherwood Forest. After joining the King's Dragoon Guards, perhaps inspired by a local Sergeant Stubbings whom he knew, Stanley quickly found himself embroiled in the Napoleonic Wars.

By 4 April 1815 Wellington was in Brussels, which had become a rumoured target for Napoleon and the army he had started mustering within days of arriving back in Paris from exile. By May, he had amassed tens of thousands of men, including experienced veterans of the Grande Armée. Wellington was in command of a mixed army of British, Dutch–Belgian and German soldiers. On 15 May Stanley wrote to his cousin Christopher Alvey from 'Brusels Flemish Flanders'. He mentioned that he was billeted with two regiments of Life Guards and the 'Oxford Blues'.[83] As one of four squadrons of King's Dragoon Guards, he would have been under the command of Major-General Lord Edward Somerset, spending mid-April to mid-June in the Dender valley in central Belgium.

In the weeks running up to Waterloo, Stanley's regiment took part in parades and field days, as well as having inspections of weapons and uniforms. The Earl of Uxbridge inspected the regiment on 6 May, the Prince of Orange on 24 May and Wellington and Blücher inspected the whole British cavalry on 29 May. There must have been a palpable and growing sense of tense anticipation among all the men; they knew they were heading for a spectacular showdown.

Stanley's farewell letter seems to have been the only correspondence that survived. It wavered from nonchalant descriptions of Belgium and day-to-day life, to quite dark, serious sentiments. He wanted to ensure his cousin would not follow him into military life and took care to remember several close relatives. Stanley also revealed something of the isolation and loneliness felt by soldiers for whom home seemed a distant memory. 'I have wrote to my sister . . . out of site out of mind' was his melancholy lament. Conversely, the letter also revealed the steadfast pride and sense of duty that Stanley – like so many ordinary soldiers – had. The field exercises and parades in the run-up to Waterloo were designed to build confidence, bolster camaraderie and instil in the men a 'conquer or die' sense of destiny. In the short farewell paragraph, the idea that he might die in the field was calmly accepted as the lot of a soldier.

> Dear Cousin,
>
> I take this opportunity of writing to you hoping this will find you all in good health as it leaves me at present I thank God for it. I have had a very rough march . . . we are only 15 miles from Mr. Boney Part . . . we expect to have a rap at him every day. We have the most cavalry of the English that ever was known at one time, and in good condition and good spirits . . .
>
> At present there is no doubt of us beating the confounded rascal. It may cost me my life and a many more. That will only be the fortune of war. My life I set no store by at all.
>
> . . . This is the finest country ever so far before England. The people [are] so civil, their land cultivated so well and they have it as clean as a gentleman's garden. They are sadly afraid of Boney's Army coming again. He distressed them so before. We have some little trouble to make them understand us not knowing their language. We do a great deal by making motions.
>
> We have one good thing cheap that is tobacco . . . 4d per lb gin is 1s8d per gallon . . . our allowance per day is one pound of beef, a pound a half of bread, half a pint of gin but the worst of all we don't get it regular and if we don't get [it] in the day it is due we lose it . . . I hope whatever may come across your mind to trouble you which, I hope nothing will, I hope you never will think of being a soldier. I assure you it is a very rough concern . . . I have not had the pleasure of lying in a bed since in the country – thank God the weather is fine which is in our favour. We get no pay at all only our bread and meat and gin. We have 10d per day [subbed] from us which we shall receive when six months is expired. I thank God I have a friend with me which I find very useful to me I assure you. I hope you will excuse my bad . . . spelling. My love to Aunt and Cousins, Mrs Darby, Cousin Joseph and my family . . . and all that thinks well to ask after me. My duty to mother when you see her.
>
> If you think well to answer my letter wish I should be very glad you would I should be very glad to hear from you all . . . So no more at present from your ever well wisher Stanley. God bless you all.[84]

No doubt the gin allowance helped dull the nerves, but at three o'clock in the morning of 16 June Stanley's regiment were given orders to march to Enghien. There would be no going back. At eight o'clock they paraded at Ninove, making slow progress towards Nivelles, finally arriving at Quatre Bras at eight o'clock. Here they camped in a wheat field for no doubt a fitful few hours' sleep. At two

Brussels Flemish Flanders May 15 1815

Dear Cusson I take this Oppurtunety of
Riting to you hoping this will find you all
in gud helth as it leves me at Present I
thank God for It I have ad a very Ruf march
Since i sow you at Booton we am only 15 miles
From Mr Boney Part harmeys wich we expect
To have a Rap at him Every Day We have the
Most Cavilrey of the English that Ever was
None at One time and in gud Condishon and
Gud sperrets we have loot a few horses by hour
Marching I have the Plesure to say my horse
Is Better Every Day Wich i think im to be the
Best frend i have at Pressant there is no dout
Of us Beting the Confounded Rascald it ma Cost
Me my Life and a meaney more that will only
Be the forting of War my Life i set no store
By at all this is the finest Cantrey Ever iss
far befor England the Peepel is so Civel thare land
Cultevated most of them as a littel Land and thay
have it as Clen as a gentelman gardin tha are
Sadley a frad of Boney harmey Comming agane
he District them so before we have sum littel
trubel to make them Understand us not noing thare
Langwige we do a grate del By makin moshens ___

3 Part of the letter from Charles Stanley, 15 May 1815 (with kind permission of Peter Galloway).

o'clock the following day, the enemy was spotted just a few miles away and the men were ordered to retreat in three columns along the road, with Stanley's regiment providing rear-guard cover as French lancers pushed onward and were forced back a number of times. The French stopped surging forward and the allies continued to retreat slowly, finally taking rest at the farm of Mont St John that evening. It was a wet night that left men cold, sodden and subdued and creating a quagmire of the fields around them. At daybreak, preparations for battle began once more. Horses were groomed, equipment prepared and by six o'clock the regiments were massed together – ready for battle.

At twelve noon, French cannons started blasting the men, and by early afternoon the allies were scrambling forward, frantically attacking the French cuirassiers. It was a hand-to-hand sword fight; a bloody and chaotic attack. Swords slashing and indiscriminately slaughtering as they surged forward, the King's Dragoons moved towards the farm at La Haye Sainte. Already the regiment's casualties were numerous – five entire troops had been taken out, as well as some key commanding officers. With depleted men, the regiment fought on – a desperate struggle of inner will as much as combat skill . In total, only fifteen King's Dragoon Guardsmen survived out of 530 who had set out that morning. Stanley was one of those who fell – although his body was never buried in a marked grave. Nobody knows exactly how he died, caught up in the maelstrom of swinging swords, cannonades, charging horses and incessant musket fire. A description of the battlefield afterwards made for devastating reading:

> the sight was too horrible to behold . . . The multitude of carcasses the heaps
> of wounded men with mangled limbs unable to move, and perishing from
> not having their wounds dressed or from hunger . . . every tree is pierced with
> bullets. The Barns are all burned down and in the courtyard it is said they have
> been obliged to burn upwards of a thousand carcasses, an awful Holocaust to the
> War-Demon.[85]

Recovering, identifying and burying all bodies amidst this hideous scene would have been a near-impossible task. Confirmation of Stanley's death was not immediate. The regimental pay list up to 24 June 1815 recorded him as 'missing', as did the subsequent pay list up to 24 September. Indeed, his death was only confirmed in the 'supplementary pay list for Men in consequence of having served in the Battle of Waterloo' as 'Killed in action 18th June 1815'.[86]

Charles Stanley's letter was discovered lodged in a Victorian writing desk bequeathed to several generations of family and then friends in the Northamptonshire area. The man who uncovered this moving note uses the letter as a teaching aid in schools, revealing that, some two hundred years later, the words still prompt tears from children learning of the fate of the writer.

THE AMERICAN CIVIL WAR

August 7th 1861

 Dear Mother. I am going on a dangerous scouting excursion tonight. I have not tried as hard as I ought to be good, yet I trust in God I mean to do my duty. Good bye. Do not know unnecessary trouble about me. Should any accident occur to us you will hear of it immediately. I hope your prayers for me are not in vain. Rest assured my death *shall not* be that of a wicked coward, but that of a God-fearing Patriot if I am to perish in the cause. Do not be uneasy. The expedition may be bloodless.[1]

WHEN CIVIL WAR BROKE out, few could have envisaged the horror and bloodshed it would cause. Over 600,000 men were killed – more than the American dead of the Revolutionary Wars, 1812 War, Mexican War, Spanish-American War, First and Second World Wars and Korean War combined.[2] It was a bloody testament to the advances of the industrial revolution in terms of weaponry, warships and troop movement. It was also a conflict that could be dubbed genocide; an aggressive war that pitched American against American.

 Abraham Lincoln emerged as the saviour of the Union. He came to power in 1860 with just 39 per cent of the vote, mainly from the North: there was an acidic divide between the slave-owning Southern states and the free states of the North. Within weeks of Lincoln's arrival in Washington, Southern states started seceding from the Union over the inflammatory issue of slavery. Led by Jefferson Davis, they wanted to push westwards, exploiting the rich land for cotton growing and using slaves as their economic engine. They formed a Confederation, pitched against the Union men.

 On 20 December 1860 South Carolina broke away, and on 1 January 1861 Georgia volunteers sailed down the Savannah River and occupied Fort Pulaski. Over January, Mississippi, Florida, Alabama, Louisiana and Texas all separated. On 12 April South Carolina's Confederate gunners opened fire and bombarded Fort Sumpter, and a day later Lincoln ordered the blockade of the Southern ports. It was a bloodless prelude.[3] The stage for an atrocious war had been dressed, the actors were positioned, and the curtain ready to rise. Along a thousand-mile front, in over ten thousand sites and involving three million men, the odds were long for the Confederates, outnumbered by the Unionists in the North.

Nevertheless the first few years of the war went badly for the Unionists, especially in Virginia. This was a 'green' army on both sides, with ageing generals and few men who had ever led in the field. Although there was no shortage of volunteers, these war virgins would be learning soldiering on the job.

Lincoln declared secession was the cause of war and not slavery, but was soon under pressure to consider emancipation.[4] The recruitment of black slaves into the Union army was the turning point of the war – and a turning point in American history. Lincoln as commander-in-chief went for the Southern jugular, proclaiming, 'We will teach them the folly of starting a war.'

Letters to and from home were a vital comfort among the conditions of warfare, and men could be moved to tears if they did not receive post. 'Dark and gloomy would be my existence while soldiering down here were it not for those heart-cheering words of love and comfort from . . . the heart of one in whom I ever *have* and ever *can* confide,'[5] admitted soldier William Ruse. Home comforts were welcome, particularly food, candles and clothes. Soldiers bought paper, ink and envelopes from sutlers,[6] and stationery makers indulged a demand for patriotic paper, envelopes bearing slogans and even specific regimental headers, and men added their own embellishments of cartoons and drawings. The Union army had its own post office near forts, Christian organisations distributed free paper, and in 1864 Union soldiers were allowed to send free letters. The Confederates were not so lucky, and acute shortages as the war raged led to theft and desperation, with some soldiers writing on mere scraps of paper. Nevertheless, their letters are a snapshot of their emotions and lives in the heat of battle. There was no censorship, which allowed for visceral descriptions, the naming of traitors and unfettered sentiment about the morals and progress of war. It would be unheard of for a soldier in the 1940s to divulge 'the next forward movement of this expedition will most likely occur in the direction of . . . Charleston,'[7] as one Unionist did in 1862.

The Civil War raged for five years until the Confederates surrendered on 8 April 1865. 'I am so happy . . . At last we have really broke the back-bone of the rebellion,'[8] wrote Private William Smith. Conversely, Confederate soldier Dewitt Clinton Gallaher wrote, 'we heard Lee had surrendered. We did not believe it as first but soon learned the worst.'[9] Two hundred and eighty thousand Confederates had died and the Southern landscape had been devastated. It had been a war that affected virtually everyone in the country, who would have lost a son, brother, husband, cousin, uncle or friend. Poetry by Confederates and Unionists, written in response to men killed, was indistinguishable in sentiment: 'Where fiercest grows the battle's rage / And

Southern banners spread; / Where minions crouch and vassals kneel, / There sleep Virginia's dead,' were the words of a Confederate poem, while this was written by a Unionist: 'A soldier had fallen! 'Tis well that we weep! / O soft be his pillow, and peaceful his sleep! / Far, far from his home, and the friends he loved most, / He fell in the conflict, and died at his post.'[10] Whole communities had a generation of men simply wiped out. Death became a macabre unifying force as a period of long and painful reconstruction and reconciliation began.

THE DECLARATION OF WAR: CELEBRATION AND DUTY

In the Confederate South, men were waved off to war along flag-lined streets thronged with cheering crowds and brass bands performing songs such as 'Bold Soldier Boy' and 'God Bless the Boys'. In the states that wanted to secede there appeared to be a real hunger for war. Eddie Neuville proclaimed, 'If those infernal Yankees don't get more hot lead than they can digest in a year, then I don't know anything about Southern pluck and shooting.'[11] Similarly, Unionist volunteer W.E. Camp wrote in April 1861, 'The mildest state of excitement reigns here our best men have tendered their services . . . everybody left back is anxious to go.'[12] Although slavery was leading the political argument for war, for the ordinary soldier on the ground, surprisingly little mention was made of the issue in letters home on either side. Granted, slavery in many parts of the South was not seen as an 'issue'. Slaves were just an economic resource, and Unionism threatened their land, personal interests and patriotism. It was also an affront to the self-government and self-determination fought for by their fathers in 1776. John H. Cochran wrote to his mother:

> I think now the air is redolant with the fumes of powder and I believe we will have war with the North in less than sixty days. If Virginia refuses to go out there will be a revolution in this state which will be the special wonder of the world and go down to posterity as the bloodiest picture in the book of time. I have said before and I say now that I will be free and will maintain my rights even though I have to fight 'looking a halter gallantly in the face.' I am a man who knows my rights and knowing dare maintain. One of those rights is secession but if the convention refuses to give us that there is another which I will maintain even at the foot of the gallows and that is rebellion . . . But like that gallant Henry who rose in rebellion against the mightiest empire on earth my words are 'give me liberty or give me death.'[13]

The word 'slave' was rarely mentioned among the rank-and-file Unionist soldier either. 'This was war gotten up by a party of traitorous politicians at the south, who wished to enrich and aggrandise themselves at the expense of the nation,'[14] blasted one Unionist volunteer. Another, Alex Cressler, did put an end to slavery at the top of his agenda:

> . . . the secessionists will have to leave to escape being imprisoned for treason, and then western Virginia will extend her government over the whole dominion and abolish slavery herself, because the non-slaveholders will carry the elections, and after Virginia becomes a free state and presents to the other southern states her advantage gained by freedom and their dis-advantage incurred by the curse of slavery they will gradually one after the other become free, and those who live to see it will behold the whole union cemented together by bonds of common interest and brotherhood, this is my opinion of the result of this war.[15]

Once men were mustered at camps, they received basic training in musketry and infantry tactics, and would do company and battalion drills daily. The common soldier who, on average, was twenty, was paid just eleven dollars a month – the equivalent of a pair of boots. In December 1861, the Confederate government promised men furloughs[16] and bonuses if they enlisted. William Margraff affirmed,

> We are going to get . . . one hundred and sixty acres o land when the war is over. They say we are going to get one hundred dollars bounty and I think that the war will be over by next Spring and if we get killed there in the war our folks can draw the land and the pay too.[17]

Often decked out in tatty old militia uniforms, and with little or no experience of warfare, many farm-boys volunteered in a spirit of making history through creating a new land and order. Over a hundred thousand soldiers were under fifteen, and some were as young as twelve. Many men who would be travelling out of their state for the first time were unwittingly redefining their American identity. As war drew on, more and more men were drafted, although for around three hundred dollars it was possible to buy your way out of the military call-up. In 1862 the Confederate Congress introduced conscription for all white men between the age of eighteen and thirty-eight, with the upper age limit rising to fifty by 1864.

It was not just Americans who fought in this conflict. 'Britishers', including over nine thousand Welshmen who had emigrated to America to escape poverty, also fought in the Unionist army. Many were Nonconformist Christians, passionately opposed to slavery, and inspired by abolitionist preachers. Singing 'raly [sic] round the flag . . . Hurah for the union down with the traitors,'[18] wrote Corporal John Griffiths Jones in 1862. Some regiments contained whole companies of Welshmen, and letters to family back in Wales were hungrily received, often reprinted in local newspapers.

The majority of soldiers were Protestant, but there were also Jews and Catholics. Despite the disparities, there was strong religious cohesion between the men. Chaplains and pastors would make themselves available to all faiths, and interdenominational services and societies were normal. When it came to the imminent battle, men would invoke God, regardless of their beliefs.

There were also huge numbers of black soldiers who fought in this war – and even 166 black regiments that served in the Union army. It was controversial. Abolitionists asked, 'Will the Negro fight?' but their courage under fire soon proved their commitment and must have changed many Northern attitudes to race. 'It really makes one's heart pulsate with pride as he looks upon those stout and brawny men, fully equipped with Uncle Sam's accoutrements upon them, to feel that these noble men are practically refuting the base assertions reiterated by copperheads[19] and traitors that the black race are incapable or patriotism, valor or ambition,'[20] wrote black Corporal James Henry Gooding.

There were few people who believed the war would rage for as long as it did, and many entered into battle believing it would be a largely 'bloodless revolution'[21] or joined in a spirit of eager anticipation. 'Everything is excitement here, we are preparing for Battle,'[22] wrote Theodorik Montford. At some of the early battles spectators turned up with champagne picnics, waving handkerchiefs as the firing started. The illusion of this being a valiant, bloodless adventure was swiftly shattered.

BLOODY REVOLUTION: A NEW WARFARE

The industrial revolution made this a new type of war in terms of weapons. Musket shot could penetrate almost two feet of earth, and twenty-four-pound cannon-balls could break through thirteen feet of earth. Grape shot of iron balls and chain shot consisting of iron chains wreaked havoc on the battlefield. 'To hear a large shell or ball whittling through the air which you can hear for three miles is not a very pleasant sound,'[23] divulged Theodorik Montford. Men learned to recognise the bumblebee-like whistle of musket balls, and were all too aware of the damage they could inflict. 'Eighteen hundred years of Christ and five thousand years of historical experience and today we are slaying each other with no better instincts than prehistoric brutes with improved machines to accomplish it,'[24] wrote Benjamin Abbott in horror. The descriptions of injuries in the field made for grim reading. Private Jacob Middower described how 'the damn rascals would throw a mortar shell . . . it blowed a nigger up about 40 feet one day and he came down dead as hell.'[25] The carnage of battles such as Cold Harbor, which caused seven thousand Union casualties, remain etched into the psyche of modern America.

Men witnessed death at close quarters; often bayonet to bayonet. They would fight until dark or until the weather set in, often too exhausted to press home advantages gained. Mistakes and confusion were commonplace: 'it was not a fight but a Slaughter without a chance for our men to see who or what they were fighting with or against it is thought that half of our men were killed by our own men it was so dark that they could not tell friend from foe,'[26] blasted Calvin Shedd after the siege of Battery Wagner in 1863.

This was a real war of attrition: Winchester in Virginia changed hands over seventy times during the course of the war. In letters home there was little boasting about killing the enemy. Many had friends and even relatives fighting on the other side, and there was clearly empathy with the fellow soldier. William White described 'one of those horrid sights of mangled humanity . . . a wounded Yankee. An Enfield rifle ball entered the back part of his right jaw, passing inside his mouth, tearing the tongue out by the roots and shivering the upper jaw into small fragments. He was indeed an object of pity . . .'[27]

Following battles, the field would remain strewn with bodies and bones, with many men comparing scenes to farmyard slaughter pens. When battles were refought in the same areas, bodies could emerge from shallow unmarked graves. The descriptions of the groans and screams of men dying in agony were chillingly recounted in letters home. In many cases there was a palpable unburdening in letters as events were described in toe-curling detail, like this from John Hagan, in 1863: 'His head was half shot off, his brains all flew about four feet and mostly fell in a pile.'[28] Admittedly, few of the most gruesome descriptions found their way into letters destined for mothers, but wives and siblings were not spared. Achilles Tynes made no apology for his frankness in letters to his wife: 'I remember you are a Soldier's Wife, hence I shall talk plain. It has always been my habit to talk plainly to those I love. Therefore do not let what I am going to say disturb or make you sad.'[29] On the battlefield, men had to fight on stoically despite the bloodshed and dead bodies. Letters were an outlet for frank, bald reflection.

Although there were field ambulances and hospitals, thousands of men died from shock, injury, infection or even ptomaine poisoning from badly tinned goods. Moreover, diarrhoea, smallpox, malaria, scurvy and pneumonia claimed lives, and there was a resurgence of several childhood diseases such as mumps, measles and diphtheria, as many men had never previously been exposed to them. It was a sobering statistic that for every man killed in battle, three would die from disease.

A Soldier's Life: Belief, Stoicism, Duty

This was a stop–start war, so there would be weeks when men were waiting in camps, or marching across country. They passed their time with camp competitions, singing, music and storytelling. Alcohol was freely available, and gambling was prolific, despite being 'officially discouraged'. Nevertheless it was an unrelenting existence. Boots that fitted were hard to come by and ever more expensive as the war dragged on. There were instances of men trudging barefoot in the snow. Lice or grey-backs were also a terrible problem, as Frank Rosenbery recounted:

> Put them in a small tub. Put some salt in the tub. Then put some boiling water on the shirts. Those grey backs are not the body lice but still they know how to bite. I washed the shirts some time ago. I did not notice any of the gentlemen about them. But they can easy be seen when they come to a full growth.[30]

Vegetables were often in scant supply, forcing men to steal from fields and orchards. Beef was perhaps too plentiful, so there was always some relief when men camped near rivers or the coast and could catch crabs and fish. Some men even tracked game and rabbit. On the march moreover, supplies often lagged behind, giving rise to some ingenious improvisation on the part of soldiers who made their own soap, smoked thistles and made beer from artichokes. Union soldiers had it marginally better than their Confederate counterparts. For a start, they were well fed and well groomed. Corporal Jones noted that he and his comrades had all gained weight since leaving camp, and that 'fat cattle'[31] were plentiful. Blockades and lack of industry exacerbated the suffering in the South, while rising prices and inflation were equally debilitating. In mid-1862, flour doubled in price and some soldiers were marching with wooden pikes as there were not enough guns. 'I can take two blankets and lie down in a pile of rocks or in mud on frozen ground, or anywhere without anything to shelter me. My cartridge box makes a soft pillow, the mother earth makes an easy bed, the heavens make a good shelter, the Lord is a good general,'[32] wrote James Thompson of army life.

'Nor must Uncle Sam's web-fleet be forgotten. At the watery margins they have been present,' wrote Abraham Lincoln. Conditions at sea, on the Atlantic coast and along western rivers were equally tough. Many men were swiftly promoted in the navy, with around 80 per cent never having previously been to sea.[33] Contrabands[34] were charged with the heavy, dirty work of coal heaving, and many suffered 'land-sickness' – a desire to escape sea air and a longing for dry land. All men faced the deadly force of torpedoes: 'While we honour the living soldiers who have done so much we must not forget to whisper for fear of disturbing the Glorious sleep of the many who have fallen.

Martyrs to the cause of Right and Equality,'[35] recorded William Gould in his diary. Conditions were damp and stuffy. Sailors would begin their exhausting days before first light, when a bugler sounded the reveille. A well-trained crew would be expected to stash hammocks and muster in seven minutes. Each day the ship would be washed down, fittings polished and guns cleaned. Food was monotonous and drill continuous. There would be a twenty-four-hour rolling watch, with men never knowing when blockade runners or a mine might blow.

'Three words . . . dearer . . . than any other in our language . . . Heaven, Home and Mother,'[36] wrote an exhausted and homesick William Ruse. It was largely to religion that men turned to help them tolerate battle and conditions. Matthew McCann admitted, 'we Stand in the Presence of Grim Death & know Not but in a few Moments Some of us Shall be fast in His Embrace,'[37] and Hiram Camp assured his mother,

> it looks like the Lord is on our side and I hope he will soon deliver us out of the trouble that is now all over our new Confederacy. Ma, I want your prayers and pray that we may be able to live in the discharge of our duty both as a Christian and a soldier. For the Bible says that the prayers of the righteous availeth much.[38]

Religion offered men strength and comfort in the fight. 'I take great delight in the rich truth of the Book. I can say it is a spring to the thirsty traveller or as a cooling breeze to the body. God be blessed for his holy word,'[39] wrote John Carnahan.

Love was another sustaining force, and conditions of battle prompted remarkably emotional letters for some. In the maelstrom of war, desires and unspoken sentiments were unleashed on paper, making for some exquisite, deeply moving letters to loved ones. Lieutenant Stamper wrote to his sweetheart Miss Walker with hope that 'the happy day will soon come that I can call you my own. I intend to be true to all my promises to you. You are the girl that won my heart and you are the one that I intend to marry . . . I still remain your true lover until death . . .'[40] Separation from wives and children was keenly felt, regardless of age. Surgeon Harvey Black wrote to his wife to say, 'may I ever be a husband worthy of your warmest affections. May I make you happy and in so doing be made happy in return. A sweet kiss and embrace to your greeting. But maybe you will say it looks ridiculous to see a man getting grayhaired to be writing love letters . . .'[41]

As months became years, war-weariness inevitably set in on both sides. 'If this is independence I don't want it, I had rather take bondage,'[42] admitted William Stillwell. By late 1862 onwards, many men had crises of conscience when they wondered whether the fight was worth it. William Latham Candler despaired:

We have been kicked, 'cursed' and butchered; and are tired of it. I don't like to acknowledge to myself the feelings that seem to be gradually imbuing the entire Army; but there is no use denying it. I actually believe that peace, today, would be welcomed by three fourths of the Army in the field and an equal number of citizens.[43]

Patriotism was a powerful impetus nevertheless, as was the severe punishment for desertion, as Jedediah Hotchkiss described:

Yesterday a deserter was shot. He wept bitterly, wishing to see his family – he fell dead, pierced by five balls – poor fellow – it seems hard, but in no other way can the discipline of the army be maintained . . . a good many have been shot, some whipped, some drummed out of camp and then put to labour with a ball and chain, some branded on the backsides with the letters D. or C. for desertion or cowardice . . . When will wars cease and the necessity no longer exist for such brutal punishments.[44]

As the war wore on into 1864 there was a gnawing realisation by many Confederates that defeat was inevitable. Some men wrote letters home urging families to accept the Union, and questioning whether they were right to rebel. At the same time, there were still huge numbers unwilling to succumb to the Yankee 'blue Devils' and saw the conflict – to the end – as a straightforward choice between liberty and death. Tom Dowtin wrote:

I trust that the God of Battles will be on our side and conduct us safely through the wars and crown us with victory! I am determined to fight if there is any done, as I had rather die on the battlefield than live and see my country needing my services. I am ready and willing to devote my all to my country.[45]

The human toll provided powerful and nagging food for thought, as Confederate Benjamin Moody encapsulated in a last letter home: 'I want to meet in a better world where all wars will be won, where pain will be felt no more, where Christ sets on the right hand of the Father and liveth to make intentions for the saints.'[46]

FAREWELL LETTERS: COMMON THEMES

Final farewell letters from the front line took many forms during the American Civil War. There were instances of locks of hair being sent home and even items made from the detritus of the weapons that killed a soldier. It was an age when the importance of being with family at the moment of death was deeply ingrained and letters became that final familial link – a way of being with your family to the end. One mother paid for a daguerreotype of her son, 'should any misfortune befall him, I would wish some likeness of him preserved,'[47] and likewise many men were recorded as having died clutching images of their loved ones to their chest.

For this reason, perhaps, farewell letters written as a man lay mortally wounded were as numerous as letters and wills written months before a death. This conflict saw many 'ordinary' letters written home over the course of the years, displaying what we may today consider to be a rather morbid preoccupation with saying goodbye. This was the culture of the time in many ways, but also a primitive reminder of the sheer scale of death and destruction men would encounter during their time in battle. It was also symptomatic of the unpredictability of battle – where life could be snuffed out by a single musket ball. William Stillwell – who survived the war – wrote:

> Molly I think of you while the cannon roar and the muskets flash. Never have I been so much excited yet but what I could compose myself enough to think of you, and I have often thought that if I have to die on the battlefield, if some kind friend would just lay my Bible under my head and your likeness on my breast with the golden curls of hair in it, that it would be enough. Molly I shall have to close for my eyes is bathed in tears, 'till I can't write. May the God of mercy and goodness be with you and bless you, preserve and protect, guide and direct you and yours always in the prayer of your ever disconsolate Husband.[48]

Dealing with the death of a soldier was all the more difficult if there had been no communication found on the soldier, and perhaps that was why letters saying farewell were so much more ubiquitous during this conflict than others. Many soldiers pledged to write condolence or final letters for one another – for example Williamson Ward of the 39th Indiana made a pact with each comrade that they would do this for the other if the worst happened.[49] Newspaper lists of the dead and wounded were at best incomplete and often inaccurate, carrying the scantest of detail. Letters, if drafted by the individual, or communicated verbally to doctors, nurses or fellow soldiers, could tell the real story of how that person felt in their dying moments. Confederate surgeon Dr Holt recalled this letter dictated by a soldier for his mother:

> This is the last you may ever hear from me. I have time to tell you that I died like a man. Bear my loss as best you can. Remember that I am true to my country and my greatest regret at dying is that she is still not free and that you and your sisters are robbed of my youth. I hope this will reach you and you must not regret that my body cannot be obtained. It is a mere matter of form anyhow. This letter is stained with my blood.[50]

Many last letters concerned instructions for children, wives and parents. Some were matter of fact and rather practical. H.C. Kendrick wrote:

Ma, please make me a coat for next winter. It may be, that I will fall on the battle-field, but if I should, my clothes can benefit some of my brothers. I know this is calculating further ahead than I have any assurance of living, but if I fall, be you well assured, I will sacrifice my life upon the alter of my country.

William Clark Corson was also in practical mode when he wrote, 'If I had property of my own to leave you in the event of my death I would beg that our nuptials be celebrated the first time that I should come home, but the thought that I might be suddenly snatched from you and you left worse off than when I married you is too serious for me to contemplate.'[51] The majority of letters home were also desperate expressions of love. 'Your letters are received by me with the greatest pleasure and a beating heart . . . if we never again met on Earth, I shall ever cherish the fond remembrance of thee, and think of the pleasant hours passed in your society,'[52] wrote William Ruse to his sweetheart Maggie.

One overriding characteristic of the last letters from this conflict was their fervent religiosity. Men went to lengths to stress that their death would be painless; it was a passage to, and acceptance of, the afterlife. Tracts were distributed to Confederate soldiers by the Presbyterian Church that hailed the importance of death: 'Death fixes our state. Here everything is changing and unsettled. Beyond the grave our condition is unchangeable.'[53] In many ways, chaplains prepared men to embrace a death that many saw in premonitions or felt was inevitable. Levi Pennington claimed,

I think it is not right for people to crave riches in this world. For if a man passed the world, it would do him no good in the world to come. We had better try to lay up treasures in Heaven. Where moss nor rust doth corrupt. Where war, sin nor pain dwell but all one in Christ. I want you all to see the Lord and obtain a pardon for you sins and be prepared to meet me in Heaven where we will part nor more . . . Children, above all things obey your Mother for she will give you good counsel. Rachel, do all you can to get you children to do right.[54]

The final theme in last letters from this period was how political and patriotic they were – whether shrouded in the rhetoric of religion or not. There was a blurring of lines between duty to God, and duty to one's country. 'He loves your children and will be a father to them if their father should fall in the Defense of their country. God tempers the wind to the shorn lambs,' was the poetic farewell of John Carnahan.[55]

Cementing the political nature of many farewell letters were those that mentioned individuals they considered to be traitors or heroes. 'Aunt Stacey is no copperhead,' wrote Colonel Matthew Starr, while an indignant Private Morrison divulged,

> Bill Brabazan was telling around that he was wounded . . . Bill has made his brags too many times publicly . . . I suppose he would like to get his descriptive role but he will be there a great while before he gets it . . . I think if he is sick it is a judgement on him for trying to play off.[56]

It was a final chance to put their view across, and settle rumbling scores.

The farewell letters from this war gave a sense of immortality to the fallen soldiers. They were particularly important to families who found that the war deprived them of attending a proper burial or funeral. Thousands of men were missing or buried in unmarked graves when the war ended; if the family had no headstone, at least they had a letter. Despite the gulf of time, the words and sentiments are as insightful today as they were back then. They open a window on the hopes, fears and opinions of men who changed the course of American history.

MAJOR SULLIVAN BALLOU

Killed in the First Battle of Bull Run, 28 July 1861

BORN ON 28 MARCH 1829 in Smithfield, Rhode Island, Ballou was educated at the Philips Academy in Andover, Massachusetts, before attending Brown University, and then the National Law School in New York, where he taught elocution (Plate 3). His father Hiram had died when Ballou was just six, and he was raised by his well-to-do Huguenot relatives. By 1853 he was appointed to the Rhode Island Bar. A passionate public servant, in 1854 he was elected as clerk of the Rhode Island House of Representatives, and unanimously voted speaker a few years later. By the end of the decade, he had returned to Woonsocket in Rhode Island and settled into life as a lawyer.

On 15 October 1855, Ballou married Sarah Hart Shumway of Worcester, with whom he had two sons, Edgar and William. Just two years after the birth of William, Ballou enlisted as a major[57] in C Company of the Second Rhode Island Infantry, on 5 June 1861, and was soon on the way to Washington with the regiment. Men knew they would be moving towards the Manassas Junction in Virginia where the Confederate army was waiting. Indeed, in late July, Ballou's unit was heading for Confederate lines as part of Major General Irvin McDowell's army. One week before the Battle of Bull Run, Ballou was certain it would be a ferocious, dangerous fight. His letters were a physical link to home, and he could imagine himself there for a few precious moments:

> I never knew the longing of a father for his children before. And you can scarcely imagine how my blood dances – my nerves thrill and my brain almost whirls, when with eyes wide open the world all becomes blank to me, and I see my little boys going through their childish pranks, and hear their singing voices, and even stretch my arms to catch them, and awake to touch the white walls of my tent.[58]

On 14 July 1861, at Camp Clark in Washington, Ballou poured out his heart in what has become perhaps the most famous civil war letter in history.

My very dear Sarah,

The indications are very strong that we shall move in a few days – perhaps tomorrow. Lest I should not be able to write again, I feel impelled to write a few lines that may fall under your eye when I shall be no more. Our movement may be one of a few days duration and be full of pleasure, and it may be one of severe conflict and death to me. 'Not my will but thine O God be done' if it is necessary that I should fall on the battlefield for my Country I am ready. I have no misgivings about or lack of confidence in the cause in which I am engaged, and my courage does not halt or falter. I know how American Civilization now bears upon the triumph of the Government and how great a debt we owe to those who went before us through the blood and suffering of the Revolution; and I am willing perfectly to lay down all my joys in this life to help maintain that government and to pay that debt.

But, my dear wife, when I know that with my own joys I lay down nearly all of yours, and replace them in this life with cares and sorrows – when, after having eaten for long years the bitter fruit of orphanage myself, I must offer it as their only sustenance to my dear little children – is it weak or dishonourable, while the banner of my purpose floats calmly and proudly in the breeze, that my unbounded love for you, my darling wife and children, should struggle in fierce, though useless, contest with my love of country?

I cannot describe to you my feelings on this calm summer night, when two thousand men are sleeping around me, many of them enjoying the last, perhaps, before that of death – and I, suspicious that Death is creeping behind me with his fatal dart, am communing with God, my country, and thee.

I have sought most closely and diligently, and often in my breast, for a wrong motive in thus hazarding the happiness of those I loved, and I could not find one. A pure love of my country and the principles I have often advocated before the people and 'the name of honour that I love more than I fear death' have called upon me, and I have obeyed.

Sarah my love for you is deathless, it seems to bind me with mighty cables that nothing but Omnipotence could break; and yet my love of Country comes over me like a strong wind and bears me irresistibly on with all these chains to the battle field. The memories of the blissful moments I have spent with you come creeping over me, and I feel most gratified to God and to you that I have enjoyed them for so long. And hard it is for me to give them up and burn to ashes the hopes of future years, when, God willing, we might still have lived and loved together, and seen our sons grown up to honourable manhood, around us. I have, I know, but few and small claims upon Divine Providence, but something whispers to me – perhaps it is the wafted prayer of my little Edgar, that I shall return to my loved ones unharmed. If I do not my dear Sarah, never forget how much I love you, and when my last breath escapes me on the battle field, it will whisper your name.

Forgive my many faults and the many pains I have caused you. How thoughtless and foolish I have often times been! How gladly would I wash out with my tears every little spot upon your happiness and struggle with all the misfortunes of this world to shield you and my children from harm but I cannot I must watch you from the spirit world and hover near you while you buffet the storms with your precious little freight and wait with sad patience till we meet to part no more.

But, O Sarah! If the dead can come back to this earth and flit unseen around those they loved, I shall always be near you; in the gladdest days and in the darkest nights amidst your happiest scenes and gloomiest hours always, always; and when the soft breeze fans your cheek it shall be my breath, as the cool air fans your throbbing temple, it shall be my spirit passing by. Sarah do not mourn me dead; think I am gone and wait for thee, for we shall meet again.

As for my little boys they will grow up as I have done and never know a father's love and care.

Little Willie is too young to remember me long but my blue eyed Edgar will keep my frolics with him among the dimmest memories of his childhood. Sarah I have unlimited confidence in your maternal care and your development of their characters. Tell my two mothers I call God's blessings upon them. Oh! Sarah I wait for you then come to me and lead thither my children.

Sullivan.

On 21 June the men marched to the front lines, negotiating the trees that had been set to block their path. By nine o'clock, they were on the Manassas Road, and came under a hail of fire from the enemy. Ordered up a hill, many Rhode Islanders reached the crest, only to come under more fire from Confederates, 'scattering death and confusion everywhere'.[59] Hours passed as more and more men were felled in a maelstrom of sword-blows, bullets and musket balls.

Ballou's regiment was ordered to move, and he rode up in front of them on his horse, Jennie. Turning his back on the Confederate army, Ballou was hit by a six-pound shot that decimated his leg and killed Jennie. He was evacuated to the field hospital at Sudley Church as his men continued to stand their ground and return fire. Ballou's regiment suffered ninety-three men killed, wounded and missing. The battle ended as a Southern victory, despite the Unionists' initial triumph.

As a prisoner of war at the hospital, Ballou must have been in agonising pain and despair. A Confederate surgeon amputated his leg a week later, but Ballou could not survive the trauma. At four o'clock on 28 July, he died and was temporarily buried in the grounds of the church.[60] Ballou's farewell letter was never posted home, unlike the many other letters he wrote from the field during his short war. It was found among his personal belongings – including a lock of hair – when Governor Sprague travelled to Virginia in March 1862 to retrieve the human remains of several Rhode Island officers who had fallen there. At the end of March, Ballou's remains were back in New York, and the local militia escorted the coffins through streets crowded with onlookers. He had a full military burial with musket fire and bells ringing. When Ballou died, his wife was just twenty-four. She later moved to New Jersey and lived with her son William until her death at the age of eighty. She never remarried, and ensured she was buried next to her husband at Swan Point Cemetery in Rhode Island.

Second Lieutenant Ira P. Woodruff

Killed in the Battle of Seven Pines, 31 May 1862

THERE IS SCANT RECORD of Woodruff's early life, save for the information that his father was called Richard and was a miller who later became a commissary supplying food to soldiers. Ira Woodruff enlisted and was commissioned as second lieutenant in the Confederate army on 31 August 1861 in Atlanta, and was assigned to the 23rd Regiment of the Georgia Infantry as they moved to Virginia.

In November 1861, Woodruff was at Island Mills in West Virginia. This was an enormous flour mill that on the outbreak of the Civil War was donating huge quantities of grain to Union soldiers. In October, Confederates burned down the mill; one would assume that Woodruff was involved in this attack. By December 1861, Woodruff was onboard a steamboat 'plowing our way down the dark rolling waters of James River' to Yorktown in Virginia. Here he was posted on artillery duty at the Kingsmill plantation lands, as defences were built outside Richmond, and naval skirmishes occurred along the river.

At this time, he wrote to his cousins, with prophetic words at the top of the letter. 'Farewell home, and farewell friends;/Adieu each tender tie: Resolved, we mingle in the tide,/Where changing squadrons furious ride,/To conquer or to die.' A sign that Woodruff was aware of the scale and implication of events came in his description of his letter as 'a history'. In it, he described the regiment's orders to move to Yorktown and the snowy, unsheltered conditions. He was also missing home deeply:

> I have been sitting by the rivers side today thinking of the comforts of home. I thought of you all as my imagination soared with an even flight to the sun bright clime of Good Old Georgia. The price of Liberty is eternal vigilance and it takes hardships to achieve its gilded meteor. The river here is seven miles wide and you may imagine my feelings as I was gazing upon this expanse of water and thinking of my sweet friends far away. We are expecting some desperate fighting as soon as we get to Yorktown.

The letter gave some vivid insight into the reflections of ordinary soldiers facing an uncertain future,

> talking about the hard fate of a soldier. I have just remarked to them that this is only a small foretaste of what we will have to encounter. They are beginning to think a soldier's life is a hard one but they all say if they can get a chance 'They are bound to whip the Yankees the whole hog or none'.

In January 1862 Woodruff was still at Yorktown and had experienced first-hand that battle was not the only danger for soldiers. Two friends had been discharged with illness, and two in his company had died from pneumonia. Indeed, Woodruff himself had fallen ill over Christmas, 'but by a speedy application of medicinal remedies I avoided a sever attack'. Death and disease were certainly making Woodruff consider his own fate: 'I can only surrender myself into the hands of a kind and protecting Providence who does all things for the best. The dispensations of Providence to the Eyes of man are sometimes hard to Comprehend and they often seem as if they are unjust but we should try and be reconciled to all the dispensations of Providence.' Woodruff would have known that battle was surely imminent, and his thoughts turned not only to God, but to home. 'I would give anything in the world to see my dear cousins and aunt at this time and also I would like to have some of your butter milk and chicken pie.' By May 1862, the regiment were finally involved in their first major battle at Seven Pines.

Also known as the Battle of Fair Oaks, the Confederates were attempting to oust General George McClellan's 100,000-strong army from their position just a few miles outside the Confederate capital of Richmond. Occupying both sides of the Chickahominy Creek, the Confederates were in a precarious position; their commander, General Joseph Johnston, had over sixty thousand men to call on, but in the melee of battle was unable to get all of these men into the action. On the morning of 31 May the plan was to attack from the south, marching into position at four o'clock and reaching position at eight. Due to a lack of communication and poor organisation, the Confederate plan was late in starting out. Battle raged throughout the day in dense woods and putrid swamps as more Union reinforcements piled in. Woodruff was fighting from the Chickahominy Bluffs – a huge defensive earthwork – that was slippery, boggy and muddy due to heavy rain. At around four or five o'clock, Woodruff's company was ordered to move to support soldiers coming under fire from heavy musketry. They themselves were facing shell bursts and consistent fire from the Union army. As the light started to fade, the Confederates were losing momentum and stalling, and retreated the following day. The Battle at Seven Pines caused an estimated 13,736 casualties; 5,739 Union soldiers and 7,997 Confederates. Ira Woodruff was one of them.

There was no record of how Woodruff was killed, or what happened to his body. 'He left neither wife not child,' according to his service record. However, he did leave behind a moving and heartfelt farewell letter, sent to his cousin Mattie. Woodruff had in fact written the letter just a few months after volunteering, when things were still relatively quiet. Perhaps it was then that he had time to contemplate and prepare himself for the worst that would soon come.

The time draws near when perhaps we will bid each other a long farewell, for the decrees of fortune are uncertain and no one with our limited capacity can penetrate the murky curtain that veils the unknown future. Perhaps if we could read the record of futurity as it stands systemized by Him whose brow has glittered with immortal majesty from the hoary annals of eternity, we might not pass through the fires which lie before us. I go forward to brave the dangers by which we are today threatened, with victory or death emblazoned in living characters upon my ensign.

It is to perpetuate the liberties and honours you proudly enjoy that I leave the bosom of my friends and especially those who lie near to my heart by the kindred ties of relationship that I leave all behind that is sweet to enjoy and march with proud and rapid steps to the rescue and defence of my suffering country. This land of ours has many sweet and delightful associations that proudly cluster around its imperishable history. I go to contend and plead for the rights of that land that gave me birth, which is sacred to me, and will ever be as long as memory holds its position in my brain.

When that dear land shall be polluted by the filthy tread of our enemies that are now waging an unjust war upon us, I hope that it will take place after my remains sleep in the lonesome grave of the soldier. If it should ever fall to my lot to face the instruments of death, where perhaps cannon balls may rain around me, I shall think of my own sweet friends that I have left behind me. If I fall while fighting for my country, I want you to honour me as a fallen soldier who fought for the honour of his own dear land. If I never meet you again in this world, I hope that we will meet each other in that land of love where our names will glitter like sparkling diamonds upon the tablets of eternity!

Your affectionate cousin

Ira P Woodruffe.[61]

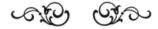

Captain James E. Rearden
Killed at Chickamauga, 26 September 1863

James – or Jas, as he called himself – Rearden was born in Edgefield, South Carolina, in 1840. He was married by the age of twenty to Mary Magdalene, and they lived with his mother Nancy. Rearden was twenty-one, with a personal estate valued at $160 and working as a farm operative[62] when civil war broke out. He decided to volunteer and enlisted in the Confederate 7th South Carolina Infantry – a regiment that had been assembled at Columbia, South Carolina, during the spring of 1861. Rearden's service record described him as five foot six, with a light complexion, black hair and dark eyes. He enlisted in June 1861 for twelve months at Camp Buller. A month after enlisting, Rearden and the regiment moved to northern Virginia.

After fighting in Bonham's Brigade at First Manassas,[63] the unit participated in the campaigns of the army of northern Virginia from the Seven Days' Battles to Gettysburg. The 7th South Carolina Infantry was a part of General Joseph Kershaw's brigade known as the Bloody Seventh because of the heavy losses suffered during their numerous battles in the Civil War. This regiment totalled 581 officers and men in April 1862; by March 1865 only 222 men remained.

On 26 July 1861 Rearden wrote to his sister. It was days after the First Battle of Bull Run; just one month into his term this engagement would have provided a sobering jolt.

I now take my pen in hand to answer your kind letter which came to hand the day I left Fairfax and I haven't had a chance to write before . . . I didn't believe we could stand so much, Sally there was alarm a few minutes ago and I put this letter in my valise and got my arm and started to the battlefield to die . . . I expect you want to know what my arm is. They are called . . . bowie knives a foot long and sword. You must take care of my baby . . . Give my love to all my friends and to all of my Sunday School chums and tell them that I am well . . . and to all the Sunday School teachers I will write to you all again as soon as I can. Hereafter one letter must do you all for I haven't got envelope or paper nor can I buy them. So I must close with my few lines so nothing more at present but remain your ever affectionate brother James.

Attached to the letter to his sister was a farewell letter that Rearden had written to his mother and wife, in which he was now keenly aware of his own mortality. Although it starts confidently enough, Rearden could not stop himself penning some words to prepare his family – and no doubt himself – for the worst.

Dear Maggia, Dear Mother,
    I have seated myself down this morning to drop you a few lines to let you know how I am getting along. We are stationed at Vienna [Camp] 14 miles off Washington. We expect to stay here a few days then expect to move but I don't know where . . . Mother we had an awful fight Sunday and there was thousands slain but as good luck happens I was not one of the slain. The enemy attacked us Thursday on the right flank and on the left flank . . . rifle balls hit our battery that we had made of dirt and completely carved up the right of our company and if we had not been lying down they would have been several killed. I tell you Maggia and Mother that was pretty close . . . When they retreated they left everything that they had. We took 1200 prisoners, 300 wagons . . . 42 pieces of artillery and 20,000 . . . small arms. I took a fine Minnie[64] rifle that I am going to bring home when I come. If I live mother I would be the proudest in the world to see your loved ones at home. I didn't know what it was to have a sweet home before Maggia. I want you to take good care of my sweet baby and if I never get back, teach her to love her country.
    I can't write much, I feel very nauseous. I wrote to you yesterday morning with a pencil. I couldn't do any letter that time so I will close. So nothing more at present, but remain your affectionate husband and son.[65]

VIENNa Camp 7 Regsec
Dear maggia   July 26 186

Dear mather i have Seated my Self
down this marning to drap you afew lines
to let you no how i am ageting along
we are Station at veanno 14 mile of washing tyn
we exspect to stay her afew day then
i exspect to move but i dant no wher
but i understand we are a going to the
Kellgape of mangland mather we had
a ffull fight sunday and ther was
thausands slayn but as good luck
happen i was not one of the slayn the
enmy attacked us thursday on th
Right flank and on the left plank
sunday in time of the fight sunda a rifle
ball hit our battry that we had made
of durt and campletely caverd up th
Right of our campany and if we had
not bin lying down that wauld bin seral
Kill i tell maggia and mather that
was pretty clase cutten when the
Retreated tha left aver thing tha had
we take 12 000 prissners 3 00 woagens
2 00 000 42 peices of artlery and
20 000 stand of smal arrms i taken a
fine mine rifle that i am ogoing to bring

4 Part of the letter from James Rearden, 26 July 1861 (Special Collections, University Libraries, Virginia Polytechnic Institute and State Univeristy).

Following this letter, Rearden took part in many more battles, including the Yorktown siege, Williamsburg and Virginia's Seven-Day battles over June and July 1862. He obviously impressed with his military prowess, and on 17 September 1862, the day of the Battle of Antietam, was promoted to captain. He wrote as often as possible to his family in Edgefield, grabbing whatever scraps of paper he could find. There must have been occasion for celebration on 10 February 1863, when Rearden came home for the first of twenty-seven days' furlough. When he returned, the regiment saw action at Chancellorsville in May, and then Gettysburg in July. It was at Chickamuaga in September 1863 that he finally fell.

The Unionists' victory at Gettysburg had bolstered their confidence, and their next target was to seize the Chattanooga–Atlanta railway line. Chickamuaga was a battle that pitched 60,000 Federals against 62,000 Confederates. According to Kershaw's report, at midnight on 18 September the troops gathered at Catoosa Station before marching the next morning to Ringgold. As night drew in on the 19th, the men were ordered across the nearby Alexander Bridge, where they made camp after midnight. At eleven o'clock on 20 September the men moved to the rear of the front line. It was an area of dense forest, and shells rained in from unseen directions. Some hours later, the men were ordered to advance, bayonets fixed, at the enemy soldiers, who were positioned across a field in a patch of woodland. Under severe artillery fire, men were mown down on both sides. Reinforcements arrived at three o'clock. 'It terminated at sunset,' Kershaw baldly stated, although he was moved to mention that 'Officers and men each acted as if impressed with the feeling that the destinies of the country depended upon his own faithful, earnest, and intelligent discharge of duty.' During the first charge on 20 September the 7th South Carolinas had helped capture masses of artillery and ammunition, and it was hailed a Confederate victory. But it came with a price. Casualties were enormous – 2,312 Confederates killed and 14,674 injured, against 1,657 Federals killed and 9,756 injured. Thousands of men were missing. The following day was spent by Confederates clearing men from the battlefield and burying the dead.[66]

Rearden may have been one of those men lying injured on the battlefield. He had been wounded in the leg – most likely shot with a ball that would shatter bone on contact. Hospitals at this time were frequently dirty, crawling with parasites and lice. It was decided to amputate his leg. Gangrene was so prevalent that amputation was seen as a preventive measure. Anaesthetics and chloroform were in use, but in short supply. The standard surgery textbook of the period described in excruciating detail the agonies that Rearden would have endured: 'The patient is to be placed on a firm table, with his back properly supported by pillows, and assistants, who are also to hold his hands, and keep him from moving too much during the operation. The ankle of the sound limb is to be fastened, by means of a garter, to the nearest leg of the table.' With tourniquet fastened, the text advised how to prevent the 'violent struggling' of patients. Scalpels were used to cut through the flesh, before the bone submitted to the surgeon's saw. 'If the bone should break, before the sawing is finished, the sharp projecting spiculae . . . must be removed by means of a pair of bone-nippers,' advised the text. Arteries were tied and ligatures applied to prevent haemorrhage. The stump was then dressed with bandages and ointment.[67]

Despite 75 per cent of amputees surviving at this time, Rearden did not. Lack of sterilisation and resultant infection, blood loss or shock could have caused his death six days after being wounded.

When his wife Mary filed to claim Rearden's outstanding pay of $372.66 in November 1863, she had to submit to an official process, which must have been desperate and upsetting. Cash then – as now – would have been scant comfort for the loss of a husband and son, though they undoubtedly sought solace that he had been able to say goodbye in a letter.

Colonel Thornton Fleming Brodhead
Killed in the Second Battle of Bull Run, 2 September 1862

Thornton Brodhead was born on 5 December 1820 in New Hampshire, the son of Mary Dodge and John, a clergyman who founded Methodism in New England and Canada (Plate 4). He had military ancestry stretching back to the seventeenth century. The youngest but one of six siblings, Thornton's older brother John had studied medicine at Dartmouth before being appointed to the Treasury. Thornton studied law at Harvard and worked as a lawyer in Gross Isle, Michigan. He served in the Mexican War of 1846–8 as an officer with the 15th Infantry and was twice promoted for bravery. Resuming his career after the war, he was elected to the State Senate as postmaster of Detroit in 1852, and edited the *Detroit Free Press*. Brodhead married Archangela Macomb Abbott on 27 June 1849, and they had six children – five girls and a boy – all of whom were baptised. [68] Thornton enlisted near the start of the Civil War, on 22 August 1861, and was made a colonel at Camp Lyon near Detroit, directing the First Michigan Cavalry and serving under Generals Banks, Fremont and Pope. The First Cavalry had 1,144 officers and men on its rolls; Brodhead was well respected and had a reputation for courage.

On 29 September the men left camp under orders to proceed to Washington. Brodhead wrote to his mother on 8 October 1861 in sombre mood, 'I have a fine command but my dear mother, I have had to fight harder . . . than I ever expected to fight against this traitorous enemy.' Nevertheless, his belief in the cause was undimmed: 'I have felt & do feel that our cause is just. It *must* prevail or this Providence in which we all believe turns out a failure.' He also remembered his emotional goodbye to his wife and children, which left them 'a little damp about the eyes'.[69] For most of the winter he was in camp at Frederick, Maryland.

Into early 1862, and the regiment were part of General Banks's force, guarding the Potomac Line. In March Brodhead grabbed a few moments from the 'never ending spinning excitement' to pen a few lines to his mother and reassure her he was safe, although others had been wounded. He described the tumult of battle – 'charging through . . . and facing the unearthly music of their guns . . . blazing ridges' – in confident, strident tones. He took immense pride in his men and the 'chivalry of the old dominion'.[70] It was clear that Brodhead's war had become his passion and that honour and duty were attributes to be admired.

On 12 June the regiment entered Virginia, where they soon joined the General Pope campaign, clashing with Confederates in July and August. On 20 August 1862 Brodhead was promoted to brigadier-general.

Brodhead and his men moved to Centreville, where they would contest the second famous Battle of Bull Run. In total, seven men were killed, thirteen wounded, and 115 captured and missing. The battle began sporadically on 28 August, reaching full momentum by the 29th. Armies were now bigger and more experienced, and the Federals held their position. General Pope was unaware, however, that massive Confederate reinforcements had arrived, and he prematurely announced victory. His illusion was soon shattered the following day as the now ill-prepared Unionists were battered by the onslaught; there were twenty-five thousand casualties.

On 30 August Brodhead and his men were at Bull Run Creek, preparing for an attack on the Second Virginia Cavalry, who had support from the First West Virginia and First Vermont at the rear. At the command of 'Draw Sabres' and the deathly sound of a bugle, the men advanced. It was a typically chaotic battle as men, horses and artillery swept the area. The Confederates charged headlong into Brodhead's men, forcing them into retreat. Brodhead tried desperately to round his men up and form a defensive line but found himself face to face with Adjutant Lewis Harmon of the 12th Virginia Regiment. Refusing to surrender, Brodhead was shot twice; he was blasted off his horse and taken prisoner. Brodhead's pension record affirmed that he was killed 'by two bullets entering his left breast and passing through his body'. He died of his wounds a few days later.

Knowing he was ebbing away, Brodhead pencilled a letter to his brother on a piece of discoloured paper, apparently torn from an account book and spotted with his blood.

> I am passing now from earth, but send you love from my dying couch. For all your love and kindness you will be rewarded. I have fought manfully, and now die fearlessly. I am one of the victims of Pope's imbecility and McDowell's treason. Tell the President, would he save the country he must not give our hallowed flag to such hands. But the old flag will triumph yet. The soldiers will regild its folds, polluted by imbecility and treason. John, you owe a duty to your country. Write; show up Pope's imbecility and McDowell's infamy, and force them from places where they can send brave me to assured destruction. I had hopes to live longer, but I die midst the ring and clangour of battle, as I could wish. Farewell! To you and to the noble officers of my regiment, I confide wife and children. Thornton.[71]

On 31 August Brodhead wrote a more personal – though still incredibly proud – farewell letter to his 'dearest wife'.

> I write to you, mortally wounded, from the battle field. We are again defeated. And as this reaches you, your children will be Fatherless.
>
> Before I die, let me implore you that in some way it may be stated, that General Pope has been outwitted[72] and that McDowell is a traitor. Had they done their duty, as I did mine . . . the dear old flag had waived in triumph . . .
>
> Today is Sunday. And today I sink to the green couch of our final rest.
>
> I have fought well, my darling, and I was shot in the endeavour to rally our broken battalions. I could have escaped; but would not run till all hope was gone; and was shot about the only one of our forces left on the field. Our cause is just. And our generals – not the Enemy's have defeated us. In God's good time he will give us victory.
>
> And now, good bye, wife and children. Bring them up, I know you will, in the fear of God and love for our Saviour.
>
> But for you and the dear ones so dependent, I should die hapy. I know the blow will fall with crushing weight upon you. Trust in him who gave Manna in the Wilderness.
>
> Dr. Nash is with me. It is now after midnight; and I have spent most of the night in sending messages to you.
>
> I send my silver watch to Johnny. And all my military equipment at home, guns, saddles etc are his. The Rebels took my horse, saddle, pistols, and sabre from me as soon as they shot me. It is lucky that I had this pencil and paper in my pocket so as to write you.
>
> Two bullets have gone through my chest; and directly through the lungs. I suffer little now, but at first the pain was acute. I have won the Soldier's name, and

am ready to meet now, as I must, the Soldier's fate. I hope that from Heaven I may see the glorious old Flag wave over the individual Union I have loved so well.

Fair well wife and babes and friends. We shall meet again.

Your loving Thornton.[73]

When Brodhead finally died, his body was transported to Alexandria, where his brother was formally notified of his death. He was laid to rest at the Elmwood Cemetery in Detroit. His wife was left with six children under the age of sixteen, and Brodhead's army pension of $30 per month. Thornton's farewell letter to Archangel was made public after his death, and his treasonous comments led to an inquiry into McDowell's actions, although he was fully exonerated. Mistakes and chaos had become inescapable in the frenzied tumult of this war. Brodhead was an impassioned soldier to the end, and refused to believe the Confederates could triumph. He was ultimately right, but his dying words in the heat of a battle still raging betrayed his anger and bitterness. In the same note though, he was able to include the words of love that his wife and children, would have desperately sought.

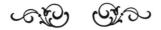

GALUTIA YORK

Died 14 May 1863

BORN 1843, GALUTIA YORK was the eldest son of a farming family from Hubbardsville, New York. His parents Zebulon and Lucy had seven children – four boys and three girls – and a personal estate worth $350. At Hamilton on 12 August 1862, nineteen-year-old York, who was a labourer on the farm, volunteered to enlist with G Company, 114th New York Infantry Regiment. Mustered on 3 September 1862 under Colonel Elisha Smith, only days later the regiment sailed by canal boat to Fort Monroe at the mouth of Virginia's James River, and then on to Baltimore.

On 10 September 1862 York was in high, patriotic spirits, writing, 'tell Henry, Emily, Irene, Adelbert and Delly that I am a going to kill each of them a rebel if I can.' Just leaving New York was a huge adventure for York. His letters revealed his wide-eyed wonderment at the wider world and his ever-expanding horizons. 'I have seen some great wonders since I started from home or they are wonders to me. I have seen the railroad and steam-ships . . . as you may say all kinds of vessels and above all, all kind of folk. The folks down here after you take out the soldiers are half negroes,' he wrote from Camp Belger in Maryland in October 1862.

Many recruits during this war had no military background and largely learned to soldier on the job. At camps there was daily drilling, but for many – including York – this was the first time they had ever wielded a gun. In November, realising action was drawing closer, and expecting to be sent to Texas, he rather shakily revealed, 'I don't know whether I could shoot a rebel or not, for I never shot my gun but we are going at it tomorrow. They are going to put us right through the picker now.'

York was a prodigious letter-writer, sending notes to his family and siblings every ten days or so. In return, their letters to him were a huge comfort and 'put new life right into me'. His letters reveal him to be a high-spirited young man, with a fierce loyalty to his family and his duty. His writings also underlined how young, inexperienced and often homesick, he was. Army life gave him his first introduction to alligators and orange trees. He was at pains to reassure his mother that he had not started smoking and was reading his bible regularly. He had a particular preoccupation with his health, frequently letting them know how his diarrhoea and other bodily functions were coping! Many of York's letters were filled with the minutiae of soldiering life, giving us a remarkable snapshot of the deprivations and hardship in this conflict. He painted a vivid picture of the lice that plagued soldiers: 'it is quite a sight to see a thousand men drawn up in a line of battle along the seashore, all stripped bare-assed, fighting lice; body lice I mean. Them that is larger than a cornel of wheat with US under their tail and there is some that has got US marked on their backs.'

His descriptions of camp life in particular told of how rife sickness and disease had become. As early as September 1862 he said, 'Captain Tucker is pretty sick. There is quite a number sick in this regiment. One man in company A is dead and there is one of the Lieutenants that cannot live.' By October the ravages of poor sanitation and arduous work were taking their toll on his health (he was suffering diarrhoea) and his kit. 'I want a little money to get my boots taped with. That is something that I didn't calculate for . . . The soil down here is very coarse sand and it wears shoe leather the worst thing . . . the bottoms of a good many of their shoes are all gone.' He told of increasing numbers of men lying sick in hospital and two more who had died. In October 1862 the regiment was at Camp Belger in Maryland, and the end of war seemed a distant prospect to York: '[I] should not wonder if we should stay here all winter. That is the calculation now I believe. The war is not ended yet nor won't be in a good while yet,' he wrote in a letter also asking for butter, cheese and milk from home. Having grown up on a farm, no doubt York was used to his own produce, and Unionist fare did not quite measure up.

Reaching the James River in November, York penned a somewhat awed description of the stockpile of weapons at an army fort: 'I saw a quarter of an acre of ground covered 4 feet with canon balls . . . there was a pile of grape shot as large as our hop house or very near it and there was over 300 canons . . . there was 2 canons that weighs over 60 tons apiece. Them is what you might call popguns . . .'

When General Banks took over control of Louisiana, Texas, Alabama and Mississippi from General Butler, the 114th Regiment sailed for New Orleans. They saw action at Fort Bisland (where eleven of the regiment were wounded or killed), but York was ensconced at Chesapeake Hospital. He remained here for over two months. Measles had ravaged the camp and as a boy who had never left New York, it was inevitable that York would succumb.

On 8 February Galutia York penned what was his farewell letter. The farewell was rather flippant, but deeply telling of his justifiable worries about dying from disease. Smallpox and other infections were felling men all around him, and he was suffering a heavy cold. It must have been a depressing prospect to face what would have been considered a most ignominious death at the hands of fever rather than fight. York wrote to his parents in morbid, miserable mood.

It is with much pleasure that I once more take my pen in hand to let you know how I get along. I am not very well. I have got a hard cold and a very hard cough but I hope this will find you all well and in good spirits. I ain't in very good spirits today for they have got us down to quarantine again. We have been here 3 days. We went up to New Orleans as I wrote to you but just as we got up there, there was 2 men come down with the smallpox and then we had to come back to this hospital, for this is a hospital where they keep smallpox. I suppose that I shall have it and all of the rest of the men on board and probably the most of us will kick the hospital-bucket. I don't know when I shall see the 114 Reg. again for we shall have to stay here 1 or 2 months and if we stay on this ship as we be now, we shall all have the ship fever and go overboard faster than sheep with any distemper. The mumps is on board. Jud has got them. His chops swelled up like a Chipmunks . . .

I saw a lot of nice Plantations when we went up to New Orleans. I picked me out one where I am going to live when I get through soldiering . . .

The 114 Reg. is in Texas doing guard duty. They have all of the milk and molasses that they can eat. They are having a first rate time down there . . . goodbye for this time. This from your ever loving and affectionate son Galutia H York . . .

His experiences in hospital and the stifling conditions of Louisiana (which also brought mosquitoes and rats) was making York reconsider his initial enthusiasm for soldiering. On 19 February 1863 he confessed,

there ain't but one place that I should like to be any better and that is HOME. But
I ain't there, but I shall be sometime, and if it is God's will, it won't be many long
months . . . I dreamt about being home last night and finally I dream about being
. . . home every once in a while but when I wake up I am in my tent as usual.

York also urged his younger brother Henry to 'grow young one year' and so
avoid being drafted.

By April 1863, York was vaccinated against smallpox and back with his unit.
He was still not fully recovered, and the regiment was still plagued by illness.
York was disillusioned with the army:

there is a lot of men hear that had ought to have their discharge but they will get
it by going to their graves before Uncle Sam will give them one. I have been with
the Reg. 5 days but I ain't seen the Captain. He is sick. God knows I would get my
discharge or a furlough if I could but there is now use talking.

Because of his illnesses York had still not been in battle and was itching to do
so. At Brashear City, the Unionist army was 'right in sight' of the Confederates
and he believed, 'they will probably have a battle at Vixberg within a week.
Well let them fight. I ain't hardly able to help now but shall soon if nothing
happens and they will have to look out.' His letters throughout April revealed
that he was engaged in light duties and was confident that the war would be
over by 'next hop time'.

On 8 May 1863, York wrote what would be his last letter home. Ironically,
he said,

[I am] feeling first rate today for I had a good lot of beef tea for my breakfast and
have got a good chunk of beef steak for my supper . . . but Oh my God what I
would not give to sit down at the corner of the table at home and take a meals
victuals. Will that time ever come? Yes and may god grant that the time is not
far distant.

He mentioned in passing that he was suffering with a bad cough and
ended the letter somewhat prophetically with the words, 'when this you see
remember me. Good bye. That's all.'

Like the majority of men who died during this war, his death was not due to
a bullet or shell.[74] Six days after writing to his parents, Galutia York suddenly
died. A letter to his family from his uncle revealed that he had suffered a
'convulsive fit' at camp and complained of chest pains. Drinking a cup of tea
in the hospital, he remarked, 'it was the best tea he had tasted since he had
been in the service. He sat up in bed with the cup of tea in his hand. All at
once he let the cup fall and leaned over back and was dead. The Doctor . . .

says it was a disease of the heart.' The letter went on to describe his burial in a white wooden coffin on the sandy bank of a river where other soldiers had been buried. A pine board etched with his name marked the spot. 'His death has cast a gloom over all who knew him . . . Alas how many hearts have been made to bleed by this cursed war? How many places are left vacant? God grant peace may soon crown the effort of the Union armies,' he concluded. York's so-admired captain, Charles Tucker, wrote his sympathies to the family, urging them to find solace in religion. He paid a fitting tribute to York in his letter, describing him as:

> a *good* boy. An *intelligent, obedient, uncomplaining, well drilled Soldier.* And though he never faced the enemy, yet we know he *would* have done it had Providence allowed him to have been with us. He has fallen, in the service of his country. He lies buried in his uniform. He fills a patriot soldier's grave . . . He is today awaiting us in a land where sickness & death are felt afeared no more.[75]

Shepherd Green Pryor

Survived

Born on 7 December 1828 in Sumter, Georgia, Pryor's parents Robert and Lucinda were a farming family. They described themselves as simple God-fearing folk who were well respected in the community. Pryor's father died in 1841, and his uncle Spencer assumed guardianship of Shepherd and his sisters. Spencer fell in love with his brother's widow and they married. They went on to have two sons and two daughters, and they all grew up together on a sizable estate valued at $5,000.

Shepherd Pryor was of a sturdy build, with blue eyes and brown hair. At twenty-three he married Adaline Tinsley, daughter of another farming family. They married in 1851 and had a daughter, Margaret Lucinda. Tragically, Adaline died soon after giving birth, although Pryor had remarried by 1853, to Penelope Eudora Tyson, the educated daughter of a judge. By 1861, they had three more children, Ada, Ella and Robert, and a fourth on the way. Owning a farm of around six hundred acres, Pryor struggled to clear enough land to grow sufficient crops and support the farmstead. The buildings were somewhat ramshackle, and Pryor had debts – it left him unsettled and restless with agricultural life. When the opportunity came to join the Confederate army in June 1861, he took it.

He joined up with his half-brother William and set off with the Muckalee Guards – a company comprising neighbours and friends. On 26 June 1861 they were officially mustered into the Confederate army for the duration of the war as Company A, 12th Regiment, Georgia Volunteer Infantry. Pryor was second sergeant. The 12th Georgia Regiment would become a famous unit, seeing action at the bloody Battle of McDowell in May 1862, and then Seven Days, Fredericksburg, Chancellorsville and Gettysburg, to name but a few.

In one of his first letters home, on 28 June, Pryor was in optimistic mood: 'Since I got here I cannot hear much news about the war. I don't think there will be any fighting soon.' Nevertheless nerves were mounting: 'I have been feeling very bad. I hope that I'll not be . . . homesick as I have been. It is a bad feeling when there is no remedy.' At Camp Reservoir near Richmond in July, he was confident of Confederate success, though this was tempered with trepidation. 'Be assured our army will make its mark where it goes. The men here seem to go into it with that determined spirit to conquer or die. I feel more resigned to my fate this morning than I ever have.' Camp and marching conditions were arduous and he was missing his watermelon patch. Penelope was very much on his mind, and he described making her rings from laurel branches. 'I was sergeant of the guard Thursday night which was two nights without sleep. I was . . . worn out entirely this morning . . . I get cold every night; get up in the morning and shiver around the fire for an hour.' The reality of what lay ahead was starting to manifest itself in his letters and he confessed,

the prospect ahead looks dark . . . I have been in twenty miles of the enemy, have seen twenty yankee prisoners and if I am ever brought into action I'll make my mark. I feel that I can stand and face the enemy. I may be killed but I don't believe it . . . I am perfectly resigned to my fate. Let it be what may. I know that the supreme being reigns above all who rules all. In him it is that I have and put my trust believing that he'll manage things knowing that his will shall be done.

On 26 July 1861, close to the time he would see his first major action, Pryor was compelled to write a farewell letter that he sent home to Penelope.

Dear Nep,

I take the opportunity this morning to write you a few lines I wrote you yesterday in haste . . . We have prayer every night in our company. I attend worship regular. My only hope is in that supreme being who rules all who can say peace to this nation and we'll have peace . . . If I fall in this struggle I feel that I fall in a good cause and have faith to believe that I'll be happier than I've been in this word of trouble. That should be our great aim in life to be sure to prepare for death, then let this be our aim. If it is not the will of our heavenly father for us to meet on this earth let us meet above where we'll see no more trouble, where there shall be no more wars to interrupt our peace. If I fall in this cause and you should be permitted to live and raise our little flock, try and learn them to know and love their creator whilst young. I have no notion but that I'll get home. I have that presentment that I am sure to get home and live with you and enjoy your society again. That is my daily prayer – that is if I do fall I may be prepared to meet our heavenly father and it is to live, to see you again at home . . . my firm conviction now is that our side will be victorious.

On 4 October Pryor described his first battle at Greenbrier River in a letter to Penelope from Camp Bartow. For nearly five hours the Confederates faced waves of attacking troops and heavy artillery fire before successfully forcing the Federal forces back to their fortifications at Cheat Mountain, twelve miles away.

This morning about 6 o'clock the enemy commenced firing on our picket about two miles from camp. The enemy supposed to be between 4000 and 5000 strong. Our grand guard was about 100 strong . . . The enemy then commenced firing their cannon into our camp, shooting shell and solid shot by the quantity. But we had cannon too, and men to man them that knew how to shoot them. Our grand guard killed near 100 of them. The cannonading lasted three hours. The enemy killed ten or twelve of our men and horses . . . we killed at least 250 or 300 . . . When our officers saw them making for our right flank, we was ordered across the river to meet them. We went in a run, waded the river, it near waist deep, got back about 100 yards on the opposite side . . . We were ordered not fire a gun until we could see the whites of their eyes. We lay still, awaiting them to get near enough to fire on us. They came up in about 400 yards of us and commenced firing on us with their long-range guns, but killed none, wounded two. The balls went 'zip' all around us. They found that they could do nothing without coming close up to us, and one of the cannon opened on them with the grape shot, and they retreated in quick time . . . This ended the first battle I ever was in, and General Jackson gave the 12th Georgia the credit of repulsing them . . . I can't describe my feelings when the battle began. I could but think of you at home so far away and me here in the fight with the balls flying around me and the shell bursting around me, thinking that the next moment one might get me. Musket balls struck within twelve inches of my head . . . I do thank Heaven that I am alive today.[76]

There was bloody fighting on 12 October at Culpepper in Virginia. Pryor wrote of how quickly time passed in battle, but how these actions caused a myriad of fatalistic emotions to whirl around his head. He encapsulated the heightened state men would have been in, never knowing if each day might be their last.

[I go out] with the expectation of being shot every minute . . . This is the place that tries men's souls . . . I ask you now to think of this, and prepare yourself for any news you may hear if I fall in this war. There will be thousands of widows and orphans that will perhaps be in a worse fix than you would be if I should fall. You know that life is uncertain and death is sure, and let us be at all times prepared to meet it . . . there isn't a day passes over my head but that I think of death and its consequences. Those are serious thoughts, dear, but when acted out properly they are good for one's soul . . .[77]

He described his own role in the battle, taking command of the sharp-shooters of his brigade. On 13 October Pryor was hit by a rogue piece of shell that created 'a very ugly ragged flesh wound' above his knee.

Shepherd was a good soldier; he was physically fit and fiercely loyal. He did have a minor skirmish with the law when arrested for pilfering apples to make a pie,[78] but despite this minor indiscretion, he was promoted to captain on 8 May 1862. This coincided with the Battle of McDowell in Highland County, Virginia, where he was wounded slightly in the foot.

By December 1862, Pryor was desperately homesick and weary of war. He had fought and survived several major battles, and was facing the prospect of at least another twelve months in the army. He took courage from the fact that he was still alive, and was more fearful of losing a limb in battle. In early May 1863 he was fighting at the Battle of Chancellorsville, in charge of the sharp-shooters, and again in July at Gettysburg, where he was cited for gallantry. That would be his last major action.

It was not until December 1863 that Pryor finally returned home. He had been hospitalised for a wound that had become infected, and was invalided out of the army. Penelope apparently ran out to embrace her husband as he limped towards their log house on crutches. It was a moment so intense that their two-year-old son remembered it vividly.

Pryor never bore a grudge against the Unionists. His time on the battlefield had engendered a great respect for these men as soldiers. He returned to a farm that was in remarkably good shape, and decided to remain in Sumter County. In January 1864 he was elected sheriff, with one of his main duties being to round up runaway slaves. It was a role he was thought to have hated, and he only served one term. On 10 February 1864 he finally resigned his commission in the army. For many years, Pryor managed the farm, as well as setting up a blacksmith's forge and a shop repairing wagons and making furniture. Shepherd and Penelope went on to have five daughters and four sons, two of whom died in early childhood. The others grew up, married and brought up children of their own. The war had had a profound effect on both Pryor and his wife, particularly in terms of religion – so much so that they founded a small Methodist church in the woods that they named Mount Zion. They held meetings and neighbourhood services there, and lived a resolutely religious life. Shepherd felt that God had preserved his life, and a debt was thus owed.

He never severed ties with his military comrades and kept in touch with the men of the 12th. Pryor had repeatedly survived ferocious battles that killed so many others. His letters revealed that he fully expected to die at any point, and his farewells remain a poignant legacy of an impressive military career. Pryor died in 1911 at the age of eighty-three.[79]

~ 3 ~

THE ANGLO-ZULU WAR

Fire away boys, death or glory. I am done.[1]

There is about 16,000 Zulus waiting for us the other side of the river. Don't vex about me if I die like a soldier.[2]

THE ANGLO-ZULU WAR, WHICH started in January 1879, was the culmination of longstanding tensions between Britain and various factions in South Africa itself. Military units were already in the country, fighting the frontier wars on the Cape when this conflict broke out. The powerful independent Zulu nation – which extended along the south-eastern coast of Africa, between the Indian Ocean and Drakensberg Mountains – was an irritating obstacle to Britain's desire for a federation of colonies and dreams of white supremacy. Disputes over boundaries and compensation for Boers living in Zulu territory were intensifying by 1877, and Sir Henry Bartle Frere, the high commissioner, saw the Zulu nation as a threat. The perfect opportunity for invasion came when Zulu King Cetshwayo KaMpande refused to comply with Frere's demand that Zulus who had carried out suspected atrocities be handed over to the authorities. Cetshwayo wanted to avoid conflict, declaring 'Go back and tell the white men this, and let them hear it well. The Governor of Natal and I are equal. He is the Governor of Natal and I am the Governor here.'[3] Delays in communications with British Prime Minister Benjamin Disraeli's government allowed Frere to forge ahead unimpeded, with a draconian ultimatum to Cetshwayo to disband his army and military system. To all intents and purposes, it was a declaration of war.

Lord Chelmsford, Commander-in-Chief, expected it to be a 'short, sharp, brutal and decisive'[4] war, and was confident that there would be a British victory before the government at home had time to intervene. In his eyes, it was a foregone conclusion that Britain, with what he believed to be superior guns and military might, would triumph. To be certain, he planned an invasion to coincide with the Zulu harvest and when rivers were at their highest, forming natural defences. His arrogance would be quickly deflated.

Most rank-and-file soldiers were from the working classes and had signed up in a bid to escape manual labour and to travel the world. In an age where life expectancy was just thirty-eight, soldiering offered an escape from poverty, disease and unemployment. In fact, during Victoria's reign, conscription was unnecessary because of the huge numbers of men signing up voluntarily. In theory, the soldiers had to be over seventeen, but boys as young as fourteen became soldiers at this time. By November 1878 Chelmsford was starting to raise colonial corps, made up of proper soldiers and disparate volunteers – eager to protect the colony rather than feeling any patriotism or wider allegiance to Britain. The war began with 5,128 British infantrymen already present, and reinforcements (affectionately called 'fresh lobsters'[5] by soldiers on the ground) en route. This was an army of class opposites: drunkenness was an issue among the rank and file, and officers – who could buy their commissions – employed a 'theirs is not to reason why' attitude towards their men. Even so, the lower ranks' written opinions on leadership and strategy were authentic and descriptive, and were largely well-written and eloquent. By 1877, 76 per cent of recruits could read and write,[6] and soldiers enjoyed compulsory education. Few could have envisaged the horror awaiting them in South Africa, and virtually all underestimated the enemy they would face, dismissing them as savage wild animals; a swarm of bees that could be swatted aside.

On 11 January 1879 a war broke out that would shake Britain to its core. More than a thousand British and over seven thousand Zulu lives were lost in a conflict that cost £5 million and lasted just less than seven months. Proportionately it was worse than the bloodshed of the Crimean War. At Isandlwana, 95 per cent of the soldiers in the battle were killed. Despite these grim statistics, it took a Hollywood film to revive this war in the public consciousness. In the 1960s, Cy Endfield's *Zulu* reignited people's interest in a war that had virtually faded from memory, and made it one of the most iconic struggles of modern history. The ferocity of battle was keenly felt on both sides, and at the end of it Cetshwayo spoke for all when he concluded, 'An assegai[7] has been thrust into the belly of the nation. Here are not enough tears to mourn for the dead.'[8]

THE START OF WAR: CONFIDENCE AND JINGOISM

When war started, confidence that it would soon be over suffused letters home. There was a sense that it was a marvellous, breathless adventure. Captain W.R.C. Wynne remarked, 'we are ordered up to the front at once. It is overwhelming to me.'[9] Another, Captain Anstruther, proclaimed, 'I really expect the thing will be over in 3 months,' and then, months later in April, was still hopeful: 'This thing will be over in 6 weeks or a couple of months.'[10] Even after the horrific losses at Isandlwana, there was a carnival atmosphere onboard the ships that brought reinforcement troops. Anstruther again noted, 'We played music from 8–10 . . . the catcalls and encores from the cavalry were quite alarming,'[11] not to mention the sore heads from the copious ale available onboard. Even for some in the field, it was a boy's own adventure. Lieutenant General Sir Edward Hutton wrote in April 1879, 'I am rather ashamed to own it, but I like this life, and I am as happy as the day is long. It is to me like a shooting expedition, with just a spice of danger thrown in to make it really interesting.'[12]

There was a confidence that the British would win the fight and clear contempt for their enemy before the fight began. A jingoistic fervour pervaded letters home: 'I long for nothing more than to see the country laid waste and the ground strewn with black carcasses.'[13] In a letter published in his local newspaper, Private Owen Ellis warned, 'King Cetywayo will be made into atoms if captured by us.'[14] The language in letters – shocking in hindsight – was normal for the age. 'Sodger boy' wrote, 'although I have not yet practiced on a nigger's vile body with my revolver, I may have that pleasure, perhaps soon.'[15]

The Reality of War: Harsh Conditions, Harsher Enemy

Once in the field, soldiers found themselves in a land that was alien in so many ways. Private Griffiths wrote home with talk of '"grasspopers", birds, monkeys and river Buffilo', and his delight at plentiful orange trees in this 'strange country'.[16] Captain Anstruther relayed his delight at seeing ostriches for the first time.[17] Initial glee at this far-flung environment soon gave way to irritation with the conditions and unique South African wildlife – which included puff adders and swarms of flies. 'In England a wave of the hand will drive a respectable fly away, but here if you are eating marmalade, you first push the brutes off when about to lift the desired piece to your mouth, then raise it to your opened jaws, shove them off again by physical strength and pop it in before they make another fiendish attempt,' wrote one disgruntled soldier.[18]

Conditions were not improved by torrential rain and the fact it was a highly mobile conflict. Royal Engineer, Captain Warren Wynne wrote, 'Overwhelmed with work and scarcely time even for a farewell. We march to-morrow.'[19] Each battalion carried their own ammunition, tents, tools, medicines and food across swollen rivers and muddy terrain. Supplies were hardly plentiful – one soldier wrote of having to cook over dried cow dung due to the lack of wood – and the cramped conditions men and animals lived in were breeding grounds for disease. Letters home revealed the frustrations of daily life: 'the 8 ounces of biscuit we get daily being maggoty and mouldy . . . no vegetables . . . exposed to all weathers . . . no tents',[20] wrote Gunner Carroll. Private William Lloyd described the men as 'a lot of mud turtles. By jove you would stare if you saw our sleeping places. Each man lies down in the mud quite contented'.[21] Tuberculosis from infected animals and their milk, horse sickness, enteric fever and diarrhoea were all common, and seeing comrades die from disease played on men's minds. Private G. Griffiths wrote home from a camp riddled with disease to reassure his family: 'I am safe and healthy at preasant . . . Dear Father and Mother I hope that we shall meet once more if the Lord pleace.'[22]

Men could be up and working as early as three o'clock, and kept busy until eight in the evening, digging ramparts and reinforcing camps. As well as the physical strain, there was unimaginable mental pressure. Troops were continually on guard against surprise ambush attacks from the Zulus. Private Alfred Davies revealed, 'We lie down with 100 rounds of ammunition round our waists, and our rifle by our side, as we should be ready at a moment's notice.'[23]

The Zulu tactic of deception and surprise attack had devastating effects at Isandlwana. With that massacre came the realisation that this would be no small, swift war and that Britain had woefully underestimated its enemy. The Zulu impi[24] was organised into units that were highly disciplined and incredibly fit. The men could march for up to sixty miles per day barefoot, with just a pouch of dry meat for sustenance. In advance of attacks, doctors administered special potions to make the Zulu soldier feel invincible, and they fought with an intensity and courage that came to be grudgingly admired by the British. Cetshwayo warned, 'Do not put your face into the lair of a wild beast for you are about to get clawed,'[25] and British soldiers in letters home likened this enemy to fearless lions.

BATTLE HARDENED: SINKING MORALE AND GROWING CRITICISM

The Battle of Isandlwana on 22 January 1879 marked a change in morale, opinions in Britain and the soldiers themselves. Fifty-two officers and 806 NCOs died and, at least a thousand Zulus were believed to have been killed. It was a wake-up call for all involved and there was palpable relief in those who survived. Private George Smith wrote, 'I am thankful I have been saved from the cruel slaughter and bloodshed . . . My dear wife I trust you will feel thankful to God for having preserved my life.'[26] Soldiers found themselves suddenly confronting their own mortality. 'It is turned out very bad for our troops,'[27] wrote Private Joseph Morgan to his father.

Many men wrote home to describe the shocking scenes they witnessed, among them one Sergeant Warren: 'I could not help crying to see how the poor fellows were massacred. They were first shot and then assegaied, the Zulus mutilated them and stuck them with the assegai all over the body. There were bullocks, horses and mules lying dead . . . waggons thrown down deep precipices . . . our tents burnt and torn up to ribbons.'[28] Surprisingly, there was no marked increase in farewell letters, despite this battle. On the whole there was a staggering lack of emotion or perturbation at what the soldiers had witnessed, such as the Zulu practice of disembowelling fallen soldiers,[29] heavy rains that washed open shallow graves, scalping, men strewn on the battlefield for weeks – even months – after the fight. Journalist Archibold Forbes went some way to describe the horrors: 'dead men lay thick, mere bones, with toughened discoloured skin like leather covering them . . . Some were almost wholly dismembered, heaps of yellow, clammy bones . . . Every man had been disembowelled. Some were scalped and others subject to yet ghastlier mutilations.'[30]

The Victorian stiff upper lip still reigned supreme. It seems that men did not want to dwell on past events if they were to be able to continue the fight. 'I could describe the battlefield to you, but the sooner I get it off my mind the better,'[31] wrote Private Meredith, who also described seeing young boys stripped and hung from meat hooks.[32] For some soldiers, events in January 1879 simply hardened their resolve. Robert Head wrote, 'I am ready and willing to lose my life to win back for our sister battalion . . . renown.'[33]

The Battle at Rorke's Drift provided a welcome counter to Isandlwana and has since become a byword for bravery. Newspapers at home seized on this demonstration of pluck and spirit whereby British soldiers, outnumbered by forty to one, triumphed with just fifteen casualties. Conversely, 'the dead Zulus lay in piles, in some places as high as the top of the parapet.'[34] There was a newfound respect for Tommy Atkins – the common soldier – and newspapers heralded his loyalty, steadfastness and bravery. Music halls celebrated this victory with songs and skits. 'And when Rorke's Drift he'd pit against / Ten thousand blacks' concussion / This ragged silk defied them and / Will do so ever more.'[35]

There was a renewed hunger for information back home, and newspapers printed swathes of soldiers' letters. Amid tales of derring-do, the horror of battle and particularly criticism of those leading the troops were also starting to emerge. Lord Chelmsford was blasted as a hopeless plodder whose poor decision-making had cost lives. A letter published in the *Aberystwyth Observer* blasted Chelmsford's standing: 'the men . . . look upon him as a very inferior general . . . now he is over-cautious as he was before over-rash.'[36] By February 1879 even Chelmsford himself was feeling the 'strain of prolonged anxiety and exertion'.[37] Letters home revealed a war-weariness and regret at having signed up. John Price wrote home to ask 'Harry not to enlist for God's sake, or else he will be sorry for it',[38] while Private Joseph Morgan felt, 'unless we have more troops sent out soon I think all the men shall be killed. Dear mother, I hope you won't vex for me.'[39]

LAST LETTERS: COMMON THEMES

Writing letters in itself was no easy task during this conflict. Writing paper and stamps were in short supply, there were few flat surfaces on which to write, and rain was a constant problem. Private Ellis Edwards revealed, 'It is very hard to get any paper or stamps in this part of the world. I have been forced to steal out of the way every time I want to write because we haven't got one moment as we can call our own . . .'[40] On average there was just one bottle of ink per three tents of men, so some came up with their own novel solution – mixing gunpowder and water, and making their own envelopes. Despite these problems, it was a war of prolific letter-writing. Letters took, on average, three weeks to arrive. The delays in correspondence must have been excruciating. 'Poor old mums, what a state you must have been in on first hearing the news from here . . . I hope you will know in a day or two if you have not already, that I am all right.'[41] Few men may have admitted to a fear of dying to their loved ones, but it was a sentiment keenly felt by wives at home: 'What shall I ever do if I am left a widow . . . If our poor men fall.'[42] At the same time, there were financial reasons for wives to fear the death of their husbands because there were no statutory payouts, only voluntary collections often made by fellow comrades.

Farewell letters from this conflict were remarkably stoic. Lieutenant Baillie's dying words were rumoured to be, 'Never mind me; save the Colour.'[43] However, it was an era when post-traumatic stress and depression were little understood, and soldiers tended to put a brave veneer on their words. Outpourings of love familiar to virtually all other conflicts are noticeably absent in farewell letters from the Zulu War. With men perhaps bottling up their emotions, it was hardly surprising that a number ended up in asylums or killing themselves after this war. Letters were matter of fact and unsentimental. 'It's the fortune of war and somebody must go to the wall,'[44] wrote one soldier home.

Although most farewell letters mentioned God, it was almost in passing. Private Joseph Morgan wrote, 'If God spare me – and if not I shall be killed – I will live to come home again.'[45] Sergeant Lennon declared, 'if please God thanks I am spared. I must hope & pray that I may be spared to see you and all that is near and dear to me soon,' and in a letter to his sister revealed that those at home were clinging onto God as a means of comfort: 'Dear Alice I am more than gratified to you for your great encouragement in Divine Providence respecting my safety in the battle field.'[46] On the whole, the few soldiers' letters that were overtly religious stand out for that very reason. For example, a farewell letter from field camp worker Ted Turner said, 'In case you shouldn't see me again, and the worst we dread should happen you will find all our books in the Milners' safe . . . We are in His hands, who says, "Not a sparrow shall fall to the ground without His permission; fear ye not, therefore, ye are of more value than many sparrows." Goodbye.'[47]

The unwavering belief that Britain would triumph over the Zulus meant that men were not consumed with thoughts of dying. Letters home revealed a sense of pragmatism and acceptance of death in the field. Harry Lugg simply wrote, 'We will fight of it, and if we have to die, we will die like Britishers,'[48] while Ellis Edward stated, 'Should I be killed in this place, my friend will write home and let you know. I gave him my address in case of something should happen to me, so that you can claim my money. He will give you the full description how to get them. At the same time, I trust my Almighty Maker will protect me.'[49]

The brevity of farewell notes was also a feature of this conflict. They almost always consisted of one or two brief, unemotional and succinct lines within a regular letter home – again an example of Victorian stoicism and the sense that death would not happen to them. 'My dear mother and father, if I should fall don't vex about me, as it is my own fault,'[50] wrote Private Alfred Davies. The ordinary rank-and-file soldiers wrote with mush less bravado than their superiors, Private Isaac Morris simply stating, 'Farewell in the event that I shall not write again.'[51] It seemed that some men did carry wills on them in the event of their death – a newspaper reported that Bandmaster Bullard of 2/24th had 'in his pocket a watch, two rings and his will, dated January 18th 1879'[52] – but these were largely official, financial documents without any personal message.

Paradoxically, the overriding theme of last letters from this conflict is the lack of them. The element of surprise in battle frequently left soldiers off-guard, with no time to write a letter – it was then left to colleagues to write home to a loved one. Colonel Glyn at Helpmekaar on 16 April 1879 wrote how he 'got from Melvill's pockets a white silk pocket handkerchief, ten shillings and sixpence in silver, a little dog whistle and his gold watch and chain which I shall keep carefully until I hear from Mrs Melvill what she wishes done with them.'[53] It is clear, though, that soldiers verbally related messages 'in the event of my death' to one another to pass on. Piet Uys promised Colonel Wood: 'Kurnall if you are killed I will take care of your children, and if I am killed you do the same for mine,'[54] and Sergeant Edward Daly wrote to the widow of Sergeant McCaffery, killed at Isandlwana, 'I happen to know your address, as I have often seen McCaffery direct letters to you . . . So, in compliance, with a promise made to him when alive and well, I wrote hoping this may find you.'[55]

The letters from this conflict reveal a unique insight into the mind of the Victorian soldier – less emotional, more battle hardened and perhaps more positive about survival than soldiers both before and since.

THE PRINCE IMPERIAL LOUIS NAPOLEON

Killed near Ityotyozi River, 1 June 1879

WHILE IN AFRICA, THE Prince Imperial (Plate 5) revealed to a journalist: 'If I had to be killed, I should be in despair at the thought of falling in [a minor battle]. In a great battle, very well; it's for Providence to decide; but in an obscure skirmish – ah, no, that would never do.'[56] He could not know how prophetic those words would be; he was killed in a casual ambush in a war in which he was not 'officially' serving. Furthermore, it was only through fortune of birth that this death was recorded and remembered as more than just another grim statistic of war. Ordinary soldiers who died in this conflict routinely had their service records destroyed – leaving little trace for historians to explore.

Born to a hail of gunfire from Les Invalides on 16 March 1856, the Prince Imperial was heralded as the future, legitimate sovereign of France. His father was determined that Louis should be a soldier so he was commissioned into the First Imperial Guard as a baby. Louis dreamed of walking in his great-uncle Napoleon Bonaparte's footsteps and bringing military glory on himself and France. He grew up to be an outstanding horseman and skilled swordsman. War with Prussia was his first experience of real combat at just fourteen, and the slaughter he witnessed horrified him. It was a debacle: a poorly organised and equipped army, with no leadership. The Empress Eugenie deposed her husband and brought her son back from the front. The Second Empire was in tatters.

The royal family took refuge in England, where they received an enthusiastic welcome from the people – and eventually the queen. Louis was listless and bored, however, until a visit to the Royal Military Academy at Woolwich. It revived a passion for the military and he was duly sent there in 1872. At his graduation three years later, Louis topped his 'shop' in riding and fencing, and was seventh overall in a cadet class of thirty-four. In the meantime, his father had died, and Louis had grown ever closer to his mother. France was politically stable and chances of the Bonapartes returning were unlikely, given the hostile press they received from the French. The people labelled him an idiot and branded his military training a farce. Brushing this aside, in England, Louis was a central figure on the aristocratic social scene – the focal point of parties and subject of a rumoured romance with Princess Beatrice. He travelled across Europe and joined a battery for annual manoeuvres. He also had a strange feeling that he would die violently and once sketched himself as a young hero with the Angel of Death – a chilling prediction.

In 1879 and aged twenty-two, Louis started to display a greater maturity. He wrote speeches and articles and began to gain a grudging respect from France. Then came war in Africa and the tragedy of Isandlwana. With reinforcements mustered, Louis wrote to the Duke of Cambridge and begged to be allowed to go to the front to fight his first campaign for England, his second home. Moreover, a military record against a savage nation would hardly harm his claim to the French throne, as revealed in a letter he wrote: 'The time I shall devote to witnessing this conflict of civilisation against barbarism will not be lost for me. Afar, as near, my thoughts will constantly be directed towards France.'[57] Disraeli was reluctant to sanction the prince going to Africa, but bent to pressure from Empress Eugenie and the queen, who could not conceive that a royal would be in any danger in that environment. The Prince Imperial was dispatched to the veldt under strict instructions that he was there only as a spectator, but with an ominous note of caution that 'he is *too plucky* and *go ahead*.'[58]

Before leaving in February, Louis prayed and breakfasted with his mother, who pledged to wear her emerald clasp every day until his safe return. She cried as they travelled to Southampton, and wrote, 'May God protect him! Have prayers said for him, that he may find an opportunity to distinguish himself, and may return safe and sound.'[59]

On 28 February, the Prince Imperial set sail from Southampton on board *Danube*, with drafts for the 3/60th Rifles. It was onboard ship that he wrote his will and final farewell. Given his exuberant and confident character, writing his letter allowed him to dream what an honourable death would be, and was a clear insight into the mind of a man who desperately wanted France to take him to its heart once more; it was a portrait of how he wanted to be perceived in life as well as death.

This is my testament:
1st.   I die in the Roman Catholic and Apostolic faith, in which I was born.
2nd. I desire my body to be laid by that of my Father until such time as both are transferred to the resting-place of the Founder of my house, in the bosom of that French people which was so dear to us, as to him.
3rd. My last thought will be my country's; it is for my country I should wish to die.
4th. When I am no more, I trust that my mother will keep me in tender memory, as I shall keep her until my last moment.
5th. Let my private friends, my servants, and the partisans of the cause which I represent, be assured that my gratitude towards them will cease only with my life.

6th. I shall die in the same heart-felt gratitude to H.M. the Queen of England, to all the Royal family, and to the country where I have found so warm a hospitality for eight years.

To my beloved Mother, I bequeath all of which I die possessed, under the following charges . . .

Louis then went on to list a number of people to whom he wanted to leave money, including his childhood school tutor Filon and Bachon, his former equerry. Finally, 'all but the last I shall have worn [i.e. weapons and uniforms] . . . I bequeath to my Mother.'[60]

Danube reached Durban on 31 May, and the prince came ashore to crowds of people. He was attached to an artillery battery and awaited his call to the front. He was impatient and desperate to fight, but Chelmsford – mindful of the Duke of Cambridge's warnings to keep Louis safe – asked if he would serve on his personal staff as an aide-de-camp. This was a safe enough position that would occupy him, but keep him out of immediate danger. Louis revelled in a military way of life; he enjoyed roughing it in camp – 'If you saw the extraordinary position in which I'm writing to you, squatting on my heels and using my saddle as a desk'[61] – made copious friends of all ranks and was the first to volunteer for any duties. He had a knack of taming troublesome horses and a skill in using his sword to slice potatoes, flung at him as he rode past.[61] 'For two days I have not had my boots off, but this life pleases me and is good for me,'[63] he wrote in a letter to his tutor.

Louis was attached to the staff of Colonel Richard Harrison, who was in charge of the Royal Engineers transport and reconnaissance towards the Zulu capital Ulundi. The prince was always supposed to have a strong escort party and in reality he was far too inexperienced for the patrols he carried out. He proved himself headstrong and impetuous, often riding out ahead unaccompanied and under-armed. He was almost ambushed on one occasion when he ignored orders in a party led by Colonel Redvers Buller. On 31 May 1879 Harrison agreed that Louis could ride out early the next morning with a party of scouts, believing that the route ahead was clear of Zulus. The prince's pocket-book entry for that mission – which would be his last – simply read 'escort under Captain Carey'. He also wrote what would be a final letter to his mother, betraying no fears of dying. In his mind, the only reason for no further letters would be due to postal arrangements. 'I didn't want to lose this opportunity of embracing you with all my heart. Your devoted and respectful son. Napoleon.'[64]

Louis was eager to leave camp and make headway, so the group set off without their full escort. In bullish mood, Louis nominated himself in command, despite Carey's superiority. They stopped at what appeared to be a very recently deserted kraal in the valley of the Tsotshosi River, and made some drawings of the locale. They lit a fire but crucially did not post a lookout. Chatting animatedly, the men sat drinking coffee. As they were preparing to leave, at least ten Zulus ambushed the kraal.

Louis desperately tried to mount his horse and managed to get one foot in the stirrup as it tore off down the valley. However, the horse then threw him and Louis was left on foot and without a sword. The pursuing Zulus attacked the prince, who continued to fire shots, despite being speared in the shoulder and thigh. He eventually fell over and was rushed by Zulus, who speared him to death. The doctor's report corroborated the fact that the prince had faced his enemy head-on.

A recovery party was sent out at first light to find the body. It was stripped naked, bar one sock and a religious medallion. A cut up the abdomen to release the spirit had been made, and many stab wounds had been inflicted after death, including one through the right eye socket. A stretcher was fashioned from blankets and the body solemnly returned to camp.

Only five men survived the skirmish, including Carey, who had abandoned his comrades and ridden away in a desperate panic. He was the first to break the news to camp. That night he wrote despondently to his wife:

I am a ruined man, I fear . . . My own darling I prayed as I rode away that I should not be hit and my prayer was heard . . . As regards leaving the Prince, I am innocent, as I did not know he was wounded, and thought our best plan was to make an offing . . . Poor boy! I liked him so very much . . . I shall be blamed, but honestly, between you and me, I can only be blamed for the camp.[65]

It was Captain Carey who took the brunt of the blame for Louis Napoleon's death. He was subjected to an inquiry and court martial, and was largely shunned by fellow officers until his death in India in 1883.

Napoleon's death sent shockwaves through Europe, and the newspapers clamoured for eye-witness accounts. 'I am very sorry to tell you of the sad misfortune which befell the young Prince Napoleon whilst scouting out in the wilds of Zululand. After the Zulus had killed him they stabbed him in fourteen different places. I was one of the men who removed his body . . . to send it home to England . . .' wrote Ellis Edwards,[66] while Captain Anstruther described events as 'A dreadful calamity'.[67] Music halls rang out with songs mourning the prince's death.

His mother the Empress Eugenie crumbled. In a cruel twist of fate, she received two optimistic letters from her son on the day she learned of his death. The news was broken by the Duc de Bassano, her chamberlain, and she fainted on hearing it. She stayed in her darkened bedroom for over a month, and when the coffin came home she hugged it and refused to leave it for a day.

She wrote to the Duke of Cambridge in an open letter published for the world to read.

> The one earthly consolation I have is in the idea that my beloved child fell as a soldier, obeying *orders*, on a duty which was *commanded*, and that those who gave them did so because they thought him competent and useful. Enough of recriminations. Let the memory of his death unite in a common sorrow all those who loved him . . . I, who can desire nothing more on earth, ask it as a last prayer.[68]

In March 1880 the empress went to Africa on a pilgrimage to retrace her son's final moments. She trekked across the veldt and slept in tents, re-reading the letters her son had sent her – proof indeed of the irreplaceable value of letters as a last link with that person. Writing home, her grief was palpable. 'Everybody speaks of him in terms which make my grief more intense, but which at the same time appeal to my pride as a mother . . . Oh, why was he taken so soon, and why was I left behind?'[69]

At the spot where Louis had been killed, she placed a wooden cross and spent the night kneeling and praying by candlelight. The next day, she planted a willow and ivy she had brought from Camden Palace and sought out the exact spot her son had sketched on that fateful day. 'My soul is full of bitterness, regrets and sorrow; it is a curious thing, but I can only find peace near these stones which mark the spot where he fell, fighting, with his last breath, "like a lion" as the Zulus say.'[70] While it was the privilege of status that allowed this pilgrimage to take place, the grief that she felt would have been common among families who had lost loved ones in this conflict. Likewise, the desire to know every detail of how and where a death occurred has been a virtually universal desire for bereft relatives.

Passing through the battlefield of Isandlwanda on their return, Eugenie took up a spade and joined in the effort to bury the bones of soldiers still strewn across the field. She brought home seeds and filled her home with the flowers that reminded her of the Zulu battlefield.

Louis's death gave Eugenie a newfound unfettered zest for life: she bought a yacht and travelled widely, even climbing Vesuvius; she rode a bicycle, drove a car and built a villa on the Côte d'Azur. In short, in her late seventies, perhaps she finally started to live the life her son would never have. Nevertheless, Eugenie carried her son's death with her until her own, building a Gothic abbey church to him and expanding it into a fantastical chateau. Louis's Chistlehurst study was faithfully recreated as a museum-cum-shrine, and the house filled with portraits and trinkets. Eugenie wore black for the rest of her life.

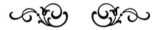

PRIVATE FRANCIS HORATIO WARD

Survived

THERE IS A QUESTION-MARK over Ward's real age: his service record had him born in 1852 while a census record estimated his birth year to be 1846. Regardless, this was one instance where a recruit was at least not pretending to be old enough to sign up. By 1871, Francis was a blacksmith, married to Jane, and they had a child with the unusual name of Lusegham, aged two. They were far from wealthy and shared a house with another young family – George (also a blacksmith) and Mary White and their one-year-old daughter.

Ward was born in Merthyr and grew up in nearby Bedwellty in Monmouthshire. In the Victorian period this was a solidly working-class area, with high unemployment that left many people living a hand-to-mouth existence. The army offered an escape from the drudgery of hard, manual labour and a regular wage. Francis Ward signed up and joined the 2/24th Foot Brigade (which would become the South Wales Borderers) on 8th December 1877: soldier number 1486. Ware was five feet five and a half inches tall, with dark hair, hazel eyes and a dark complexion.

Ward achieved a third-class educational standard – the average for someone of his background. This meant he could read and write easy narratives and solve basic mathematical problems. Nevertheless, his letter was remarkably well written. Newspaper editors would frequently correct spelling and grammar, but the words Ward wrote seemed to be too vivid, personal and descriptive to belong to anyone else. Even if written by someone more literate, the sentiment within must have come from Ward himself.

For men who had possibly never travelled out of Wales, the opportunity to serve on the other side of the world must have been a most attractive prospect. Ward took his attestation oath at Brynmawr and within three months was at the eastern frontier in eastern Africa, fighting in the Ninth Xhosa Cape Frontier War. While he was in Africa, Ward suffered from the first of many gastric illnesses that would blight his military record and lead to his discharge. Recovering from this first bout, Ward was posted to Natal in August 1878, so would have been on the ground and called to action at the very start of the Zulu War, crossing the Buffalo River into Zululand on 11 January 1879.

From his letter, however, it was obvious that the military dream had quickly soured.

I am glad to say that I enjoy capital health and hope to continue so. I am fully aware that you know I have enlisted. I am now indeed sorry for it. I was under the influence of drink when I did so.[71] I have already served fifteen months of my time, and I must go through it the best way I can.

For Ward and his comrades in Africa, it was a tough, unrelenting life. They covered hundreds of miles and did their best to fortify their camps in spite of the lack of entrenching tools and the tough terrain. No major battles had yet taken place, imbuing soldiers with mistaken bravado and confidence, which were shattered following the attack on Isandlwana.

Ward's farewell letter to his aunt was written in the aftermath of Isandlwana and Rorke's Drift. For his regiment in particular, Isandlwana was a shock awakening to the realities of war and must have made many men start to question their decision to sign up, and whether or not they would survive against such a formidable enemy. The 24th Foot suffered 540 dead, including the 1st Battalion's commanding officer. For Ward, who encountered the horrific aftermath and suffered a personal loss, it became the prompt for his farewell letter. Despite the description of the scene, the farewell element was unsentimental: a calm, practical instruction; perhaps even the words of someone who was resigned to the ultimate sacrifice he might have to make.

Ward's letter to an aunt who was landlady at the Prince Albert Inn in Aberdare would have almost certainly been passed around the pub for reading. It was, as were so many letters home, also printed in the local paper – the *Aberdare Times* – in March 1879. Local newspapers clamoured for news from the front and took immense pride in printing the words of 'our boys'. Following the remarkable triumph of Rorke's Drift and the carnage of Isandlwana, letters from local Welsh boys were of particular interest. They offered a very personal link to the conflict and became the unofficial commentary on the war for their readers – often containing news of other local lads serving in Africa.

LETTER FROM AN ABERDARE SOLDIER IN SOUTH AFRICA.

5 Headline from *Aberdare Times*, March 1879

I have already served fifteen months of my time, and I must go through it the best way I can. Ever since we arrived in this country we have been on active service and, most likely, operations will not be over for the next twelve months. I hope and trust that God Almighty will guide me safe through all, so that I may return to my dear native country once more. I daresay that you are aware that Tom Jones, Aunt Betsy's son, was in the same regiment as myself. It is with very deep emotion and regret that I have to acquaint you of his death. He was killed on 22 January at Isandhlwana Camp in Zululand, the territory we invaded. There were lost on our side 993 men. I can assure you, dear aunt, it was a most ghastly sight to witness. After our poor fellows were shot, they were brutally mutilated. Kindly write to poor Tom's mother and let her know of his death. I was speaking to him the night before and he requested me to write home if anything should happen to him, also he said he would do the same for me; but, as I said before, I have to perform the painful duty of acquainting you.

He was on guard this day, and the company he belonged to sent out with five other companies, we having been acquainted that the enemy was not far distant. We left camp at daybreak. In the meantime, the enemy was watching our movements and marched on our right flank towards the camp, which they captured after a terrible struggle. They cut up every man of ours, except three that managed to escape. The enemy brought a force of about 15,000 against our handful of men. Our aide-de-camp was sent out after the column to fetch them back with all haste, the reason being that the enemy had captured our camp. We arrived near camp when it got dark. We opened into skirmishing order and we had four 7-pounders in the centre of the column. They throwed some shells and rockets to the left of camp; also we fired a few volleys as well before we advanced towards the camp. We had our bayonets fixed; we captured the camp; but the enemy had disappeared – but before they retired, they burnt all the things that belonged to us and took away with them one million rounds of ammunition and the colours of our battalion; and the first battalion of our lost five companies of men and officers; also the artillery and volunteers lost every man; indeed it was a terrible calamity.

Dear aunt, I wish I had listened to your good advice and give up the drink, I would not be where I am at present. Now I must draw to a close, and please write to all my sisters, and tell them I am quite well at present, and please God I hope to see you all some day . . .

If I should have the same fate as poor Tom, tell Mary, my youngest sister, to claim what belongs to me to the War Office but I sincerely hope that I shall be spared to return home again. There will be many poor fellows yet will have their heads laid low before the war is over . . . .

Now I must conclude, and please give my kind love to all my relatives and friends, and accept the same, dear aunt and cousins, many times. Please write back soon, as I am anxious to hear from you.[72]

At Natal, Ward suffered a back injury and also dyspepsia – a digestive condition linked to women, alcohol and environment – and it was recommended that a change of climate was the best course of treatment. By July 1879, while war continued in Africa, Ward found himself back in Brecon, suffering from chronic hepatitis caused by enteric fever. This disease swept through camps in Africa – the insanitary and crowded conditions producing perfect conditions for rampant contagion. It lasted a considerable time and Ward ended his military career in Devonport, where he made a full recovery.[73]

Ward may seem an unremarkable character; indeed, he received no badges for good conduct and no special mentions. He does, though, exemplify many young men who fought in this conflict. Poorly educated, wanting to expand their horizons and experience real excitement, it was men like Ward who made up the majority of troops and carried out some remarkable feats of bravery. His farewell letter gives a powerful picture of what so many of these men felt about the war and their positions. Many soldiers who were just like Ward died without writing any kind of farewell letter. The fact that his was printed in a local newspaper preserved it for posterity, ensuring that Ward at least, would never be written out of history.

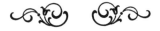

PRIVATE ASHLEY GOATHAM
Killed at Isandlwana, 22 January 1879

ASHLEY GOATHAM WAS JUST twenty-four when he was killed in Africa, thousands of miles from his home in Kent (Plate 6). He was born in 1855 to parents George – a carpenter – and Hannah, and lived in the small village of Bredgar, where generations of Goathams had grown up. At seventeen, he joined the 24th Regiment and by 1872 was stationed in Gibraltar. In 1877 Goatham was in South Africa, fighting in the Border Wars, where he wrote countless letters home to different members of his family.

Having been in Africa for some time before the outbreak of the Anglo-Zulu conflict meant that he was accustomed to the harsh weather, terrain and living conditions of the African bush. Battle with the Xhosa had brought him face to face with death and he was desperately missing home. His letters were confident and breezy, despite (or perhaps because of) having had a bullet pass through the helmet, narrowly missing his head. In a letter written in 1878 he wrote, 'I have pulled through 23 years I hope to pull through many more.'

By October 1878, and while in South Africa, Ashley had married and had a son with Susan Seal. She was in Durban, he was at Fort Glamorgan – a post at the head of the Buffalo River that was guarding the supply line to King Williams Town. It was unclear whether Ashley had even seen his son at this point, 'I am quite glad to state that I am at present quite well only anxious to see you and the little chap . . . I am quite broken-hearted and do not know what to do . . . accept my kind love and sweet kisses from your affectionate husband.'

Ashley was there from the start, from the declaration of war against Cetshwayo, marching forward under Lord Chelmsford as battle commenced. In a letter to his sister he set the scene for war.

> We hear that he (that is Cetewayo) has 15 days to consider what he is going to do . . . Now they have made us into the main attacking column . . . There are columns around him (Cetewayo) on all points. So we are only waiting to strike the blow for the revenge of the poor unfortunate women that his black devils outraged and massacred. I think, according to talk, we will get some stiff work settling him as he has on reliable sources, 47,000 armed men. They might stand well a couple of hours. I can tell, although large and powerful, they have not the pluck and martial spirit of an Englishman.

The confident belief that the Zulu army was no match for the British was commonplace. At the outbreak of hostilities nobody thought the war would last long or that ill-equipped 'savages' would pose any serious threat. Despite earlier weariness with life in South Africa, on the eve of war Ashley was enthusiastic and eager for action. By 12 November 1878 he had reached Camp Helpmekaar near the Tugela River. This camp comprised a handful of zinc sheds, storing ammunition and supplies, and hundreds of tents where the men slept. There was even a field bakery here, producing fresh bread each day – some comfort to men living cheek by jowl and with little sanitation. In November Ashley was still confident that, despite being outnumbered, they would triumph. It was clear by this point that soldiers were being carefully briefed on the rather unique enemy they would face, but still there was no hint of foreboding or nerves at what was to come.

> We have the strongest column under the command of Colonel C.B. Glyn. The whole force on our side is estimated at 16,000 men while that of the enemy is, according to the most reliable source 47,000. They are taught by deserters . . . but all the drilling in the world is no good to them. They are all very well until they begin to see a few fall and then off they go in disorder. Their arms are good we all know. But they don't know how to use them. I don't suppose any of you would really know me now as I have grown so much stouter and whiskers as well.

As the inevitable battle drew closer, anticipation was palpable. Goatham may have grown from boy to man during his army service, but British soldiers had not faced a Zulu impi of this scale during their time in Africa. On Christmas Day he wrote to his younger brother Arthur: 'Here we are going into Zululand on January 2nd and the stakes are 10-to-one that we will all come out alive. But still, I am happy and contented with my lot. If I ever live to reach old England, I will make up for this.'

Days later, he wrote to his parents. The 24th had still not moved into Zululand at this point, but the sense of trepidation was clear; this seasoned soldier was longing to be home once more.

Things are looking very crooked out here at present. A dispatch came in last night from Captain Shepstone at Rorke's Drift and it said the scouts came in and said that the Zulus were assembling in great force the other side of the river. My dear parents, I am so longing to get this affair over, and when I once get home they don't get me out of England again.

By 6 January Ashley was at Rorke's Drift, keeping watch for the expected Zulu invasion and awaiting more columns in support. It must have been a tense time, but he was once again in bullish mood. No doubt as they sat waiting for the storm, soldier bolstered fellow soldier with tales of how they were the superior force, while Chelmsford's confidence had clearly been passed onto his men. 'Ketchwayo sent word that he . . . would eat us up every white skin in the country . . . little does he think what we can do we have sufficient artillery to blow him and his country up . . . The general says we shall have him . . . quite subdued and annihilated in 15 days.'

Goatham was one of four thousand men that made up Glyn's central column, and by 20 January they were camped at Isandlwana. Just two days before he died, Ashley again wrote home to his parents. It was a letter that was part farewell and part reassurance, but also incredibly poignant. The farewell sentiments were short and understated but had a profound effect on Ashley's family, who received the letter some weeks after his death.

I am sorry to see you so distressed and cut up about me.
    Never mind about me. I hope to pull through all safe by the help of God.
    Think of it yourself – miles and miles away from old England's shores tramping and tearing over tracts of wild wastes in search of them black skin beggars.
    . . . You don't know what trials and tribulations a poor British soldier has to put up with. Colonel Pearson's column was attacked fourteen miles from us and the enemy attacked him on all points almost numberless.
    . . . We do not know the minute that we will have another engagement . . .
So, my dear mother, cheer up. Time might come when I shall come home and surprise the lot.[74]

Ashley was killed on his birthday; his parents were left distraught. His wife was forced to bring up their child without a father. In 1880 she wrote to Ashley's sister, admitting 'he [their son] will sometimes ask me to let him see his papa.' She enclosed a lock of his hair to be given to Ashley's mother, who also took possession of his service medal and personal effects. Susan and the child remained in South Africa, where – despite what had happened to his father – Ashley's son went on to fight and survive the Boer War, while his grandson fought and survived the Second World War.

PRIVATE GEORGE MORRIS
Killed at Isandlwana, 22 January 1879

AFTER SERVING IN THE Royal Monmouthshire Militia, 610 Private George Morris enlisted with the 2/24th Regiment. Hailing from the industrial town of Pontypool, whose ironworks had been hit by recession and high unemployment, Morris was one of a number of local men who 'took the shilling' and joined the army in search of brighter prospects. He sailed out to Africa in 1877 to join the First Battalion, where he was detached to the gunners. In a letter home to his father in March 1878, when he was caught up in the Ninth Frontier War, it was clear that he was not revelling in soldier life. He wrote from Fort Wellington, where he was in charge of 'rocket operations':

> For the last four months I have been unable to procure either stamp, pen, ink or paper. I have been nearly all over Africa and have not know what it is to sleep in a bed for that time. My clothes are worn to rags and I have not a boot to my feet and God knows when I shall get any . . . We have about 2 miles to go for water. God knows I have had enough of campaigning this last few months; the weather has been very bad and wet, and many of our poor fellows have died from dysentery. I am not in the best of health myself . . .

Six months later, George was still in South Africa, in King William's Town. Demonstrating a shrewd financial brain, here he arranged that ten shillings would be sent home each month to his parents. By this time, there were rumours afoot of a new military campaign in South Africa and he wrote home tensely, 'I am greatly afraid we are going to Natal.' Homesickness was evident in his letters; not only was he requesting local newspapers, but his father had died. 'How I wish I was once more at home with you. You must feel so isolated by your poor self . . . .' Even so, he was not in a hurry to return: 'I am thinking of stopping it out here with the 2nd Battalion until I have my term of service in; then when I come home I shall be a free man. What do you think of it?' If a soldier served his five years in Africa, he could take a share in the money generated from selling captured cattle – and money-savvy George Morris was evidently aware of this.

By November 1898 Morris seemed ready for action as a change from the rather mundane daily routine of camp life at Fort Glamorgan.

It is a fine healthy station but it is very quiet, no life whatever . . . How are things looking in Pontypool. I am much afraid that it will be some time before I shall see it again. We are under orders to proceed to Natal, and it is thought we shall have some hard fighting up there as there are not sufficient troops in the country to properly rout the rebels . . .

On 28 December 1878 the regiment were poised to march into 'King Cetshwayo's country' – land of the wild animals and mosquitoes that were a 'popular nuisance'. Although George, like so many others, expected this to be a swift battle that would bring him home by the summer, nerves were starting to show. This letter contained his farewell sentiments:

I have now been about 18 months in the field but thank God I have come safe through all . . . I suppose by the time or before you receive this we shall be on active operations against the Zulus and they are very numerous and well armed . . . I do hope you will not grieve yourself for me as I trust God will bring me safe out as he has before.

By 10 January 1879 George was at Rorke's Drift, where he wrote a rather anxious letter home, again referring directly to death and the enemy ahead. It would be his last letter and became his final farewell.

Dear Mother
    I received your very kind and welcome letter, dated 3rd Dec 1878 and am glad to hear from you and . . . to hear that you are in better health as I am very happy to inform you that I am myself in the best of health. This place is in the heart of the enemy's country at the side of a very large River called the Buffalo. We are waiting here to make a pontoon bridge across the river to go in pursuit of the enemy. Our force is about 6000 of all armies. Dear mother you say that I never say anything of the State of this Country. Well it is in an awful state the natives murdering all the farmers and traders that they can, but an awful retribution is awaiting them.

We have had several engagements with them and killed a lot of them. I expect we will have some hard work with them as they are in strong fortified places called military kraals, and we shall have to fight hard to get them out of them . . . There have been several of our men wounded but thank god I am alright myself and by his kind blessing I shall remain so . . . .

    With kind regards to all love to Maggie and fond love to yourself to console and believe me Dear Mother.

    Your affectionate Son.

    George Morris.[75]

George was killed at Isandlwana, alongside many friends. On his death, his mother as his legal representative, received a payment of £9.13.2 from the War Office – small comfort for the death of her son in a distant land.

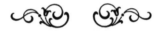

Private Henry Moses

Survived

Born in 1858 in the small South Wales village of Panteg, Henry was the eldest son of Sarah and John, a wagoner and labourer in the local ironworks. They lived in nearby working-class Sebastopol. By the age of thirteen, Henry was also working in the ironworks as a heater in the forge.

On 2 June 1878 he joined the 2/24th Battalion, aged nineteen, in Newport, the nearest city. At this point he was a labourer – probably still in the ironworks. He was one of over a hundred men from the area who joined this regiment, most of whom would have worked in the iron industry, and may well have joined together, or urged each other on. Henry was just under five feet seven inches tall and had a sallow complexion, hazel eyes and dark brown hair. His character was described as 'fair, latterly good' and his education was fairly basic – at class four – although he was literate.

Henry arrived in South Africa on 2 December 1878 and stayed until 12 January 1880; he was on the ground for the entire conflict, yet avoided illness and injury.[76] Despite this good fortune, the dream of army life being a welcome adventure away from the drudgery of the industrial South Wales was turning into something of a nightmare. On 2 February 1879 Henry wrote a farewell letter that was published in a number of newspapers, including the *Western*

Mail. The shock of Isandlwana was palpable in Henry's letter, as was his regret at signing up.

> Dear Father, Sisters and Brother,
>   I take the pleasure of writing these few lines to you, hoping to find you are all well, as I am, so far. I know what soldiering is now. We have marched 200 miles and haven't had a night's sleep this month. We are in fear every night, and have had to fight the Zulus, who came on us and killed 800 of our men. They were about 25,000, and we killed 9000. I wish I was back in England again, for I should never leave. It is sad times here, and we are on the watch every night with our belts buckled on and our rifles by our side. It is nothing but mountains here; all biscuits to eat. We killed about 10,000 Kaffirs, and they killed about 800 of the 1.24th, and 170 of our men. Dear father and sisters, and brother, good-bye. We may never meet again. I repent the day I took the shilling. I have not seen a bed since I left England. We have only one blanket, and are out every night in the rain – no shelter. Would send you a letter before, but have had no time; and now, you that are at home stay at home. Good-bye, if we never meet again, and may God be with you. Give my kind love to all friends . . .
>   Yours affectionately,
>   Henry Moses, Private 24th Regiment.[77]

Henry wrote his letter after the slaughter of Isandlwana, when he had arrived at Rorke's Drift. Although his estimates of Zulus killed were a huge exaggeration of reality, many letters home expressed similar statistics, suggesting that the sheer might of the Zulu impi they faced en masse at Isandlwana appeared to number tens of thousands. Having fought at Isandlwana, the fact that Henry wrote his farewell letter from Rorke's Drift suggests that he went there as part of the relief garrison the following day. The previous day, that place had made history when a small British garrison of 140 men – many of them sick and wounded – fought for twelve hours to repel repeated attacks by up to 3,000 Zulu warriors. Their heroic defence was rewarded by Queen Victoria's government with no fewer than eleven Victoria Crosses; the most ever awarded in a single action. On 23 January Chelmsford ordered columns to head towards the post and the Zulus retreated. Eye-witnesses reported that many Zulus, lying wounded nearby, were shot or bayoneted by the British in desperate, anguished revenge.

Despite his fears of dying and of the Zulu army invading Natal, Henry survived the Zulu War and went on to have a six-year army career, serving in India between 1880 and 1884, and earning two mentions for good conduct. The only slight blemish on his army record was treatment for gonorrhoea in 1880. However, he was a young single man and venereal diseases were rife among such soldiers, for whom willing women were a welcome perk of a job away from home comforts.

Compared with many men who had fought in Africa and struggled to come to terms with what was undoubtedly post-traumatic stress, Henry's life seemed to return to normal on leaving the army. Having witnessed the horror of war, the humdrum of working-class industrial life was, if not more appealing, then perhaps his only option of employment. In 1889 he married Jane from the Forest of Dean and returned to work in what had now become a steelworks as a smelter – a rather skilled job at the turn of the century. Jane and Henry went on to have five children: George, Bertice, Edith, Harry and Bertie.

Sapper H. Cuthbert

Killed at Isandlwana, 22 January 1879

Sapper Cuthbert was one of just seven Royal Engineers to be killed in the field during the conflict. The Royal Engineers had an illustrious history and role in conflict, with the 5th Field Company having been formed by Royal Warrant at Plymouth in 1787. Perhaps their most famous lieutenant of the Zulu War was John Chard, who commanded the successful defence of Rorke's Drift, earning a Victoria Cross in the process.

Two field companies were sent out to South Africa on 2 December 1878 to join the 7th Company, which was already there. The Royal Engineers played a vital dual role in South Africa, building bridges and pontoons as well as carrying out the duties of ordinary infantrymen.

Cuthbert's first letter home to his wife was written while he was en route to South Africa on 3 December 1878. Although there was no direct reference to the prospect of death, the farewell at the end of the letter was significant for the number of kisses. Although he had not reached the theatre of war, Cuthbert was clearly consumed with thoughts of his family – and wanted them to know that. The repeated use of the word 'good buy' rather than the customary 'yours affectionately' also seems to hint that Cuthbert had a sense of foreboding about what lay ahead; perhaps a sixth sense that he would not be returning.

My dear wife
I now take the pleasure of writing these few lines to you hoping to find you and the dear little ones quite well as it leaves me the same just now Thank God my dear I with these lines [am] as neear as I could [be to] you neear Dungerness

We started saill on Monday about 3 o'clock we anchored on Monday night neear the Goodwin Sands started again on Tuesday morning about 1/2 past six My dear I write these few lines to just send of to you the first port we shall call into that I could not tell you in this letter I will let you know in the next letter you will be able to see I think buy the post marks My dear I am coooks maite for the seargants and I mess with them we get fresh bread and meeat every day and one pint of beear My dear theirs about 7 hundred on board beside the ships crew My dear I will tell you moor the next time I write

So good buy till you hear frome me again
Good buy and God bless you all
From your affet husband H. Cuthbert
With kindest love
Kiss the dear little ones for me
Good buy

The Royal Engineers arrived in Durban on 4 January 1879. Colonial engineers also joined their ranks; some with rifles, some with assegais and shields. Cuthbert became part of Colonel Glyn's column, which would start their penetration from Helpmakaar and Rorke's Drift. On 11 January Glyn's column crossed the Buffalo River, and it is likely that Cuthbert was brought into Isandlwana on 22 January, the very morning he was killed. As scouts brought in mixed messages about the numbers and proximity of the Zulu impi, tension must have been almost unbearable for the men waiting for the attack. 'The lives of all on foot must have been lost . . . an example of noble self-devotion'[78] was the description recorded in the official account.

Cuthbert's second letter was sent from Port Natal, just ahead of what would be an exhausting march to war. Again, Cuthbert's cheerfulness was tempered with a sense of homesickness and anxiety as he mentioned sending money home, and the 'unhapy' Christmas he had spent in the field. This would be his last letter home – written just sixteen days before his death at Isandlwana. The stark fact of Cuthbert's death was relayed home with an envelope bearing his name and unit details, and the word 'DEAD' scrawled across the top.

My dear wife
I now take the pleasure of writing these few lines to you hoping to find you and all quite well as it leaves me the same thank God My dear we had a splended journey to the Cape we stopped at the Cape 2 days but are going to Port Natal from the Cape It was very rough indeead it was realey expected the ship would turn up side down My dear we have got about 700 miles to walk up the country beafore we commence any fighting actule My dearest wife the officer is a going to send home some money to the mens wifes so you might expect to hear some

thing about it soon after you received this letter My dear I do not know how you are getting a living in Chatham I do not know what you are to do if you should have to leave where you are you had better leave your address so they will know where to re-address the letter to My dear I am now beginning to find out the comforts I have left behind My dear I have no idea what kind of a Christmas you spent but I desay it was a very unhapy one which my dear mine was a very unhapy one all though I had a very nice dinner the seargents had a gose 2 ducks and a leg of mutton 2 plumb puddings 2 bottles of Port . . . we left all the married women in Cape Town in Castle Barracks and poor Jonny Galds to look after them on account of him having rumatic . . .

Judging from a gap in the letter, the following was added as a postscript some days later while Cuthbert was on the march. It is clear that the prospect of facing the enemy was imminent; although brief, this acted as his final farewell to his wife and children.

> . . . My dear give my kind love to Bill and to all My dear I have no moor tim to say any moor so good buy and may God protect you and the dear children
> Good buy all
> Kiss the dear
> little ones
> For theirs H. Cuth[79]

Like most soldiers, Cuthbert's final thoughts were of his family. There is no record of what exactly happened to him at Isandlwana, and it appeared that by 1881 his wife and children were no longer in Chatham. His words bore testament to the voice of the ordinary soldier who managed to say 'good-buy' – albeit in the briefest of ways.

~ 4 ~

THE BOER WAR

There is one thing, dear mother, if we do get there, & get snowed under, I hope it
will be as a soldier should fall, with his face to the front.[1]

While a patrol was out yesterday, Pt Hennessy found the body of a British soldier
only a few miles from this camp, he must have been killed in the battle . . . and
no one found him; all he had on him was a sixpence, and a letter half wrote to his
sister, it started by saying, by the time these few lines reaches you I will be well on
my way . . . but he never got time to finish it.[2]

T HE SECOND ANGLO-BOER WAR of 1899 to 1902 was the result of two
hundred years of imperialist expansion and subsequent conflict between
Africans and the British; 364,693 imperial and 82,742 colonial soldiers fought in
the war. Official records reveal that over 22,000 men died; more of them from
preventable diseases such as typhoid than from bullets. It has been estimated
that as many as 28,000 people perished in concentration camps, and the figures
for black Africans killed are still unknown. In comparison with previous wars,
it was a hideous death toll.

Many young middle-ranking officers such as John Denton French and
Douglas Haig would become the future field marshals of the First World
War. In South Africa they fought a stop–start battle: static in the later stages
as blockhouse lines penned in the Boers, compared with periods of intense
mobility early on, tracking down Boer commandos – units of up to a thousand men. The Boers were fewer in number but were virtually all mounted
cavalry, whereas just an eighth of British troops were on horseback. It was this
disparity in numbers that led the press to dismiss the outbreak of conflict as
a mere war in a teacup. Few believed it would amount to much – as echoed
in soldiers' letters home: '. . . I expect it will be over in a month or two.'[3] They
were sadly mistaken.

THE BUILD-UP TO WAR: PATRIOTISM AND ADVENTURE

Despite Liberal opposition to the war, largely spearheaded by David Lloyd George, on the whole there was support for it. Newspapers carried stories of crowds waving off their men, and there was no shortage of philanthropic parcels of socks, chocolate and tobacco being sent to South Africa. There was similar excitement among soldiers heading overseas. Syd Critten wrote to his father on arrival in South Africa, 'Am perfectly happy and would go through twice as much roughing it rather than not have come . . . You need have no fear for me as Jack held my hand before I left England and said I should not be shot in this war, and I believe it.'[4]

At this time, there was no censorship of soldiers' letters, and newspapers in particular relished printing news from the front line. It became the first real war to be well covered in newspapers, with many sending correspondents out to the front. Indeed, fifteen journalists were killed or died during the conflict and a young Winston Churchill writing for the *London Morning Post* was captured, but escaped with a £25 bounty on his head.

Many letters displayed a rather bloodthirsty desire to give the Boers the 'skewer'. One soldier wrote in his diary, 'If we Canadians caught any Boers would we torture them. Scottie didn't forget to tell them how we would string them up and set fire to them.'[5] In many cases, though, hatred for this unknown enemy often turned to a grudging respect, particularly as the war progressed.

Men from Australia, New Zealand and Canada joined the imperial force, and expressed their patriotism and loyalty in letters home. Watson Augustus Steel of the New South Wales Mounted Rifles wrote in his diary on 15 May 1900: 'Those who doubt the military strength of Britain should see it here, and this is only a portion of it. It is open to doubt whether any nation in the world could have done the same.' Indeed, throughout the period of conflict, it was rare to find any mention of the possibility of overall defeat.[6] Walter Moodie wrote home to say, 'We have all seen what war is now we have seen our dead and we feel now that the quarrel is certainly ours.'[7]

THE REALITY OF WAR: SHOCK OF THE UNEXPECTED

Following the initial shocking defeats of Black Week, when, between 10 and 15 December 1899, the Boers defeated the British in a series of bloody battles and besieged the key towns of Ladysmith, Mafeking and Kimberley, the mood at home sobered. Soldiers and families started to realise that this might not be the short, straightforward conflict they had expected. This reaction was summed up in a letter that the deputy prime minister Arthur Balfour wrote to his brother: 'I not only think these blunders have been committed, but I think they have been of the most serious kind, imperilling the whole progress of the war.'[8]

As a result, there seemed to be a hardening desire that people should know the reality of conditions at the front. Churchill himself wrote during the siege of Ladysmith,

We have hardly any force to stop them and no cavalry . . . A long and bloody war is before us, and the end is by no means as certain as most people imagine. The Boers have already captured twice as many soldiers as have been hit – not a pretty proportion. They firmly believe they will win and although I do not share that opinion, it must be admitted that it does not sound so unreasonable as it did only a month ago.[9]

Lance Corporal Wicks survived the Battle of Magersfontein and delivered this description. 'Of the awful sights and privation I won't speak, only I must say . . . we had no water for 32 hours and dozens died through want, wounded of course. I got through with my helmet knocked off, two bullets through the kilt, and one through my spats. Do what you want with this letter, it is all the truth.'[10]

David Morrison Stewart recorded in his diary,

If there is anything that will put the fear of death into a man, it is those cursed pom poms they fire a small shrapnel shell; they have a range of 3000 yards and can fire 300 shots a minute . . . You hear a pom pom, pom pom, and then if you have cover, it is just as well to put your head behind it.[11]

The Boers were consummate horsemen and adroit at guerrilla warfare. Organised into commandos, every man between sixteen and sixty was obliged to join up, although there were reports of boys as young as twelve on the front line. It became the most expensive, bloody and vicious war since 1815, and, as Rudyard Kipling put it, the Boers gave the British 'no end of a lesson'. Many imperial soldiers had no experience of shooting or riding, and 32 per cent of the British army was thought to have been made up of unfit men. Nevertheless, the Boers came in for criticism from their own ranks. Gideon Sheepers wrote, 'we are all very angry that such a large number of Boers could not fight their way out – a real disgrace!'[12]

As in previous conflicts fought thousands of miles from home, the importance to morale of letters sent and received could not be underestimated. There were two main post-offices at Cape Town and Pietermaritzburg as well as field post offices and travelling rail-carriage post offices. Biscuit tins served as post boxes, and bicycle orderlies would bring letters to and from the main post depots. During this conflict, an estimated fifty thousand letters arrived each week. Letters were repeatedly the target of Boer attacks – mainly to loot them for stamps and postal orders. As well as countless attacks on the mail wagons, town sieges also caused severe disruption to letters getting through.

War-weariness crept into letters almost as soon as soldiers found themselves confronted with hard, bloody combat. They were fighting an unfamiliar enemy, in conditions that were largely alien. 'Last week we had our first experience of an African sand-storm. The sand came down like hail stones, cutting one's face and hands till it brought the blood. Our tent blew down and our horses got frightened and stampeded.'[13] Many letters spoke of the terrible weather and incessant insects, including tarantula spiders. Supplies were scarce on both sides, with many soldiers writing about their ragged uniforms – 'We arrived looking like people on whom the Salvation Army would almost close its doors' – and uncomfortable conditions. 'No shelter only the bare stones which are often too hot to touch, while the water in our bottles will almost scold one . . . I have burnt my face by picking the field glasses off a stone in a hurry to look at some body of troops advancing.'[14]

As the length of the conflict extended beyond six months there was a realisation that the Boers were a serious enemy who would not give up easily. 'There is no doubt our enemy is as cunning as the proverbial fox and no bait, however alluring, will entice him out of his lair.'[15] The Boers regarded themselves as superior fighters: 'Remember that one Boer is equal to 10 Englishmen,'[16] wrote Mike du Toit to his brother.

Private Edwards wrote to his parents after the terrible battles of Paardeberg and Driefontein, 'I have been in two fierce battle and two skirmishes but the two terrible battles will never be forgotten by any of us that have the luck to get thru it all and home again safe.'[17] Private Clarke Gamble admitted in a letter home, 'there is a good deal of fear about camp quite a number of deaths in the Regiment.'[18]

As war progressed, the debate on the need for censorship grew louder, as soldiers became increasingly critical of those in command and the strategies they were being asked to follow. In a letter to his mother, Bertram Lang referred to that 'incompetent idiot [Field Marshal Paul] Methuen'.[19] George Harris of the South African Light Horse expressed similar disdain toward British military leadership in a letter to his mother on 25 October 1900: 'I can tell you something now that is not known at home and it is this that Roberts [Lord Roberts, British Commander in Chief] is not at all the popular man with the troops that he is supposed to be.' Following the Battle of Magersfontein, Private Smith complained, 'Why weren't we told of the trenches? Why weren't we told of the wire? Why were we marched up in column? May Tommy Atkins enquire?'[20]

In most letters there was clearly a degree of self-censorship from soldiers not wanting to worry their families, in contrast to previous conflicts. Perhaps having a better understanding of the impact of graphic descriptions on the home front during the previous Zulu War had made men a little more circumspect in their writing. 'There is absolutely no need to be anxious as you put it from the day we land in South Africa; anxiety is all tommy rot and does nobody any good so buck up.'[21]

Soldiers' letters also painted a rather different portrait from that created by Rudyard Kipling, who depicted the common soldiers as foul-mouthed, godless and with little concern about their wives and children at home. Instead, the letters, written in childlike hand, with poor spelling and grammar, reveal a lack of education alone.[22]

LAST LETTERS: COMMON THEMES

The majority of letters referenced God and faith: 'Dear Mother, I now write to you, But this will be my last; A rifle bullet pierced me through, my strength is failing fast. Grieve not for me my mother dear, though here I wounded lie; For I'm a Christian volunteer and not afraid to die.'[23] Furthermore, virtually every letter contained expressions of love towards wives, parents and children at home. 'My last and heartfelt love you have and always will have to the end of all things,'[24] wrote Sergeant John King to his wife. At this time, only 20 per cent of British people were thought to be attending church or chapel regularly, although this varied according to geography. Soldiers from rural areas were rather more devout than their urban counterparts. There was a feeling that many rank-and-file soldiers resented religion being forced upon them, and were generally suspicious of chaplains. However, when it came to addressing the profound questions of life and death, it seemed that the majority of men found some comfort in appealing to God, whether they were overtly religious or not. Charles Rickett wrote a farewell note to his wife, in the event that 'I shall have passed over the place into the unseen . . . this is the will of our Father & however unacceptable it may appear to us there *must* be a good and sufficient reason for it.'[25]

On the whole, letters home were generally short. There was a shortage of paper, it was difficult to carry ink, and pencils broke. The Boer War was very much a mobile conflict and long days marching across the veldt were not ideal conditions for writing or posting letters. This may be one reason why higher ranks, seated at desks, often wrote much longer, sometimes more emotional, letters home.

It was a characteristic of this conflict that many soldiers just did not have the chance or inclination to write a final letter. The Victorian stiff upper lip was certainly an overriding theme. Many letters contained just a few lines with practical instructions on what to do if the writer was killed. Lieutenant James

Annat told his wife that he had done 'everything I can think of in case of accident to fix things up comfortable for her'.[26] Private E. Bogan wrote, 'I address my letter as Mrs instead of Mr . . . because I have made my Mother my next of kin so if anything happens to me you get the lot mother.'[27] Meanwhile, Charles Rickett was at pains to reassure his wife that 'the past 2 years have been the sweetest I have ever spent. Life has been fuller, richer & happier in every way than it has ever been before,' but also had rather practical concessions to his farewell:

> And now dearie as to the future. I have no intention to make any alteration to my will but I wish you as far as possible to save the capitol of what I leave you & only use the interest . . . when [Charlie] comes of age or when you feel the time is ripe . . . If you should marry again (and if you do may the marriage be as happy as ours; I can wish you no happier) pray all the money is absolutely settled on the little ones *before* you marry.[28]

Private James McIntosh was one of the few soldiers who wrote a farewell to his beloved grandmother, rather than to his parents:

> Now dear you must not be grieved at what I am going to write, but you must know that there are a few who go out to where we are going who will not come back and as no one knows who may be among that few I intend to make my will before I go. There is not much to leave you dear but better you have it than the Government so that if anything happens to me after everything is squared up you would get about £14..0..0 . . . And if it be His will to spare me to see you all again but that we must leave to him and him alone.[29]

Soldiers on both sides wrote farewell letters. Boer commando O.V. Oosthuizen wrote to his wife and children from Magersfontein to say, 'We have . . . every hope that the future battle will go off well. Do not lose hope, and take the necessary measures just as if I were not coming home.'[30] Likewise Mike du Toit asked a colleague to pen this to his sister as he lay in hospital: 'Be sure Katie that if I do die tomorrow my last thoughts will be of you.'[31]

Many who did not write an actual letter left final messages. General Sir Penn Symons wanted to 'tell everyone I died facing the enemy' as he lay mortally wounded in a field hospital. Captain Childe indicated that his epitaph should read 'All is Well with the Childe.'

The dearth of long, considered farewell letters may be largely due to the fact that most men were reservists and volunteers with no concept of what they would experience in South Africa. Many signed up eager for a foreign adventure – and death was scarcely on their minds. Those who did write letters have left us with an invaluable record of their hopes, fears and opinions on a conflict whose ramifications continue to this day.

SAPPER JOHN BLYTH

Died 13 June 1900

JOHN BLYTH (OR JACK, as he preferred to be known) was a sapper in the Royal Engineers. Born in Scotland, he sent this letter to his sweetheart in Holyhead, Anglesey, just over six weeks before he died.

John Blyth was most probably stationed at Ladysmith from June 1899, and from there the Royal Engineers deployed sections in charge of balloons, communications, fortifications and supplies. The corps was instrumental in mobilising steam engines, which could then support the subsequent fighting along the line of the Tugela River, as well as repairing telegraph lines and building bridges. Given the guerrilla nature of much of the conflict, it was extremely dangerous work. Mines were frequently planted on railways, and repairs meant venturing into enemy territory. As well as this work, the brigade also saw frontline action and Blyth would almost certainly have fought at Spion Kop in January 1900 and Paardeberg in February the same year. Lord Roberts praised the corps for their work on the march from Bloemfontein to Pretoria, where the engineers repaired twenty-seven bridges, forty-one culverts and laid ten miles of railway track.

It is likely that when he wrote this letter John had already picked up the enteric fever that would kill him at Marizburg Hospital. Born in 1880, his sweetheart Louisa Evans was a dressmaker and the daughter of an Anglesey stoker employed on the cross-channel vessels. She may have met John fleetingly, as many soldiers and ships passed through Anglesey en route to Africa. By 1901 Louisa had married a navy writer called Henry Mapp and went on to have four children, three of whom died. Poignantly, John's deeply romantic letter was never kept by 'Louis'; it was submitted to the War Office as an 'informal will' and filed.

25th April 1900

For you love cheer up xxxxxx

Elanslaagate
My Darling Louis,

I received your most welcome letter last night. Do you know we are surrounded by the enemy here or rather nearly surrounded. They attacked us the day before yesterday with their big guns, they threw two or three shells into us doing very little damage . . . They are quiet at present if they come to attack us they will come to

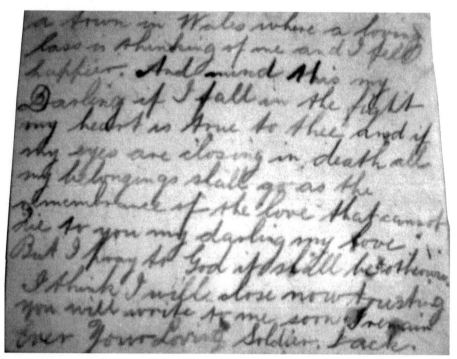

6 Part of the letter from John Blyth, 25 April 1900 (National Archives of Scotland).

their doom for if they come into the plain below our position our cavalry are ready to charge them and our bayonets are as deadly. As ever General Buller is only laughing at their challenges. The Boers gave us 9 days to clear out or they would kill us all. Buller's message was come and put us out of it we are here ready for you and we don't mean to move a step for all the Boers in South Africa. I don't think there will be much more war now about another two battles and the relief of Mafeking will finish it I think. I won't speak much more about it as I have no doubt you are reading full particulars my dear. One half of our company half passed away – the deaths are terrible. Here we bury 3 and 4 every day died from Interric [sic] fever. Our company alone there is out of 220 only about 100 are left, the rest are in hospital, some invalided home and the rest are dead. I am in good health yet. I am very thankful for the little present you are sending me. I haven't got it yet but I have no doubt I shall receive it with the next mail. It will be a God-send to me my love. I am afraid I can't send you anything in return for there is nothing here but a railway station and a few coal-mines – no shops here . . .

You ought to see [my uniform] it is dirty, full of holes and getting worn out. I am writing to you now every week and I hope you will do the same. I am always thinking of the brave little sweetheart who is keeping true and who is wishing me well. And I who am far away across the sea, far out now on the African Veldt, my heart is filled with the love and kindness for the fidelity of only a soldier you know but for an hour. And your loving words make me go through everything with a lighter heart and when we are lying out at night under fire, when it rains in torrents and brave fellows curse the day they became a soldier and say they are deserted by all sympathy from the world, I look back across the sea for a town in Wales where a loving lass is thinking of me and I feel happier.

And mind this my Darling, if I fall in the fight my heart is true to thee and if my eyes are closing in death all my belongings shall go as the remembrance of the love that cannot die for you my darling love. But I pray to God it shall be otherwise. I think I will close now trusting you will write to me soon. I remain ever your loving soldier, Jack.[32]

John Blyth is commemorated on the Boer War Brompton Arch Memorial at Chatham.

LIEUTENANT PETER JOSEPH HANDCOCK
Executed at Pretoria Gaol, 27 February 1902

BORN IN FEBRUARY 1868 in Peel, New South Wales, Handcock was the ninth of ten children of an English father William Handcock – a farmer – and his Irish wife Bridget (Plate 7). Peter Handcock was a blacksmith by trade, a Catholic and married to Alice by the age of twenty. He had two sons and a daughter and is thought at some point to have studied at the Royal Veterinary Institute in London. In November 1899, whilst labouring on the railways in Bathurst, he enlisted as a shoesmith in the 1st New South Wales Mounted Rifles.

The outbreak of war in South Africa coincided with a move towards the federation of the Australian colonies and became a conflict that laid the foundations for the newly formed Australian Imperial Force. Joseph Chamberlain's 3 July telegram to the governor of New South Wales, asking for a show of support in terms of extra troops, was hardly enthusiastically taken up. At that point, the government was not inclined to spend money sending Australians into a conflict that was deemed unthreatening to Britain or the colonies. As time went on, Queensland was the first to send men, sparking other colonies to raise contingents and do the same. Among the lower rural classes, it was less about serving Queen and Country than an opportunity for adventure and employment following depression and drought. Peer pressure undoubtedly played a part. Letters revealed there was also a desire to prove to the British that their 'natural bushman' skills would be highly effective against the Boers. The Australians would be a fighting force with which to be reckoned and the Boer War was their chance to assert a new national identity. Around sixteen thousand Australians served in South Africa, embedded into British columns. They signed up for twelve months, after which many signed up into British irregular units.

Handcock at the time was estranged from his wife and signed up. His squadron, commanded by Captain J Antill, arrived in South Africa on 6 December 1899, working in the Orange River and Prieska area, avoiding heavy losses. In January 1900, the unit was in Naauwport in the Central Cape, seeing successful action in Colesberg and then on through the Orange Free State. In February 1900, Handcock was promoted to farrier-sergeant, then enlisted into the Railway Police.

It was on 21 February 1901 that Handcock joined the detachment that would lead to his death and notoriety in Australia. He signed up to the largely Australian Bush Veldt Carbineers as a veterinary lieutenant, operating from a base headquarters at Pietersburg in Northern Transvaal. Paid five shillings a day, irregular units such as the Carbineers were seen as independent from the formal military structure, and lived up to their reputation as fierce fighters with a cavalier attitude to warfare. The Bush Veldt Carbineers were a counter-insurgency unit charged with fighting in the wild terrain of Northern Transvaal. They were effectively mounted policemen whose plan was to establish outposts as Henry Plumer's column marched north to Pietersburg. They would replace Boers with economically revived colonials, patrolling until these outposts were up and running. They worked tirelessly to turn local allegiances away from Kruger and towards Edward VII – denying locals sustenance and weapons until they fell into line. They were also charged with ensuring Plumer's supply trains ran smoothly, given the Boer's repeated attempts to blow them up.

In June, Handcock joined a detachment under British/Australian officer Captain Robertson at Fort Edward in Spelonken. Later Robertson was dismissed and replaced by Captain P Hunt, another British officer. Alongside Hunt at Fort Edward was his friend Lieutenant Harry 'Breaker' Morant. The unit was singled out for praise by the area commandant Lieutenant-Colonel Francis Henry Hall and acted as scouts for General Plumer.

As Plumer marched onwards, some of the regiment stayed in Pietersberg under the overall command of Lieutenant Colonel Hall. They continued to establish outposts, confiscated crops and cattle and crushed opposition where they could. Over April and May, hundreds of Boers were captured or surrendered. It was a fragile existence, though; tensions simmered between Boers, 'henshoppers' who had accepted imperial rule, and particularly within the Carbineers themselves – who counted among their ranks many Boers who had switched sides. By the middle of 1901 there was increasing frustration among the troops, leading to increased reprisals on both sides.

On the evening of 5 August, Captain Hunt and seventeen men went to a farmhouse at Duivalskloof to capture Veldt Cornet Viljoen. It was a bloody confrontation. Hunt was killed and reputedly mutilated afterwards. Morant, deeply embittered at this and other atrocities, assumed charge of the unit, claiming he now would follow instructions to 'take no prisoners'. Six prisoners had been shot under the orders of Captain Alfred Taylor, a British intelligence officer, prior to Captain Hunt's arrival, and Hunt strengthened that order. Some of the men claimed Hunt had received these verbal orders from Lieutenant Colonel H. Hamilton, General Kitchener's military secretary. Morant, abetted by Captain Taylor and later said to be 'unhinged' by grief, took up the orders with a vengence.

Morant set off with a group of Carbineers and days later attacked a party of Boers. The attack was bungled and they caught only one man – Visser – whom Morant claimed was wearing Hunt's clothes. A hurried court martial ensued and Visser was executed. It marked the beginning of a brief yet bloody vendetta led by an unrepentant Morant. Violence seemingly bred violence and the killings increased. That month, a German missionary named Reverend Heese was murdered near Fort Edward after speaking to Boer prisoners. It was this murder that attracted the attention of the military hierarchy, and a full investigation was launched.

Provost-Marshall Robert Poore was in charge of rounding up witnesses and statements. Seven Carbineers including Peter Handcock, were charged, arrested, handcuffed and put into separate cells in Pietersburg. At the Court of Inquiry on 6 November Handcock was persuaded to make a confession of sorts. During the trial he testified that 'I have had a very poor education. I never cared about being an officer; all I know is about horses, though I like to fight . . . I did what I was told to do.'[33] They did not deny the killing; their defence was that they were following orders. Several Carbineers corroborated those orders, while others spoke of a reign of terror. Handcock and Morant were found guilty of murder, inciting to murder and of manslaughter. Despite numerous pleas for mercy, their punishment was execution. J.F. Thomas, defending officer, wrote, 'I am seriously dissatisfied with the severe punishment meted out, which has astounded, I think every unbiased person . . . Over Handcock's death I have suffered deepest grief.'[34]

Handcock wrote to the Australian government asking them to care for his children, and then wrote a farewell letter to his elder sister Jane.

Dear Sister,

I have but an hour or so longer to exist and altho [sic] my brain has been harrised [sic] for four long weary months I can't refrain from writing you a last few lines, I am going to find out the grand secret, I will face my God, with the firm belief I am innocent of murder. I obeyed my orders and served my King as I thought best. If I over stepped my duty I can only ask my People and country for forgiveness. Tell poor Polly to take care of little Eileen for me at all costs. They

7 Part of the letter from Peter Joseph Handcock, 17 February 1902 (Australian War Memorial, negative number (3DRL/3834), and with kind permission of the Handcock family).

were my greatest comforts at Home & my greatest trouble now I hope my country will see my children cared for I will die brave for the sake of all, God, forgive any enemys [sic] & give you peace for ever I have not heard if our Brother Eugene was killed in this retched war or not. But if not tell him & Will I have gone to rest. Tell Peter and Willie to be good to their sister, God, be with you in your trouble.

From your fond brother

P.J. Handcock

Australia Forever

Amen[35]

On 17 February 1902 Peter Handcock was shot by eighteen soldiers at Pretoria Gaol, under the command of Major Souter, who described Handcock as a 'charming young man'[36]. Handcock was buried in front of thirty Australians in the town cemetery, in a single plot, along with Morant; ignominiously they were not laid to rest in the military sector. Peter was estranged from his wife and nobody informed her of events officially. 'Would you think that the British authorities would treat a widow and three children as I have been treated? My husband has been dead a month, and not one of us has been acquainted of it. I've heard of the cruelty of the Boers spoken of, but could anything be more cruel than this treatment?'[37] There was some comfort in a letter from the prison warder, who wrote to the family following Handcock's execution, convinced of his innocence.

I hope you will Excuse Me for taking the Liberty of writing to you it is with regret I have to Do as I was the last warder on Duty over your Brother *an my* friend . . . on the 22 your Brother and Morant an 2 more *Lieutenants* 1 Victorian an one from Newzeland 4 in all 2 sentensed Penelservitude an the other 2 shot the fased Death without A Murmour an *had* only 48 hours notce of the fact your Brothers trouble Was you an his *children* the faced Death as *Brave* as men could an I was with them until the last the shot 30 odd Boars on Acount of the Boars shooting there Captain the say the are not Guilty of the charge the were sentenced to Death for shooting there mates it was as nice A funerl as Ever Left the Gaol . . . Everyone that look on said it was A shame to shoot 2 so brave men I Hope you will for his mates sake an your Brothers do your Best for the children his Person Belongings will Reach you Later on when the are given out from the Prison . . . Good by God Bless you all from your sincere friend.

In a war where the chain of command was unclear and men unquestioningly followed the orders of their superiors, what they had done was no worse than others were doing elsewhere.

Indeed, long before the Visser shooting, Kitchener instituted an order that Boers could be court-martialled and executed for wearing khaki deceptively.

The court denied such an order despite its general circulation. Breaker Morant's final poem summed up his disillusion with the imperial cause.

> If you encounter any Boers
> You really must not loot 'em
> And if you wish to leave these shores
> For pity's sake don't shoot 'em.[38]

The case caused outrage in Australia. Handcock was the first Australian national to be executed for war crimes, and his sentence passed without the knowledge or consent of the Australian government. Many felt – and still feel – that Morant and Handcock were scapegoats. A letter to the Colonial Office after the event proclaimed:

> The other officers implicated possessed wealth, rank and political influence enough to shield themselves from . . . punishment . . . the Australian officers sprung by merit from the ranks were . . . poor and without official backing and were therefore chosen on that very account as scape-goats to carry by the ending of their lives the misdeeds of a collection of British officers . . . all the feelings I may entertain as to the injustice of the execution will not restore the poor fellows into life again. Though their sad and undeserved fate will ever awaken feelings of regret.[39]

Peter Handcock has never been pardoned, despite an ongoing campaign to reopen the case.

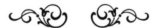

Field Marshal Jan Christiaan Smuts
Survived

Smuts went on to serve in the First World War and became prime minister of South Africa, but his heroics during the Boer War bolstered his record (Plate 8). Born in 1870 in the Western Cape, he was educated at Cambridge, gaining a double first, and was called to the bar in Britain. He was unable to settle, though, and returned to Africa, where in 1897 he married an Afrikaner. Sybella Margaretha 'Isie' Krige was the daughter of a leading local farmer and they settled in Johannesburg.

Smuts had a long-standing interest in politics and by 1898 had become state attorney and adviser to the Executive Council of the South African Republic under President Kruger. Smuts was a prolific planner, passionate strategist and scathing of the perceived British military strength. He worked hard to turn Afrikaners against Britain and had absolute confidence in the skill and might of Boer soldiers to achieve their aims. At the outbreak of the war he wrote:

> Brother Africanders
> Once more the day has dawned in our blood-written history when we are compelled to take up arms and renew the struggle for liberty and existence . . . history will prove conclusively that the allegation of humanity, civilisation and equal rights, upon which the British Government bases its actions, is nothing but a cloak for that hypocritical spirit of annexation and piracy which has always characterised her actions in all her relations with our people . . . Whether we conquer or whether we die . . .
> Africa for the Africander[40]

At the same time, Smuts had a deep-seated belief that reconciliation and finding common ground could bring the war to an end. As the pace of war quickened, he was instrumental in planning the extended guerrilla warfare, and rose to the rank of general. In June 1900 he left his home to lead what he hoped would be a republican victory. His wife, knowing her husband to be a grand prize for British intelligence, went to extraordinary lengths to cover his tracks. She hid secret telegrams in a curtain-pole, sewed gold into a money belt, hiding it in the depths of a copper, and cut up all her husband's letters, stuffing them into a cushion – never to be seen again. British intelligence had circulated a slightly inaccurate description of Smuts, who was known for his piercing blue eyes, as six feet tall, with brown eyes, dark hair, dark brown moustache and French cut beard.

Smuts knew that warfare involved desperate choices, which he characterised as 'capture or annihilation'.[41] By December 1900 he proposed taking control in Western Transvaal where infighting between troops meant that headway was slow. Smuts was well liked and known to be fair and just. He enforced tough discipline and developed a code of conduct whereby no prisoners or spies would be ill treated, whether black or white. He also introduced proper trials for transgressors before any punishment was meted out: the lawyer in Smuts was certainly within Smuts the soldier. He appointed new commando leaders, expelled traitors and took full advantage of British carelessness. On 3 December, Boers seized a supply convoy at Buffelshoek and, following a fortnight of clandestine spying, attacked a camp at Nooitgedacht. Unfortunately an easy victory slipped through Boer fingers as some British survivors escaped. Large-scale offensives were not suited to the poorly organised Boer commando forces.

On 4 January 1901 Smuts wrote a farewell letter to his brother. It was a world away from his enthusiasm and energy of previous correspondence; 'I have hardly any hope of seeing you in this life.' At this point, Boer troops were barely 25,000 in number, and the ravages of the British scorched-earth policy and concentration camps were taking their toll. He described the conflict as a 'hopeless cause'.[42] However, later that month he fought at Moodersfontein where the Boers beat off 2,500 men, inflicted heavy casualties, took two hundred prisoners and were able to replenish supplies of food, water and ammunition.

Throughout the conflict, his wife received few letters from Smuts. When their son died, a telegram she sent did not reach him, and most news of Smut's actions came from scaremongering propaganda in English newspapers carrying repeated rumours of his death. Finally, on 2 June 1901 Smuts was able to send word to Isie and, despite his outward optimism, there was no disguising a dark sense of foreboding. This was his farewell letter.

> My Dearest Isie . . . I warn you not to be influenced by anything you may see in the papers about my being ill or wounded or dead. Should I be seriously wounded or killed you will be officially informed of the fact. So don't worry yourself with groundless fears. I have never been in better health or spirits in my life. Military life agrees wonderfully with me . . . But more than all I have felt for you in all your sore trials and disappointments. I can fathom the depth of agony which you must have endured especially since I left Pretoria a year ago. But I have been cheered by the certainty that your heroic spirit would bear up against all misfortune and that in adversity no less than in prosperity you would be approved as a worthy daughter of your little people. Our future is very dark – God alone knows how dark. Perhaps it is the fate of our little race to be sacrificed on the altar of the world's Ideals; perhaps we are destined to be the martyr race . . . In any case there is nothing worse awaiting us than death . . . Do not expect a letter from me again. Farewell.[43]

Smuts wrote this letter following months of exhaustive raids and repeated political movements towards a peace agreement. His wife responded, giving a poignant insight into the emotions that came with waiting without word, and the impact that Smut's letter had on her.

> Now I shall be able to live on those loving words for the many weary weeks to come . . . Don't worry about me Boetie; I am quite well and my spirit is still strong as ever . . . I am satisfied that my husband is doing his duty bravely and fulfilling the difficult work allotted to him as a worthy son of our little race . . . Take care of yourself Boetie, and remember that your wifie is with you in thought and prayer wherever you are, by day and by night, and her spirit is ever hovering around you

to cheer you in danger and watch over you when the bullets fly around . . . O that I might be beside you in very deed and share every danger with you![44]

As war continued into the next few months, Smuts led commando raids and had hopes for a unified uprising against the British. Moving across the Free State on 7 August 1901 he described 'Dams everywhere full of rotting animals; water undrinkable. Veld covered with slaughtered herds . . . the horror passes description . . . Surely such outrages on man and nature must move to a certain doom.'[45] Smuts's diaries reveal that he had a number of near-misses on the battlefield through the course of August and September. His commando had suffered since crossing the Orange River with dwindling ammunition, countless horses dead and little food, and had been attacked as they trekked southwards.

On 7 September at Moordenaarspoort he recorded, 'I alone escaped in miraculous fashion,' following an ambush on a scouting mission that left his three companions dead. Following that, Smuts found himself surrounded by British columns, but he and his commando staged a miraculous escape down a near-vertical incline at Boshoff's Kraal in particularly bad weather. Knowing of the battles still ahead, it prompted another letter to Isie. 'Who knows what is still in store for us – what losses, what disappointments, what renunciations – but there are treasures of the soul, of love and truth and endeavour which no many can ever rob us of.'[46] The letter was written just days before the Battle of Eland River, where the Boers defeated a squadron from the 17th Lancers and destroyed a field gun. The encounter gave Smuts and his commando renewed confidence. Guerrilla raiding raged on but finally, by May 1902, was fizzling out and hopes of peace took centre stage.

On the surrender, he was sanguine, restrained and hopeful: 'I accept my fate – it is the only manly thing to do . . . Let us do our best to bind up the old wounds, to forgive and forget, and to make the future happier than the past has been.'[47] He attended the Vereeniging Peace Conference in 1902 as legal adviser to the Transvaal government, and after the war campaigned for the establishment of the Union of South Africa.

In later life, Smuts reflected on the Boer War, describing it thus:

a story of disaster, but of a disaster which did not unnerve or paralyse the defeated but spurred them on to even greater efforts in which, in spite of their weakness and ill-success, they sometimes seemed to rent the very fetters of their fate. It was a Titanic struggle fought, if one may say, by pygmies, and constitutes a record of dauntless battling against invincible fate.[48]

PRIVATE EDGAR HALLETT

Died at Bloemfontein, 10 June 1900

PRIVATE EDGAR HALLETT WAS the son of Jane and Benjamin Hallett, and grew up in Lenton, Nottingham. He enlisted and was posted to South Africa in 1899 as part of the newly formed 2nd Mounted Infantry Company of the 1st Battalion Sherwood Foresters, commanded by Captain Leveson Gower. When men who had signed up as reservists marched through the streets they received a wild reception: bunting lined the roads, people stood on roofs to wave them off and their train was cheered until it was out of sight.

The 1st Battalion would remain in South Africa for the duration of the war, taking part in all the major battles and trudging hundreds of miles across country. On one occasion they marched four hundred miles in little under two months, engaging with the enemy on countless occasions.

The unit was stationed in Malta when war was declared. Shortly joined by a number of officers and reservists, they at once sailed for Africa on *Dunera*, with a brief stop at Zanzibar – the first British battalion to land on the island. During the voyage, training continued in drill and musketry so that the men would be ready to go into the field immediately upon arrival. They reached Durban in December 1899 during 'Black Week', when the British army suffered three heavy defeats at Stormberg, Magersfontein and Colenso. It was on 17 December 1899, mindful of what lay ahead, that Hallett wrote his last letter home.

Dear Mother,
I write the few lines to you hoping to find you quite well as it leaves me at present. We arrived at East London South Africa on Friday after a very good voyage from Malta. I wrote a letter from Zanzibar but I think you will get this one first as the mail only calls there once a fortnight. I am writing this letter while we are staying for the train to start again we have been travelling all night and have still to travel all day today. As we are going to join a brigade at the front and expect to see some fighting by Monday. I will take the opportunity to wish you all at home a happy Xmas and a happy New Year as it will be passed and gone when you get this. When we got on board at Malta I met Titch Wardle and Longley and they didn't seem to like the idea of being called up again. Give my best love to all at home from your loving son Edgar and if we do not meet again, Goodbye.
Edgar.[49]

This note was evidently a treasured family heirloom; it is the only surviving letter in the family that has been passed down to different generations for safekeeping. Edgar's farewell to his mother is almost in passing. His letter outwardly betrayed no fear about what might lie ahead and in that way he was typical of so many men who joined up, never really thinking that anything could possibly happen to them. Nevertheless, these few words conveyed the niggling doubt that must have been at the back of nearly everyone's mind at this time. In fact, Edgar had had a premonition he may not return from the war and hurriedly penned this letter home to ensure he had said goodbye.

Sadly, six months after writing to his mother, Hallett was dead – floored not by a Boer bullet but by enteric fever. A form of typhoid, enteric fever took around four weeks to manifest itself and was caused by the appalling lack of clean, safe drinking water and by poor sanitation. The cramped conditions in which soldiers were living meant it spread rapidly. Hallett's battalion alone lost sixty-five men to enemy action and fifty-three to disease. The first cases of enteric fever and dysentery came in February 1900 during months of waiting in a standing camp at Looperberg.

It is likely that Hallett was struck down by the disease at Edenburg, where the battalion concentrated in April, rebuilding railway bridges and roadways to get much-needed supplies through.

Edgar Hallett was buried in Bloemfontein Cemetery.

Major General John Emerson Wharton Headlam

Survived

Born on 10 April 1864, John was the son of Marley Headlam of Gilmonby Hall in Durham (Plate 9). He became a lieutenant in the Royal Artillery in 1883 and was made captain in 1892 when working as an instructor at the School of Gunnery. He married Mary Wilkinson in 1890, and they had two daughters. Headlam was a hardworking devout man from a deeply religious family who cared greatly about the welfare of others. His great-uncle was archdeacon of Richmond, his uncle a clergyman and his cousin later became Bishop of Gloucester. Indeed, among John's most treasured possessions was a well-thumbed copy of the Bible, which he carried throughout his time in Africa. At this point he was deputy assistant adjutant general of the Royal Artillery.

On 7 March 1900, during the Battle of Poplar Grove, he wrote a farewell letter to his wife. On paper it should have been an easy battle to win against the outnumbered, poorly equipped Boers.

> My own darling love,
> I don't think I can attend to a pause in the fight better than by writing a letter to you. We are sitting on the top of a rocky kopje – just like one of the Tors at Okehampton – a glorious morning and the most interesting spectacle in the world – a great battle developing at our feet. The little chief and Kitchener are about ten yards away and everyone is very cheerful for we have seen the daring spectacle of several hundred Boers running like hares! We got up here about 5.45 am – just as the son rose over the enemy's position and then we had to wait, for the Cavalry Division had started early to make a great turning. Suddenly the Boers appeared coming through a neck in the hills with our horse artillery skills all on them and we saw them all clustering . . . and they galloped like mad for the next hill with our shells dropping among them. Now we are waiting whilst the infantry come up before pushing our main attack, but the beginning has been all in our favour and we have turned them right out of the position occupied by their left flank . . .
> Now sweetheart good bye for the present if it comes to hand fighting later, I hope I shall not disgrace you and you will know darling that if anything happens to me I thought of you and loved you to the last . . . I enclose some little flowers picked on the field for you and the chicks.[50]

Poplar Grove was fifty miles from Bloemfontein, set among rolling hills, and was where Christiaan de Wet was firmly entrenched with more than six thousand men. He was determined to withstand Lord Robert's confident advance from the west. It should have been easy defeat for the British, who, well equipped and thirty thousand strong, planned to attack from the rear and cut off any escape route to Bloemfontein. After this, the Boer trenches would be attacked, supported by an artillery barrage. However, the Boers did not wait to be encircled and fled the scene. General French did not chase, and the artillery support was slow and cautious. The opportunity to capture another Boer army slipped through British fingers.

The prize that the British really wanted was Bloemfontein. Despite the debacle of Poplar Grove, it was clear that the next few days would require decisive, bloody action. Realising this was perhaps the prompt for the darker sentiments in Headlam's letter.

Just a matter of days later, though, the British had seized Brand Kop: a decisive moment that meant that Bloemfontein was finally open to be taken. At home, the news prompted rapturous scenes for many. Both Houses of Parliament gathered at Buckingham Palace to serenade Queen Victoria with the national anthem. It seems that this victory gave Headlam a renewed confidence. He made no further mention of death or defeat in any letters. Fortunately, he survived the Boer War, was awarded the DSO and the two South African campaign medals. He attained the rank of major-general during the First World War, was made a KBE and received several foreign decorations. He retired in 1921, and eventually died in 1946.

Sergeant Major Robert Cornelius Gifford
Wounded at Pieter's Station, 18 February 1900

11th December 1899.

Dear Tom,

We are right up to the front near Ladysmith, there are about 25000 men in this camp. I go out on patrol nearly every day. There have been a lot of farmers living here, but they have left their homes. The Boers have smashed all their furniture and commanded all their cattle and horses. There are dozens of railing buildings burnt and bridges blown up. If you do not hear from me again do not fail to apply to the officer commanding the South African Light Horse for my medals, you are entitled to wear them if I am shot. I have a dangerous position being a ground scout. I gallop ahead and find the best track for the troop.

. . . I go out on patrol every fourth night, one never knows the minute one may be shot down. I always have my rifle ready to shoot.

With best and fondest love to dear mother and all at home.

I am, dear Tom, yours ever Bob.[51]

THE SON OF JOSEPH and Pauline Gifford, Robert Gifford was born and brought up in Bombay near Braidwood, New South Wales. Many of his letters appeared in his hometown newspaper throughout the course of the war; it was a close-knit community that was extremely proud of their soldiers and eager for tales of breathless escapades from the front line.

Bob Gifford set sail for Africa on board *Salamis* in October 1899, before any of the official regiments had even left Australia. Perhaps he thought that the fighting would all be over before a New South Wales contingent could reach the front. Arriving in Cape Town, by November he had joined the South African Light Horse as a sergeant major, under the command of Major J.H.G. Byng of the 10th Hussars. Three squadrons were then commanded to Natal, where Gifford was put in charge of an outpost twenty miles from Bloemfontein and within months was heavily involved in some of the bloodiest skirmishes of the Boer War.

He wrote the above letter in the run-up to the Battle of Colenso. The Boers had already inflicted two humiliating defeats on the British, the first at Stormberg on 10 December, and the second at Magersfontein on 11 December – the day Gifford wrote his letter. Already there was growing unease at home and among troops about the tactics of their generals, who persisted in frontal attacks, only to be outwitted and their men left exposed.

The aim at Colenso was to defeat General Louis Botha, whose eight thousand men were holding the approach to Ladysmith at the Tugela River. Under General Sir Redvers Buller, a British army of eighteen thousand men marched forth. It should have been a whitewash but Buller underestimated Botha's skill in command, and woeful communication between commanders meant there was no coordinated attack. For two days, nobody really knew the exact position of the Boers. As troops pushed forwards from right, left and front, the Boers unleashed fire. Gifford was under the command of General Dundonald on the right flank.

Although his letter seems to revel in the danger of battle, Gifford's matter-of-fact instructions should anything happen to him revealed that death was in his thoughts – albeit at the back of his mind. Gifford displayed a clear pride in his role and almost boyish excitement about what he was doing, despite the fact that he was undertaking one of the most dangerous and exposed jobs in the battle.

Gifford's squadron were commanded to move at four o'clock in the morning towards Hlangwane Hill. Their attack was initially successful and they made good progress. However, there was inadequate infantry support and the mounted men found themselves exposed. Gifford's regiment lost four men, with nineteen wounded and thirteen missing. In total, 143 men were killed and more than a thousand wounded, compared with seven Boers killed and twenty-two wounded.[52] It was a bleak culmination to a tragic run of defeats, although Buller recognised the efforts of Gifford's regiment: 'I cannot speak too highly of the manner in which the mounted Volunteers behaved.'

Gifford survived, and his regiment pushed on towards northern Natal. On 15 February he was severely wounded at the Battle of Pieter's Station along the Tugela River. Once again the British army far outnumbered Botha's by almost three to one. The fight had been raging for nine days when Gifford's regiment attacked the Boers entrenched on a kopje known as Hussar Hill. Despite heavy fire, the infantry pushed on, but on reaching the top of the kopje found that the Boers had already gone. The men were now exposed on the Boer's right flank and artillery fire started once again. Robert Gifford had just saddled up when he received orders to mount. He described what happened in a letter to his brother.

27th March 1900

. . . a volley from the neighbouring kopje brought me and my horse to ground. My horse was shot through the neck, while a Mauser, glancing from my spur, tore its way through my left foot and embedded itself in a horse nearby. Severely hurt by my horse falling on me and with my wounded foot, I suffered the most excruciating agony. The next day had far advanced before I was picked up by the stretcher bearers, and sinking from loss of blood, I was quite faint when I was placed on the train for Pietermaritzburg, arriving there after a weary journey.

Gifford was taken to the Assembly Hospital at Pietermaritzburg, where he remained for almost two months before rejoining the front line in April. He was evidently a plucky fighter, and received the Distinguished Conduct Medal. In September he was mentioned in dispatches for special acts of bravery, arduous reconnaissance and dangerous duties over the previous year.

Gifford's Boer experience had a happy outcome and he started a new life. He survived his wounds, and his Australian sweetheart Rose Pike of Araluen travelled out with her sister to marry him in South Africa in August 1902. Robert then worked in the South African Constabulary. By 1909, they had three children and as Rose was again pregnant, they decided to return home to Australia. The Pikes' farm had been sold but the family lived on the upper floor of a family-owned produce store in Sydney.

Private James Coulter
Died at Bloemfontein, 18 May 1900

SCOTSMAN JAMES COULTER VOLUNTEERED in early 1900 and joined the 7th Dragoon Guards. In February 1900 he sailed on *Armenian*, arriving at the Cape on 1 March. The Guards became part of the 4th Cavalry Brigade under Brigadier General Dickson. Coulter would have seen almost immediate action and wrote his farewell letter to his wife as his brigade pushed towards Bloemfontein. At De Aar in April hundreds of men were dying from diseases such as enteric fever and typhoid, which were spreading rapidly through camp. Literally meaning 'artery', De Aar had a vast underground water supply that could have easily become contaminated as troops passed through. Witnessing death from disease, and the battle action that Coulter experienced on the march northwards to relieve Wepener, may well have been the prompt for his letter.

Like so many soldiers, Coulter was not felled by a bullet. After winning two Queen's Medals, he fell victim to disease. It is likely that by the beginning of May Coulter was hospitalised at Bloemfontein while the rest of his regiment marched on towards Pretoria. He died in hospital and his farewell letter was the first and only communication to his wife while in South Africa.

April 1st. De Aar.

Dear Jill. Just a note to wish you many happy returns of the day. I have not forgot your birthday. I am well . . . we were up at five with Kitchener's column, the rebels surrendered without fighting. We are going up to Bloemfontein this week . . . we are expecting the biggest battle of the season but it will be over I think before you get this and as one never knows what will happen I now take the opportunity of telling you 1 very thing that I am entitled to. I have signed over all to you but I would not have told you this if I had not expected the last battle fought before you get this. And if anything happens to me you will have seen my name in the papers. Oh Jill if you knew how I feel to tell you this perhaps I have not been so good always as I might have been. No man is perfect dear wife. If ever I am afraid to come home again Jill you will never have any cause to find fault with me. I would give ten years of my life to see you and Isabel for a few seconds but I see you a thousand times in the day and night and I wonder what you will say & if you will be so nice to me again if I am spared to come home to you again. I am glad I have some one that I know thinks of me and loves me to perfection for I know you love me as we desire . . . Dear Jill I do not require to tell you I know you can & will care for our little one. For the sake of some happy times we have had should I not be able to come home, I trust you to have a fatherly and mother's care over her from me. Fetch her up as like yourself & she will not have many enemys in the world I hope. But you have not to take this letter too serious Jill I could not help telling you . . .

I will close now with love to you and the baby. I remain your loving husband James Coulter.[53]

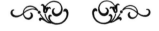

CORPORAL RODNEY DEVEREUX

Killed at Rietfontein, 29 November 1900

RODNEY TALBOT DEVEREUX WAS a New Zealand warehouseman and farmer, living in Epsom, Auckland. Son of Henry – a customs officer – and Maud, he had four sisters and three brothers, and was educated at St John's College in Auckland. He volunteered for service in South Africa and set sail on board *Waiwera* on 10 January 1900. He was a corporal in the 2nd New Zealand Mounted Rifles Contingent; his service records reveal that he was twenty-three, stood five feet nine inches tall and weighed almost thirteen stone.

The Boer War was the first overseas conflict to involve New Zealand troops. Premier Richard Seddon offered Britain troops in late 1899, just weeks before the conflict broke out. Hundreds of men volunteered – including Devereux, who already had military experience with the College Rifles and Waiuku Mounted Rifles. Over the course of the conflict more than six thousand New Zealanders sailed to Africa. Seventy men died in action, with over a hundred more dying from disease.

Devereux wrote regular letters home to his father. In April 1900 he described six days of marching after having orders to go to the front. 'The marching we have done is record marching never been done before in S. Africa.' There was little sign of any war-weariness; instead he was more concerned about his horse Brian, who had developed 'a bad back caused by riding him with a wet blanket'. There was a glimpse of homesickness in his wish that 'I would be glad of our Weekly News now & then if you would send me one.'

In mid-May 1900 the first three New Zealand contingents were organised into one regiment. They took part in the advance through the Transvaal to Johannesburg and Pretoria, which would both be in British hands by mid-June. On 14 June 1900 Devereux wrote, 'The forces are only some 15 miles away & we hear nothing at all about them, a rumour goes about camp that the different forces, Buller, Carrington & Roberts are gradually closing in on the Boers. Now & then we hear a distance Boom! Boom!' It was clear, however, that the ravages of war were taking their toll: 'I wish you could see us now all in rags & boots with no soles, you would not know us.' Nevertheless, he remained chirpy and was even thinking of joining the police – 'a good billet' – despite the fact it would mean his stay in South Africa might be extended.

By late November most soldiers really believed the war was virtually over. Indeed, it was in the final battle of the war that Devereux was killed. On 29 November the Battle of Rietfontein Farm took place at Rhenoster Kop, east of Pretoria, when imperial forces attacked a Boer contingent. Five men were killed and twenty-one wounded.

The battle started at four o'clock and lasted for seventeen hours. The sun was blazing and the New Zealand contingent had little water and a dwindling supply of bullets. Two or three men made it back to camp to bring back supplies amid the fighting. Had the Boers advanced, they almost certainly could have overrun the force, but they missed their opportunity, with one newspaper reporting, 'we, with the exception of the poor fellows who were "wiped out" are still sailing under the British colours instead of kicking up our heels in a Boer prison.'

That same newspaper carried an account of what happened to Devereux:

At the time he was shot he was kneeling up, covering the retirement of our guns, and the bullet passed through his arm and heart. Throwing up his arms he fell, never to rise again, and death must have been instantaneous . . . our Auckland boys volunteered to go out and fetch the body in, but as it seemed but certain death to allow them to move out in the face of such a hail of bullets, they were prevented by the officers from doing so. They were simply pouring in on us, both with the big guns and the rifle.

The killed and wounded had to be left on the field in the blazing sun all day, and could only be brought in at midnight after suffering terrible agonies. The ambulance, with the red cross flying, was sent out earlier, but its appearance only called forth a hail of bullets, the flag being simply riddled through and through . . .

Altogether it was a terrible day, and the wonder to me is that any of us are alive to tell the tale.

Devereux did not get the opportunity to write a last letter. Instead his comrades penned a beautiful poem that became his final farewell to friends and family.

RODNEY DEVEREUX
(*One of the Best*)

Stalwart, sturdy & strong,
Open & frank of face
Stamped with the attributes that belong
To the best of the human race;
Tall of stature & stout of build
Broad of shoulder & deep of chest;
By this & that we remember him
Rodney Deverex one of the best.

Voice sounding deep & rich,
Eyes looking blue & clear,
With a brace, bright smile on the features which
Showed a heart devoid of fear
Showed a life joy filled to the every brim

A happy which by the face exposed;
By this & that we remember him
Rodney Devereux one of the best.

Born of a noble name
Type of a nation free,
What wonder that when the war-call came,
There in the war was he.
We watched with pride, tho' our eyes were dim
The ships that bore him towards the West;
By this & that we remember him
Rodney Devereux one of the best.

To more in pride we yield
Of our gallant island band
Who fought on many a hard-won field,
From Reinburg to the Rand
And mid the first, this good & ill
Who ever foremost, onward pressed,
Was he whom well we remember still
Rodney Devereux, one of the best.

But dear was the price of failure
And in blood we had to pay
For the deeds that have made our island's name
A household word today.
And many a comrade true and tried,
In that distant land has been laid to rest,
And he is numbered with those who died,
Rodney Devereux, one of the best.

Died on the Rietfontein,
In the charge that now the day
That tinged our name with a golden sheen
And sealed our fame for life;
And tho' hearts are heavy & eyes are dim
Our grief is with glory and honour blest,
His with pride & love we remember him –
Rodney Devereux one of the best.[54]

After his death, Devereux's effects were returned home by his comrade Lieutenant Banks, although there was a lengthy delay in this, which caused

Rodney Devereux
(One of the Best)

Stalwart, sturdy, & strong,
Open & frank of face,
Stamped with the attributes that belong
To the best of the human race;
Tall of stature & stout of limb,
Broad of shoulder & deep of chest;
By this & that we remember him —
Rodney Devereux one of the best.

Voice sounding deep & rich,
Eyes looking true & clear,
With a brave, bright smile on the features
                                        which
Showed a heart devoid of fear.
Showed a life joy filled to the very brim,
A happy mind by the face expressed;
By this & that we remember him —
Rodney Devereux one of the best.

Born of a noble name,
type of a nation free,
What wonder that when the war-call came,
there in the van was he —
We watched with pride, tho' our eyes were dim,
the ship that bore him to-wards the West;
By this & that we remember him —
Rodney Devereux one of the best

8 Part of the poem to Rodney Devereux (Auckland War Memorial Museum).

Devereux's father to write anguished letters to the military authorities, begging for his son's letters, photographs and pocket-book. Devereux's father was invited to receive his son's medals at the Auckland presentation ceremony. He was buried at the Diamond Hill Garden Cemetery in Donkerhoek.

~ 5 ~

THE GREAT WAR

23rd April 1915.

 Dearest we have just received orders to embark on the shores at 10.45 a.m. tomorrow . . . In case the worst happens and I am unable to make any more entries I will take this opportunity to bid you goodbye dear girl. I trust that I will come through, but it is impossible to say, and I must do my duty, whatever it is. But if I am to die, know that I died loving you with my whole heart & soul, dearest wife that a man ever had. Kiss little Gwen and our new baby, who perhaps I may never see, and never let them forget Daddy . . . You will always find a good friend and counsellor in Jack Mossop, and I would like you to trust him. If dear, in some future time – I know you will scorn the idea now, but time brings many changes – if in some future time you should think of remarrying, always know that I would wish you to do whatever is for your own happiness. But think well, dear, and make sure what manner of man you take won't you darling . . . And now, dear, dear sweet heart, goodbye goodbye.[1]

THE HUGE MILITARY CEMETERIES that almost characterise the landscape of France and Belgium are testament to the near-inconceivable loss of human life during this conflict. The statistics of human sacrifice in the First World War are both shocking and sobering. Almost a quarter of the British adult male population passed through the army during this war, with nearly five casualties for every nine who went to war.[2] On the German side, four years of conflict created around six million casualties.[3]

 The rows and rows of identical headstones in immaculately manicured graveyards in some ways de-personalise the human story behind each death. Official histories talk of casualty numbers and strategic gains: human emotion seemingly has no role in our understanding of how the war was won or lost. It is through the personal letters of men who fought this war, though, that we can put real faces and voices to the war. Desperate, philosophical, stoical, political and emotional letters of men facing the grim possibility of death are a window on the reality of this conflict for the men who fought.

 The war to end all wars split Europe as two camps developed out of alliances, broken promises and German naval expansion. The murder of Archduke Franz

Ferdinand of Austria in June 1914 was a spark that ignited more than three decades of suspicion and mistrust into a global war on a devastating scale.

ENLISTING: PASSION AND DUTY

'Kitchener's Mob' – just like the French 'Poilus' and the German 'Kaiser's Men' – was a massive number of volunteer soldiers, many blithely unaware of the horrors that lay ahead. Those signing up sought adventure and foreign travel, and for the many living in extreme poverty, war offered clothes, shelter and food. Australian soldier Percy Mansfield wrote excitedly, 'I will have to thank the Kaiser for a grand trip and experience.'[4]

Passion for the cause was a powerful, unifying force that drove thousands of men to enlist. It was a fervour explicit in virtually all letters home – whatever the nationality. In Britain Private James Goodwin wrote, 'Strengthen us to quit ourselves like men in our right and just cause. Keep us faithful unto death, calm in danger, patient in suffering, merciful as well as brave; true to our King and country, and colours. If it be Thy will enable us to win victory for Britain.'[5] In Britain alone, within the first five months of war breaking out, more than a million men had volunteered for the army.

It was no different in Germany. Walter Roy proudly wrote home in November 1914 to say, 'Only one thing is real now – the war! And the only thing that now inspires and uplifts one is love for the German Fatherland and the desire to fight and risk all for Emperor and Empire.'[6]

The First World War saw the British introduce a £5 payment if a serviceperson was killed in action. For the soldiers themselves, this was a source of bitterness and anger – referred to as the 'blood bounty'. Private Espie was suitably curt about the money in a letter to his mother on 25 September 1914: 'I have signed a will if I get killed that you shall get the lot my blood money is five pound.'[7]

Despite the encouragement to make a will, and ever-growing numbers of casualties, there was a palpable sense of invincibility among the soldiers going off to fight. Indeed, to a large degree, this reflected the very young age of millions of recruits in this war, who simply thought it would not happen to them. 'I don't think a German could hit me with a stick let alone a Bayonet or Bullet,'[8] wrote Private Patrick Steele, while Ted Whiteaway affirmed, 'I am not going to write in the goodbye strain as I have the feeling that all will be well. If not well no Englishman could have a better end.'[9]

THE CHANGING TIDE: DWINDLING ENTHUSIASM

From letters sent home, it was evident that, particularly after events on the Somme in 1916, there was a growing realisation that this was no short skirmish. What Richard Holmes aptly described as 'a war of attrition' was slowly grinding men down – particularly those who had fought throughout the war. Letters became more questioning, and patriotism was not quite so clear cut. This war-weariness was evident in Reggie Crooke's letter to his friend Len Ornellas on 3 September 1918: 'Please don't think that I am not as true a soldier as I used to be but I have seen and done what I have never before, and it must tell on one. Nature will not allow one to carry on in this strain for too long a period, and I am just beginning to feel it.'[10]

Some soldiers admitted to deliberately missing shots at the enemy, while other letters revealed a remarkable developing relationship with the enemy, with truces, night-time banter across the trenches and even rare instances of 'trench-hopping' to swap stories and anecdotes. Letters were becoming more reflective; moreover, there seemed to be a growing unease and fear that it was only a matter of time before a soldier's number was up, keenly felt on both sides. Rudolf Fischer wrote home to say:

> The whole life here at the front is permeated with a sublime solemnity. Death is a daily companion who hallows everything. One no longer receives him with pomp or lamentation. One treats His Majesty simply and plainly. He is like many people whom one loves even though one respects and fears them. Nobody will come through this war without being changed into a different person.[11]

LAST LETTERS: COMMON THEMES

The majority of 'farewell letters' from this conflict took the form of a few lines within a 'normal' letter, or notes in a diary. Indeed, many diaries had a scrawled frontispiece that it should be sent on to a loved one in the event of its owner's death. Other diaries had goodbye notes in them, implying that it was assumed they would find their way home and be read by the right person eventually. Corporal Henry Taylor wrote in his wartime diary,

> We are just off to the front & may be in action in a few hours time . . . in case of my misfortune to go under . . . to my boy I wish him to be a good, brave & real English laddie . . . Do not worry or fret as that is no use but be as cheerful as possible to help others.[12]

Private Alfred Young penned this poetic farewell: 'Like the creaking beams of a well stormed sea-tub, groaning as the storm beats against her timbers, unwilling to give in, but sooner or later must fall a victim to the tempest.'[13]

Unlike in previous conflicts, there seem to have been very few letters written as a man lay dying or mortally wounded – although such letters existed. German soldier Eduard Bruhn managed to scribble the following lines to his parents: 'I am lying on the battle-field badly wounded. Whether I recover is in God's hands. If I die, do not weep. I am going blissfully home . . . Jesus is with me, so it is easy to die. In heartfelt love.'[14]

The hundreds of farewell letters that survive from the Great War have three recurring characteristics. First, in a stark reminder of the youth of so many soldiers, they were overwhelmingly written to mothers. Many of the men would have been away from home for the first time, and virtually all were still reliant on mothers for endless supplies of cigarettes, socks and chocolate!

Secondly, letters revealed an immense sense of comradeship – more explicit than in earlier conflicts. Undoubtedly this was due to the huge amount of time men spent together, often in very close proximity. Harsh circumstances forced close friendships, and whether they shared their feelings or not, each man understood he was going through the same as his comrades. There was an unspoken bond between men who knew they were sharing the burden of impending death and through friendship could – if not alleviate – then better face those fears. It was rare that one man *alone* would go over the top: they all would go. If they were hurt or killed, they hoped someone would pick up the pieces.

Finally – regardless of nationality – there was an overwhelming spiritual element to these letters, ironically suggesting that in the field bloodthirstiness was next to Godliness. Few soldiers saw any conflict between believing in Christ and killing the enemy. Many saw the war as a quasi- religious mission. In their eyes it was a battle between right and wrong; a battle for honour, integrity and country.

Chaplains preached the gospel of self-sacrifice and duty. At the outbreak of war, there were 117 British padres. By November 1918 this number had swelled to 3,457 – all volunteers. There were instances of soldiers being baptised in the field, and on the eve of key offensives or pushes, chaplains would find their oft-makeshift churches full to bursting. Chaplain Julian Bickersteth had an underground chapel so large it could hold up to a hundred men, and in the run-up to the Battle of the Somme he was holding Holy Communion services on a daily basis.[15]

It was the chaplain who was so often privy to the thoughts of dying soldiers and became the physical embodiment of a farewell message: a sole living witness who could pass it on to a loved one, or write themselves and tell of final moments. The Reverend T. A. Williams wrote to the mother of a soldier in 1916:

I was with him to the end. He did not suffer long and his last words were 'Goodbye Sir' . . . He gave me a message for you when he realised he was going home. He said tell my mother that I died trusting in Jesus as my Saviour and that I shall meet her yonder. He also sent his love . . . Being Welsh myself I sang Welsh hymns and prayed in Welsh with your son. He joined me in these readings and prayers.

No doubt it was known that a family would take great comfort from knowing that their dying son was 'resigned to God's will and patiently awaited the end'.

The farewell letters of the First World War shed light not only on iconic battles, but also embodied the universal themes of that conflict. Wherever a soldier came from, his letters revealed youth, optimism, camaraderie and belief. Over ninety years later, the farewell letters of soldiers killed in the Great War carry great resonance. They are a surviving memorial to the fallen; a voice that still speaks clearly and loudly on behalf of those killed.

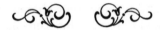

CAPTAIN ERIC FOX PITT LUBBOCK
Killed at Ypres, 11 March 1917

ERIC FOX PITT LUBBOCK was born on 16 May 1893, the son of Lord and Lady Avebury (Plate 10). He was the 'absolute apple of his mother's eye'. An accident-prone questioning child, he was extremely bright, and went to school at Eton. After his death a friend remembered him as 'a rare character with wonderful understanding and sympathy'. On 7 October 1912 he started university at Balliol College, Oxford, and his diary there captured the outbreak of war: 'For three or four days there had been one strange word whispered by everyone . . . War. It sounded terrible enough, and yet, to the initiated, it was a word of excitement, it almost sounded romantic.'

On 6 November 1914 Lubbock went to the Royal Automobile Club and enlisted. After training, he was posted for service with the 69th MT Company ASC, Lahore Division. His first visceral introduction to war came in December 1914 when evacuating a hospital at Chateau Gorre – near Béthune in France. Under shell-fire he recalled the 'awful sights . . . There were Gurkas with no trousers and no socks, with half their faces off. Terrible.' As so many other men fighting on the front, he had one wish for the New Year: 'May it bring peace, a long and lasting peace and victory. The victory must however be complete or the peace will not last. This you know is not life. Our life ended last August and this is an interregnum of chaos and sin. For some life will start again, but alas, for many it is ended.'

By October 1915 he had been promoted and transferred to the Royal Flying Corps (RFC), qualifying as an observer after forty-two hours of flying with Major Robert Loraine in a variety of planes.[16] His commanding officer noted that he was a 'keen and promising officer'. Indeed he would go on to win the Military Cross.

Lubbock certainly had no qualms about the enemy. He claimed to have seen evidence of German atrocities against women and children, and his letters revealed a venomous dislike of them, an unshakeable conviction in the war effort ('playing a part in the advancement of human nature'), and a belief that everyone should do their bit. These feelings were coupled with almost uncontainable glee and delight at the thrill of attack.

On 26 October 1915 Lubbock was flying a Vickers Gunbus on a reconnaissance flight that lasted one hour and fifty minutes. They went from north of Boesinghe to south of Ypres.

> Yesterday Loraine & I had an exciting adventure. We sighted a Hun about 4 miles off . . . We both opened fire at about 50 feet. I fired again at 25, firing 26 rounds, & then my gun jammed . . . [Eric managed to un-jam his gun] . . . Then our machine turned downwards. As I fired my last shot I had seen the German turn down also – I knew that if he got below us my machine gun was the only one that could fire at them. We were diving, I almost standing in the front of the body. Then we turned level . . . Then there was no Hun. But our guns had jammed at the same moment. [He fixed his gun and Loraine's] . . . We saw another enemy coming in the distance. Loraine went all out to climb & attack while I put my stiff & aching hands in my mouth praying for sufficient life to come back to them, they were frozen. Then our engine stopped & we were helpless, so we turned and glided homewards. Unable to reach the aerodrome we landed in a plough; a beautiful landing.

Apparently a crowd surrounded them as the farmer rewarded the crew with some steak and coffee, and a fellow soldier gave him a well-deserved cigarette. Machine-guns jamming was a common problem – on 28 October Lubbock's log book talks of chasing the 'Hun' near Armentières: 'Fired 5 drums but both guns jammed owing to bad bags.'

Indeed, for much of the war, German pilots had the advantage of better planes and training. In addition, the Western Front's prevailing winds favoured the Germans. Pilots of the RFC developed a reputation for aggressive and courageous flying in the face of all this, despite very heavy losses. The ratio of British losses to German was around four to one at some periods.

Eric wrote an undated farewell letter in 1915, certainly it was begun before November that year. Perhaps, in spite of all the bravado and adrenalin of that chase, in cold, sober reflection, Eric may have realised that life in the air could be extinguished in a second. First World War aircraft had open cockpits, no heating, no oxygen, no landing brakes, and no parachutes were worn.

My darling Mum.

One is here confronted almost daily with the possibility of Death, & when one looks forward to the next few months this possibility becomes really a probability. I am therefore setting down now to write to you briefly a few words which in the event of my death I hope may help to comfort & to cheer you. That is my purpose in writing, for as my object in life is to comfort & help you, so is my last hope if I should be taken from you, that I may not cause you too great a grief. The thoughts which I here intend to write are those which I have had on occasions when it seemed that my life was about to be cut short. Also. I know that if in my last hour, I am conscious, my chief consolation will be to feel that these thoughts may reach you. I shall therefore simply write down my ideas about it all & I hope thereby to enable you to feel that though I may be taken away yet that fact is not all grief..

Now one of the questions one asks oneself about it all is do you fear Death? And I have I think convinced myself that I do not.. My reasons for this I will show later. Of course it is the natural instinct of a human being to avoid Death in all possible ways, "life every man holds dear", yes & every animal of God's holds this great gift clear,

9 Part of the letter from Eric Lubbock, 1915 (Imperial War Museums).

My Darling Mum

One is here confronted almost daily with the possibility of Death, and when one looks forward to the next few months this possibility becomes really a probability. I am therefore setting down now to write to you briefly a few words which in the event of my death I hope may help to comfort and to cheer you. That is my purpose in writing, for as my object in life is to comfort and help you, so it is my last hope if I should be taken from you, that I may not cause you too great a grief. The thoughts which I here intend to write are those which I have had on occasions when it seemed that my life was about to be cut short. Also I know that if in my last hour, I am conscious, my chief consolation will be to feel that these thoughts may reach you. I shall therefore simply write down my ideas about it all and I hope thereby to enable you to feel that though I may be taken away yet that fact is not all grief.

. . . Now my reasons are two (1) love and ambition (2) that I know my death would cause pain to you and I don't want to do that. My love is firstly love for you, secondly love for others, and thirdly love for the world in general. I love you and all my brothers and sisters and friends, and as you know I have loved one person very deeply for several years, but of that I will speak later. My love for you and for my brothers and sisters and friends makes me long for life because with it I hope to be able to help you all and add to your happiness. And my love for Dad makes me want to live because I hope that perhaps in some small way I might carry on one of his great works and in so doing honor him. My love for the world in general makes me hope that before I go I may be able to make it in some way (however small) just a bit better than I found it.

Ambition I should perhaps better call interest, it is simply the desire to learn something more of this wonderful and beautiful world before I leave it.

And the other reason, which is more the cause of my dreading death than anything, is why I am writing now.

To fear or dread death for its own sake is absolutely against all reason, and I want to point out to you that you must not grieve too much if I die.

You my poor Mummy suffer a lot from sleeplessness. But suppose now that you went off to sleep at 10 one night and woke up at 8 next morning having had no dream or consciousness at all would not that seem to you a blessed 10 hours? Now death at its *very worst* is that, absolute blank, and therefore why fear it?

But I do not believe that death is that. I believe it is something very different.

You and I know very well that there is what we call right and wrong. We also know that if there is right there must be reward for right doing, and if there is wrong there must be punishment. Now in this world that is not always so, for many are happier and 'better off' as we call it for doing wrong. Now if this world were the end then our wonderful consciousness, and our knowledge of right and wrong is 'altogether vanity', and life is a hopeless failure. If this world is the final end, this imperfect world with all its sorrows and griefs if this is the best we can attain to then the Great Giver of Life is but a torturer and if you love me you will rejoice that I have left so miserable an existence and lost so painful a consciousness before I suffer any more.

. . . What I have meant to say is that either Death is the end or not the end. That it should be the end is inconceivable and if it is not the end then that which comes after must be better and higher than this world.

. . . Of course I know that this is not going to relieve you of the first pangs of parting. You will say I might have been spared for some time to help and comfort you. Yes and I hope I may be spared. We mortals have such deep feelings in the world that it is inevitable that we should have pain at parting. But I hope you will let me help you even if I am not alive, by believing that I do that we cannot judge for ourselves, and that we cannot here on earth see everything in true proportion. Is not the sorrow of a child when it loses its doll a very real and great grief? And yet, although it is not much use saying to the child, we know that it doesn't much matter.

So Mummy if you love me try not to let it be too great a blow to you, try and conquer your own sorrow and to live cheerfully. You have great work before you in caring for Moke and in bringing him up to be the great and good man he is going to be. And you have got to help Urtie, who, although she is so wonderfully strong and good, needs help to bring up her children, and help which you more than anyone can give. Live for them cheerfully.

. . . And to one friend in particularly, Winifred, whom I have always loved. I tried hard not to love her, and even though I found I couldn't help it, for some time I did not admit it to myself. Now I do, and I know what it is to love. God bless her and keep her always happy.

So with all my love my darling Mum I now say goodbye, just in case. Try to forget my faults and to remember me only as your very loving little son.

Eric Lubbock

10/11/15

This was written some time ago. Now I have again suffered the most awful pain a man can suffer, that of losing the girl he loves. I know that in your heart you fear it may make me reckless. It will not, you must trust me that I have strength enough not to let it. But Mummy could you see her for my sake and tell her to the end I loved her. Be kind to her.

His mother never acknowledged Winifred Martin-Smith as Eric's sweetheart, and the family are still unsure why this was. Perhaps it was simply because Lady Avebury did not want to share Eric, whom she absolutely adored. In the shadow of that stifling love, perhaps simply nobody was deemed to be good enough for this extraordinary young man.

In 1916 Eric was still in France and relishing the thrills and challenges of wartime life. Now qualified as a pilot, he was undertaking night flying, although his first attempt on 31 May 1916 was 'not good as I under/overestimated the hight & undershot'. Nevertheless, as Eric himself admitted, luck was on his side and his passion undimmed. His letters brought that excitable passion to life; when reading them, one is with Eric in that aircraft – along for the thrilling, almost primeval excitement of the ride:

> All the luck seems to be my way. I went up today to take some photographs. We were soon attacked by a Hun & each fired one drum. He was getting out of range when up came another. Then followed a series of twists & evolutions & I fired & Powell . . . fired & the Huns fired & we turned over one round the other till I felt giddy almost.

Eric's last letter home was written on 9 March 1917. It is poignantly abstract and innocent – blithely unaware of the fate around the corner. He talked of eating tinned lobster and oysters. He ended with the prophetic 'we are once more calm and collected'. Eric's log book, filled with his unmistakable exuberant notes and handwriting, has notes written in a different hand for 12 March 1917.

> Live patrol, northern sector. Two machines were on this patrol (Lubbock & Bowden). They encountered two German single seater Albatross scouts. A hot fight ensued in which both Lubbock & Bowden (with Thompson & Stevenson) were shot and brought down in our lines in the Ypres Salient. Lubbock's machine fell from a great height and hit the ground at a point . . . The place is very near a small farm house which stands rather alone . . . WR Read.

A captain wrote and told Eric's mother of his funeral: 'It was just a small field that was set aside as a burial ground, just a corner of a ruined land, and in that field lie the bodies of some of England's bravest. The little crosses stand there as proof of England's greatness, proof of her sacrifice, proof of her integrity.'

Lady Avebury was devastated by Eric's death. She wore black for the rest of her life, and wrote on black-edged paper until she died on 11 March 1947. She commissioned a stone model of an aeroplane as a memorial to Eric, which was in the family graveyard in the woods below the Farnborough parish church. She published his letters and diary in a privately circulated volume, and wrote her own heart rending reaction to both the farewell letter and Eric's death:

> There is nothing conceivable that could possibly be desired for the most unspeakable kind of Hell that is now taking place at this moment and has been taking place for over two and a half years on this earth, but then comes the feeling – How is it possible that we who thought this world was so vastly improved,

so civilized, could possibly come to this . . . however bad our lives have been, I cannot feel that this ghastly torture is not absolutely inadequate and brought about by a few utterly heartless, gross, ambitious men throwing the whole of the world into depths of despair and suffering and cruelty which, as I say, the worst description of Hell imaginable would not come up to what is taking place on this beautiful earth. It is not God who allows it, *but we are being tried very high*. It is the outcomes of men's selfishness and lust and we have to work out our own salvation or else no merit or sense well doing . . . One has often thought one would like to know what was in store for us, but had I known what was in store for me and all the ghastly suffering, it would have made existence always impossible.

. . . It seems impossible to believe that Eric has gone out of our lives – he seemed to wear a charmed life and one never could think it possible that Eric should not be alive. How he was beloved on all sides – and how it helps – and I have always the past. It was a most perfect relationship – separation cannot touch that . . . I recall every gesture, every look, and I have to remind myself that Eric has actually left this world . . .

Well as I knew him and deep as our talks had always been yet I marvel more and more at all he had thought out in his short life, and how like his splendid, thoughtful self to leave me behind such a letter as he did to help me always even if he was taken from me.[17]

Second Lieutenant Eric Rupert Heaton

Killed on the first day of the Battle of the Somme, 1 July 1916

Born in Hove in Sussex on 12 April 1896, Eric Heaton was the youngest son of the Reverend and Mrs Daniel Heaton (Plate 11). Educated at Kingswood School, he was fiercely intelligent, winning the Dux Prize. At Guildford Grammar School he started studies to help him fulfil his ambitions of joinging the medical and dental profession. War upset his plans to enter Guy's Hospital and he volunteered in March 1915. Eric initially joined up with the 14th Battalion Middlesex Regiment before joining the 16th Battalion Middlesex Regiment (86th Brigade, 29th Division) on the Western Front in February 1916. He also had two older brothers who joined up – Captain Douglas Heaton and the Reverend Wallace Heaton – both of whom survived the war. Eric joined up with gusto and threw all his energy into his training at Colchester and Shoreham. His notebooks are evidence of his diligence as he scribbled instructions and wrote down useful bits of advice.

Raids on Enemy Trenches
Armed with revolvers and truncheons
Grenade carriers
Steel helmets
Faces blackened

His notes conjured up an image of a Boy's Own hero, dashing into action. It was an ironic foreshadow of how he would die on the Somme. Like so many young men, his bookish notes were sanitised and innocent, and a world away from the real experience of trench raids: frightening, deafening, stinking and horrifying.

Eric wrote to his parents every few days and his early letters revealed the boyish innocence of someone aged nineteen – almost at odds with the fact he was a commissioned officer. The 16th Battalion was a Pals Public School Battalion where 'gentlemen' were encouraged to apply for commissions. A private education instilled a thirst for adventure and a keen intellect, but was poor preparation for the horrors to come.

On 14 February 1916 he wrote from,

Somewhere in France. The officers are quite a nice lot and the men are a good lot. I have a platoon No 1 in C Company. They have lost six officers since coming out. To-day we go into the trenches for how long I do not know, a week or so I suppose and I shall get my 'baptism of fire!' I think things are rather quiet in this part of the line, at least I hope so . . .

Monday February 21st
    We are in rest just behind the firing line, behind us are some big howitzer guns which the Bosche does not like at all, but they shake what remains of this place pretty badly, when they fire. One does not realize the destructiveness of this war until you are actually on the scene, but what strikes me is the awful monotony of it all. Our Tommies are Marvellous, how they can have stood month after month in the trenches is wonderful . . . I shall be all right; you may be sure I shall not put my head over the parapet unless it is necessary!

War forced boys to grow up quickly, and Eric was mindful of what lay ahead. Hundreds of other letters written at the time still expressed hope that the war would be over by Christmas, but on 2 March 1916 he bleakly wrote, 'This war is by no means finished I fear.' Like so many others at the front, Eric had been as close as twenty yards from the German line. At this range, you kept your head down and simply absorbed the constant sound of artillery fire. The idea that at any moment a mortar could strike your position must have been an agonising mental pressure for the men. Little wonder that Eric was 'looking forward to the time when I shall see the shores of dear old England again'.

The Battle of the Somme has become etched in the public consciousness as the British army's bloodiest day of the First World War. There were nearly 58,000 casualties on that first day – a concentrated barrage before the attack was so thunderous that it was heard in London. The 29th was one of thirteen British divisions in the front line. For many men, this was to be their first real action of the war, thus expectations were high for a decisive victory. On the eve of battle, they were warned that surrender was not an option. Along the twenty-two miles of trenches, commanders must have been rousing their men with similar speeches: 'success will mean the shortening of the war, failure means the war prolonged indefinitely.'[18] In the bright, optimistic minds of men facing what would be an Armageddon, was the belief that this was the battle that could end the war.

Two days before the battle, Eric crouched in his dugout and wrote a farewell letter:

June 28th 1916

My darling Mother & Father,

I am writing this on the eve of my first action. Tomorrow we go to the attack in the greatest battle the British Army has ever fought.[19] I cannot quite express my feelings on this night & I cannot tell if it is God's will that I shall come through – but if I fall in battle then I have no regrets save for my loved ones I leave behind. It is a great cause and I came out willingly to serve my King and Country. My greatest concern is that I have the courage and determination necessary to lead my platoon well.

No one had such parents as you have been to me giving me such splendid opportunities and always thinking of my welfare at great self sacrifice to yourselves.

My life has been full of faults but I have tried at all times to live as a man and thus to follow the example of my father. This life abroad has taught me many things chiefly the fine character of the British Race to put up with hardship with wonderful cheerfulness.

How I have learnt to love my men. My great aim had been to win their respect which I trust I have accomplished and hope that when the time comes I shall not fail them.

If I fall do not let things be black for you. Be cheerful and you will be living life always to my memory.

I thank God for my brother and sisters who have all been very much to me.

Well I cannot write more now. You are all in my thoughts as I enter this first battle. May God go with me.

With all my love to you all.

    Always

      Your loving son

        Eric

10 Part of the letter from Eric Heaton, 28 June 1916 (Imperial War Museums).

Eric did not post that letter home. He gave it to the company quartermaster sergeant just before he went over the top – with instructions that it should be passed to his friend Captain Wegg if anything happened.

That day, he wrote a further letter – which he did send home – and the tone and contents could not have been more different. He cheerfully thanked his parents for a parcel, discussed the weather and how the padre was organising a boxing contest. He closed with an emphatic 'Well let us hope the Bosche is done for this time, he will get it strong on all sides! . . We move soon now I believe – may it be to victory.'

The two letters highlighted the torment of a soldier's mind – particularly when facing action. On the one hand they were forced to confront their own mortality and wanted to take steps to say goodbye. On the other hand they were cheerily convincing themselves as much as family at home that they were confident and ready for what lay ahead. This admirable stoicism was a prerequisite for keeping a steady head and trying to stay alive.

On 1 July 1916 Eric's battalion was one of the main units preparing to lead the attack towards Beaumont Hamel and Hawthorn Ridge – in perfect view of the enemy positioned on the higher ground opposite. They were ordered to advance along a hundred yards of front line and immediately came under fierce machine-gun fire. On that day alone, the battalion lost 522 men.[20]

Captain Wegg wrote to Eric's mother the next day, enclosing his last letter and describing what he knew: 'Pte Henry saw this officer hit in the knee – in fact he says that the knee was almost blown off – 2/Lt Heaton was bleeding very badly and Pte. Henry thinks he must have bled to death. Nothing further has been seen or heard of this officer.'

Shortly after came the telegram bearing the message 'Missing Believed Killed'. One can only imagine the impact of such a telegram and the glimmer of hope those words offered. Eric's parents refused to give up hope and relentlessly sought more information and confirmation in the weeks and months that followed. Two weeks after that fateful day, Eric's brother Douglas wrote home to say, 'I cannot but think that he is perfectly safe, although perhaps wounded. I want to know as soon as there is any more news of him . . . I think it will probably be some time before you have news of Eric; do not be downhearted.' It must have been tortuous – they had the comfort of his farewell letter, but no proof their son was actually dead.

The family had to wait until 6 September 1916 to receive the official report of their son's death but it took until 14 May the following year to receive news of his burial 'at a point 200 yards from Beaumont Hamel Road and 50 yards from mine crater Auchonvillers'.

Eric was left £55.10s in army pay. There is no doubt that his family took great solace in the farewell letter he sent as they kept it in a scrapbook with all his wartime ephemera. The scrapbook contained heartbreaking clues as to the effect

Eric's death had on his parents: palpable bitterness in the mass of newspaper cuttings relating to the Somme. Even into the 1930s they were religiously collecting reports of 'The Great "Ifs" of the Somme' and articles decrying Kitchener's poor command, 'lost minutes', first-day failures and poor training.[21]

Eric's death affected his whole family. In the family scrapbook was a letter from 1979 when Eric's sister was still trying to understand every possible detail of that fateful day. John Wilson survived the battle and wrote: '[The attack at Beaumont Hamel] was catastrophic. Looking back and viewing the battle from a layman's point of view, I would sum up in a few words, a wicked waste of life. This battle will never be eradicated from my mind.'[22]

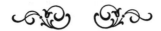

PRIVATE ALEXANDER WUTTUNEE DECOTEAU
Killed in the Battle of Passchendaele, 30 October 1917

ALEXANDER DECOTEAU WAS BORN on the Cree Red Pheasant Indian Reserve in Battleford, Saskatchewan on 19 November 1887, to Dora Pambrun and Peter Decouteau (Plate 12). He had two brothers and one sister, and in his teens he moved to Edmonton in Alberta, where he became a policeman (the first Aboriginal and motorcycle cop in Edmonton) and distance runner. He twice won a celebrated road race called the Calgary Herald, and competed in the 1912 Stockholm Olympics in the 5,000-metres.

When war broke out, he was still working as a police sergeant, but by April 1916 had been inspired alongside countless others to enlist as a private in the 202nd Infantry Battalion – a battalion renowned for its sportsmen. His father had fought against Canadian militia during a local rebellion fomented by his chief, Poundmaker, in the 1880s. He achieved warrior status in the Cree Indian community, and it was thought that Alexander Decoteau was strongly influenced to serve for that reason.

Decoteau wrote home to his sister, as his mother could not read or speak English. A handful of those letters have survived, giving an extraordinarily vivid insight into his mindset and those around him. Whilst still at Sarcee Camp in Calgary on 4 October 1916 Decoteau sent an innocent letter to his sister that would become cherished as his farewell letter. It was clear that the thought of dying was one he had considered, but in purely practical terms. It was one of four letters that the family kept; a symbol of the importance it held to them.

My Dear Sister,

.... We all had to make out our wills the other day, so that looks as if we must be going pretty soon, doesn't it? I made out my will to you. I have not assigned my money to any one yet. You know when we get to England they give us only half our pay. The other half is kept in trust for us in some Bank, unless we assign it to some person who will keep it for us. So I am going to make over half my pay to you before we leave Canada. You can leave it in the Bank till I come back or (go where I won't need it). Of course if you should need any of it before I do, I've no objection to your using some of it. I suppose the proper thing to do would be to leave it to mother, but then she can't read or write and I'm afraid they would take advantage of her if they wanted to be crooked . . .

Of course, Sis, if anything happens to me and I fail to come back, don't forget poor mother. I haven't much to divide but I should like her to have a little. I did not consign my (money) pay to her because I figure on coming back and will need some money and am afraid she couldn't keep my money as well as you could. I hope the tone of this letter has not given you the blues, Sis. My reason for writing this, is because one never knows when the authorities may take a notion to give us our marching orders. The 151st I understand had only 60 hours notice before they left here. One can't do very much in that time. We might get our orders to move tomorrow and we'd be so very busy packing for the rest of the time that I'd have no time for writing.

. . . Well Sis, remember me to Dave and the children. I do hope to see you all before long, if only for a little while. Be good to yourself and don't work too hard.

As ever,
Your loving brother
Alex

On 2 July 1917 it was clear that the big question of 'what if' was certainly still on his mind – and Decoteau was still suitably pragmatic about it: 'I'm sorry I wasn't able to make any arrangements about my money before I left for England. So you'll have to see to it yourself if "my number is called". I have over $100.00 to my credit now.'

In July 1917 Decouteau had joined the 49th Battalion in France, having come through the Arras offensive, and were repairing trenches and strengthening outpost lines. The entry in the battalion war diary reveals that on the day before Decoteau wrote this letter, parties were being sent to reconnoitre the front line. The men would have been very aware of the impending push.[23]

By September, still in France, the battalion was under constant heavy shelling and suffered high casualties. Decoteau was clearly war-weary, describing soldiering as 'a thankless job'. He wrote to his sister on 10 September 1917:

. . . Well sis, in spite of the fact that we are used very decently by the French people, there's no use denying the fact that we are all aching and longing for our own beloved Canada. Of course there's work to be done yet and I s'pose will stay there till it is finished. A man has lots of time to think of his people and home out here, and one does get awfully lonesome at times. I know in my last trip to the front line, I dreamed of home and about 'all the mothers, sisters and sweethearts' I ever had.

. . . Most of the boys turn Fatalists. I don't know if I've got it spelled right, after a few month fighting. They believe that everything is prearranged by Divine Power, and if it's one's time to die no matter what one does, one has to die. Their motto is 'If my turn comes next, I can't do anything to avoid it, so I shouldn't worry'. They don't worry either. Of course there are lots who suffer from shell shock or nervous breakdown, and they can't fight against fear, but most of the boys have a keen sense of humor, and laugh at almost anything. I know of one in particular, a corporal. He is the life and wit of our party. A shell landed close to him one night and the concussion threw him on his head several yards away. The shock stunned him for a minute and when he came to the first question he asked was 'Is my head still on?' That sent the rest of us into a roar, and only a minute before they were all ready to beat it to the nearest dugout. It's the likes of him that make army life bearable, and the army is full of such as he.[24]

The battalion were training regularly in gas and wiring drills by this time, in preparation for the Passchendaele offensive in the Ypres Salient. It was a unique location, with two armies almost surrounding each other, each refusing to relinquish their lines. At 5.40 am on 30 October, the attack that would cost Decoteau his life began. It was cold, wet and windy. Guns and howitzers created a hellish maelstrom of noise as the Canadians advanced. Eight minutes later, the enemy returned fire with a vengeance, from machine-gun posts and concrete pillboxes. The 49th Battalion were one of the hardest hit, yet still managed to capture Furst Farm: Indeed, overall, the Canadian forces gained up to a thousand yards of the almost three-thousand-yard line. They paid the price, though: 884 men killed, 1,429 wounded or gassed and 8 taken prisoner.[25] Canadian riflemen did their best to pick off the enemy and provide cover, but Decoteau – like many others that day – was caught by the bullet of a sniper.

Alexander Decoteau was buried in Belgium, but in 1985 his relatives and friends performed a special ceremony to bring his spirit home. In Cree culture, without a Cree burial, a spirit wanders the earth. An Edmonton piper played 'Amazing Grace' as Decoteau's memory and spirit was finally laid to rest.

PRIVATE GEORGE HENRY DAVIES
Killed at Messines, 12 July 1917

ORIGINALLY BORN IN MONTGOMERY in February 1889, George grew up in Much Wenlock in Shropshire, and was one of two sons of John and Lilla Davies (Plate 13). While his parents remained in Shropshire, George emigrated to Australia as a Protestant missionary.

On 21 January 1916 George decided to join up 'to make a sacrifice on behalf of my country', and enlisted at Coffs Harbour in New South Wales. In July that year he sailed for England on the *Beltana* as part of D Company, 36th Battalion, Australian Imperial Force. Many recruits had been targeted by a recruitment drive among the rifle clubs of New South Wales, led by government minister Ambrose Carmichael, who himself served as a captain in the battalion.

Davies's army records show that he was five feet six inches tall, with brown hair and blue eyes. His distinguishing marks included a crushed thumb and forefinger on the right hand, and a slight disfigurement on the left – not that this in any way impeded this voracious writer. His record as a soldier contained just one minor indiscretion when he went absent without leave for three hours (from six until nine in the morning) while at Broadmeadow Camp in May 1916. He was punished by being 'confined to barracks'.[26]

Davies was a qualified signaller by the time he left his training camp at Larkhill in Wiltshire on 22 November 1916, and had been nicknamed 'Smiler' by his fellow soldiers there. His faith, however, was his passion and driving force. His letters and diaries, more than any others written by clergymen, are vehemently religious. For him, the war was the opportunity to preach in several countries, and he talked excitedly of holding a service in Amesbury Chapel while training in the area, and of preaching evening service at the YMCA on the line at Armentières.

While Davies's faith imbued his letters with an exuberance and excitement, his experiences made him passionately opposed to war as a means of conflict resolution: 'If I live . . . I shall seek to do all I can to crush any military tendencies in my nation, I will make my name heard against money grabbing, and other evil things, and will uphold the highest and best socialism and I will try to make life more like Christ's life.' Despite his opposition to warfare, he clearly had little fear of what front-line fighting warfare would entail, as death would simply deliver him to God. Throughout his wartime service, George kept a detailed diary of his experiences, and his opening words in it were evidence of a head consumed with thoughts of death and the afterlife.

> In the event of my death at the front, I would esteem it a great privilege if some friend would hand this record of my doings, my thoughts and spiritual desires to my adopted brother, Willie Scott Ross of 79, Manningtree Rd., Hawthorne, Melbourne, as an appreciation of his love and abiding sweetness and purity of life, so it may be a guide and an inspiration to him . . .

George was clearly incredibly close to Willie Ross, whom he called his adopted brother, and the strength of feeling revealed in his diary was almost stifling. Perhaps it was his deep Christian faith that made him feel so protective of his 'orphan' brother, and speak to him as a surrogate parent. Being so far away from his own parents and brother in England, it is perhaps no wonder that he sought another 'family' in Australia.

The unit's first major action was at Messines, in the Ypres sector in Belgium, June 1917. In the months leading up to the attack, the men were involved relieving trenches, as well as still training. The battalion war diary recorded almost daily accounts of heavy shelling and casualties on both sides.[27] Despite these losses, on 31 March 1917 George wrote home to his mother in ebullient spirits:

> Here I am again in the trenches and somewhere near the front line. Fritz has been trying to frighten us by putting over minnies[28] and coalboxes[29] but we refuse to be bluffed. He puts up 'fairy lights', 'levey lights'[30] is the proper name I think . . . Well mother dear what do you think of the way things are going on now on the different fronts, some of our boys say they will be back again in their homes by Xmas week. I hope they are right and I hope I am with them. Peace will come much sooner than we think and I can see it in sight . . . Well mother I am longing to see you again, how nice it would be if I have you a surprise one day . . . Ta ta for the present with very best love.

In spite of this apparent optimism, the thought of dying evidently pressed on his thoughts as his diary was filled with farewell messages. George's archive truly stands out in this period for the sheer number of messages and the preoccupation with potential death. Before each concerted action he wrote messages just in case; testament to an increasingly exhausted mind.

When he wrote on 6 June 1917, there was palpable excitement that the hour was drawing closer, tempered with a calmness prompted by his deep religious faith:

> News has come in that Fritz is completely demoralized. The hour is approaching!!! All preparations are being made for the 'great movement' . . . Today is the

day when we proceed on our way to the trenches for the final effort . . . I am ready for every eventuality, expect it will arrive soon . . . All the boys are like this, no extra excitement, no flurry, no growling, but on every face there is a new look . . . I too, never felt so calm, and have set my face toward the inevitable, whatever that may be.

On the same day, George Davies also wrote a farewell letter to his beloved 'adopted brother', in his diary:

Dear Willie,

This will be the last time I shall write in this diary before the 'Great Push'. It may be the last time I shall ever write. I am just taking these last few minutes at my disposal to pen this letter to you, and even as I write I am expecting to be called away.

The time is now ripe for the moment when we 'go over the top' and advance on the enemy trenches; I am to go with the boys and am not sorry to be able to do so.

I leave this diary for you, dear Willie, whatever may happen to myself, whether I live or die. I am quite ready dear laddie, I have made my peace with God, and am trusting in Christ my Saviour to bring me to Eternal Light. I may be killed, I welcome such a death as freedom from this hell upon earth. I may only be wounded and will go home to my parents, but I may never see you again till the Golden Day breaks and that is why I am writing this diary for you.

I am leaving you all my books, excepting a few theological ones which are for Mr. Charles Cox of the Oara, NSW. All my Poet's works are yours and all other literature. I hope you will read them as they will make your life beautiful and sweet.

I also leave you my bicycle, which you will find at Walter McGraths of Brooklana or East Dorringe near Coramba NSW. Any other personal effects of mine in Australia are for you, and I have left you and mamie £5 of my money, which you will doubtless receive as time goes by.

I am looking forward to this 'push' to bring me a happy release from further military life which I hate, and I hope to be wounded and sent home, or else be killed, either are preferable to this hell on earth.

Now Willie dear, you will see in this diary how I love you; you are my adopted brother, your sweet, beautiful 'boy' influence lingers with me as I write these last few lines, and I want to say that I shall think of you right to the end, and I shall pray to God to keep you in His Care.

You will remember our last words together on Melbourne station, 'We will meet in Heaven'. If I die I shall be looking for you Willie, I know I shall see you again with your mother and mine in the Fadeless Morning on the Eternal Shore. I want you to be always good, spurn from your heart all evil and impure thoughts. Keep looking upward and onward to Him who loved you and me. Fill your heart with love for erring humanity. Two things laddie as true and as useful as of old.

'Love God with all your heart, and your brothers and sisters in the wide wide world as yourself.' So will your life be supremely happy and peaceful.

If I live Willie, I shall seek to do all I can to crush any military tendencies in my nation, I will make my name heard against money grabbing, and other evil things, and will uphold the highest and best socialism and I will try to make life more like Christ's life. If I die I would like you to do this for me. Set your heart against all greed, selfishness, lust, and dirt my laddie, and remember Jesus Christ IS a stronghold in Whom we can hide.

. . . Good-bye,

Your ever loving brother,

George Davies.

Prayer

Oh God keep me from all harm in these dangerous hours, bless the little laddie with no mother or father, keep him pure and holy, useful to his generation, and may we meet bye-and-bye in Thy Presence. Through Jesus Christ's Sake.

Amen.

He also wrote a farewell letter to his mother that – perhaps having premonitions that this would be his final hour – he posted home:

Dearest Mother,

. . . I am now ready for the 'big push' ready in body, mind and spirit, I was never better in health than I am now, my mind is just as clear, my soul has been purified, and the whole is in God's hands. If I die, do not fear for me, I will wait for you my loved above all, and for my father and brothers and sister too . . .

I give my life willingly for my country knowing that it is given in a righteous cause. I can do no more, I give my love to you all and to Jesus Christ My Maker . . . military life [which] I hate with my intensest hatred as an unworthy and despicable means of settling affairs. If I live I shall stand by red hot socialists and peace cranks to stop any further wars after this one, but while I am at it I will fight like only one facing death can fight.

Best love to all, Mother dear I will never forget me, think of me always.

Your ever loving son,

George.

The writing didn't stop. That evening, he added more to his diary. This was either a man keen to meet his maker, or perhaps his torrent of thoughts were the product of simply having to sit, wait and wonder.

The time is near at hand; Jesus Christ went all the way to the Cross. I can meet my Gethsemane and my cross in His strength. I am ready for all things; Jesus is

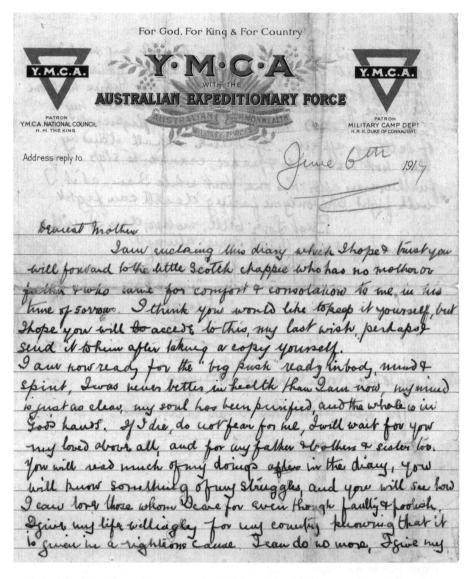

For God, For King & For Country

Y.M.C.A.

Y·M·C·A
WITH THE
AUSTRALIAN EXPEDITIONARY FORCE

Y.M.C.A.

PATRON
Y.M.C.A. NATIONAL COUNCIL
H. M. THE KING.

PATRON
MILITARY CAMP DEP.T
H. R. H. DUKE OF CONNAUGHT.

Address reply to

June 6th 1917

Dearest Mother

I am enclosing this diary which I hope & trust you will forward to the little Scotch chappie who has no mother or father & who came for comfort & consolation to me, in his time of sorrow. I think you would like to keep it yourself, but I hope you will to accede to this, my last wish, perhaps & send it to him after taking a copy yourself.

I am now ready for the "big push" ready in body, mind & spirit, I was never better in health than I am now, my mind is just as clear, my soul has been purified, and the whole is in God's hands. If I die, do not fear for me, I will wait for you my loved above all, and for my father & brothers & sister too. You will read much of my doings after in this diary, you will know something of my struggles, and you will see how I can love those whom I care for even though faulty & foolish. I give my life willingly for my country knowing that it is given in a righteous cause. I can do no more, I give my

11 Part of the letter from George Davies to his mother, 6 June 1917 (Australian War Memorial (negative number 2DRL/0789)).

my Saviour, in Him I trust and I know He will bring me Home to Glory. God was never nearer than he is now, even as the shells burst all round me . . . I have not been all I might have been, but I feel my sins forgiven through His love for me. We all feel this in our innermost hearts, we say very little, but we think of Him now, and we know He is capable of bringing us through more than conquerors. Self sacrifice for righteousness sake is the grandest thing in life. No man can do better, Jesus Himself did just this. With these last few words I close this diary and await with calmness and patience the time of fighting.

Finally, also on 6 June 1917, George wrote a will. In it he bequeathed all of his real estate to his father and brother Bryan. His personal estate he left to his mother. All of his personal effects and £5 each was left to Willie Ross and his sister Mamie.

That night, the battalion marched to Nieppe, to get in position for battle at the southern end of the line. The Messines–Wytschaete Ridge was a key strategic position that the Germans had held since the start of the war. The Battle of Messines is notorious for the tunnelling that had taken place beforehand under Hill 60, near Ypres. General Plumer, commander of the Second Army, famously stated on the eve of the battle, 'Gentlemen, we may not make history tomorrow, but we shall certainly change the geography.' The next day, six hundred tons of explosives were detonated under the German positions, immediately killing around ten thousand men. It was a meticulously planned operation, combining artillery, tanks, engineers and aircraft.

The battalion war diary revealed that D Company was the brigade reserve, providing cover and support for the troops as they advanced under a coordinated bombardment. They encountered very heavy shelling as well as gas attacks, especially in Ploegsteert Wood.[31] Ultimately they achieved their objectives, but George Davies was one of over fifteen hundred Australian soldiers killed in action at Messines.

There were few details about his death. Instead, the letters home regarding his loss focused on his vibrancy in life. A condolence letter sent by Methodist Chaplain Alf Nells spoke of Davies's 'bright winsome personality that owed much to his manly Christian faith'. When he was killed the contents of his pack were sent home; among the items were his diary and, of course, his Bible.

Otto Heinebach

Killed in the Battle of Verdun, 14 September 1916

Born on 14 August 1892, by the time war broke out, Heinebach was a philosophy student at Berlin University. His letters home – mainly to his father – reveal him to be a deep thinker, someone highly sensitive to the carnage and bloodshed of war, who had a growing hope that peace would come. In fact, it is in reading the letters of German soldiers that one is reminded of the similarities with their enemy counterparts. They too went into war on a patriotic crusade, and many quickly became disillusioned by the barbarism of what they experienced. These letters provide a revisionist standpoint to the pervading views of letters that talked about the dastardly 'Hun' and his savage spirit.

In an early letter to his father dated 22 September 1915, Heinebach was desperate to recount a terrible experience:

> Less than three hours ago, our dear, good H., my best comrade, was killed by a shell which gave him a terrible wound in the body . . . I hurried to the dreadful spot and found him lying in a pool of blood with his abdomen torn open . . . I couldn't bear the ghastly sight for long, but I stayed with him, in the next bay, so that I could hear everything he said . . . Oh, what a passion of rage against this vile war rose up in me when I saw that dear, splendid man, who was so full of high aspirations and carried such a noble soul within him, laying there on the ground, hideously injured![32]

It must have been an inconceivable hell to see a close friend killed, but war allowed little time for grieving or reflection. Duties continued, and soldiers must have carried huge emotional scars from what they had witnessed. Letters, of course, were one way to channel high emotion, and certainly in those of Heinebach one can see that the level of detail was due in part to some need for catharsis and to make sense of the nightmare around him.

By late December 1915 Heinebach was at Achiet le Petit, a small village south of Arras subjected to frequent shelling from enemy forces in trenches and in the air. Following a particularly fierce aerial bombardment on the station and anti-aircraft positions, Heinebach wrote home in hopeful mood.

> December 30th 1915 . . . Sometimes it seems to me as if the universal longing of all nations for peace *must* finally put an end to this murder. I heard yesterday on good authority, that after the ghastly affair at Loos, there had been at one place on that Front an absolute cessation of hostilities, as if by mutual consent; both sides walked about quite unconcernedly on the top, in full view of the enemy, who was only a few yards away, and not a shot was fired . . . I can imagine that the general

war-weariness might at last reach such a point that it might lead to a similar 'entente cordiale' between the opposing armies . . .[33]

There was no swift end coming to the struggle, as we know, but it is terribly poignant that Heinebach had to gear up for the Battle of Verdun with such hopes uppermost in his mind. It was a battle that, with the benefit of hindsight, Crown Prince Rupprecht of Bavaria called 'a crazy offensive'.[34] Verdun was the longest battle of the war, raging for an agonising ten months until it reached an inconclusive end, leaving a million men dead. Verdun could be attacked from three sides and had a long history in Franco-German conflict. It was of strategic as well as symbolic significance; a target the French would not easily relinquish. The German Fifth Army launched their attack on 21 February 1916. Three days earlier, Heinebach took the opportunity to write a farewell letter while crammed in a 'stiflingly hot dressing-station dug-out'. It is a haunting image.

A little while ago we heard that the attack had again been postponed for twenty-four hours, and just now came word that it was fixed for 20th.[35] Packs are to be worn, but everything not absolutely necessary is to be left behind.

I say good-bye to you, my dear Parents and Brothers and Sisters. Thanks, most tender thanks for all that you have done for me. If I fall, I earnestly beg of you to bear it with fortitude. Reflect that I should probably never have achieved complete happiness and contentment. Perhaps my life would, to the very end, have been cleft by the impossibility of reconciling desire and fulfilment, struggle and attainment, yearning and actuality. This is the tragedy of moderately gifted natures, who, never being able to reach the heights of creative genius, come eventually, through constant self-criticism, to complete disaster – and I have always been of a melancholy temperament.

. . . And so, in imagination, I extinguish the lamp of my existence on the eve of this terrible battle. I cut myself out of the circle of which I have formed a beloved part. The gap which I leave must be closed; the human chain must be unbroken. I, who once formed a small link in it, bless it be for all eternity. And till your last days remember me, I beg you, with tender love. Honour my memory without gilding it, and cherish me in your loving, faithful hearts.[36]

The target for the Germans was Fort Douaumont, which stood on a commanding ridge over a thousand feet high. It was defended by fewer than one hundred French soldiers and was thus captured relatively easily by the Germans on 25 February 1916. Heinebach was gravely wounded by shell-fire in the struggle to reach the fort. He was transferred to the military hospital at Frankfurt, where one imagines his family was able to be with him until the end. He eventually died from his injuries on 14 September 1916.

Lieutenant Giosuè Borsi

Killed in the Fourth Battle of the Isonzo, 10 November 1915

Born in Livorno, Italy in 1888, Borsi was the son of journalist Averado Borsi, who owned a chain of Florence newspapers (Plate 14). His father was a vehement critic of the Catholic Church and raised his son in an atmosphere of religious hostility – although Borsi's Catholic mother ensured her son was baptised. A gifted child, he studied at college in Guerazzi and published the first of two collections of poems in 1907. Possibly Italy's leading Dante scholar, Borsi found God when a series of tragic deaths hit his family. First his father died in December 1910 (and Borsi took over as editor of the *Nuovo Gionale* at the age of just twenty-two), then his sister Laura in June 1912, following a long illness. In 1913 he lost his nephew Dino. For Borsi, these deaths demonstrated the solemnity of life and brought him in contact with the Franciscan monks of San Miniato. From a child brought up to despise the tenets of the Catholic faith, Borsi became one of its fiercest converts and apologists.

In May 1915 Borsi volunteered to serve with the Italian army, feeling it was his sacred duty to fight for his country. He immediately began to keep a diary of his talks with God and daily recorded his thoughts. Borsi went to war in the firm belief that a Christian soldier was the embodiment of patriotism and love:

> O Lord; enable me to overcome easily the last difficulties, shorten the days I shall have to remain here, hasten the day when I shall be fighting on the battlefield . . . I feel in the depth of my heart that this war is just and holy, and . . . will make us more worthy to love and serve and know and praise the Lord.[37]

He became a lieutenant in 125 Infantry Regiment 'La Spezia', a corps that was largely made up of young and uneducated men who liked Borsi a great deal.

Perhaps most famous as the backdrop to Ernest Hemmingway's *A Farewell To Arms*, the Battles of the Isonzo are largely unknown struggles in the histories of this war. Following the signing of the secret Treaty of London in April 1915, Italy declared war on neighbouring Austro-Hungary on 23 May. In an unforgiving environment along the banks of the Isonzo River (between Italy and modern-day Slovenia), countless offensives were launched, creating a circle of vicious fighting as the Italians sought to liberate their fellow citizens from contested Habsburg control and seize territory. The Italians called these

1 Arthur Rowley Heyland, 1781–1815; killed at Waterloo, 18 June 1815.

2 Karl Theodor Körner, 1791–1813; killed at Leipzig, 25 August 1813.

Background: part of letter from Samuel S. Barrington, 1796–1815; killed at Quatre Bras, 16 June 1815.

3 Sullivan Ballou, 1829–61; killed in the First Battle of Bull Run, 28 July 1861.

4 Thornton Fleming Brodhead, 1820–62; killed in the Second Battle of Bull Run, 2 September 1862.

5 The Prince Imperial, Louis Napoleon, 1856–79; killed near Ityotyozi River, 1 June 1879.

6 Ashley Goatham, 1855–79; killed at Isandlwana, 22 January 1879.

7 Peter Joseph Handcock, 1868–1902; executed at Pretoria Gaol, 27 February 1902. Background: part of letter from Handcock.

8 Jan Christiaan Smuts, 1870–1950; fought in the Boer War and First World War.

C. Strick

PRETORIA
S. Africa.

9 John Emerson Wharton Headlam, 1864–1946; fought in the Boer War.

10 Eric Fox Pitt Lubbock, 1893–1917; killed at Ypres, 11 March 1917. Background: part of letter from Lubbock.

11 Eric Rupert Heaton, 1896–1916; killed in the Battle of the Somme, 1 July 1916.

12 Alexander Wuttunee
Decoteau, 1887–1917; killed in
the Battle of Passchendaele,
30 October 1917.

13 George Henry Davies, 1889–1917; killed at
Messines, 12 July 1917.

14 Giosuè Borsi, 1888–1915; killed in the
Fourth Battle of the Isonzo, 10 November
1915.

15 William Robert Jones (1895–1919) and his company; Jones was killed in South Africa, 7 June 1919.

16 William Barclay Binning 1897–1916; died in Belgium, 24 April 1916.

17 Leslie Abram Neufeld, 1922–44 (on the right); killed at Varaville, 6 June 1944.

18 Friedrich Spemann, 1897–1965; fought in the Second World War.

19 Goulden Oliver Webster, 1913–40; killed over Berlin, 20 November 1940. Background: part of letter from Webster.

第3独立飛行隊　久野　正信　中佐
昭和20年5月24日　　愛知県・29歳

20 Masanobu Kuno; killed 24 May 1945.

21 Eugene M. Courtright; died at Iwo Jima, 18 March 1945.

22 Michael Andrew Scott, 1916–41; killed over the English Channel, 24 May 1941.

23 Glen Robinson-Moltke; killed in the Falkland Islands, 25 May 1982.

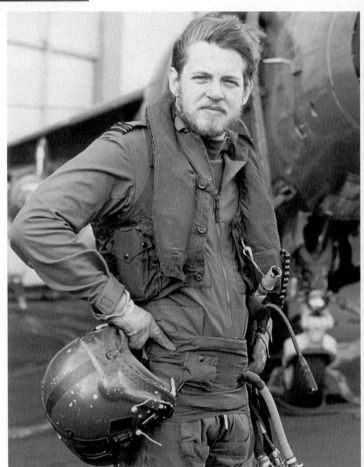

24 David Morgan, b. 1947; fought in the Falklands Conflict.

25 Herbert 'H' Jones, 1940–82; killed at Goose Green, 28 May 1982.

26 Chris Howe, b. 1956; fought in the Falklands Conflict.

27 José Antonio Scaglia, b. 1962 (on the left); fought in the Falklands Conflict.

28 Lee Thornton, 1983–2006; killed in Iraq, 7 September 2006.

29 Jesse Givens, 1969–2003; killed in Iraq, 1 May 2003. Background: part of letter from Givens.

family:

I never ... would be writing a letter like ... ly don't ... start I've been getting bad t... h and ... I am ta... to you, Dakota, and the bean. ... my lif... and I found it in you. I think th... positive difference in your never ... e up for the bad I am so s... happiest moments in my life all deal with my ... ly. I will always have with me the small momen... shared the moments when you quit taking life so...

Sm... ound... ... b... le... no... lonliness and tau... ught me how to ... a world I never ... on the path you... ortant again, You a... Dakota you ar... can only hope I ... ny" but; no matt... se me. You laugh... ut me how to ... serious and some... utiful heart. Th... w it. Never be a... ur park when you dream so we can still play. I ... day you will have a son like mine. Make them ... shine just like you. I love you Toad I hope

30 Jamie Hancock, 1987–2006;
killed in Iraq, 6 November 2006.

31 Tony Downes, 1986–2007;
killed in Afghanistan, 9 June
2007.

32 Andrew Olmsted, 1972–2008; killed in Iraq, 3 January 2008.

frontier provinces 'Italia Irrenta' – unresolved – and under the command of Chief of Staff General Luigi Cadorna they were determined to secure the lands for Italy. The plan was to advance towards Austrian Ljubljana and Trieste in a series of assaults supported by light field artillery, in the hope of a breakthrough.

The sixty-mile Isonzo River was prone to flooding, and the Austro-Hungarians had built up strong mountainous defences and strongholds along a four-hundred-mile front. Borsi had already fought three major battles, starting on 23 June 1915. He was in the midst of frantic fighting, seeing massive loss of life and cholera outbreaks in his battalion. There can be little doubt that those experiences provoked his farewell letters. Indeed, in a letter he wrote to Lieutenant Mazzinghi on 18 October 1916 it seemed that Borsi was having premonitions of his death that coloured all his writing from then on:

> I have made up my mind to do my duty to the end and to be a good example to
> my soldiers . . . If I am sure of victory and of the unfailing triumph of our army,
> I am not equally sure that I shall see all these beautiful things here below. On
> the contrary, my presentiment is that in moving to the assault I am going to be
> released from the ties that bind me to this world. I do not know why, but I could
> almost swear to this.[38]

On the eve of fighting, Borsi wrote, 'I know my platoon now, I know my sergeants, my corporals, my privates; I feel that in the first attack I shall lead them all in a dash, and then throw myself forward into the tempest of fire crying, Avanti! Savoia! Viva il Re! Viva l'Italia! And thus I shall die, die happy and exulting.'[39]

Just five days after the Third Battle of the Isonzo had ceased, the fourth began, on 10 November 1915. It opened with a thunderous bombardment and repeated infantry attacks. It ended a month later thanks in no small part to the onset of bitter winter weather and exhaustion. Italian losses stood at 49,000. Borsi was shot through the heart as he led his platoon at Zagora on Monte Cucco, and died immediately. In his uniform pocket was found a volume of Dante's *Divine Comedy*, still wet with his blood, and an incredibly long farewell letter to his beloved mother that he'd written on 21 October 1915. As he lay dying he asked a fellow soldier named Ezio Barbieri to 'Give that to my mother. May my sacrifice and her sacrifice be acceptable to God.'

> Mother
>   This letter, which you will only receive if I should fall in battle, I am writing
> in an advanced trench, where I have been since last night, with my soldiers in
> expectation of the order to cross the river and move to the attack. I am calm,
> perfectly serene, and firmly resolved to do my duty in full to the last, like a brave

and good soldier, confident to the utmost of our final unfailing victory; although I am not equally sure that I will live to see it. But this uncertainty doesn't trouble me in the least, nor has it any terror for me. I am happy in offering my life to my country: I am proud to spend it for so noble a purpose, and I know not to thank Divine Providence for the opportunity – which I deem an honour – afforded me on this fulgent autumnal day, in the midst of this enchanting valley of our Venestia Guillia, while I am in the physical prime of life, in the fullness of my physical and mental powers, to fight in this holy war for liberty and justice.

In the world there are so many battles to fight, for love, for justice, for liberty, for the faith, and for a time, I must confess, I presumptuously presumed myself predestined and assigned to the arduous and terrible task of winning one or another of these battles . . .

. . . And as I am about to speak of forgiveness, dear mother, I have only one thing to say with all simplicity: Forgive me! Forgive me all the sorrows that I have caused you: all the agonies you have suffered on my account every time I have been ungrateful, stubborn, forgetful, disobedient towards you. Forgive me if, by neglect and inexperience, I have failed to render your life more comfortable and tranquil since the day when my father, by his premature death, entrusted you to my care. Now I understand well the many wrongs I have been guilty of towards you, and I feel all the remorse and cruel anguish now that, dying, I have to entrust you to the providence of the Lord. Forgive me, lastly this final sorrow that I have inflicted upon you, perhaps not without stubborn and cruel inconsideration on my part, in giving up my life voluntarily for my country, fascinated by the attractions of this beautiful lot. Forgive me also if I have not sufficiently recognized and tried to compensate the incomparable nobility of your soul, of your heart, so immense and sublime. Mother, truly perfect and exemplary, to whom I owe all that I am and the least good I have done in this world . . .

Love and freedom for all, this is the ideal for which it is a pleasure to offer one's life. May God cause our sacrifice to be fruitful; may He take pity upon mankind, forgive and forget their offences, and give them peace. Then, oh! dear mother, we shall not have died in vain. Just one more tender kiss.[40]

In twenty-nine months of conflict at Isonzo, there were 1,100,000 Italians killed, wounded or captured, and 650,000 Austrians.[41] The fight for territory lasted until the bitter end of the war, when the Austro-Hungary monarchy – and its war effort – collapsed.

Borsi lived on through his published writings and there is no doubt that his farewell letter – immortalised in print – was proof of how treasured it was by his mother to the very end. It was the calm, serene voice of a man who seemed to know he would die, and wanted to take practical, spiritual and filial measures to ensure he was able to say goodbye.

∽❀❀⌒ ⌒❀❀∽

DRIVER WILLIAM ROBERT JONES
Killed in South Africa en route home, 7 June 1919

WILLIAM 'WILLIE' ROBERT JONES, born in August 1895, was the second son of Henry Rochard and Alexandrina Jones of 'Armondale' in Carrick, Tasmania (Plate 15). They had a large family: William had four brothers (Hector, Vernon, Norman and Colin) and four sisters (Myrtle, Olive, Hazel and Heather). Vernon described William as 'a good horseman and excellent rider from an early age'.[42] William and his brothers attended Launceston Church Grammar School, although he left in 1911 to help run the family farm. Like countless others, William enlisted on 20 September 1915, despite the fact his work on the farm qualified as a reserved occupation. War was a big adventure for William, and he was rarely without his prayer book and camera, taking countless photographs of his first years in France and Belgium.

William Jones enrolled as a sapper with the 18th Battery Divisional Ammunition Column although his parents had to sign a form to allow him to go to the front, in accordance with Australian military code, as he was underage at twenty. His sister Hazel was just eleven at the time: 'We were very proud of him in his uniform, and the last recollection I had of him was a fine figure of a soldier, joking and smiling as he said goodbye.' His army service records revealed that he was five feet seven inches tall, with green eyes and dark brown hair. His distinguishing feature was a scar on his big toe. That might sound like a useless piece of information, but the weapons being used at the front could blow a soldier apart, leaving perhaps only an arm or leg by which to identify someone. Therefore, any mark on the body was grimly noted in the records. William set sail for Egypt in November 1915, and from the start his letters revealed that army life was not quite the blissful, fun adventure he had envisaged: '21st November 1915. They cage us up like sheep on board and do not feed us too well but I suppose it is all in a soldier's life.'

By December he was settled at Tourah Camp in Egypt, and facing the prospect of action in the months to come: 'Dear Mother & Father . . . [I] expect to be in action in about 2 months time and the sooner the better as I am about sick of this messing about . . .'

His training continued, but by February 1916 it was clear that men were hoping for an end to the conflict, and a creeping sense of war-weariness penetrated his thoughts. Active service curtailed the choice and liberty he had enjoyed at home: 'Feb 20th 1916 . . . There are great bets here over the war as to when it will be over . . . My word I can assure you that once you join the Military you lose your freedom they can do anything they like with you.'

Just over a month later, Jones was transferred to the Brigade Ammunition Column of the 22nd Howitzer Brigade, and was en route to France. Soldiers were well aware of the fierce fighting on the Western Front and the high casualties, and William's division was one of the first to go there, charged with taking over the 'nursery' section of Armentières. It was on 22 April 1916 that his parents received a farewell letter. The prospect of fighting on the Somme had obviously caused William to think about his future.

> My darling mother
> I am writing this here as I think they may not see it to censor it. Should anything happen to me I want you to give my money to Olive as you know I think the world of her and she deserves it most for she is a very good girl. I suppose you are having enough to do now with baby growing up. Don't stop Vern enlisting as you may be sorry if conscription comes in and I think it will. I have found out what it is to leave home now and should God spare me I will never do it again.
> Your very loving son Will.

His parents filed the note away – desperately hoping they would never need to reread it or act on its instructions.

On 1 May William was still in the thick of action in Armentières, and working flat out looking after twenty-six mules as 'shrapnel is dropping all around'. Weeks after writing his 'just in case' letter, William was back in high spirits – or perhaps just protecting his parents from his innermost fears:

> I am happy as a lark now as I am in the 104th Battery, 4 Field Artillery Brigade, 2nd Australian Division, AIF and I am also a gunner now which is very exciting. Well dad I think farming is nice and quiet but to see life you can't beat what we are at now. I will be able to tell you some things about war that will surprise you when I get back . . . If I get through this all right.

By August that year, William had faced death and destruction at extremely close quarters. On 27 July his division had captured Pozières heights, but at great cost in casualties. On 7 August 1916 he wrote home with devastating news:

> I am writing this to let you know I have just lost the best pal I ever had. It happened last night about midnight, a large German shell burst right in the gun pit and buried four of them one of which was Tim. I felt very cut up when I first heard of it but it is all in wartime. I saw his body this morning and smothering you can guess what his face looks like. We are going down to his grave tonight and I expect we will make some mark of respect for him.

My darling Mother I am writing this here as I think they may not like it to censor it. Should anything happen me I want you to give my money to Olive as you know I think the world of her, and she deserves it most for she is a very good girl. I suppose you are having enough to do know with baby growing up. Don't stop Vern enlisting as you may be sorry if conscription comes in and I think it will. I have found out what it is to leave home now and should God spare me I will never do it again. Your very loving son Will.

12 Part of the letter from William Jones, 22 April 1916 (Tasmanian Archive and Heritage Office).

In the following months William himself had a narrow escape and was wounded in action. He was transferred to hospital in England, where he was treated for a gas inhalation, intensive bruising from a shell burst and shell-shock. William wrote home in surprisingly matter-of-fact terms, which suggests that he was becoming hardened to the realities of trench warfare and the ever-present dangers.

Well the officer I was with the night I got gassed died a few weeks ago, but he was foolish as he would not put his gas helmet on after we had smelt it. We were on observation duty for the attack he sent gas shells all around us, so I can safely say the gas-helmet saved my life that time. The piece that hit me in the back was about six inches long and about two inches wide, and it bruised me very badly but luckily it did not break any bones so I was right into about five weeks. Well after we left the Somme we went to Ypres and I was just about myself when I had the misfortune to get buried by a large trench mortar shell known as the 'Minnie-Werfer' about the largest mortar he has . . .

On 23 August 1917 William was transferred to the 2nd Division Signals Company and was back in France. He was in confident mood when he wrote home on 10 October 1917 amid the fierce fighting of the Battle of Broodseinde in Ypres.

> I had some very close shaves but that is all in the game as a man is very lucky to get out at all. Our boys did wonderful work up there in fact they did what was considered by the Imperial troop to be impossible . . . you could throw all Gallipoli, Pozieres and Bullecourt[43] into one and they would be no worse than what this is. Poor old Fritz is getting an awful bashing here.

It seemed as if William Jones had luck on his side. He was gassed once more at Passchendaele ridge but survived and was transferred to Beaufort War Hospital in Bristol.

> The official report was that there were 13,000 gas shells landed on our small section in two and a half hours. I am burned badly between both legs and all round my hips but they are healing up well. The worst of the lot is my eyes which have been totally blind for twelve days but I am able to see a little today . . . We were with the infantry when I got this and out of eight men in our section only two got out of it alright.

In December William was still at the hospital, receiving treatment – apparently successfully. But there may have been another reason for his recovery. He had fallen in love with a nurse named May McIlroy who 'plays the piano nicely'. In fact, William got engaged privately to the nurse while in England and did not tell his parents.

By September 1918 William was back in France as his unit headed for Mont Saint Quentin, and fighting on to the Hindenburg Line. The 2nd Division was the last Australian formation to be withdrawn from the action, and William one of the few who survived over three years of war. In December 1918 he could finally write home knowing the peace he had so craved had finally been declared. 'The war is really over and I don't think I could possibly imagine the jollification you will all have when peace was declared.'

The absolute tragedy in the story of William Jones is that he was killed on his way back home. The inquest into his death makes for sobering reading. He was onboard HMAT *Ypiranga*, sailing via South Africa. On 7 June 1919 he was granted leave to go ashore and he, along with two friends, decided to have drinks at a nearby hotel or two. After numerous beers, two double whiskys and a fish supper, William was sufficiently unsteady that he needed to be helped to a room, where he sat out on the balcony for some fresh air. About fifteen minutes later he fell from the balcony to his death. It was a cruel end for a soldier who had survived so much. Like thousands of men, he took the chance of leave to celebrate the end of war and the prospect of home. Perhaps he also wanted to leave behind the horror he'd encountered. He had always suffered from vertigo, which, combined with alcohol, was lethal on that dark balcony. William was buried with full military honours at the Woltemade Cemetery in Cape Town.[44]

When his parents received the news of his death, their world crumbled. They had been overjoyed their son had survived bombings and gassings, and was finally coming home. It was a bitter twist that their beloved son should fall at the very final hurdle. They never really recovered. Up until his death in 1929, William's father would go to his desk twice a week and reread William's letters, dreaming of what might have been. William's sister Hazel still remembered vividly the day when the news came of his death: 'We girls were kept home for a half day and had black bands round our arms. Mother's grief was silent, she could not bear to discuss the tragedy.'

Towards the end of William's mother's life, the family remember her talking openly about William's death. She said, 'We took it quite differently, your father and I. He couldn't keep still, he walked very quickly round and round the room, but I – I dropped like a stone.' A few days later her hair went grey. The girls remembered their father putting his head on the mantelpiece, staring into the fire and literally groaning.

It was a death that affected the whole family – and still does today. William's memory lived on, as his brother Vernon named his first son in his honour – though he insisted that he never enlist for war.

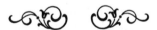

SECOND LIEUTENANT WILLIAM BARCLAY BINNING
Died in Belgium, 24 April 1916

WILLIAM BARCLAY BINNING WAS the eldest son of Sydney and Jane Binning, of Cowdenbeath in Scotland (Plate 16). He had two sisters and a brother (Annie, Isabella and John) and attended Beath Higher Grade School, where he won the Dux Prize. After hearing of his death, the headmaster W.A. Guthrie wrote a letter to the family, praising William as 'by far the brightest lad I had under me'. Indeed, William had aspirations to become a doctor and went on to study medicine at Edinburgh University.

In December 1914 he volunteered for active service and was commissioned into the 11th Battalion Scottish Rifles. During training in Edinburgh, he started to feel the enormity of what he had signed up for, writing with foresight in his diary on 7 January 1915, 'Am just beginning to feel want of my life.' Nevertheless he proved himself a studious and eager trainee soldier, passing his drill, musketry, map-reading and discipline papers at the end of January. His report was 'consistently good' and his conduct 'exemplary'.

On 3 October 1915 William sailed for France from Folkestone Pier, sending a breezy telegram home: 'Crossing tonight Cheer Oh.' By 15 November his battalion was in the trenches of Armagh wood just south-east of Ypres, and conditions were miserable. William's letter home revealed the rigours of trench life and the never-ending routine of trench fortification and repair that was every soldier's lot:

> My Dearest Dad . . . Well we got in last night after a perfect march of 8 miles – bright moonlight and a hard frost. It was glorious. But, oh, when we got into the trenches. Two weeks constant rain has turned them into a quagmire – and 2 days artillery bombardment has just put the finishing touch – it is work, work, work every hour of the day trying to get things straightened up . . .
>
> This place at times is absolute Hell dad – very peculiarly though we lose comparatively few men. We have been in the front line trenches in these parts for almost 18 days – not at a time of course – and have lost very few even although the Huns take it into their heads to shell us with every genus of shell for 5 mins at a time – and it's quite long enough!

William's pocket diary reveals him to be a man with a cheery disposition, although acutely aware of ever-present danger. On 29 January he was near Ploegsteert, which he found 'much better than the beastly salient', and two days later suffered his first war wound. 'Ricochet gets me in the arm. Thank God it was nothing worse.' Trenches were no safe haven and William's injury testified to the fact that even if your head did not go above the parapet, every man was still at risk. Little wonder he recorded that he was 'Looking forward to leave – terribly anxious.'

During February, William returned to Scotland on leave, and it is possible that he may have become engaged to a girl who had attended the same school and who won the Dux Prize two years after William. Jean Kelso was referred to as J in his diary, and frequent enigmatic entries concerning her suggest that William was smitten. He rejoiced in receiving letters and writing to her, and while home on leave, he recorded 10 February as 'Our Happy Day' in Lochgelly.

By late February his battalion was in the Le Bizet sector in Belgium, facing frequent bombardments on trenches and barbed wire, multiple casualties, and bitterly cold weather. The battalion war diary recorded that the enemy sent over 7.7s[45] in response to the twenty deliberate and twenty rapid rounds of fire, along with trench mortars and rifle grenades. Then the Battalion HQ was shelled.[46] It was around this time that William sat down and wrote his heartfelt goodbye letter: frightened, fearful and prepared for the worst.

On 29 February William was part of a working party heading for the front line at Le Touquet. He was heading into more heavy fire. On 6 March he had a 'narrow escape' from enemy shelling that left him 'fed up and out of sorts'. All through March there was constant shelling, which took its toll. He recorded that 19 March was a 'beastly day for frightfulness', with gas, shells and machine-gun fire aimed at the trenches. From these descriptions it is incredible that more men did not succumb to shell-shock – although for thousands of men the mental pressures remained internal, ever-present and debilitating for decades after the war. This was a war when post-traumatic stress disorder (then known as shell-shock) had no effective treatment and was often undiagnosed. A dark, almost desperate sense of humour marked William's diary entry on April Fool's Day – 'Here we are still fooling about in France.'

William's time in France was reaching its portentous end. His last diary entry came on Saturday 22 April 1916. That night he was fatally wounded and taken to Number 2 Casualty Clearing Station, and the sister in charge wrote to William's parents to break the terrible news:

We are taking care of your son . . . I am sorry to say he has been severely wounded in the abdomen. Everything possible is being done for him & he is having every care & attention but you will, I feel sure, prefer to know his exact condition, & I much regret to say the chances of his recovery are very small.

Sydney Binning, William's father, was able to piece together the events of that night from the accounts sent to him by fellow soldiers.

[the battalion waited at] the end of the communicating trenches till it was dark on that Sunday night. The Germans had been shelling pretty heavy all that day . . . the above mentioned Trench and the front line Trenches were on an open piece of ground just at the back of Le Touquet Station – in fact just the goods side or siding. This ground was screened from the German side with the station and Willie's dugout was underneath the station at the time the regiment was waiting. Willie was getting out his machine guns along with 2 gunners preparatory for going into the firing line with the regiment that night. Just as these incidents were taking place this Cowdenbeath sergeant and an officer standing under the parapet of the communications trench heard a suppressed groan and the sergeant was asked to go over the top to see what had happened and Willie was lying in this yard . . . We gave him first attention turned him over to see if the bullet had went through but it was evidently nearly spent and it has just penetrated his bowels. We tried him with water but he was quiet unconscious only his pulse was beating – then of course he was taken away.

On the night he lay dying, William asked the sister in charge to send home his final letter and will.

My Dear Parents,

Don't grieve dearest mother and father. I should so much have liked to live and show you what good there was in me but still I am happy for I have done something. I shall be happy in His care and will look forward so much to our re-union. Don't let any thought of me or my welfare worry you for I am going to Him and will be safe in His keeping.

You might check all my affects father if they ever reach you. I have noted whom I would like them to be given to. The others you will just have to keep. Give Johnnie every chance of realising his ambition and tell him I expect him to do well.

Give Belle, Annie and Johnnie my very best love.

Don't worry dear ones; I am safe in His keeping. I have tried to do my duty but I have failed sometimes.

With love to all,

From your loving son

Willie.

Most probably there will be some money at Cox's[47] Father. I am enclosing a holograph will[48] so that you can get it without difficulty.

Ironically, on the day the family received the telegram informing them of William's death, a letter arrived from him as well. His farewell letter arrived some days later and they were so distraught that it had to be read to them by a minister. The effect on the family was devastating. William's mother never really recovered, and his father bottled up his feelings, rarely speaking of William. William's nephews John and Sydney remembered their grandmother always dressed in a black Victorian mourning dress, and are convinced that William's death at the age of nineteen sent her to a premature grave. William's father refused to accept the 'blood bounty' for his son's death and the money William left was spent on items of furniture that have since been passed down through the family.

The Binning family kept all of William's belongings alongside a treasured memorial book, which serves to underline how dear he was to them. Following

> "My dear parents,
>   "Don't grieve dearest mother and father—
> I should so much have liked to live and shown
> you what good there was in me but still I am happy for I
> have done something. I shall be happy in His care and
> will look forward so much to our re-union. Don't let any
> thought of me or my welfare worry you — for I am going to Him
> and will be safe in His keeping.
>   "You might check all my effects, father, if they ever reach
> you. I have noted whom I would like them to be given to — the
> others you will just have to keep. Give Johnnie every chance
> of realising his ambitions and tell him I expect him to do
> well.
>   "Give Belle, Annie and Johnnie my very best Love.
>   "Don't worry dear ones. I am safe in His keeping. I
> have tried to do my duty but I have failed sometimes.
>   "With all Love to all,
>   "from your loving son
>   "Willie"

13 Part of the letter from William Binning, 24 April 1916 (with kind permission of the Binning family).

his death, future generations of Binnings were brought up on tales of William's bravery. William's brother John was a master plumber when the Second World War broke out; it was a reserved occupation, which allowed him to play a vital role in the war effort, and – to the relief of his parents – meant he was never posted to the front line.

Nobody knows how Jean Kelso reacted to the news of William's death, or whether she received a farewell letter. Many years later she actually married one of his friends who had served in the Border Regiment. When Jean died in 1989 her family found among her personal possessions a small pendant shaped in the form of part of the cap badge of the Scottish Rifles – a soldier's sweetheart pendant given to her by William and kept all her life.

Testaments to William's popularity came in the flood of letters that arrived after his death, alongside numerous announcements in the newspaper. His former teacher, college tutor, company commander and friends all wrote with glowing words about William. Perhaps the humblest tribute to William came from his servant, Private 'Jas' Dyce:

> There is not a man in the Coy. but what has a good word for him and he is often talked about by us. We can never get another one like him. He was always very good to the men . . . he always stuck up for his men when they got into trouble. We know a difference here already without him. Things don't run to be going on

the same at all. It is very disheartening for the like of us out here when we lose a good Officer . . . When Mr. Binning was here he could get more work out of the men than any of the other Officers in about half the time just simply because he was well liked by them . . . I wish it was all over. I have had enough of it.[49]

~ 6 ~

THE SECOND WORLD WAR

... if by some chance, I should not finish my tour, you will know just how I feel about things and it may help to ease the suffering and sorrow you will endure at my loss ... I have enjoyed my Air Force service as I have enjoyed no other years of my life and I have been completely happy the whole time ... This war was inevitable and I could never have been content unless I did my share, so never regret having given me your consent to enlist. I have been very proud to wear my uniform and have always strived to bring credit to the service as a whole. I believe in the cause for which we are fighting and I am equally sure that our actions are justified in the eyes of God ... I want you to know therefore that if I should die I shall not be afraid because my heart is at ease ... I love you all very dearly ... Please don't think I'm pessimistic but I do realise what the odds are and I have seen too many of my friends pass on without leaving any words of hope or encouragements behind. Cheerio and keep smiling though your hearts are breaking.[1]

BETWEEN 1 SEPTEMBER 1939 and 2 September 1945 most of the world's nations fought in a global war, creating over fifty million casualties. One hundred million military personnel were engaged, and the key participants called on civilians to play a crucial role on their home fronts. It was a war without comparison in terms of loss of life, weaponry or sheer scale. It was a war fought on land, at sea, in the air, in deserts, on islands and among mountains. It was also a war that pitted ideologies against one another and gave rise to indescribable acts of inhumanity. This war saw the first use of nuclear weapons: 'The "thing" created the brightest light and the loudest roar of anything yet known to man,'[2] wrote one soldier about the atomic bomb. Amid the individual stories of heroics and daring was a bigger story of whole populations galvanised into action against enemy nations. It was a collective effort involving men, women, children and animals; a global event that would shape the character of nations for decades.

The euphoria following the end of the Great War gave way to a general abhorrence of war, and a feeling of 'never again'. Führer Adolf Hitler's aggression in Europe made the declaration of war in September 1939 a truly 'bitter blow' to a strategy of appeasement. Britain was woefully underprepared – the navy was full of ageing ships and the army numbered fewer than one million. Britain and France together barely matched the military might of Germany. With conscription and enthusiastic volunteers, those numbers increased rapidly.

The war was a period of intense emotions, where death was commonplace. Despite strict censorship – which left families and loved ones often ignorant of where or when their men were fighting – messages of love and honour did get through. The uncertainty of life gave rise to an incredible amount of letter-writing where the true feelings of people (of all nationalities) has helped to unveil a different picture of the experience of war – with human emotion at its heart, instead of bald statistics.

MOBILISATION: A UNIVERSAL WAR EFFORT

The armed services during the Second World War were vast, encompassing all classes in society, most of whom were absolutely committed to achieve victory. Even those with reservations about the morality of war seemed to be swept along in a patriotic fervour. Many conscientious objectors volunteered to work as bomb disposers or in the ambulance services, while women and children were all encouraged to do their bit. It was a truly universal war effort – inspired in no small part by the rousing speeches of Churchill, Mussolini, Hitler, Roosevelt, Stalin and Tojo and the ubiquitous propaganda of posters, films, songs and newspapers conveying both patriotic and psychological encouragement.

Nevertheless, when men left for duty and active service it was difficult to say personal goodbyes – whether Tommy, Ivan, GI or *Landser*.[3] German soldier Rudolf Halbey recorded in his diary, 'How strange this last get-together! Sad and dreamlike. I will remain strong. Tears come to mother anew. I take her in my arms, she kisses me and whispers in a tear-choked voice.'[4] Reverend Peter Sutton recalled his final phone-call before embarking for France: 'utterly miserable as I knew only too well this would be the last time for many months I would hear her voice, possibly the last time of all, for who knew what lay ahead?'[5]

Despite its long duration, there was optimism throughout the war either that it would soon end, or that the turning point was imminent. E.F. Fry wrote to his mother in September 1940, 'the more racket you can stand – the shorter will be the War – believe me . . . I'll be home soon,'[6] and in April 1942 Corporal Ravenscroft believed, 'it can't last such a long time now . . . soon we shall see signs of the eventual end, though, by that, I don't mean that it will be over in five minutes so to speak.'[7] The Second World War did not appear to have engendered the same level of war-weariness in men as previous conflicts; although many were homesick, they were rarely driven to disillusionment.

Throughout the war, many men displayed feelings of invincibility in their letters. Indeed, once men had survived a near miss, they often felt that they would outlive anything, and to write otherwise would tempt fate. In common with other conflicts, there was little point going into combat consumed with morbid preoccupations. T.S. Bigland admitted that by 1941 he was 'not nearly so windy of things as I was'.[8] Thinking positively kept up morale at home, as well as bolstering the men's own confidence that they would survive: 'Don't worry about me – I am fit and well, and well cared for by Dame Fortune,'[9] wrote Captain Thornton on the eve of D-Day. Lance Corporal Branston assured his parents, 'Don't worry about me as I will be o.k, we have no worries as we are very confident as to what the result is going to be . . . None of us are sorry to be going.'[10] When soldiers did allow the 'what if' thought to infiltrate a letter home, it was frequently fleeting and matter of fact. Sergeant Gould wrote home in 1944 to let his family know, 'I have everything signed & sealed & if anything should happen which it won't don't forget thousands of airmen have walked back or got out so don't pay any attention to the missing list. If it does tell Marg I love her. Don't worry though as the casualties are almost nil nowdays.'[11]

THE TOLL OF SUSTAINED WAR: CONDITIONS AND REALITIES

Writing and receiving letters was of paramount importance to combatants during the Second World War. Letters were a vital reminder of their home and thus the reasons for fighting. One commander of the 3rd Panzer Army went as far as describing letters as 'a blood donor for the belief and will of families'.[12] Letters were a temporary respite – especially when they included treats such as cigarettes, balaclavas, mints, crosswords and cakes – from soul-destroying combat conditions. German troops in freezing Russia described urinating on their chilblain-swollen hands and boiling the lice out of their cardigans. Rudolph Kurth wrote to his wife to complain about his wet feet: 'Your feet quickly become sore . . . Until now I've survived these rigours . . . But . . . on a muddy forest track, my left boot got stuck and I ripped the sole off. So marching like this is shit.'[13] British troops in India wrote of food and blood poisoning, and in Holland complained of the incessant rain – 'the tap is never turned off here.'[14]

Letters also gave men a part-cathartic, part-compulsive avenue to talk about their experiences. Men rarely admitted fear to one another, therefore a letter was one recourse. Despite censorship of places or names, on the whole, many military men did not hold back in their descriptions of battle – although they were at pains to stress that all was well, so as not to cause consternation at home. Indeed, for many it was initially a relief actually to see action after months of training and waiting. War was exciting and breathless for Sergeant Pilot Bushell, describing one aerial adventure during the Battle of Britain:

> Suddenly, the front of this box lit up with flame after flame as if someone were flashing mirrors in the sun, and an instant later we were in a hail of shells and machine-gun bullets. We persisted on our course, and half a second later, we were ploughing through them like a hot knife through butter, firing as we went.[15]

There was a healthy dose of honesty in the letters; men expressed their fears and thoughts amid the tumult of battle. On the eve of the Normandy landings, Private John Folley described how 'The suspense was almost unbearable . . . men in their thousands, deep in thought and as if mesmerised . . . I became conscious of the pulsating pressure from my steel helmet, my body now tense and with clammy hands subconsciously gripping my rifle.'[16] Also during D-Day, American soldier Carl Schluter was honest in his fear that,

> every time a shell started to whistle in, I was beginning another prayer. As one of the 'doughfeet'[17] put it, 'I may not get the Purple Heart[18] for being wounded but if they give them out for being scared as hell I certainly rate one', and that's no kiddin.[19]

In reality, though, it was impossible to convey the absolute terror men must have experienced in the thick of battle: 'With a terrifying roar, the steel monster was upon us, the ground shook and to be truthful, so did my whole body.'[20] Fear was no respecter of nationality. One German soldier wrote,

> It is impossible to describe the terror of that experience. We pressed our faces to the ground and waited for a direct hit, or flying fragments, to take our lives . . . Oh, I wish I could tell you, my beloved ones, what we are going through in this campaign! Our infantry suffers even more. Yesterday I lost a very good comrade. Everything is against us . . . The future looks terribly dark . . .[21]

Going into battle was often the prompt to say farewell. Lieutenant Ian Anderson wrote from 'a state of acute tension here in Malta . . . I should hate to die without making a farewell of some kind.'[22]

The war brought men sharply to confront death, whether it was the name of a pilot scrubbed off the chalk-board following a mission, or in the field, at first hand. Driver Cassidy recorded in his diary, 'Begin to feel queer as we passed dead Tommies on the road with fresh blood on them.' Every encounter with death must have been sobering, and men dealt with it in different ways.

Some refused to dwell on the human fallout and ploughed themselves into work with renewed gusto. Others turned to the comfort of religion. For many, however, being surrounded by death or the threat of death slowly drove them to desperation. Post-traumatic stress (albeit undiagnosed) meant a lifetime of nightmares, flashbacks and restlessness for many veterans. Some were unable to sleep in the same bed as their wives, and others could not ride on buses or trains. Many simply never talked about what they had gone through. Alois Dwenger described a soldier's lot:

> He always peeks carefully out from cover, any moment a bullet can hit him.
> Shells strike every day . . . shaking and spraying the ground, the dugout trembles,
> shrapnel whistles overhead . . . the imagination working feverishly, he sits wrapped
> in his shelter, half freezing, hour after hour, listening with strained nerves . . . I
> believe true heroism lies in bearing this dreadful everyday life.[23]

In the field, it was not unheard of for men to self-inflict what British soldiers called a 'Blighty' – a wound through the foot, hand, leg or arm that was not life-threatening but serious enough to see them invalided home. Some letters recorded instances of men doing handstands in trenches to try and sustain a leg-wound, and upon success, 'There followed a rousing cheer of jubilation, as one can imagine echoing from a football stadium.'[24]

THE ENEMY AND THE REASONS FOR WAR

For the allies, anti-Nazi sentiment was easy enough to stir up, and people were genuinely fearful that Hitler would prevail. Newspapers ran mock 'Wanted' posters for Adolf Hitler 'alias Adolf Schicklegruber . . . Suffering from acute monomania, with periodic fits of melancholia'.[25] Private Talbot wrote in his diary, 'The only thing to do with the Germans is to get rid of them,'[26] while in the Middle East, Sergeant Glover hoped, 'they exterminate the rats'.[27] When it came to the Italians, opinions were almost overwhelmingly scathing. Captain Hay wrote 'The only thing I hope is that both those bastard little Musso brats get shot down in flames & burn quite slowly.'[28] In training, men were urged to remember the mantra of kill or be killed, and that the only good Italian or German was a dead one. Many soldiers carved a notch in their rifles for each German killed. Of course the Germans were no different. Harry Mielert wrote, 'in war shots are fired in order to kill people . . . I also had to think: the man over there . . . was after my blood and without doubt would have been happy if he had bumped me off.'[29]

There were, too, men who acknowledged the 'good and bad in every race',[30] with mounting respect for the *Schütze Arsch*[31] as war ground on. In essence, they might be the enemy, but they were also the victim, and suffering the same hell. 'In character, almost the same disposition as ourselves . . . a clean fighter with compassion',[32] wrote Private Folley.

War forced men to consider their politics and morals, and gave rise to conflicting feelings as well as a strong sense of duty. Before what would be his final sortie, Sergeant William Borthwick wrote:

> I'm convinced the bombing of the enemy is having a decisive effect – so we'll carry on till they give in!! . . . I don't think that I'm becoming cold hearted or callous – on the contrary. I have come to realise how beastly war is in every phase of the struggle. How aimless and futile it all is – to think that in this modern age with so called civilisation reaching a crest of perfection we are rushing like a pack of wolves at each other's throats.[33]

German soldier Adolf Dick wrote how 'we must make our contribution to the greatness and existence of Germany . . . The slogan was that we're fighting for our loved ones at home.'[34]

ADIEU TO THE STIFF UPPER LIP

The Second World War was extraordinary in terms of the emotions unleashed in letters – more than in previous conflicts. It seems that the stiff upper lip was well and truly softened for many men. Perhaps the danger of war was a licence to break the rules of formality, an exhilarating freedom from the shackles of polite niceties and inhibitions. Even the emotionally self-conscious Japanese wrote beautiful sentiments to loved ones, such as pilot Norimashi Hayashi: 'I am off to fairyland, the country of Andersen's stories, and there I shall be a prince. I shall talk with the birds, the flowers and the trees,'[35] and Hajime Hujii wrote: 'It was the day when the cold wind blustered hard. Some lives went out as if they were dew.'[36]

Separation from his wife prompted 'A strange medley of thoughts – kaleidoscopic really – in my mind's eye' for Harry Dance, who wished to 'create a life together . . . hand in hand as I always think of myself with you. I look forward to that day yet scarcely dare think of it.'[37] One American soldier wrote in 1944, 'Right now I'd like to do a good job of holding you in my arms. Nicely planned . . . first a real frontal assault – in support I'd start a double envelopment & you'd find that the pincer movement put you surely in my arms – now just a slight bit of reconnaissance & I'd capture my main objective, your lips, & demand payment in full . . .'[38] Meanwhile, a German soldier was a little cruder: 'My little cock is already yearning for you again. My "stovepipe" would like so much to heat you up once again!'[39]

Farewell Letters: Common Themes

Nowhere is an outpouring of emotion and deepest thoughts more evident than in farewell letters from this period. 'God mum I am almost crying whilst writing this letter,'[40] admitted Corporal Lawrence. In common with letters from the Great War, farewells tended to contain religious sentiments, but were not suffused with religion. Many men found God only in that last moment, or as a comfort in the short term. Sergeant Sullivan wrote, 'last night whilst I was sailing over the continent, the thought suddenly came to me to say a couple of prayers. It was not that I was praying because I was scared . . . when I went to bed I offered up a thanksgiving for my safe return.' Instances of colonels articulating a final prayer to their men on the eve of action were also commonplace. Colonel Wolverton delivered one such stirring speech: 'God almighty! In a few short hours we will be in battle with the enemy . . . use us as your instrument for the right and an aid in returning peace to the world . . . if we die, that we die as men would die.'[41]

Letters where men had actively planned for their funeral were infrequent, but the ones that exist were always written by religious men, who were perhaps more at ease with contemplating death in its entirety. Edgar Rodenbeck wrote home with instructions for his memorial service: 'The hymns that I would like to have used at this service are the following: "I'm but a stranger here, Heaven is my Home." "Whatever God Ordains is Good His Righteous will Abideth." "Who Knows How Near my End may be?"'[42]

'I don't want any grieving over me for what better way can a man die, than fighting for the people and the things he loves,'[43] wrote Flying Officer Wilson. Indeed, the overriding characteristic of farewell letters during this period is that there were no regrets and no chink in the belief that death was the catalyst for change. Commander Peter Clissold's farewell read:

> Do not grieve too much. Death is preferable to blindness, paralysis or mutilation and I would never ask a better fate than to die in the service of the Royal Navy in a cause as just as ours. Though there are lots of things I'd have like to have seen or done; to marry & have a family – yet I might never have accomplished any of them. I've had over half my allotted spin – & the best half rather I expect.[44]

It is a sentiment that is found in virtually all last letters, regardless of nationality, and ironically served to underline the paradox of war. Every side believed its ideology was right and just, so while one side might win with military might, to crush ideologies would take much longer. 'We must give no quarter or expect none because if they break through, there is nothing to stop them from landing in Australia . . . When you receive this letter, please don't grieve too much as we will know that I died trying to help save Australia,'[45] wrote Stanley McTackett. One German soldier bid farewell with the words, 'You just have to think of us fulfilling our duty completely, until the very last. And if this strikes us, well, then life was beautiful & ended with the best and toughest duty a man can have for his people, homeland, loved ones and for himself.'[46] The letters and wills of Japanese kamikaze pilots, written knowing their death was inevitable, were particularly poignant. 'Even if I shall be fish feed in the Pacific Ocean, I will often be reborn and want to devote myself to this noble aim,'[47] declared Koichi Mukojima. Yoshi Miyagi wrote:

A friend said to me that a kamikaze pilot was nothing but a robot . . . who works the controls. I must have neither emotions nor personality . . . I am nothing but a particle of iron attracted by a magnet – the American aircraft-carrier. The Americans call this suicide . . . But this suicide is also a form of sacrifice which can be understood only in Japan, the country of idealism . . . Tomorrow a man in love with liberty will leave this world . . . at the bottom of my heart I am happy to die.[48]

Men during this war seemed to have a deep understanding that they were sacrificing themselves for the freedom of future generations, and took the opportunity in farewell letters to emphasise this point. E.F. Rawlings affirmed, 'I'm fighting so that in the future people will have the chance to live as happily as we all did together before the war without interference.'[49] Flying Officer Roxburgh addressed this message to his newborn nephew:

I am doing all I can . . . to bring about a condition which will cause tyranny & oppression to leave this world so that you & your future friends & playmates may never know what those words mean. You should be able to face life with the prospect of being able to live in close harmony with all peoples & at the same time be encouraged to speak your mind as long as 'fair play' becomes the first condition in the relationship of men.[50]

In letters there was a pervasive feeling of the seismic change this global conflict would surely bring about, and to be a small cog in the machinery that prompted that change was worth writing home about. The worst outcome of a death would be that it was in vain. Flight Sergeant James Dunlop bid his farewell with these words:

Firstly, I want you to realize and, try even to be proud, that you have given a man to the cause of human liberty . . . If there is any message which the coming generation should have from mine let it be a message from us who have fought and died to make future generations of human beings possible. Let the message be this – We have cleared the site and laid the foundations – You build. This time let us hope they take the plans out of that hip pocket.[51]

As with many ordinary letters home, farewell letters from the Second World War stand out for the romance and emotion they hold. War was a powerful aphrodisiac, and a final farewell a lifelong loving bond to a family. German infantryman Mielert wrote to his sweetheart in March 1943:

> . . . you fear that if I fall you will also be quickly forgotten . . . Should I have to be in life-long imprisonment in Siberia, I would never give you up, never, and I also think that if I lay in a grave and my spiritual being had another existence I would not forget you, so that one day you must also come to me, to an absolute unification. That is the achievement of love. It goes beyond all borders.[52]

Private Ivor Rowberry, killed at the Battle of Arnhem, posthumously won Basildon Bond's best military letter with his farewell:

> Tomorrow we go into action. As yet I do not know exactly what our job will be, but no doubt it will be a dangerous one in which many lives will be lost – mine may be one of those lives. Well Mom, I am not afraid to die. I like this life, yes – for the past two years I have planned and dreamed and mapped out a perfect future for myself. I would have liked that future to materialise, but it is not what God wills, and if by sacrificing all this I leave the world slightly better than I found it I am perfectly willing to make that sacrifice . . . Grief is hypocritical, useless and unfair, and does neither you or me any good. I want no flowers, no epitaph, no tears. All I want is for you to remember me and feel proud of me; then I shall rest in peace, knowing that I have done a good job. Death is nothing final or lasting; if it were there would be no point in living; it is just a stage in everyone's life . . .[53]

The Second World War casualty rate was horrific and devastating for families. Farewell letters were small comfort at the time, but were ultimately a source of lifelong comfort and often inspiration. 'But now you are the comforter, and keep,/From out the shadows, watch, lest I should weep,'[54] wrote Vera Bax following the death of her son in 1942, while German soldier Hubert Retz reassured his wife, 'I think of our motto – weeds don't die – and I still hope that we'll see each other again . . . A loving kiss.'[55]

Private Leslie Abram Neufeld
Killed at Varaville, D-Day, 6 June 1944

Born in a small log house on 17 January 1922, Leslie was the third son and child of Anna and Henry Neufeld, a noted specialised seed grower (Plate 17). Leslie grew up on a farm in the Lost River District of Saskatchewan – a pioneering Mennonite[56] community – in a large family of nine children. The community promoted farming, education and family values, and the whole family attended church. He went to high school in Winnipeg, Manitoba, and then to Altona High School, where his uncle was the principal. Outside school, Leslie helped out on the farm with his siblings, but was also a keen gymnast and showed a gift for poetry. When war broke out, Leslie was seventeen and in secondary school. At this time, the family had moved to Codette to be nearer a railway line that would better serve the family's seed business, and were attending the United Church of Canada. Neufeld's father was the choirmaster, and Leslie himself was a keen singer. His parents hoped he would work in the family business, as he had displayed an aptitude for business, and after graduating from high school he worked as a general store clerk.

On 13 January 1942 Leslie followed his two older brothers, Leonard and Richard, in enlisting in the Canadian army. Most young men in the community were volunteering at this time, simply feeling it was the right thing to do. He joined the Royal Canadian Army Medical Corps and sailed to Britain on the same boat as his brother Leonard. When the Canadian army called for volunteers for the 1st Parachute Battalion in February 1944, Neufeld enthusiastically put himself forward. Between February and May 1944 the unit underwent intense training on the British X-type parachute (which had no reserve chute and was designed to be used at a much lower altitude than the standard chute) as well as mortar, machine-gun and anti-tank handling, and wireless communications. They were becoming a well-oiled, battle-ready machine and would have known that the long-awaited invasion of Europe was imminent. On 24 May 1944 the unit moved from Greenock in Scotland to Down Ampney in the Cotswolds, where they were briefed on Operation Overlord – better known now as D-Day. Neufeld's company were to be the lead Canadian company, dropped into Normandy on 5 June 1944. In fact, the company had prepared to depart on 4 June, but at the last minute the invasion was postponed. During that agonising wait, Leslie wrote a farewell letter to his family:

Dear parents, brothers and sisters,

My time for writing is very limited. However, I must write a few words just to let you know how things are going.

First of all, thanks a million for the cigs and parcels and letters. Received your letter, Dad, just a day ago. By mistake I received Len's cigs too.

Sorry Mum that I don't have time to answer all your questions now.

Dad, the time has come for that long awaited day, the invasion of France. Yes I am in it. I'll be in the first one hundred Canadians to land by parachute. We know our job well. We have been trained for all conditions and circumstances. We have a fair chance.

I am not certain but I expect Len will be coming in a few days later.

To go in as a paratrooper was entirely my choice. I am in no way connected to any medical work. This job is dangerous, very dangerous. If anything should happen to me, do not feel sad or burdened by it, but take the attitude of 'He served his country to his utmost.'

With that spirit I am going into battle.

And let it be known that the Town of Nipawin did its share to win the war.

I have full expectations of returning and with God's strength and guidance I'm sure He will see me thro' all peril. My trust is in God.

Your loving son,

Leslie[57]

Just before midnight on 5 June 1944 Neufeld's company took off in twelve Albemarles from Harwell Airfield. C Company would lead a clandestine operation to parachute into Varaville (a town where the Germans were dug in), with the aim of destroying bridges over the River Dives, thus preventing the deployment of German troops from east of the river. By six o'clock on the morning of 6 June, Private Neufeld was with Corporal Oikle at Chateau Varaville, and using the only weapon they had available – a PIAT gun[58] – fired against the enemy. Unfortunately, the projectile fell short. The enemy retaliated with a high-explosive shrapnel shell that penetrated the chateau's wall and set off Oikle's remaining PIAT bombs. Private Neufeld was killed instantly, buried beneath a pile of masonry. He was twenty-one.

Neufeld's letter arrived after his parents had received the telegram notifying them that Leslie had been killed. The telegram was a profoundly bitter blow, 'the only time I ever saw my father cry', recalled Leslie's brother Edward. His mother was bereft, in deep despair, comforted only by her religious faith. Edward remembered that, while the letter did not ease the pain, 'by bringing Leslie's voice and spirit into the home as he had been so close to the day he died, was forever a precious balm to help my parents and all the family live with the bitter reality of his death. It was as if his voice was forever there. It enriched enormously the family's memory of him.' Neufeld's mother, who lived to be ninety-nine, held Leslie's memory dear, and every year until she died, placed a wreath on the local cenotaph in remembrance.

Edward Neufeld felt Leslie wrote his farewell letter because they were such a close family, having all grown up on the farm. Letters had flown back and forth between the boys and parents during the course of the war and Leslie

June 4 1944

Dear parents, brothers & sisters

My time for writing is very limited. However I must write a few words just to let you know how things are going.

First of all, thanks a million for the cigs & parcels and letters. Received your letter, Dad, just a day ago. By mistake I received Len's cigs. too.

Sorry Mum that I don't have time to answer all your questions now.

14 Part of the letter from Leslie Neufeld, 4 June 1944 (Canadian War Museum).

would have been keenly aware of the pending danger of the D-Day operations. 'He probably wished his parents to have a last word from him just in case, a sort of Good-Bye, and he wished in particular to assure them that he placed his fate in the hands of God. Leslie certainly would have known that his mother, a devout Christian, would have wanted to hear just that.'

The farewell letter became a cherished family heirloom and was something they could all return to, re-read, and once again feel close to Leslie. More than sixty years later, his words still resonate with the optimism, fidelity and stoicism of so many young men who died in this war.

Lieutenant George F. Morrison
Killed at El Alamein, 24 October 1942

THE SON OF ANDREW Dean and Norah Morrison, George was born in 1921 and brought up in Crieff in Perthshire. In 1942 he joined the 7th Battalion of the Royal Highlanders (Black Watch), and the months before leaving for the Middle East, passed in a blur of command exercises, marching and an inspection by the king and queen. Morale was high and the mood excited. On 18 June Morrison embarked on board HMS *Stratheden* and wrote an animated letter home:

> I know I'm going to do *better than ever now* . . . I'm all set, Mother, at last, after
> all these weary, miserable months of Young Soldiers, and hoped for parachutists!!!
> Give my best love to all at home and I will always be praying that you are all right,
> just as much as you will for me, for I know that I have the best home that any man
> could wish for, and the finest woman on earth for Mother. So keep the flag flying
> and the war will soon be over.

A family-oriented man, George was a prolific letter writer, dispatching a cheery missive home virtually every week. The boyish enthusiasm he tagged the 'Morrison spirit' leaped off the page. He was at pains to reassure his family of his safety, revelling in the fact that he was making a tangible contribution to the war effort and confident of 'knocking hell out of any Hun that I happen to come across'.

As Morrison made the long voyage to the Middle East, his mind could not have been further from what lay ahead. He wrote about the hot, sweaty conditions and told of pipe bands, three-mile runs around the ship and being 'sunburnt nearly black . . . my freckles are frecklier than ever before!' As time ticked away, he was eager to engage the enemy, telling his mother in August, 'It's amazing but as we get nearer we seem to get cheerier instead of more morose.' The Morrison spirit was as indomitable as ever.

The convoy reached Aden on 6 August, and Quassasun on the 12th. 'The desert is flat, arid and utterly cheerless, like the landscape of the moon,' he wrote. He told of his exasperation at having to shave using Vaseline as a lubricant, let alone the plagues of scorpions and mosquitoes, and sand that worked its way into every conceivable crevice. Life in the desert boiled down to four essential components: food, latrines,[59] his 'bivvy or funk-hole' and letters. At the same time, Morrison appreciated the beauty of the desert, with its bright stars and serene calm – 'unwarlike', he felt. He was less enamoured with the 'vile' natives, whose squalid living conditions made Glasgow slums seem 'positive cream' in comparison. It must have been an extraordinary arena for a young wide-eyed soldier to enter. It was no holiday, however; the men who fought in Egypt embraced a type of battle that was far removed from trench warfare in Europe yet demanded the same levels of endurance and mettle.

By 29 August Morrison had been made a navigating officer, responsible for guiding his unit through the desert using a sun compass. Things were becoming more intense amid the frequent dust-storms, and the war diary recorded a 'supposed threat'[60] from Rommel. Morrison's captain had been injured, leaving George as company second-in-command, 'The bombing isn't nice but we're giving them as much and far more than we're getting, so don't worry.' War forced young men to grow up quickly, and on 13 September he was in reflective mood: 'This life refines you, and I'm sure we'll all come out of the desert the better for it – it makes you more patient, more contemplative, and you can arrange your thoughts much better than at home.' Nevertheless, his letters were peppered with patriotic confidence, no doubt due in part to the battalion orders he was receiving. In September the talk of imminent attack was intensifying and the battalion was on two hours' notice to occupy battle positions when the bugle and codeword 'Donald'[61] sounded. The 7th Black Watch were ordered to 'hold Barrani tomb' and 'be prepared to act offensively'. They were warned that codeword 'Twelve Bore' was even more serious. All protrusions had to be levelled, defences manned immediately and there was minimum movement by day. Morrison was confident: 'The B.W. can take it all right! They have to! They have a tradition to uphold and we're showing the Hun and the Eyetie that the "ladies from hell", or rather the Fighting Forty-Two can still dole out the punishment!!!'

By 3 October 'slothful Georgie', as he was known at home, was living in a six by seven dugout, rising before dawn and undertaking patrols at night among burned-out vehicles and the odd corpse. A snatched cigarette under his groundsheet was a welcome pleasure. Water was rationed to a mere two pints per day. In his down-time, Morrison wrote short stories and poetry and had time to plan for the future. 'Aye it's queer life . . . queer, queer, and an awful waste of good years out of my life.' Ever mindful of his family's concerns, he would counter any plaintive thought with swift reassurance: 'I'm as cheery as a sandboy now that I'm really *doing* something to give these Huns hell.'

On 13 October Morrison's battalion was edging towards the Alamein Line. They all knew that the countdown to zero hour had begun. On 18 October 1942 Morrison sat down and wrote a farewell letter to his mother.

I am writing this letter to you, in case I become a casualty in this action I am entertaining now. It may be that I will be killed, and if so, then I have left instructions that this letter will be sent on to you – you are the sort of person who can stand these things better than most people, and I know you'd like to hear from me – and so I am writing this last letter to be posted *only if I am killed.*

You have always been the best of mothers to me – and I know no other woman could be so kind, so sympathetic, and so forbearing to her children. Since reaching mature years I've tried to make up to you for all the trouble you must have had when I was smaller. My family is the best ever – and I know you'll all go on and keep the colours flying, even though I'm not there to bother you any more by phone calls from obscure spots, or mad crazes after motor-bikes, or any of these things which afflict the normal youth!

This is a queer letter to write – because I'll be dead then and *if* you get it, I feel excessively cheery and optimistic right now and this death business doesn't worry me in the least! So, if I *do* get one – don't be too sad – it's too late to be sad, and I wouldn't like it. If you would just get the organist to play Handel's Largo in my memory in the kirk one Sunday morning – then that's as far as you should grieve for me. Even in heaven, or hell – I'll be all right, never fear!! I'll send you a bit of ambrosia or alternatively a piece of glowing coal!! So don't be sad please – remember this war is being fought to protect folk like you from horrible things, and it's only right that some should have the privilege – yes, the privilege to give themselves for the cause of good and the right.

I'm still firmly convinced it won't be *me* – but just in case – then you can have this letter to tell you I went out to die as cheery as a cricket, with a song in my mouth and my chanter in my small pack, and a couple of grenades in my pockets!

Runcie will be able to square off all my money – I have about £12 in the Ottoman Bank, Cairo, which he should claim from the Regimental Paymaster, Officers Accounts . . . also any credits to my pay which may be there for me.

As to all my stuff here – it will probably be sold and the proceeds sent you – my stuff at home give to anyone who needs it – young Leighton, or George Massie, and my clothes to the McLaggans or any other needy person.

For my family – I leave you my blessing, and may God protect and help you through the hard times, and give you strength, as He does for me now as I write this.

And so, Noni, for the last time good-bye, and keep that old chin up just as well as ever.

My love to Grannie, G.P. Winf., Winnie and Elspeth, the Leightons and all the rest.

God bless you for always, my dearest Mother, your loving son –

George.[62]

He closed with the Latin motto of his Regiment: *nemo me impune lacessit* – no one provokes me with impunity.

On 23 October the battalion war diary recorded heavy artillery and mortar fire as the bombardment began, 'Heavy casualties were sustained.' The Battle of El Alamein was a ferocious fight that raged over two hellish days. At 2200 hours on 23 October Morrison's battalion was on the left flank and dug in deep. The original plan that rear companies could 'leap-frog' those up front had to be changed in the face of unrelenting fire from the enemy. It was not until the following night that the leading companies were relieved, and resupplies of ammunition, rations and water reached them. Heavy shelling continued on the 24th, and five officers were killed, including Morrison. The death toll that day was heavy: 10 officers wounded, 65 others killed, and 130 wounded.[63]

It was nevertheless a turning point in the war. By 2 November Operation Supercharge was launched as armoured divisions finally extinguished the last flames of German defence. Morrison had helped achieve a decisive victory that swelled British morale. For his family to believe he had entered the fray in confident, high-spirited mood must have made his final farewell a truly moving read.

George Morrison was buried at El Alamein War Cemetery; it was not until 22 February 1943 that his family received his farewell letter.

Captain Friedrich Spemann
Survived

Born on 7 December 1897 in Würzburg, Spemann's father was the Nobel Prize-winning Hans Spemann (Plate 18).[64] Friedrich might have been physically small at just over five feet five, but had a strong presence and natural air of authority. He was an industrious, loyal and brave man who avoided unnecessary risk.

By the outbreak of the Second World War, Spemann was an experienced soldier, having already served and survived the First World War. He married Elisabeth Kliem (known as Liesel) at the age of twenty-seven in 1924, and went on to complete his degree and doctorate in biology in Frankfurt. A nature lover and early campaigner for its preservation, Spemann was a passionate teacher and gifted communicator. In 1929 he secured a job as a professor at a teacher-training academy. During his time teaching, Spemann declared that if Hitler became Führer, there would be a war. He was fired for his comments, and both he and his wife were prevented from working for five years. They were forced to live on a meagre pension to survive, and had four children – Dorle, Brita, Wolf and Bärbel. Spemann always believed there would be another war after the Treaty of Versailles; his son recalled his incredible patriotism; he was a man who would never shy away from doing his duty. He was also a Protestant, and urged his wife to find comfort in God while he was away at war. His view of the world was dominated by German idealism and he was an avid reader of Kant and Schiller. Indeed, he lived his life by Schiller's philosophy that 'if one does not live one's life purposefully, one's life will never succeed.'

Spemann had already experienced the horror of trench warfare during the Great War. On his return from that conflict, he maintained that he wanted to be cremated, having seen the visceral nightmare of men being blown apart by grenades. It had been a war of rapidly changing technologies, which unnerved Spemann; ordered to take his cavalry unit, consisting of four howitzers (artillery cannon and twenty-five horses mission, he was met by tanks and remembered feeling inferior to this new, metal beast.

In September 1939 reservist Spemann enlisted into the 29th Infantry Division as lieutenant, to take part in the campaign to invade Poland. He was forced to leave home when his youngest daughter was two, and could only snatch a precious few days' holiday every four to six months.

Although Spemann displayed no outward signs of fear, he must have been aware of what could lie ahead. Indeed, his first letter back to Liesel was his farewell letter. It was written while he was waiting for a deployment order that was expected that night: a tense, fraught wait for the call to spring into immediate action. It was an opportunity for him to think through practical measures, and to express the overwhelming love he had for his family.

Dearest . . . So I have now totally switched into the war operation, which as a soldier I must and want to perform to the best of my ability . . . So now keep your faith. Your task now is to protect the children as best you can and in the course of this to be just as energetic as you otherwise were in such matters . . . In my filing cabinet in a blue folder there is a bunch of stuff about this; also a small blue folder in the bottom shelf of the shelving next to my desk . . . You are my deputy there as always and if you have to make decisions, then listen to your inner self about what I would think and do about it, then you too will find the answers that are correct.

I am with you throughout everything for ever and ever. And if I want, then I'll cast your dear face here and look deep into your eyes, to the bottom of your heart, and you will feel it there. And you don't cry, but are proud and willing to do everything. What other people do has nothing to do with us. We do our duty, and to that end you are Elisabeth Spemann Kliem – with everything that is in my and your blood . . . If anything should happen to me, don't make my memory into a cult. I will continue to live in you and the children. And if another, whom you trust, should come after me, then don't say no.

My life with you was so full of beauty and purity and infinite love from both sides that I can only be completely grateful and say, it couldn't have been lovelier. You shouldn't always think, if Fritz were here now 'he is there and helps and takes care.' And if I have sometimes made you worry, forgive me. And do one thing – continue to live with me.

And now you know how I think. All this had to be said once. But now we don't want to talk about that any more. May fate now take its course – be as prepared as me for everything, then you'll be able to achieve everything too.

For today, farewell.[65]

It was a remarkable letter – notably different in tone to all the others he wrote home – prompted by the knowledge that the imminent action could be his last. After that letter, Spemann's correspondence rarely mentioned death. He talked of marching with 'cocked rifles and pistols through burning villages and cities, sometimes horrifyingly beautiful pictures'.[66] Writing from Poland in mid-September 1939, he assured her that he had only seen 'half a dozen Polish pilots', no bombing and that 'My work doesn't lack variety . . . On the march, I help the captain to keep the convoy together . . . We then form a "hedgehog" on all sides.'[67]

Spemann risked his life on several occasions. One story recounted to his son Wolfgang told of passing through a burning village, coming under a hail of fire from all sides. Spemann was a captain – and so was at the front – and was ordered to undertake risky reconnaissance missions right up to the front line. He recalled another occasion when he was surrounded by hundreds of Russians. The machine gun developed a fault and would not load until the machine gunner calmly disassembled, repaired and re-assembled as the enemy approached; it was an impressive reminder of the value of drills and discipline under pressure.

While he was away at war, Spemann wrote regularly every few days. His wife, 'my dear darling',[68] lived for those letters, and it seems that Spemann found it deeply cathartic to correspond so regularly – whether he was totally honest about his thoughts and feelings or not. 'I escape to my letters and I live in them,'[69] he admitted. His letters were intensely private; Spemann's children were never allowed to read them, but sensed their mother's palpable relief when one arrived. It was a sign that Spemann was alive – or at least had been three weeks ago when the letter was written and sent. In early September 1939 he laid bare his frustrations: 'In this environment, I think of you and your day – already since early this morning at 5 clock . . . Whether I can send this [letter] in the next few days, I do not know. I write when I can . . . Dear, my heart is very full and sometimes it is not easy when thinking of you.'[70]

In 1942 Spemann was attached to the German 4th Army, which went on to see action at Stalingrad. But Spemann himself never saw Stalingrad; his role was to drive trains from Charcow in the Ukraine to retrieve the dead and wounded. In 1943, however, he returned home for health reasons. His war was not quite over – in October 1943 the family was evacuated following an air attack on Kassel. In 1944 Spemann returned to teaching evacuated children. When the war ended he established a workshop for artists, and then moved back to full teaching. He did not retire until 1962, just three years before his death. His time on the front line had a profound effect. Spemann's son, Wolf, recalled that whenever his father had to make difficult decisions in life, he would seek out the graveyard of First and Second World War veterans, perhaps reflecting on how close he also came to paying the ultimate price in the presence of his fallen comrades.

SERGEANT GOULDEN OLIVER 'BOY' WEBSTER

Killed over Berlin, 20 November 1940

THE SON OF JOHN and Alice Webster, Goulden was born in Kingston in Surrey in 1913 (Plate 19). Webster was in the RAF Volunteer Reserve when war broke out, and living in Horsell near Woking. The reserve was the main means of entering the RAF, and by the end of 1941 more than half of Bomber Command was made up from members of the Volunteer Reserve.

Webster's unit, 149 Squadron, was a night-bombing unit, originally raised towards the end of the First World War. It was resurrected in 1937 at Mildenhall in Suffolk – again as a night-bombing unit – equipped with Wellington bombers. On 1 August 1939 partial mobilisation began, and by the 2nd the station was under orders to prepare for war. They carried out the second bombing raid of the Second World War in September 1939, living up to their motto of *fortis nocte* – strong by night.

Webster's farewell letter to his mother was undated, but was written while he was based at RAF Mildenhall. Indeed, men were advised to prepare wills or make financial arrangements in case of their death in action. Veterans have recalled the hours of waiting for the call to action as being the worst part of the job. It gave them time to think and contemplate mates who had not returned, near misses in the air and the possibility that each flight could be their last. Many would have written farewell letters in these quiet hours of introspection. Up in the air, adrenalin took over, and the confidence of youth gave a feeling of invincibility. Admittedly, in Webster's final letter there was a light-heartedness and a feeling that he did not really expect to be killed – perhaps to spare his mother's feelings but also to stop any self-doubt hampering his own performance in the air.

By November 1940, 149 Squadron was still targeting battleships, cruisers, submarines and destroyers. The operational log recorded frequent sorties to Schillig Roads on reconnaissance as well as hits on German submarines and spotting enemy fighter patrols on the coast. In the month before his death, Webster made long night flights on 1, 6, 8, 13, 15, 17 and 19 November.[71] Throughout October and November, pilots were plagued with severe icing and low cloud during flights, making their bombing attacks on industrial targets more difficult. The squadron was nevertheless kept incredibly busy, attacking marshalling yards at Munich and industrial buildings in Berlin, Leipzig and Cologne. It was an exhausting job – a round flight to Berlin took almost twelve hours.

Night flights were particularly hazardous. As a rule, pilots would not fly straight or level for more than twenty or thirty seconds when under threat from German firepower. Air battles were frenetic and raw. Planes could appear from nowhere, within metres of each other. It called for split-second decision-making and incredible skill from the whole crew. As well as this there were the ever-present risks of anti-aircraft fire, friendly fire, poor weather and mechanical failure.

According to the operation record for the early hours of 20 November 1940, Webster was deployed with his crew of Aircraft Captain Hide, Sergeant Vince, observer Sergeant Mitchell and air gunners Sergeants Whitworth and Wright. Nine aircraft set off to bomb targets in Berlin, and two towards Gelsenkirchen. Poor weather 'interfered' with the missions and one aircraft failed to return.[72] Webster and his men had been shot down over the port of Stettin.

When news came through of the losses, Webster's farewell letter was sent on to his mother. His older brother had already been killed during the First World War, and the consequences of losing her youngest (whom she still called 'Boy') must have been devastating for Webster's mother. The chirpiness and fear of capture – rather than death – must have made this an agonising letter to read. Webster's voice and humour still suffused the letter, and would have no doubt made his mother smile.

My dear Ma

You won't I hope even read this, but there's always the chance that one may not come back you know, well first of all, if one should be posted as missing, don't worry too much, as there's a good possibility of our being prisoners. If this does happen rest assured I shall try everything that's known to get away.

If I should in these circumstances manage to get a letter through to you either directly or through the Red Cross, or Air Ministry remember the following

(1) If I mention *food* in any way it means that there's no chance at the time of escape
(2) If I mention *clothes* in any way it means that there *is* a chance of getting away
(3) If I mention *letters* in any way it means escape imminent
(4) If I mention *beer* in any way it means either that I'm on my way out, or that I may be out any moment and *in any case* I want you to let the Air ministry know that you've heard from me to this effect, so that they can help in certain ways.

Well that's all fairly simple isn't it? In any case we are instructed to make some arrangement like this between ourselves and our parents so don't think it's just some crazy idea of my own!

If I should be just plain missing or definitely known to be killed in action, I don't want you to feel it too much either. Look at it this way, there have been hundreds of other better chaps than I that have gone before & there's hundreds more to go after before this thing is finished.

In my own case, life hadn't so much to offer after all, and perhaps in going like this I shall have in some respects have paid the debt I owe humanity in general if any! You know I've always been rather an idealist, too much so I'm afraid, and have expected too much of myself and of other people. My generation can't look upon this war as the last war of all with the certainty that they could in the last one, but we hope it will be. It's such senseless slaughter on both sides and the bomber planes have by far the dirtier job to do, not that I'm complaining. We can't all be Sir Galahads can we? No all one can hope is that the future generation will get the happiness that we missed through having too much excitement. I know remember the following

(1) If I mention <u>food</u> in any way it means that there's no chance at the time of escape

(2) If I mention <u>clothes</u> in any way it means that there <u>is</u> a chance of getting away

(3) If I mention <u>Letters</u> in any way it means escape emminent

(4) If I mention <u>beer</u>, in any way it means either that I'm on my way out, or that I may be out any moment and in any <u>case</u> I want you to let Air Ministry know that you've heard from me to this effect, so that they can

15 Part of the letter from Goulden Webster, c. 1940 (The Second World War Experience Centre).

the rest of the family will take care of you and if you should want any money don't hesitate to get into touch with S.D. Wayse of my old firm.

Well there's not much else to say except, thanks for all you have done for me, now good bye and God bless you. Say Cheerio to the rest of the family for me and to any of my friends who may enquire, and once again don't upset yourself about me, remember your old philosophy, and try I think that perhaps it was better this way after all.

Your loving son

Boy

P.S.

I've nothing to leave I'm afraid, but you might give my watch to Ronnie, it won't help him to be any more punctual than he ever was!'[73]

Webster was buried at Berlin War Cemetery, along with his crewmates; one of 55,000 members of Bomber Command to lose their lives during the Second World War. His final thought was of future generations reaping the rewards of his sacrifice, and his farewell all the more affecting for that very reason.

Captain Masanobu Kuno

Killed 24 May 1945

THE ROLE OF JAPANESE kamikaze pilots in the Second World War is still a subject that provokes strong reactions. Indeed, the terrorist actions of 9/11 and suicide bombers of Iraq and Afghanistan have been compared with kamikaze pilots. Pilots who survived offer a different perspective: unlike suicide bombers today, they were motivated by love and not hate: 'We were ready to die, but for our families and for Japan.'[74] Throughout the war, and particularly during the period when kamikaze attacks were at their height,[75] Allied soldiers' letters revealed vehement anti-Japanese sentiments; they viewed these men as fanatical, even psychopathic, bloodthirsty murderers: 'non human',[76] as one soldier wrote. Americans nicknamed their piloted glide bombs 'baka-bombs',[77] and when the tactic of using the planes themselves to blow up vessels started being used, the Japanese were further demonised. Kamikaze aircraft contained the lethal duality of a 550-pound bomb and fuel tank of equal weight.

In recent years in Japan, the letters, diaries and poetry of Japanese soldiers and pilots have started to offer different perspectives on their wartime actions. These were incredibly brave individuals who agreed to certain death in defence of Japan – their patriotism comparable with that of every other nation involved in the war. Veterans of the Second World War have largely learned to forgive, even if they cannot forget.

Literally translated as 'heavenly wind', kamikaze had its origins in thirteenth-century Japan when Kublai Khan, the grandson of Genghis Khan, attempted to conquer Japan with one hundred thousand warriors. This plan was overturned when a tempestuous typhoon storm prevented the fleet from reaching Japanese soil. Following this tradition, the kamizake pilots were charged with preventing Americans setting foot on sacred Japanese soil. The initiative to use suicide flights as a weapon originated with Vice Admiral Takejiro Onishi, and by 1944 it was a proper corps with its own uniform – seven buttons with cherry blossom petals and the navy anchor on the sleeve. Men volunteered or were officially drafted, and over the course of the war, 1,036 Japanese pilots died.[78] Lauded as 'hero gods' in the press, many of them still teenagers, pilots took part in a funerary ritual the night before their flights. Wearing white, they symbolically renounced their earthly possessions and were presented with white boxes. Inside, many put locks of hair, nail clippings and a last letter for their family. There was even a nightly radio programme in which some pilots were able to bid a final farewell to loved ones. Many pilots before departing Chiran Tachiari[79] went to a particular local restaurant for a final meal and drank shochu[80] in a solemn farewell gesture. A night watchman at the barracks recalled the whimpering tears of young pilots from underneath their blankets the night before their deaths.

Every kamikaze pilot was given a manual that was kept in the cockpit. It is chilling reading, but provides an incredible insight into the motivation for these men. The manual's jingoistic words drummed into men the importance of their role and urged them into a trance-like state. 'Transcend life and death. When you eliminate all thoughts about life and death, you will be able to totally disregard your earthly life. This will also enable you to concentrate your attention on eradicating the enemy with unwavering determination.' The idea that pilots were robotic maniacs was also somewhat undermined by the book, which stressed the importance of calmness and not eating before a flight, to avoid diarrhoea. It suggested that some men would have been paralysed with fear to the point of losing control of their bodily functions when the time came to *tai-atari*.[81]

The manual also gives a visceral insight into what one might expect to experience in the seconds before a hit. It was a cruel piece of emotional propaganda that clearly had the desired effect on the pilots:

You are two or three metres from the target. You can see clearly the muzzles of the enemy's guns. You feel that you are suddenly floating in the air. At that moment, you see your mother's face. She is not smiling or crying. It is her usual face . . . Remember when diving into the enemy to shout at the top of your lungs: 'Hissatsu!' ('Sink without fail!') At that moment, all the cherry blossoms at Yasukuni shrine in Tokyo will smile brightly at you.[82]

Over 90 per cent of kamikaze pilots were aged between eighteen and twenty-four, and many were recruited from top universities. Few fathers volunteered, but Captain Kuno was one exception (Plate 20). On 23 May 1945, the night before he knew he would die, he wrote a final letter in katakana[83] to his two children, five-year-old Masanori and two-year-old Kiyoko. The survival of the letter humanises the kamikaze pilot that so many people have been quick to despise.

> Dear Masanori and Kiyoko,
> Even though you cannot see me, I will always be watching you. Obey your mother, and do not trouble her. When you grow up, follow a path you like and grow to be fine Japanese persons. Do not envy the father of others, since I will become a spirit and closely watch over you two. Both of you, study hard and help out your mother with work. I cannot be your horse to ride, but you two be good friends. I am a *genki*[84] person who flew a large bomber and finished off all the enemy. Please persevere like your father and avenge[85] my death.
> From Father[86]

The next morning, in a Hayate aircraft, Kuno departed for his final sortie, no doubt waved off by children with cherry-blossom branches,[87] and perhaps wearing a headband bearing the words 'Perfect Win.' He was one part of Operation Kihusi, which sank over 30 and damaged over 350 American vessels between April and June 1945, causing over five thousand casualties. Kuno would have taken just under three hours to reach his target. The destroyer he attacked on 24 May did not sink.

Following his death, Kuno's wife Chiyoko received his letter and gave birth to a third child, Masae, on 18 October 1945; Kuno had not known that she was pregnant. At the end of the war, Chiyoko became a school janitor to make ends meet, and it was only when Masae turned six that she revealed the letter to her children. Now grown-up themselves, the family still talk about their father. Chiyoko says, 'Even if he had not gone as a kamikaze pilot, there were many things he could have done to serve his country, but he was a great husband.'[88]

MAJOR LIONEL WIGRAM

Killed in Italy, 3 February 1944

LIONEL WIGRAM WAS BORN to a Polish father, Maurice, who had been a Sheffield businessman, and his wife, Rebecca. Lionel had a keen intellect and won a law scholarship to Oxford University. He then set up a lucrative solicitor's firm in London's Mayfair, where his income was estimated to be as much as £30,000 by the late 1930s. It bought him a handsome house called Moray Lodge on Camden Hill, where he lived with his wife Olga and their three children: Anthony, Michael and Dena. He had a love of golf and opera – not obvious passions for a man who would become an innovating figure in the British army.

When war broke out, Wigram had been nominated Conservative candidate for Pontefract and was a territorial officer in the London Regiment. In December 1941 he was appointed commander of a newly established central Home Forces Battle School at Barnard Castle in County Durham. Here, Wigram was instrumental in an overhaul of army training. Under his vigorous almost mechanical zeal for 'real' training, the men learned battle tactics using live ammunition, smoke and the cacophonous mayhem they would experience on the front line. He wanted men to be able to think on their feet and act in a rehearsed way amid the chaos and confusion of war. Wigram had an exuberant passion to make the British army the most efficient and well-trained unit in the world. He had his men crawling through mud, charging through hedges and jumping over barbed wire. Wigram himself wanted to be 'fitter and tougher than any Nazi'[89] and threw himself wholeheartedly into every exercise he gave his trainees. He was also a maverick; he was a zealous advocate of hate training, which drummed into the men an almost irrational revulsion for the enemy. Wigram, who was Jewish, was known for his extreme anti-German feelings (perhaps, one obituary wondered, was this 'the source of the inspiration which enabled him to take a job . . . so far removed from his ordinary occupations'[90]) and spearheaded exercises with shouts of 'Kill, kill, kill,' and 'Hate, hate, hate.' Men were splattered with cow's blood during bayonet exercises and taken to abattoirs to witness the gore of a carcass torn apart from limb to limb. His suggestions for radical change in training methods were not immediately welcomed, but by 1942 the War Office finally gave its stamp of approval with the publication of *The Instructors Handbook on Fieldcraft and Battle Drill*, co-authored by Wigram. Barnard Castle became the new School of Infantry.

Wigram went to war ostensibly as a War Office observer during the Sicilian campaign, but in 1943 he took command of a company in the 6th Royal West Kents. Wigram's letters to his wife revealed their intensely personal and loving relationship. The fanatic of the battlefield was replaced by 'Bogul' who missed his beloved 'Cuddle'. Just before he arrived in Italy on 7 July he wrote, 'I haven't had a single letter from anyone at home yet and I shall certainly go half mad when I do!! Well darling, I must say goodbye now. I miss you lots and lots and lots and lots and I love you and the children more and more and more . . . .'

As soon as he landed, Wigram found himself enveloped in the commotion of conflict, from a heavy air raid on landing, to his first outing to the front line on 17 July.

> . . . there was a terrible noise of some shooting from some woods about 100 yds away and bullets whistled round our heads. Seven men were wounded. We picked up revolvers, rifles or anything we had and dashed madly forward to the edge of the olive grove and would hear and see the enemy . . . there were about 300 of them and they were hiding in the wood to do guerrilla work behind our lines. They made themselves a nuisance all that day and night and we lost several men including 3 good officers killed. The sniping at night was most unpleasant. Next day we bombarded the wood with our mortars and attacked but they showed no fight and came out and surrendered. It was very tame – quite an anti climax! I thought I had not been 'blooded' enough so I went up and rejoined the leading BN who were making a big night attack . . . I find my Battle School training invaluable: I know when I am being shot at and when I'm not whilst many 'experienced soldiers' out here have no idea and they get down in a hole just because they hear a noise.

Wigram's enthusiasm for battle shone through his letters. He enjoyed the adventure of war and relished putting training into practice, with tales of swimming along rivers and hiding in thick reeds and rushes. He had a lucky escape when, revolver empty, he encountered a German face to face, but the German surrendered. Even a war wound was glossed over: 'I look down at my hand (left!) and found I had been wounded. I hadn't even felt it! (only a graze – don't worry) . . . it was hair-raising. Every few yards there was wreckage, corpses . . .' It did seem to have momentarily checked his emotions, though, as he continued, 'darling I am going back to the battle tonight. I love you all a lot – more than I ever did. The farmer has a boy about Mike's age . . . gave me quite a 'pang' for a moment . . . PS Don't believe anyone who thinks this is a joy ride.'

His children and relatives lapped up these tales of daring do. His niece Prue asked, 'Have you started your collection of Nazis heads and helmets?' while his son Michael wondered, 'Have you shot any Germans yet?' Wigram's confidence must have had an effect on his wife, who was also doing her bit for the war effort and working in a garage. In August he wrote, 'I have always been lucky as you know – and the luck holds. We have been shelled, bombed and everything else but nothing has come near me to date and I don't think it will.'

Throughout August 1943 Wigram and his men had great successes. On 4 August they captured the fortress of Centurife during a night attack, and four days later wrested control of another town, atop a steep rockface. Confident and full of bravado as ever, Wigram's chief complaint was mosquito bites to the eyes and the resulting quinine he was forced to imbibe three times a day for malaria. War was also giving him time to contemplate politics.

His time in Italy was a 'bitter pill darling. You have such a lively sense of adventure . . . and the fun lies in doing them together. Unfortunately this is one adventure we cannot share which ruins it almost completely.' He wrote incredibly touching letters to his children – including this one in October 1943: 'My dearest babe . . . Whenever we go out at night or dig in on some remote hillside I always find myself gazing up at the stars. It is a great comfort to look up at the Great Bear and the Pole Star and to feel it getting nearer. I often picture you also in the evenings . . . with every lump I swallow there is a lump in my throat.'

Throughout his service in Italy, Wigram's confidence was undimmed: 'I am fated to do something in this war and that my name is NOT written on a bullet.' The last letter he sent home was dated 18 January 1944. As usual it was bright, breezy and self-assured. He was returning to the front following leave in Naples, where he had bought his wife perfume.

In the days running up to his death, Wigram was in the Pizzoferrato area, where the German evacuation was in full swing, and stores emptied on a daily basis as the Germans headed towards Rome. There were estimated to be around forty Germans in the town, and the Allies were making efforts to dig out the guns that had been snowed into the hills. 'It is necessary to check up on everybody . . . and, a gentle "frisking" hurts nobody . . .' noted the war diary.

It was a complex operation, with communications flying back and forth, and artillery pounding the enemy positions. Around forty-five miles of telegraph wire was in use in this area in the first week of February. Wigram was leading what the men endearingly nicknamed 'Wigforce' patrols, but there was also some light relief on 1 February with a football game, 'watched by a large and excited crowd of Italians'.

In the early hours of the morning of 3 February, 'Wigforce' was en route to wipe out the German headquarters in Cisterna. By four o'clock, having negotiated minefields, Wigram and his men were at the base of the village. With one party sent off to attack a gun position, Wigram and his men surrounded two houses and by 4.45 were in position to attack. Surrounded by Allied soldiers, a German sentry came forward. Wigram informed him, 'You are surrounded; put up your hands, we will treat you well, we are British.' With his hands aloft, the sentry walked forward and Wigram moved to take him prisoner. When they were ten yards from the house, two Germans opened fire from a ground-floor window. Wigram was shot and fell to the ground. Suddenly everyone was firing in a pitched battle involving grenades and rifles. Eventually, the Germans withdrew, taking more than fifteen prisoners and shooting fourteen men. The area was finally liberated, but there was a bitter irony that the enemy had escaped and had outgunned the father of battle tactics.[91]

On his death, Wigram's farewell letter was forwarded to his wife. Despite the heady enthusiasm of his wartime letters, he had written this in May 1943 – when he learned he would definitely be leaving for the front. Containing the unique Wigram charm and humour, the letter was also a touching admission of his fear that in the real circus of war, things were not as predictable as on the training field.

To be handed direct to Mrs Wigram in the event of my death or capture or if reported missing.

Dearest

Of course nothing *will* ever happen to me in this war but in case it should I am leaving you a few notes to help you along.

That's a bit Irish – I suppose I'm an Irishman now by contamination.

Now you're a very good business woman really! Of course I have always pretended that you aren't but you are. Look at all those bargains!

But you must be economical as a lot of my income – like Director's fees, legal practise and so on can't be earned if I'm not there to earn it. You should have at least £2000 pa to live on at least which – after all – isn't too bad is it?

I want Anthony to be a lawyer and business man. I want Michael to follow whatever line he fancies – I think he might take to writing or being a Don. I'm sure he'll be studious. Dena of course will marry very young.

I want all the children to go to Oxford.

Well dear I think that's about all. I hope you'll think of me sometimes on Wednesday nights and particularly on that day of days 21st December.[92]

We've had a lot of fun together and I have no regrets.

XXXX   For You
XXXX   For the big ones
XXXX   For the little ones
    Bogul.

Lionel Wigram was killed one day after his thirty-seventh birthday. He was buried next to the church in a small village called Casoli. After his death, letters of condolence flooded to his wife – a mark of his immense popularity among the men who worked alongside him.

Lieutenant Corporal Bryan sent his heartfelt sympathies: 'The word "all" is genuinely applicable . . . his brilliant personality and great courage made him the best known figure in the unit and one whom the men would follow anywhere. It was this courage that finally brought about his death.' Major Forman added,

'We shall miss him sadly in the mess . . . Apart from his tremendous energy and efficiency as an officer his sense of humour, his frankness, his wit and his tremendous zest for life made him a very dear friend. I knew him well enough to realise the immensity of your loss.'

In a letter to Forman, Wigram's widow's loss was all too palpable. 'We were devoted to each other, and I find it hard, impossible to believe that when this cruel war is over he won't come striding home again. Sometimes I am filled with a wild and desperate hope that it has all been a ghastly mistake.'[93]

PRIVATE EUGENE M. COURTRIGHT

Died at Iwo Jima, 18 March 1945

EUGENE COURTRIGHT WAS BORN to parents Emma, a seamstress with German parentage, and Guy (Plate 21). He had two older sisters, Maria and Lorraine, and a younger brother Theodore, or Ted. All the children were particularly close to their father, who had brought them up when he and Emma divorced. Guy instilled in his son a strong work ethic, having lived through the Depression and finally secured work as a truck driver. The tight-knit family lived in a bungalow in Glendale, southern California. Saturday nights were spent at the movies and weekends were filled with mountain hikes. Summers saw regular trips to the beach in the family's beloved Ford Model T. Each morning Eugene's father made pancakes – apart from Saturday mornings, when they were treated to waffles and bacon.

Eugene joined the 27th Marine Regiment as a private first class. This was his local unit, formed in January 1944, and based at Camp Pendleton in California. In January 1945 the unit was given its first operational duty. Operation Detachment aimed to wrest the volcanic island of Iwo Jima from Japanese control. It was a battle that claimed the lives of more marines than any other battle of the Pacific war. It has been estimated that for each square mile gained, the human cost was over three thousand men. Before deploying to Iwo Jima, Courtright wrote his farewell letter to his father.

Iwo Jima was a crucial target for the Americans. Seven hundred and fifty miles from Japan, it would be a perfect base from which to launch fighter planes and escorts aircraft on their raids. On 19 February 1945 the 27th Marines stormed the shores of the island, under orders to cut off Mount Suribachi from the surrounding land. They encountered strong Japanese resistance in the form of heavy fire, landmines and close-quarter combat, not to mention the logistical difficulties of negotiating the rocky terrain. On 16 March the island was announced as secure, but isolated pockets of resistance continued for some months.

Iwo Jima was a battle that was immortalised in an iconic photograph of American marines raising the US flag on Mount Suribachi; a defiant display of victory and American might. Behind the patriotism of the photograph lies an altogether grimmer statistic. It had been a devastating battle for the marines: in the 27th alone, 566 men were killed, and over fifteen hundred wounded. Eugene Courtright died on 18 March, most probably from wounds sustained a few days previously.

Just a few days before hearing of Eugene's death, his father had written him a long letter, destined to be unread. Courtright's father received the devastating news about his son in the 'deeply regret' government telegram that every parent dreaded. It arrived on 26 March, just before eight in the morning. There were no details of Eugene's death, only that he had died of 'wounds sustained in action'.

A small comfort from the shattering news of Eugene's death was a farewell letter he had written.

Dear Dad

Well. Pappy, we're moving out soon, so I figured I'd write you this. It's sort of a farewell letter. I just wanted to tell you these things.

I'm sure going to miss you guys, you and Ted I mean. We sure could of had some good rabbit hunting together. That's no reason why you and Ted shouldn't get a few rabbits for me tho.'

I want you to know Daddy, that you never let me down, like you seem to think you have. You were always good to us, you tried to be a good mother and father to us, and you were. I love you anyhow, you old booze hound.

If you get this letter, you'll be getting some insurance too. Buy a home with it, at least it will help buy a home. Maybe even a farm, you always wanted a farm. Do that for me will you Daddy? That would make me happier (than anything, except maybe to be with you guys again).

Ted will stick by you Pappy, he always was a better buddy to you than I was. I was always too busy. I've already lived a life-time anyhow. Naturally I'd like to come back . . . But if you can't, you can't.

I want you to know, Daddy, that I didn't quit without a fight. I probably took a couple with me. Please give my love to Ted, Marie and Lorraine, my old buddies who did so much for me.

I hope you folks remember me. But don't think about what's happened.

Love Gene.[94]

Eugene was first buried on Iwo Jima, but his father was insistent that he be repatriated, and in May 1947 he was reburied at Fort Rosecran National Cemetery. 'I want him to come home, to be near us,' his father wept.

16 Part of the letter from Eugene Courtright, 1944 (with kind permission of Ted Courtright).

Ted Courtright had been in high school when his brother was killed, and vividly remembered the funeral: the distressing sight of his father and sisters sobbing as they buried Eugene on a balmy day, overlooking the sea. Ted described Pearl Harbor and the Pacific war as the last 'good war. Never since that time has our President, the Congress and our nation been in such accord.' Every reported death in conflict since then has been a hollow reminder of the brother he lost, but through Eugene's farewell letter Ted can continue to remember him vividly and with enduring love.

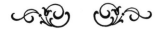

Pilot Officer Michael Andrew Scott
Killed over the English Channel, 24 May 1941

Michael 'Mick' Scott was born in 1916 to William – a doctor – and Kathleen; the family lived in Blackfriar's House, overlooking Chester Racecourse, near to William's medical practice (Plate 22). William and Kathleen had eight children, Mick was particularly close to his older sister Flora, and was profoundly affected by the death of his brother in childhood.

After leaving Shrewsbury School, Mick was working as a teacher when war broke out. Perhaps inspired by his father, who became an army doctor, Scott joined the RAF in 1939 and within nine months was flying operations with Bomber Command's 110 (Hyderabad[95]) Squadron, stationed at RAF Wattisham in Suffolk.

In August 1940, during the Battle of Britain, Scott was increasingly preoccupied with death and the philosophy of war. He wrote reams of poetry questioning why they were fighting, wishing for peace, asking whether he was a coward and condemning war as 'foul bloodstained strife'. For him war signified the intractable decimation of culture and humanity. He was free in the air; it was the 'guiltless towns' below that bore the brunt of their actions.

[I] . . . look forward to the time when Vienna will sing again, when the dome of Sacre Coeur will once more look down upon a Mass of Thanksgiving, sung by a free choir of children uninfluenced by the Nazi doctrine of fear and oppression. This Spring will come, and till it does come, we must hibernate under the anaesthetic that our work provides. The thought of coming to a sticky end does not worry me in the least . . . Life is merely a passing phase in our development . . .

On 20 August 1940, twenty miles south of St Omer, a Blenheim was shadowed by a Messerschmitt 110 and bombing over Dunkirk was 'heavy and intense'.[96] This was a very real war. Knowing this was perhaps the prompt for Scott to write a farewell letter to his father.

Dear Daddy,

As this letter will only be used after my death, it may seem a somewhat macabre document, but I do not want you to look on it in that way. I have always had a feeling that our stay on earth, that thing which we call 'Life', is but a transitory stage in our development, and that the dreaded monosyllable 'Death' ought not to indicate anything to be feared. I have had my fling and must now pass on to the next stage, the consummation of all earthly experience. So don't worry about me; I shall be all right.

I would like to pay tribute to the courage which you and mother have shown, and will continue to show, in these tragic times. It is easy to meet an enemy face to face, and to laugh him to scorn, but the unseen enemies Hardship, Anxiety and Despair are a very different problem. You have held the family together as few could have done, and I take off my hat to you.

Now for a bit about myself. You know how I hated the idea of War, and that hate will remain with me forever. What has kept me going is the spiritual force to be derived from music, its reflections of my own feelings, and the power it has to uplift a soul above earthly things. Mark[97] has the same experience as I have in this though his medium of encouragement is Poetry. Now I am off to the source of Music, and can fulfil the vague longings of my soul in becoming part of the fountain whence all good comes. I have no belief in a personal God, but I *do* believe most strongly in a spiritual force which was the source of our being, and which will be our ultimate goal. If there is anything worth fighting for, it is the right to follow our own paths to this goal and to prevent our children from having their souls sterilised by Nazi doctrines. The most horrible aspect of Nazism is its system of education, of driving instead of leading out, and of putting State above all things spiritual. And so I have been fighting.

All I can do now is to voice my faith that this war will end in Victory, and that you will have many years before you in which to resume normal civil life. Good luck to you!

Mick.

A thoughtful man of considered words, Scott wrote passionately about the politics of war and the reasons for fighting. Unlike many of his comrades, he did not enter or engage in war in a spirit of gleeful adventure, and he had moral misgivings. That he signed up to the RAF despite these reservations spoke volumes about his character and underlined the overwhelming sense of duty men had at this time, when everyone was called on to do their bit. In a letter to his father he mused that war was,

> purely economic . . . We are not fighting for Freedom but in order to retain our own spoils . . . from conquest. From our point of view it is a necessary evil, and therefore I cannot stand out and see others give up everything for my personal security. I do not believe that the average German is a worse fellow than any of us . . . I think that the R.A.F is a fine service, and I am proud to form a part of it . . . I have always wanted to fly; to cut the umbilical cord which ties me down to the earth . . .

RAF life gave crews plenty of time to sit, wait and think. During an air raid Scott was inspired to write poetry. Steeped in the cultural arts, writing was his way of coping with the devastation in which he was engulfed.

> Why do I weep the follies of my kind? . . .
> Why do I weep this man-made, frenzied strife . . .
> Nature is changeless; Earth is full with life;
> Why do I weep?

In lighter moments he wrote about missing Wiltshire and tales of boyhood scamps. It must have been a temporary relief from the underlying sense of foreboding he had.

Scott's diary reveals much about his character and his infatuation with flight. He was an accomplished pilot, gaining 88 per cent in his navigation test in early January. Being in the air was a unique experience that allowed him to be at one with the birds. He wrote of 'fiery sunsets' and extraordinary light patterns in the sky. At the start of 1941 he was hopeful that war might soon end and poignantly wondered where he would be by the same time the following year. He also kept meticulous records of the music and books he was reading. He read voraciously – from books on the Hitler Youth and Everest, to James Joyce, P.G. Wodehouse and Graham Greene. He escaped into the classical music of Haydn, Tchaikovsky and Beethoven between shooting drills. By March, despite his terror at flying Blenheims, he was up in the air and enjoying every minute: 'descended in spirals over Blighty . . . A grand life.' On 3 May Scott was becoming tense: 'soon it will be the real thing!'

On 6 May 1941 it was 'the real thing'. Six aircraft left the base at 11.15, and spotted an enemy convoy of five ships, three destroyers and a submarine. The planes were targeted with heavy anti-aircraft fire as they swooped down to spray the decks with machine-gun fire. Only five aircraft returned and later that day the planes were ordered back out to bomb the convoy at night. Setting off at ten o'clock, they bombed the ships with 250-pound bombs, and all returned safely at two in the morning. The following day, the squadron was stood down from operational flying, and instead carried out '7 local sorties'.[98]

That day, Scott wrote a second farewell letter. He had clearly been shaken by the loss of one crew, the onslaught of fire they had encountered and their retribution bombing. That same day he had been reading Keats's 'Ode to a Nightingale', and noted that he had not flown well. In the letter he seemed to have absolutely made up his mind that he would die very soon, and was apparently reconciled to that. It was written as though he had experienced some kind of premonition and that Keats's poem had reinforced the transience of life and freedom of flight. It led Scott to write an almost romanticised vision of death – an end to the living hell of war.

> Dear Mother and Daddy.
> You now know that you will not be seeing me any more, and perhaps the knowledge is better than the months of uncertainty which you have been through. There are one or two things which I should like you to know, and which I have been too shy to let you know in person.
> Firstly let me say how splendid you both have been during this terrible war. Neither of you have show how hard things must have been, and when peace comes this will serve to knit the family together as it should always have been knit. As a family we are terribly afraid of showing our feelings, but war has uncovered unsuspected layers of affection beneath the crust of gentlemanly reserve.
> Secondly I would like to thank you both for what you have done for me personally. Nothing has been too much trouble, and I have appreciated this to the full, even if I have been unable to show my appreciation.
> Finally as a word of comfort. You both know how I have hated war, and dreaded the thought of it all my life. It has, however, done this for me. It has shown me new realms where man is free from earthly restrictions and conventions; where he can be himself playing hide and seek with the clouds, or watching a strangely silent world beneath, rolling quietly on, touched only by vague unsubstantial shadows moving for the price I have had to pay for this experience. This price is incalculable, but it may just as well be incalculably small as incalculably large, so why worry? . . .
> There is only one thing to add. Good luck to you all!
> Mick

Just over ten days later, Scott's diary stated 'On the battle orders for tomorrow'. The last entry was on 18 May:

> A very heavy day. All formation flying. I found this very hard work, but it comes a bit easier towards the end . . . Apparently we are to do a show on Tuesday evening with fighter escort. May the Gods be with us! Formation flying is the most

I append a rough will, which may not be legally binding, but will, I am sure, be carried out.

There is only one thing to add. Good luck to you all!

Mick.

17 Part of the letter from Michael Scott, 7 May 1941 (Imperial War Museums).

companiable of pursuits. Twelve dots in the sky linked by a spirit of fellowship . . . What more could man ask. Today was the first day of summer.

Under the date 24 May Flora Scott, his sister, concluded his diary with the stark words, 'Missing Believed Killed. No further news of Mick was ever heard.'[99]

On 24 May, ten aircraft were ordered to attack enemy convoys around Rotterdam, Dunkirk and Gap de la Hague. They took off in formation at 11.25, and four aircraft attacked a 2,000-ton merchant ship ten miles off Borkum. Each aircraft dived as low as fifty feet, spraying the ship with machine-gun fire, dropping four 250-pound bombs, and four 25-pound incendiary bombs. The vessel was decimated. Two aircraft then attacked a stationary armed ship twenty miles from Borkum, from two hundred feet. No word of whether they had been successful was received. One of these was Scott's Blenheim aircraft, and it did not return to the base. 'This crew have been reported missing' recorded the log book.[100]

For Scott's family, it was an agonising wait for news. His death was unconfirmed. Had the crew ditched in the sea, they would have been as good as dead at this time, but had they been taken prisoner, there was still a chance. It must have been a hellish few months. In July and then November official notes from the Air Ministry confirmed that there had been 'no further evidence or news regarding him'.

Finally, on Christmas Eve 1941, came the news his family had dreaded. 'I must say that in the absence of any news to the contrary I had been assuming that your Son was a prisoner in the hands of the Germans, but unfortunately this has proved to be a false hope.'

When news came of Scott's death, his sister Flora felt immediately that he was there with her – and remained so for the rest of her life. She always kept his photograph on her dressing table, talking often and fondly of her beloved brother. Mick Scott's parents simply crumbled in the desperate atmosphere, with husband not knowing how to console wife. More tragedy was to come: the family lost another son in Mark in the war, and when Bill – who had joined the navy – survived the war, he pledged to marry and give the family three sons. At the grand age of fifty-three, he indeed married and went on to have three sons.

~ *7* ~

THE FALKLANDS CONFLICT

22nd April 1982

I hope you will not find this letter macabre, but I could not let things end on an unfinished note. Thank you for giving me ten very happy years of married life and two lovely children. Thank you for managing our affairs so well during my enforced absences. They say naval wives are a very special breed and you are no exception. Unfortunately one of the things we had to accept was the chance that one day the Royal Navy would be invited to carry out its main job for real – and now that has happened . . . You know the feelings of those who could not come with us, so I hope you can understand my willingness to be part of this operation. It will be hard for you to accept but please do not grieve for too long. You and our children still have very full lives ahead and you must fulfil them as best you see fit. All I ask is that you look back on our time together as one of pure joy, that our children remember me as their father, and that Howard retains the Prime surname. You know better what I have tried to convey than I can possibly put into words. Goodbye and God bless you my darling. With all my never ending love and appreciation. John.[1]

WHEN NEWS FILTERED THROUGH that an amphibious Argentinian force had landed on the Falkland Islands on 2 April 1982, most people's immediate reaction was to ask where the Falkland Islands were. These barren inhospitable islands the size of Wales, around eight thousand miles away in the South Atlantic, formed the gateway to the South Pole and had been colonised by Britain in 1833. Operation Rosario was instigated by the Argentinian military junta under General Leopoldo Galtieri, who hoped to boost flagging support by reclaiming sovereignty of the islands. Galtieri claimed Argentina had the rightful claim, having inherited the islands (known in Spanish as Islas Malvinas) from Spain in the division of the New World in the fifteenth century. British Prime Minister Margaret Thatcher was emphatic in her declaration that Falklanders were 'of British tradition and stock'. She dispatched a taskforce to the islands under orders to reoccupy them if the Argentinians refused to withdraw. Colonial warfare was alive and kicking – even in the twentieth century – leaving Falkland's passionately British inhabitants embroiled in an unexpected war.

Despite British confidence, the conflict had no foregone conclusion. Argentina had superior air-power,[2] although its army of conscripts was an inferior force to the skilled and integrated British taskforce. This was a war played out in colour and sound on television screens: images of men being airlifted from bombed ships, the shouts and yells of soldiers buoyed up with anticipation, Argentinian jets streaking through San Carlos 'Bomb Alley' Bay, wind-battered commandoes weighed down with combat kit stalking their way across peaty grounds and desolate hills. It was consumed by a gripped British public.

The conflict has been one mired in political controversy that should not cloud the sobering statistics of almost a thousand men killed: 255 British and 655 Argentinian. It was a conflict that continues to provoke anger and bitterness among politicians, many veterans and bereaved families. Amid the diplomatic manoeuvring, the military fight was carried on by men simply doing their job and following orders.

Galtieri's supporters have maintained that war was engineered by Britain to circumnavigate negotiations that may have led to the loss of sovereignty. To his death, Galtieri proclaimed he had 'no regrets . . . Las Malvinas son Argentinas'.[3] This, coming from a man convicted of human rights abuses and 'misconduct' during the conflict, has held little sway over the majority of Argentinians and Britons. On the British side, the decision to invade has been largely written into history as unequivocal: 'We shall remain ready to exercise our right to resort to force,' declared Thatcher in Parliament as forces set sail. By the end of April sixty-five ships were heading south, carrying over fifteen thousand troops.

To this day, British troops remain posted in the islands. Three remembrance services are held each year to commemorate the dead, and countless veterans have returned on pilgrimages to lay personal ghosts and demons to rest. Perhaps with the passage of time a more dispassionate view could be taken of the decision to commit men to war, and the political apportionment of blame finally put to an end.

Hope for a Diplomatic Solution and the Voyage to War

Emotional and jubilant scenes were the backdrop to forces leaving Britain. While Thatcher was 'talking very quietly about succeeding', war did not feel imminent for the men leaving for the far-flung Falklands. 'What we're going to do when we get there no-one knows,'[4] wrote one seaman. In early April, hopes remained high that a diplomatic solution would still triumph, but even so men were at pains to put on a brave face for their loved ones: 'This is great fun, and very much like Maggie Thatcher to stick up for our few remaining colonies with a show of force . . . the whole thing may blow over in a week.'[5]

Nevertheless, it was a wrench to leave. Captain David Hart Dyke onboard HMS *Coventry* assured his wife, 'I feel very sad not to be seeing you on 6 April. This is where you have to be a long-suffering and patient naval wife. Shall always be thinking of you and the girls very much.' He was acutely aware of the 'fearful responsibility'[6] that lay ahead. Lieutenant General Sir Hew Pike admitted, 'the whole affair is proceeding with an increasing feeling of inevitability about it, but everyone is highly confident and wanting to see it through – I hope we do.'[7]

The realisation that this was going to be a real war came as the taskforce was en route to the Falklands. David Devenny, a Royal Marine commando, recalled being issued with Geneva Convention cards and details for blood and plasma supply. The welfare officers suggested that men write wills, and amid briefings on survivability came the grim sense of events ratcheting up and a diplomatic resolution ebbing away.

Swords were metaphorically drawn as a two-hundred-mile exclusion zone was declared around the islands. South Georgia was retaken on 25 April, and on 1 May the RAF targeted Stanley airport, followed by a Harrier strike at dawn and a naval bombardment in the afternoon. The first major loss of life happened on 2 May, with the bombing of the Argentinian 14,000-ton ship *General Belgrano*, which left 368 crewmembers dead. This controversial act was ordered by Prime Minister Thatcher, who deemed *Belgrano* an intolerable threat, despite the fact that it was heading away from the islands. The attack gave rise to the famous 'Gotcha' headline in the *Sun* newspaper, which celebrated each 'wallop' with a jingoistic cheer that Britain 'had the Argies on their knees'.[8] The sinking caused consternation in Britain, and was fuel for a growing band of opponents to the war, who saw the conflict as motivated by commercialism driven by potential mineral gains in Antarctica. On the whole, Britain was behind its troops and that was hugely comforting to the men heading into the conflict thousands of miles away. 'Wars are not easily won by nations if they are divided or unconvinced as to the rightness of the cause,'[9] wrote David Hart Dyke.

A REAL CONFLICT:
BATTLE CONDITIONS AND THE 'BLUEY' LIFELINE

The voyage to the Falklands took two weeks, and was largely taken up with operational practices and briefings. Men endured incredibly rough seas, sleeping in bags tied to mattresses tied to bunks, or 'pits'. As information came in from the BBC World Service and men waited for operational commands, the mood onboard was light-hearted, at least outwardly. Brian Tucknott wrote to his mother about 'doing Fred Astair singing in the rain' in warm downpours, and of porpoises 'jumping in and out of the water, we have even seen a few sharks off the stern of the ship attacking the gash bags that are thrown overboard'.[10] Another man reassured his wife that 'we're all in good spirits on the ship, there's a feeling we're going to do something useful for a change.'[11]

Morale boosts came in simple form for the Falklands taskforce, namely food (and beer), friends and letters. Many men wrote about how a bar of nutty (chocolate) could make all the difference after a punishing seventeen-hour day, and Brian Tucknott was glad of the readily available beer. 'It's not a bad job though as the ship's crew isn't on a beer ration yet so I can still do a little business now and then, mind you I have got to be a little more careful in the future as the other morning I was accused of being seasick when it was really a hangover.'[12]

Letters were a lifeline to home, although their arrival was spasmodic. On board HMS *Coventry* the advent of post by helicopter was the highlight of the day. Rear Admiral John Lippiett recalled how the broadcast 'Mail is now ready for collection' was met with cheers. Men would read their post greedily in a moment, then re-read it in more reflective mood at night, imagining their family at home with all its comforts. 'Darling one, I long to hear all your news, even the smallest detail, for it all brings you much closer to me,'[13] wrote Lippiett.

This conflict also saw the introduction of 'familygrams', where men could send a brief but reassuring message home quickly. These became vital reassurances in the aftermath of news reports that told of deaths and hits, but often without naming the vessels. Another sign of changing technology came in the number of taped messages that went back and forth. For Heather Prime, one of her husband's tapes brought the war viscerally into her living room as she heard the interruption of 'Take cover, take cover, take cover' during a recording – a scenario that induced dread in her and glee in her young son, clamouring for news of his father's heroics.

To be able to write a few words home was a welcome escape from the pressure and uncertainty of war. It was a means of articulating the mundane as much as the profound. Hew Pike explained:

> I do feel I need to write just as much, more if anything, as I suppose one feels that much more remote . . . I think of you all constantly and please don't carry too heavy a burden of worry . . . I rather liked this extract from a letter by Marlborough to Sarah Churchill: 'My dearest soul I love you so well and have set my heart so entirely on ending my days in quiet with you, that you may be so far at ease to be assured that I never venture myself but when I think the service of Queen and Country required it.' That is exactly how I feel . . .[14]

Men at sea have described the unimaginable tension as they waited for bombs to be dropped. They were often working incredibly long hours – up to seventy-two hours non-stop in some instances. Paul Callus wrote to his parents and revealed:

> The truth of the matter is that we are all scared witless, especially after the *Sheffield* had been hit by an exocet.[15] That she got hit at all was a 'comedy of errors' only not as funny . . . I think we will be invading in the next few days. Please don't worry about me as I think they are not posing too much of a threat to us.[16]

On land, men had to deal with the disorienting terrain, and lived in four-foot trenches full of water and covered with turf. The romantic names of the Falkland mountains – Tumbledown and Two Sisters – belied the horrific actions they staged. For the Argentinian conscripts, no more attuned to this hostile environment, the conditions were horrendous. Children sent pocketmoney to buy food for these half-starved men, and the soldiers wrote anguished letters to the islanders, begging for supplies. 'Excuse me, please, I'm hungry & I wish . . . some sweet things,' begged one. Another wrote, 'We're sorry but we're hungry . . . When you see a man with stars or red lines you can't speak with us,' and requested chocolate, 'toothbrash' and a 'piece of ham'.[17] They were fed a tirade of lies by the junta, who insisted that victory was theirs at a time when they must have known the fight was unwinnable, and these pitiful letters were met with great sympathy by islanders.

THE FIRST HIGH-TECH WAR: LAND, AIR AND SEA

The Falklands Conflict was a war fought on land, sea and from the air. It was the dawn of the digital age of battle, with interconnected attacks coordinated via radio and radar. The Argentinians had longer-range weapons, but these were ineffective at night, when the British were supreme. The missiles and weapons used during the conflict were more accurate than those used in any previous war, which led to a massive reduction in casualties. Men onboard ship wore either white overalls treated with chemicals to make them non-flammable or 'Number 8s' (blue cotton shirts and trousers) and anti-flash gear (hoods and gloves worn to protect any bare skin exposed to fire, flash or explosion). When missiles struck, the results were catastrophic. Limbs blasted off, gruesome shrapnel wounds and horrific burns inflicted on men trapped inside vessels that became iron-clad fireballs came to characterise this conflict. For the countless men – many of whom were still in their teens and some only sixteen years old – this was not the war of Hollywood films.

The impact of witnessing such bloodshed and carnage left many men mentally scarred. It is no secret that more veterans have since killed themselves than were killed in the conflict. One Argentinian veteran, wracked with guilt at killing a soldier at Mount Longdon, wrote an open letter of remorse:

> We were the victims of incomprehensible humanity, your life ended and I feel your absence profoundly. I know today that deep inside I did not intend to provoke your death. I know that your family weeps for you, that your mother, your father, your wife, your brother, your son, your girlfriend, all misses you. I suffer your disappearance because I was part of it. I honour your courage by always thinking of you. I do not allow myself to forget any of your last moments, your last cries of pain, moments that are present in me, as if they had just happened.[18]

There is no doubt that many British soldiers felt these emotions as keenly.

The first major hit on the British came just two days after the sinking of *Belgrano*, with an Exocet missile strike on HMS *Sheffield*. The ship sank under tow six days later with the loss of twenty crewmen, and it sent shockwaves through Britain as the conflict suddenly snowballed. Men generally tried to protect loved ones at home from the horrors they were witnessing – in contrast to previous conflicts, where almost visceral details had been the norm. Brian Tucknott joked, 'Having a loverly time glad your not here,'[19] while on 11 May David Hart Dyke assured his wife, 'I am confident that we shall survive unharmed . . . A tumultuous homecoming is not far away.'[20] Censorship had come into force soon after the conflict started, preventing operational details being divulged in letters home. More than that, though, there seemed to be a shared and unspoken agreement among men that to dampen spirits at home with tales of destruction would do no good for morale. Hew Pike only revealed in his personal notes the 'feeling of loneliness, of insignificance, of expendability in this great enterprise . . . the accidents of war are no more than the accidents of life in more concentrated form, and in a greater madness.'[21]

SURRENDER AND HOMECOMING

On 14 June 1982 Argentina surrendered as British troops liberated Port Stanley. Thatcher's lethal gamble had paid off, and she was hailed the most popular prime minister since Churchill. Troops received a rapturous welcome home as crowds thronged harbours, waving flags and banners. At Cheltenham Racecourse on 3 July 1982 Thatcher's speech to her Conservative Party affirmed a rebirth of a resolute and patriotic Britain: 'We faced them squarely . . . Britain is not prepared to be pushed around.' It was a sentiment shared by most men who fought in the conflict, who had to believe that comrades who had been killed had not died in an inconsequential skirmish, but had died in the service of a people who clung desperately to the notion of queen and country.

It was with mixed emotions that men welcomed the end of the conflict. A relieved John Lippiett wrote on 17 June, 'The government has acted boldly and with excellent timing at every stage – without seeming too bellicose. Sounds pompous of me to say so, but I didn't think politicians had it in them to be so resolute in war! Let us hope that the final solution is a political success to follow up the interim military solution.'[22] Meanwhile Ian McKay, killed in the last days of the war, had bitterly penned, 'To be honest, once we have given them a hammering . . . the Argentinians can have the place. It really is fit for nothing.'[23] For most men there was simply quiet relief that the fighting was over.

Farewell Letters: Common Themes

Although few men headed to the Falklands with morbid thoughts in mind, that mentality changed once the seriousness of the situation was confirmed. Tragically, some had no chance to write. Pam Boggs, whose Marine son Paul Callan was fatally injured on 27 May, did not receive any post from him. Her only letter came from the padre on HMS *Uganda* where Paul died: 'I gave him the last rites. Though he was always unaware that he would die. I thought it kinder not tell him and I waited until he was unconscious.'[24] Padre Alf Hayes recalled a definite increase in attendance at Mass, confessions and prayer sessions as the taskforce neared the Falklands, and he himself took the opportunity to write a farewell letter to his father. 'It was sobering and it seemed like the right thing to do,' he recalled.

It was suggested that men should write wills if they had not already done so. In a letter home from HMS *Ambuscade* John Lippiett was careful to stress that this was simply procedure: 'The will is a requirement for everyone onboard and needs depositing with bank or solicitor . . . But *not* needed, please note!!'[25] Additionally, for the first time in combat, some welfare officers advised men to consider writing a farewell letter. Former Commando David Devenny recalled being encouraged not to leave events unresolved: 'If I die, will what I write in this letter make any matters worse?' they were urged to think.

For the majority of men, however, writing the letter was a very personal, private act, rarely discussed with colleagues:

> This is, in fact, the last letter that I will be sending for a while until Chile starts sending our mail back for us. But then, of course, it will be censored and even though only by the padre, doctor or dentist, not people who I want to read my personal thoughts to you. I love you very much indeed.[26]

There was an unspoken sense of foreboding, a silent acknowledgement that men knew they would not all return. In particular, those in senior positions – being privy to guarded information – were acutely aware of what lay ahead, and they took the opportunity to write a letter. David Hart Dyke, for instance, realised the odds were against them surviving as the conflict progressed, and that it was only a matter of time before the ship was hit from the air. Openly admitting this to the ship's company would have been disastrous for morale, so his way of coping was to write a letter:

> If you get this letter, I have slipped beneath the waves and am utterly at peace in the next world. Please try very hard not to be too sad, although I know it will be difficult. Remember, I will always be aware when you are sad and I will always be trying very hard to make sure you remain happy for the rest of your life. I will always be with you . . . Look to the future and your life with the girls – this may mean marrying again if it's the way to have a happy and fulfilled life for you all. For this reason, it will have my full blessing . . . Be brave, talk about me and laugh about me and always remember I am still around . . .[27]

Censorship came into play early on in the conflict, and some men took the opportunity to write this most private of letters before it could be read by the designated censor onboard. John Prime believed this was one reason he wrote his farewell letter at such an early stage. In addition, his mother had suffered the pain of loss during war without closure, when her husband was officially reported missing presumed killed in action in Burma during the Second World War. Fortunately, she heard six months later that he was in fact alive, albeit wounded. Subconsciously he wanted to ensure he had tied up loose ends and, although it was incredibly emotional to write, he found the letter cleared his mind, allowing him to get on with the job in hand.

Indeed, there was a tacit practicality to Falklands farewell letters but, unlike previous conflicts where men would write specific instructions home, the motive behind such letters during this conflict was to achieve a sense of closure. It was a job ticked off the list that would not then impede the mission ahead. Captain Ken Hames remembered writing a last letter to his mother on the Plymouth quayside on a scruffy piece of paper, assuring her that 'the rose bush would still grow whether I'm there or not' – this poignant farewell was in stark contrast to the fact he 'didn't sit there with tears welling up; I had too many other things to think about.'

Farewell letters from the Falklands were overwhelmingly preoccupied with the writer's love for their family, and advice for how the family should continue to live after the writer's death. There are many instances of letters that were sent that contained almost subconscious farewells, and it was only on re-reading them that men realised the underlying enormity of what they had written. John Lippiett's 10 May letter contained all the emotions of a final farewell: 'All I've got time to say is that I love you and that is the most important thing in the world to me. You are the focus of my life and I couldn't be happier than having it that way. This strange situation we are in just emphasises the point and makes it all the clearer . . .'[28]

Many men who wrote farewell letters in this conflict actually survived, allowing us a unique first-hand insight into the process of writing this letter and the events that may have prompted it. Their letters are no less poignant than their historical predecessors', though it is noticeable that they lack the same bellicosity. That patriotism and absolute sense of duty was present, but in a final letter it was love and farewell to the family that would always have the last word.

LIEUTENANT COMMANDER GLEN ROBINSON-MOLTKE

Killed 25 May 1982

GLEN ROBINSON-MOLTKE WAS BROUGHT up in Mirfield, Yorkshire (Plate 23). His father had been in the navy and passed on a love of sailing to his son. At eighteen, Glen enrolled in the naval academy at Dartmouth: the first step in a promising career. In 1972 he met twenty-two-year-old Christine Moltke at the British Embassy in Copenhagen; her father was governor of Copenhagen and a friend of the ambassador. Over cocktails, they caught each other's eye and it was love at first sight. They married in 1976 and children soon followed – Michael in 1979 and Hélène in 1981.

In autumn 1981 Glen was appointed executive officer of HMS *Coventry*, commanded by Captain David Hart Dyke. The ship sailed in January 1982 for NATO exercises in the North Atlantic and its return was planned for April. The Argentinian invasion of the Falklands scuppered those plans, leading to great tragedy for the Robinson-Moltke family.

The first indication that Glen was even heading for the Falklands came in a telegram in early April 1982. It simply stated: 'Going South. Possibly several weeks. Love and miss you all.' Christine received the telegram while staying at her parents in Copenhagen with the two young children. She remembered bursting into tears and her parents retrieving a decent bottle of red from the cellar as they took in the news. From the outset, they were all aware of the seriousness of the situation. As early as March, Glen had hoped for a non-military resolution, saying, 'if only everybody will keep talking, there may be a solution.'

His first letter from the conflict was dated 16 April:

> Alexander Haig[29] seems to be on an impossible mission as both Governments are thoroughly dug in. There can be no justification in the Argentinian case – particularly as the only race ever to have lived in the Falklands are the British. Anyone who believes there is justification would have to agree to Germany taking over Denmark! . . . We hear that the Argentinian conscript army are unhappy living in tents with little food or water. That will teach them to think they can just walk in and do what they like with a chunk of England!

There was no doubt in Glen's mind that they were doing the right thing. There was to be 'no faffing about' when it came to British territory.

Letters back and forth were 'completely vital' to Christine and Glen as the only real communication for men and their families, and Glen had always been a prolific letter-writer. From his letter of 30 April, it was clear that tension was mounting for the men at sea: 'I will not be able to relax for many nights now. My cabin is very empty: I have no door, just photographs stuck on the wall of you, Michael and Hélène. I am wearing them out I look at them so often! I need your strength so much now my darling. Keep smiling – and keep the children smiling.' Nevertheless, Glen was still clinging onto the small hope of a diplomatic solution: 'All they have to do is take their flag down and move out! Then we can talk.'

Christine recalled a clear turning point in her husband's letters even before HMS *Sheffield* was hit on 4 May 1982, an event that shook men at sea as well as families at home. Glen was already confiding in Captain Hart Dyke that he feared he was going to die. Hart Dyke recalled the 'testing' conversation they had in May when risks were mounting and they were edging closer to enemy air fire. Glen believed he would not get home. It was a courageous thing to admit, and he gained the utmost respect from his captain for being so open and honest.

Glen was a forthright and fearless man: not the type to shelter Christine from his thoughts. Inevitably, she was extremely worried, but knew that her husband would still be getting on with his job and keeping busy. Indeed, his captain remembered him as a true professional who kept morale and spirits high in the men, despite his personal misgivings. In many ways Glen's letters were an outlet for him to express his sense of foreboding, allowing him then to get on with the task of rallying the ship's company and upping the morale of his men. Christine herself found that keeping busy was the best way to cope with the news reports and uncertainty from the Falklands: 'I just thought, let's keep the show on the road.'

On 5 May, Glen reacted to news of *Sheffield* being hit: 'We now have the list of "missing" persons from *Sheffield* and 22 is a much smaller number than we first feared. The loss though is enormous in every possible aspect. I can see us losing the war if we are not careful. Everyone is very jumpy and nervous and some very dangerous decisions are being made.' On 9 May he described how they had downed an Argentinian helicopter – a vital morale boost for the men. These events clearly gave him cause for concern, however, and a letter two days later was suffused with a sense of apprehension:

I love you and the children more than you will ever know. It is strange how a lot of thoughts and values change when each word could be your last. Everything is more desperate and more honest perhaps. I have been terrified once or twice, but now I believe we have settled down and will get it right when we need to. We had better!

Christine recalled that her husband had a premonition long before the Falklands that he would die. On a Christmas walk with his wife in December 1981 he told her, 'everything is sorted if and when I get run over by a bus.' Just five days before the attack on *Coventry* that would claim his life, Glen wrote a farewell letter to Christine:

Perhaps today will be the last 'writing day' for a while as I expect to be at Action Stations for some time. The ship is pulling together well and for most of us spirits are high . . .

My darling, I have certainly not been away as long this time as in the past, but I have not left the three of you before – and certainly have never before thought that I might not see you again. I have been through a few such periods on this trip and it is very thought-provoking. Life is too short – and I started mine with you far too late.

Give me strength and pray for all of us. Keep the children happy and smiling always. Good night my darling. All my love – Glen.[30]

On 25 May 1982 the Fuerza Aérea Argentina (the Argentinian Air Force) had been given a mission specifically targeted at HMS *Coventry* and *Broadsword*. Both ships were in a precarious vulnerable spot, deliberately positioned to draw Argentinian fire so that British soldiers could land safely. Two raids were planned: the first was abandoned when *Coventry* downed one of the aircraft; the second – Skyhawks carrying 1,000-pound bombs – was successful.

Argentinian pilot Barrionuevo released his bombs, and all three hit the ship. Fitted with delay fuses, one bomb failed to explode. Seconds later, one detonated in the bowels of the ship, tearing through the port side. The third bomb had not exploded, but had ripped a massive hole through the deck. As water poured in, fire was raging through the rest of the ship. When the bombs hit, Glen was in the operations room and was swiftly engulfed in a fireball. Through acrid smoke and menacing flames, a comrade spotted him moving and dragged him up to the deck, forcing a lifejacket onto his limp body.

As the ship started listing, it was clear that abandonment was the only option, and life rafts were released. Men recalled how the calm process of evacuation contrasted with the panicked pandemonium onboard: a gut-wrenching cacophony of men shouting, fire roaring, metal creaking and groaning, and smoke billowing. Among the chaos, Glen was ordered to jump overboard. In shock and concussed, his body had completely shut down. He fell overboard, but hit one of the stabilisers, puncturing his lifejacket and breaking his neck. He was never seen again.

Back in Britain and living in Petersfield, close to the Hart Dykes, Christine soon knew *Coventry* had been hit; she was immediately crippled with fear. Cruelly, she had to wait an agonising four days – 'total hell' – before her husband's death was confirmed. The news was a devastatingly bitter relief from the tension of not knowing. On hearing the news, she broke down and was sedated for two days. Christine recalled a chaplain visiting her in bed, where he knelt and said a prayer. She remembers how, as she turned to the window, the green leaves on the trees seemed brown and wizened.

Glen Robinson-Moltke's last letter arrived after his death. Christine recalled the unbelievably strange sensation of receiving these almost ghostly words, and it ignited a tiny hope that perhaps the news had been wrong. In the days and months following his death, the letter provided incalculable comfort, and Christine found herself reading and re-reading it.

Similar to many bereaved relatives who feel an inner compulsion to retrace steps and stand on the spot where tragedy occurred, Christine has made four trips to the Falklands. On the first, in 1983, she went alone. Despite her grief, she recalls it as a 'wonderful experience'; a chance finally to be alone, reflect and be at peace. One trip allowed her to be in the exact spot where her husband had fallen: an emotional voyage onboard a ship whose sonar picked up *Coventry*'s otherworldly signal from the seabed.

Glen's Falklands letters were literally all Christine had left of her husband. Tragically, his body was never recovered, and all his valuables had gone down when *Coventry* sank. She created a scrapbook for her children, and intends that his letters will go to them eventually.

In 1998 Christine remarried, to Michael Mates, her local MP, whom she first met when establishing the Falklands Family Association. In a strange prophetic coincidence, in October 1981, Glen had spotted Mates's picture in a local newspaper and told Christine that she should 'go to him if you're ever in trouble'.

Glen Robinson-Moltke was one of nineteen men killed when HMS *Coventry* was bombed. He lives on in his children who, sadly, were too young really to remember their father but have inherited his loyal and compassionate nature as well as his striking looks. For Christine, Glen's letters are a priceless legacy. 'I'd be prepared to part with anything I have, but not the letters.'

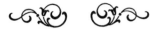

LIEUTENANT COMMANDER DAVID MORGAN

Survived

BORN IN FOLKESTONE IN 1947, David Morgan was the son of a former Fleet Air Arm Seafire pilot and a nurse (Plate 24). Brought up in and around Kent, he boarded at Sir Roger Manwood's Grammar School and harboured dreams of flying. His ambitions were temporarily halted with the discovery of a serious heart defect in 1964, but after surgery he was able to join the navy and train as a helicopter pilot in 1966 at RNAS Culdrose. Five years later he transferred to the RAF, and was based at Odiham, where he met his first wife Carol. They married in 1971, and went on to have two children: Elizabeth and Charles.

By 1982, they were living in Ilchester in Somerset. David had completed a ground tour and four years in Germany flying Harrier GR3s and was now an exchange student based at RNAS Yeovilton. Here he embarked on Sea Harrier training with 899 Naval Air Squadron. David remembered hearing the radio news that Argentinian soldiers had landed on the Falklands but did not think for a moment he would soon be en route there. Swiftly disabused of that view the very next day, he was informed that everyone would be deployed, and he would be flying as a full pilot. He returned home to pack and tell his family he was going to war. Among other things he packed three beloved books, including the Second World War poetry of John Pudney: 'my constant companion, to be brought out when melancholy strikes'. As the locals waved the pilots off the next day, Morgan mouthed a silent farewell to his loved ones.

Once at sea in HMS *Hermes* there was uncertainty and excitement over whether the situation would materialise into anything serious, though from the outset Morgan felt there was an inevitability about the conflict: 'prepare for the worst and hope for the best' was his philosophy. He wrote his first letter to his 'dearest little wife' on 15 April in confident tones:

> Morale is pretty good at the moment and we are all set to give these guys a whopping if they don't wind their necks in pretty rapidly . . . I don't think that we

have too much to worry about from the Argies, especially with a couple of nuke submarines in the area. In fact it sounds from the news as if they are getting cold feet about the whole deal, so we may not have to go all the way after all. You can always hope. You know I miss you and the kids something rotten. God knows why. I must be getting sentimental in my old age.

He knew the first task would be to block the Argentinian air force from Stanley airfield, and on the way south had to perfect 'carrier controlled approach' landings onboard ship – no easy task in thirty-foot waves and with poor visibility. En route, the ship practised the call to action stations or 'Condition Zulu' to man the defensive positions. Morgan recalled hundreds of men scrambling to put on masks, lifejackets and bulky anti-flash while closing hatches and doors. The process took thirty minutes on the first attempt, but by the time they neared the Falklands this gut-churning ritual took less than ten. Then came the broadcast that confirmed there was no going back, and to 'prepare accordingly'. With that moment of realisation, and knowing that they only had 10 per cent of the air power that the Argentinians had, David sat in his cabin and composed two farewell letters. The first was to his wife, and the second to Antje – a German woman with whom he had had a passionate affair that had ended in 1981. His wife knew about the affair and, albeit painfully, they had all moved on. Indeed, Antje was engaged. However, David had found a kindred spirit in Antje: she was someone who understood him implicitly and whom he considered his soul-mate. It was just as important that he wrote to her as well as his wife to say goodbye. David felt he needed to 'square a few things' in his letter, but freely admitted his letter was born of a somewhat personal, almost selfish, desire not to leave the business of the affair unfinished.

Well my love, I'm afraid it has happened. I am leaving this letter with Andy George, to be forwarded to you as soon as possible after my death. Please try not to be sad, I know that dying will not hurt me and I am equally sure that I will see you sometime, somewhere. All things are possible if you want them strongly enough.

If you read *Jonathan Livingstone Seagull* and *Illusions* and also *The Little Prince*, I think you might understand. Those three small books meant more to me than all the other books I have ever read put together. I am sure that what they say in them is true. Death is an unfortunate but necessary method of passing on to a new level of consciousness. Not a gateway to heaven but a chance to improve your knowledge and awareness and get a little closer to the concept of total love. It is only in the last year or so that I have really understood, or started to understand the meaning and power of love. It has to be spontaneous, selfless and all embracing. I am afraid that I wasn't really very good at it and it is a bit annoying that I didn't get the chance to practice a bit more. However, I don't think you have seen the last of me! I intend to spend a lot of time with those I love; every time you

19 Apr 82.
Hermes.

Well my love, I'm afraid it has happened. I am leaving this letter with Andy George to be forwarded to you as soon as possible after my death. Please try not to be sad, I know that dying will not hurt me and I am equally sure that I will see you again sometime somewhere: All things are possible if you want them strongly enough.

If you read J.L.S. and Illusions and also the Little Prince I think you might understand. Those three small books meant more to me than all the other books I have ever read put together. I am sure that what they say in them is true. Death is an unfortunate but neccessary method of passing on to a new level of conciousness. Not a gateway to heaven but a chance to improve your knowledge and awareness and get a little closer to the concept of total love. It is only in the last year or two that I have really understood, or started to understand the meaning and power of love. It has to be spontaneous, selfless and all embracing. I am afraid I wasn't really very good at it and it is a bit annoying that I didn't get the chance to practice a bit more. However don't think you have seen the last of me! I intend to spend a lot of time with those I love: every time you think of me I will be there, that is a promise. Please try to explain that to the kids, I will always be there in their

18 Part of the letter from David Morgan, 15 April 1982.

think of me, I will be there, that is a promise. Please try to explain to the kids, I will always be there in their thoughts to help them and look after them when they need me.

Please, none of you feel any bitterness towards anyone who was responsible for my death, they could not touch the real me and pain is only there if you allow it to be. Likewise, please do not hesitate to find someone else you can share your love with, you will most certainly have my blessing.

I would like to give you a final explanation of my feelings for Antje. I was, at first, attracted to her sexually but discovered within a matter of a couple of hours that there was an uncanny bond between us. We could literally read each other's thoughts. I must admit, it confused and puzzled me and I could not explain it to myself, let alone you, although I desperately wanted to. I thought that if I tried to explain, I would only hurt you and that you might leave me, which I could not stand the thought of. Not because of pride but because I was beginning to realise how much I really did love you, despite the problems we had been through.

Well the rest you know really. The only way I can describe our relationship is that it feels like we have known each other for thousands of years, which maybe we have, and when I met her again in London, it was just a natural progression to go to bed together. You may find it hard to believe but my relationship with Antje made me even more aware of my love for you than I was before. Probably because I became so much more aware of my own emotions and began to learn so much more about life and death. I was no longer afraid to say I loved you and I understood what I meant. Even if I showed it in funny ways sometimes! *Illusions* says it all really.

You know, we really did have some good times together and I don't think I would change much if I had my time over again, except perhaps to try harder not to be ratty! Give Elizabeth and Charles a great big hug and kiss for me. I will always love you all and I intend to look after you all, if you need it, until we meet again . . .

Take care, my love

D[31]

David's letter to 'my dearest disciple' Antje revealed his deep connection with her – and it left her absolutely overwhelmed when she read it after he returned:

When I was young I used to be scared at the thought of dying but it holds no great horror for me now. I expect it will be mildly unpleasant for a short period but pain and distress can only affect you if you want them to. I really want to thank you for changing my life. I have learnt so much about love and living over the last couple of years and I owe most of it to you . . . It is actually rather exciting to be on the brink of a brand new experience of such tremendous proportions. I am certain that I can carry my knowledge with me into my next existence . . . I will always remember your face in the moonlight and your hair streaming in the wind, and talking the night away in the clubroom at Breitscheid and the thrill of your touch and the deep longing for your body and the intoxicating smell of your hair on my shoulders . . . I have been very lucky in life; I have two children, whom I love very much, a wife whom I also loved dearly, although it took me a long time to realise how much, and of course, you, my dearest disciple, who helped me understand.

On 1 May the men were under orders to attack Port Stanley airfield, which gave rise to an anticipation akin to 'losing your virginity'. All the men survived, despite David's aircraft being hit by anti-aircraft fire. Twelve aircraft had dropped thirty-six bombs, destroyed enemy planes, decimated buildings and stores and made it back alive. Fierce action followed, and Morgan experienced the death of three comrades in the first week. There were near escapes and heady personal triumphs, including sinking the *Narwal* and the destruction of two Argentinian helicopters.

By mid-May the force had attacked the airfield at Pebble Island, but were in constant fear of the ship being hit. David had terrifying dreams as 'D-Day'[32] approached, and felt a keen awareness of his own mortality. On 22 May he wrote a breathless letter home:

Life here is far from boring . . . Yesterday we got fourteen kills (plus three probables) for one GR3. Not bad odds and the GR3 pilot is possibly a POW . . . I miss you a hell of a lot, you know. I am not afraid anymore but I wish I were back home with you and the kids and the cat and dog and goldfish and tadpoles and everything.

With each mission and each casualty, David was reminded of the fragility of life. On 8 June he witnessed the shocking aftermath of the bombing of the British landing ships *Sir Galahad* and *Sir Tristram*. It was a date etched into his mind. After sunset he shot down two Argentinian Skyhawks:[33] 'absolute hatred turned to a wave of empathy, followed by hatred.' This was no computer game, rather it was a determined kill, and he struggled to deal with it.

When Argentina surrendered, David returned home to a new cottage and transferred to the navy to train as an air warfare instructor. His Falklands demons were far from smothered, though; it took almost ten years for them to re-emerge, when the Gulf War broke out in 1990. 'It was like a hammer hitting me on the head,' he admitted, and he was grounded for medical reasons. In 1991, Morgan left the forces. The Falklands had bestowed a devastating legacy of severe post-traumatic stress disorder and its debilitating side effects: he divorced, struggled with heavy drinking, depression, considerable weight loss and endured terrifying nightmares.

Through his new marriage to Caro and intense therapy, since 1994 Morgan has flown as a commercial pilot. Once in the air, his concentration is 100 per cent and his Falklands experiences are shut in a closed box. Meanwhile, his letters are a constant reminder of an extreme episode that not only changed his life, but shaped the life he would go on to live.

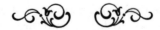

Lieutenant Colonel Herbert 'H' Jones VC, OBE
Killed at Goose Green, 28 May 1982

Born in 1940 in Putney, London, and growing up in Kingswear on the river Dart, Herbert Jones – known as H to friends and family – was one of three boys born to an American artist father Herbert and Welsh mother Olwen, who was a nurse (Plate 25). H was a determined and rather shy man who originally attended St Peter's Preparatory School in Sussex, before going to Eton College and then the Royal Military Academy at Sandhurst at eighteen. Following that, he was commissioned into the Devonshire and Dorset Regiment as a second lieutenant before transferring to the Parachute Regiment on command in 1965. He first met his future wife Sara when she was just sixteen, and they married in 1964, going on to have two sons, Rupert and David.

The couple had just seventy-two hours to marry before H was sent off on an emergency posting to British Guiana. Sara knew what life as an army wife entailed and had few qualms about her husband's job. Both of them were sunny, optimistic characters. H's fellow soldiers remembered him as a strong, charismatic commander: impatient and stubborn, but also honourable, devoted and courageous. 'He is an individualist with iconoclastic views on many of the shrines of military thought and custom. These views, combined with intelligence and a pleasantly relaxed manner, produce a refreshingly unorthodox approach to life with something always in reserve for an emergency,'[34] read his annual report in 1963.

When the Falklands diplomatic situation started escalating, Sara and H were away skiing with the children in Méribel. Hearing the news on the radio that Thatcher intended to take action to see the Falklands returned to the British, H fell silent. He stopped to call his HQ and within days was en route to Ascension Island. Sara had no idea that the last time she would see her husband would be as he left in a car with the words, 'Goodbye, see you in a week.' She recalls that there was no protracted farewell because she fully expected him to return: 'We all thought scare tactics would be enough to dissipate the Argentine threats.' As the situation worsened and conflict became imminent, Sara became nervous, yet still hoped for the best, feeling that, as a colonel, H would be well protected. Nevertheless she struggled to prevent images of the evacuation of Dunkirk racing through her mind. This would be his first 'real' conflict.

Television and radio news became a vital window on events and was avidly followed – particularly as journalist Robert Fox was embedded with 2 Para. Sara's sons were excited, though since they were at boarding school they were relatively cosseted from the reality of what a conflict would truly entail.

H had always been a prolific letter-writer, often writing every day when away on operations. En route to the Falklands he immediately started to write to Sara, telling her about how he was keeping fit and practising live firing. He wrote on 25 April from HMS *Canberra*:

I went for a run yesterday evening – ten times round the Promenade Deck . . . It is quite humid so I was sweating like a pig by the time I had finished . . . Everything seems to change here every time the clock strikes so I have no idea what's going on or when we are going to sail.

On 9 May from the cramped ship *Norland*, he hinted that the situation was darkening:

We had a good church service on the flight deck, and I went to communion afterwards. Quite a lot of soldiers turned up – a sure sign that the full seriousness of the situation is dawning on people – and all the hymns were chosen by the soldiers . . . Frankly the sooner we get ashore, where our destiny is in our own hands, the better.

'I'm a bit of a squirrel, and I've kept all of his letters,' Sara recounted. Having missed an emotional farewell with her husband, she went to Portsmouth to bid goodbye to the rest of the troops and found comfort and support among other wives in the same situation. At the same time, she was not nervous. Once he was ashore, she knew H was in his comfort zone in the job he adored. 'You will know we got ashore ok – first! And that our section has no casualties. So far so good!' he wrote in the May.

H's letters were upbeat despite the miserable conditions and a sore knee. 'Don't worry about me, I'm fine. It's cold, wet . . .' However, following the devastating hit on HMS *Sheffield*, he wrote to reassure Sara of his safety. 'I hope you're not worrying too much, poor darling. I still don't know what the actual plan is but you can be sure that we will all be very careful . . . make sure I come home to you.'

On 18 May 1982, ten days before his death, H sent a letter home containing one paragraph markedly different in tone to all the others. Read in hindsight, it was to be an achingly poignant and uncharacteristic farewell. It has become Sara's most treasured letter from her husband.

My dearest Sara,

We are now (it's evening) under 400 miles from the Falklands. I've just heard the news say that *Canberra* has joined *Hermes* and the rest of the task force, but no mention of *Norland*, as they don't want the Argentinians to know we've arrived.

I've pretty well finished packing now, my sterling magazines are filled, and it's just a matter of waiting for D Day.

As soon as the landing has been announced, Mike Beaumont, or the senior Naval Officer on board, Chris Esplin-Jones, will ring John Holborn to let me know that we are all ok and ashore. If they can't contact John, they will ring you.

I suspect that Maggie will want us to go ashore on a weekday, so that she can announce it in the house. She won't want to say anything until after first light, which is at about 12.30 your time, so I suspect she will announce it fairly early in the afternoon . . .

From now on we will be sleeping fully dressed except for boots in case there is a submarine attack, and we are all standing to before first light. It's been very calm all day, but there is an expanding grey light all the time. We expect bad weather fairly soon, which should help to stop Argentine air attacks.

It's strange to think you'll be going off to Colchester soon for the new Colours parade; I feel as if I've been afloat all my life – I'm glad I'm not a professional sailor! . . .

I had an early bed last night, and we were woken at 06.15 by 'Rule Britannia' from the last night of the Proms being played over the loud speakers! We're having 'Land of Hope and Glory' tomorrow!

We still don't know when D Day is, but it looks as if it may be Friday (21st May) since the UN have said Thursday is a key day. We are now on the edge of the Total Exclusion Zone, WNW of the Falklands. Mail closes in 30 minutes, so I had better hurry up and finish. I may write again today or tomorrow, but I doubt if the letter will get away before we go in, so this is probably the last letter I can guarantee will get to you.

By the time you get this I expect the whole thing will be all over; we will certainly be ashore and I expect we will have some sort of settlement. Most important of all, you'll know whether I'm ok or not.

I don't suppose there's any chance of anything happening to me, but just in case I want to tell you how very much I love you, and thank you for being such a super wife for the last 18 years. I know we have had our ups and downs, but despite all that it's been a wonderful time, and you have made me very happy. I certainly wouldn't want to change any of it. Marrying you was the best thing that ever

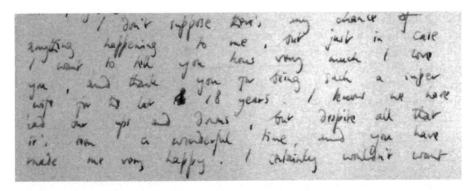

19 Part of the letter from H Jones, 18 May 1982.

happened to me, and thanks to you I can look back on a life that has been pretty good so far. I've been very lucky – let's hope my luck holds.

I've written last notes to David and Rupert, and to Dia, which will go off in this mail, too . . .

Must stop or I'll be too late. Look after yourself, darling; give Jimmy and Scrumpy my love.

All my love, darling, always.

H

On the eve of the battle, H calmly informed his colleague Hector Gullan, 'I am going to die' – it was a chilling prophecy. On 28 May, H's battalion was ordered to attack the enemy, who were well dug in around Darwin and Goose Green. They were held up south of Darwin by more than ten enemy trenches on a strategically important ridge. Under heavy fire there were numerous casualties but the men were determined to push forward and not lose momentum. Jones took his reconnaissance party to the foot of an area the battalion had secured and ordered mortar fire at the enemy trenches. Unfortunately, heavy artillery rained back, preventing any further surge forward. For over an hour the men were under constant fire in a gully and making no ground. The light was improving and could only give the Argentinians the upper hand as they drafted in reinforcements. H decided on a desperate measure to break the bloody stalemate and to prevent more casualties. If they did not secure Darwin ridge, his company were at risk of losing the first real land battle of the campaign. Grabbing a sub-machine gun and calling on those around him to 'go for it', H charged the enemy trench. Immediately exposed to fire from several directions, H was hit instantly as he charged up a slight incline; even so, witnesses recalled him continuing to clamber forwards, firing his gun. He finally fell just metres from the enemy trench at 9 o'clock in the morning. His action was typical H: he would never expect others to do anything he was unwilling to do himself. He was decisive, intuitive and took risks. It had made him an admirable soldier but tragically cost him his life.[35] The frantic message was relayed by his radio operator: 'Sunray[36] is down.' By the time the Royal Marine helicopter arrived to evacuate the casualties, H was dead.

Despite the Argentinian surrender on Darwin ridge, there was to be another twenty-four hours of fierce fighting before the two settlements were taken. Nevertheless, H's actions had pierced enemy territory and broken the Argentinian hold. The locals – imprisoned in the community hall in Goose Green – were released and over twelve hundred Argentinian soldiers surrendered.

For Sara, it was enough to know that her husband had been killed. 'I was a bit of an ostrich,' she recounted, 'I didn't want to know every detail.' H was posthumously awarded the Victoria Cross.

Sara heard the news about her husband's death the day after it had happened. There was an army policy that bad news was never broken in the early hours. It was half-term and Sara had been to collect her sons from the train station, passing newspaper headlines declaring victories. Of course there were casualties, but no names were mentioned, and Sara recalled feeling elated that Britain seemed to be winning. At home she received a phone call from the regiment, warning her to 'guard against too much enthusiasm'. A few hours later, the regimental colonel arrived at the house. His words have been blocked from Sara's mind but came against the poignant backdrop of her sons playing croquet in the garden. Luckily, a friend and her mother happened to be staying at the time and Sara remembers having bought a large bottle of sherry from the NAAFI and swiftly getting stuck in. The family were shattered and in shock, but insisted on carrying on with everyday life in true stiff upper lip fashion. They were quickly inundated by press eager for the inside scoop on such a high-ranking military casualty; H became 'H for Hero' in a barrage of newspaper headlines that, at the time, simply reinforced Sara's loss.

In the hours and days following the news Sara kept busy; refusing to dwell on the tragic events. Letters arrived from H – a surreal, rather macabre shock, but incomparable with the blow felt when a bundle of Sara's letters arrived home unopened. They had not reached H in time.

The day after Goose Green surrendered, H was buried in a large temporary grave above Ajax Bay in a simple ceremony that was televised. The horror of watching H's silver body bag with the name etched in black marker pen was inconceivably painful for his loved ones in Britain. When asked if she wanted H to be repatriated Sara was insistent that, true to soldiering tradition, he should lie where he had fallen and H was thus moved to San Carlos cemetery. In 1983 Sara and the boys made the journey to his final resting place. They felt that it was important that they follow in his footsteps and were drawn to experience the alien, faraway spot where his life had ended. They found soothing catharsis in the journey and in the immense gratitude of the islanders. Sara has returned four times since and plans to return once more on the thirtieth anniversary in 2012.

At her Wiltshire cottage, Sara still plants a tree each year in memory of her husband – an annual ritual now involving grandsons; the four boys each have Herbert as one of their names. Both Rupert and David joined the army – the Devon and Dorsets, their father's original regiment – fulfilling ambitions they had held long before their father's death.

H's letters are stored in a plastic box in the bedroom cupboard. Sara does re-read some of them on occasion but still finds them overwhelming. Almost thirty years later, H's words evoke raw tears and sadness when she reads them – a powerful testimony to this 'bright star'.[37]

PETTY OFFICER CHRIS HOWE

Survived

ALTHOUGH HIS FATHER AND grandfather had done national service, there was no tradition of a military career in Howe's family; he decided with a schoolmate that they would join the navy straight from school (Plate 26). Living in Leighton Buzzard, where university was never considered an option and factory life a foregone conclusion for many, it was easy to choose a seafaring career. On 2 August 1972, at the age of sixteen, Chris signed up for the navy. His parents were happy and supportive: a naval life would lead to a long career and job security.

Before the Falklands Conflict, Howe had seen action in Cyprus during an evacuation in 1974, but the Falklands would be his first conflict. HMS *Coventry*, where Howe was stationed, was one of the first ships to be diverted when the command came to go to the Falkland Islands after Argentina invaded South Georgia. He scribbled a note home to his wife, Margaret, who had been expecting him home to spend Easter with her and their two sons, aged four years and ten months. On receiving this letter, Margaret had a sense of foreboding and realised how serious this operation might be.

We have just been diverted along with about 14 other ships to sail south to South Georgia, Falklands. The Argentinians have invaded our sovereignty and we are going to get it back, somehow. Well we have enough ships with us, but we have a big problem with food and stores. So that is what is happening and why we won't be back for about 6 weeks. That is an outside estimate. We might even be turned round at any time; it all depends on the Argentinian actions. I'm so sorry about this, but it can't be helped. I know you must be feeling pretty low, but some of us are quite hacked off as well.

Howe remembered a general sense among his shipmates that Argentina was firmly in the wrong, and they had no qualms about entering the fray. His role as an assistant intelligence officer and electronic warfare director saw him plotting enemy positions and using above surface radar to formulate operational strategies as part of the taskforce that included HMS *Sheffield* and *Glasgow*, forming a shield ahead of the British fleet. Howe recalled that writing his will was a difficult thing to do at the invincible age of twenty-five: 'Why am I writing a will? The MPs will sort it out and I'll be home in a few weeks.' His will was basic and matter of fact, but the implications of having written it were profound, and he mentioned it in a letter home to his wife.

I know how this must read, but I have been told you must know of me making one. This must all be upsetting you by now, so I will leave it at that. I'm very sorry, I don't want you upset for the world but I think you'll understand how it is for me down here, we are all on edge and disturbed about the future few weeks.

While Howe was in the Falklands, letters went outwards and homewards with a four- or five-day delay, although sometimes there would be nothing for up to a fortnight. Howe remembered men writing farewell letters, but nobody actually talked about doing it. 'You never really thought I'm not going back, but I think subconsciously you wrote in a way that you might not come back.' A heart-stopping emphasis of this came when Admiral John Forster Woodward, the Commander of the British Naval Force in the South Atlantic, boarded ship and bleakly informed the men that it was likely some would not make it home.

By 11 April, war was becoming ever more likely, although hopes still remained that President Galtieri could be persuaded to negotiate and avoid a bloodbath. Howe wrote home to break the news:

. . . if we go in it is going to be a big ding-dong and a long time before anyone gets home, about 3 months at the earliest . . . I love you all very much, it is times like this when I really appreciate how things are taken for granted. Let's just hope that it is all over soon, at least then we'll know I'm coming back, no matter how long it takes, I think you'll agree with that . . . at the moment I've got a lot on my mind, and I can tell you we are all rather 'scared' if you like, because we are all doing jobs that aren't natural to peacetime operations.

On 14 April 1982 Chris wrote a farewell letter to his wife. It was a letter he blanked from his memory, and only discovered when he later re-read his letters.

This might be my last letter for quite some time, we are leaving this area for operations further south and we have been told we will be away for a long time. Anything could happen, and I mean anything, so remember I love you very much and I always will. This might seem a last letter home darling, and it well could be.

As you know talks haven't gone well and we could be going to have a set-to, but I'm sure everything will be alright.

Well, mail closes in 5 minutes as we have only just been told where we are going, please keep writing we might get some mail from somewhere.

I love you very much, please take care of my bairns . . .

This letter was a change in tone for the normally positive Chris. For Margaret, letters from her husband were a lifeline that she was totally reliant on. She remembered waiting for the postman each day, and the sheer relief when a letter arrived. The letter of 14 April arrived at an already distressing time for Margaret: her father was seriously ill and died just two days later. Caught in a maelstrom of emotion, she remained glued to the television and tried to prevent her mind from wandering and pondering the worst. She knew there was always a chance of things going wrong in a combat situation but tried not to dwell on this. Being alone at night-time was difficult; worry and anxiety kept creeping in.

A letter Howe wrote twelve days later revealed his confidence in a British victory. 'We are all certainly ready anyway and I feel we are far superior to them any day, so we should have an upper hand whatever happens.' However, niggling apprehension about full-scale conflict with the Argentinians was also clear. 'I don't really know what else to say but I love you and am missing you very much indeed. I know this might sound daft, but I keep thinking my whole life has changed because we just don't know what will happen to us. I can't really explain but I hope you understand.' The orders were to bring down enemy aircraft in San Carlos Bay using Sea Dart surface-to-air missiles – four-metre-long missiles that could travel twice the speed of sound. HMS *Coventry* was out in front and thus most exposed.

By 5 May 1982 British confidence had taken a huge knock with the loss of HMS *Sheffield* to a supersonic Exocet missile and the shooting down of a British Harrier. Margaret Howe remembered the hit on *Sheffield*: 'I think it brought it home to me that maybe the same could happen to us, and I wouldn't know what to do without Chris.' It had also affected Howe, who wrote an emotional letter home:

It has also given us all a shock and we are still in a state of shock and 'confusion' over how the hell we let it happen . . . It will have to be a very clever Argentinean to get anywhere near us, all our exercises have paid off at last. Believe it or not, I am trying to let you know we are going to be ok, but at the same time I must make sure you really understand what is happening down here . . . It nearly brings me to tears when I look at my pictures of you and my two little laddies, I carry them around in my top pocket now everywhere I go. I am always getting them out and looking at you all, soon I hope to be able to hug and kiss you all, and I will, just you wait and see.

The ship brought down a number of enemy aircraft on 24 May. On the following day, however – Argentina's National Day – a message was intercepted, and the ship's company knew that their position had been spotted. Radar picked up four enemy aircraft tearing towards them. One bomb skimmed the ship and exploded into the sea. Seconds later, two 1,000-pound bombs hit port side. The explosion ripped through the ship. In the computer ops room, Chris was choking on smoke and engulfed in flames. He managed to get to the starboard passage, where his best friend Sam MacFarlane guided him up to the next level. His clothes had been blasted off – save for his collar, boots, wedding ring and a Saint Christopher that he wears to this day. As the ship started to lurch and sink, Chris was hurled overboard. The cold salt-water provided immediate first aid as he had suffered 27 per cent burns to his body, and had lost a tremendous amount of fluid. After thirty minutes a life raft picked him up and took him to the escort ship *Broadsword*, where he was transferred to a Sea King helicopter and hoped he would be taken to the field hospital. Through the headset Chris heard not only that there was an unexploded bomb in the hospital, but that the helicopter had taken off with precious little fuel. He was taken onboard the hospital ship *Uganda* instead; his six-hour ordeal was over. Chris was in shock and his wounds infected, but he was alive.

Back home it was a different story. Margaret heard on the news that a ship had been bombed and feared it was *Coventry*. Glued to the radio and television, the following morning she received a telephone call from a neighbour screaming that it was indeed *Coventry* that had been hit. 'It was panic stations,' she recalled. 'Nobody knew anything.' A vicar arrived at the door with bible in hand, and Margaret immediately feared the worst. When she finally heard the news that Chris was alive, the worry did not dissipate: she knew the extent of his burns, and felt 'utter despair and shock; it was touch and go.' When a phone call a few days later eventually reassured her that Chris would live, relief flooded her body. 'One thing that sticks in my mind, is my mother putting her arms around me and saying that she could have broken her heart for me during all that time and wanted to cry with me, but didn't dare,' recalled Margaret.

Howe recovered from his burns, but the trauma of what he experienced has never waned. He suffered flashbacks and nightmares. 'I keep seeing the ops room ablaze and everybody screaming and panicking and rushing everywhere just to get out . . . I've been told it will fade as time goes by.'[38]

HMS *Coventry* brought down more enemy aircraft than any other ship. Howe went on to serve twenty-six years in the navy and was awarded a military MBE. He now works as an electronic warfare director. His Falklands experience shaped his life, and the farewell letter he wrote acts as a continuing reminder of the fragility of life as well as an insight into the mind of a man who faced death – and survived.

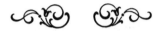

Private José Antonio Scaglia
Survived

BORN ON 16 JULY 1962 in Buenos Aires, Scaglia grew up in the small town of Rosario, three hundred kilometres from the city, and dreamed of becoming a pilot (Plate 27). One of seven children, Scaglia had a difficult relationship with his father, who was not keen on his son's ambitions, instead pushing him towards a career in medicine. José's father was a compulsive gambler and the family's fortunes constantly swung from luxury to abject poverty.

In 1981, Argentinian men had to undertake compulsory military service and were posted according to a lottery draw – the last three digits determining where a man would be assigned. Scaglia found himself bound for the Marines. At the age of nineteen, he saw the prospect of war becoming inevitable but felt immortal. 'Nothing could happen to me; I knew how to look after myself,' he remembered. However, he entered the conflict with mixed emotions:

> I couldn't understand (and I still can't) how in 1982 we could decide to kill another person because they clashed with my objectives, my interests, or my opinions. Despite everything, the strong media reporting had a strong impact on our patriotic feelings. I believed in my flag more than in any political ideals . . . Despite everything, at the time I wouldn't have hesitated if I'd had to kill someone.

In 1982 Scaglia found himself on an alien island, fighting a pointless war with which he did not agree. He felt young and out of his depth, not understanding the reasons for the conflict and hoping that a peaceful resolution could be found through talking and negotiation. Scaglia arrived at the Falklands on 2 April 1982. He wrote home almost immediately.

MALVINA ISLANDAS. Sunday 4 April 1982
    Dear parents:
    Above all, I hope you are not worrying about me, because fortunately I'm alive and quite well . . . we were woken up at two thirty in the morning on Saturday the 27th . . . and we were told we were being sent to the Malvinas because we were in war with the English. Just imagine what we felt at the time. We left at midday on Sunday the 28th. The trip was terrible. It lasted five days, and to cap it all we were travelling on a vessel with no keel across the ocean. We couldn't tell if it was a ship or a blender for all it swayed. In fact, in five days I only ate three times . . .
    We came here loaded with weapons. The tension we experienced (we still do) is tremendous. Believe me when I say that I didn't think I would live so long. There were random shots, a fair pair of losses, but thank God I didn't have to go in on the taking of the Government House. Just imagine, things were so bad that I'd even written a post-mortem letter. Out of the entire battalion, I was the only one left here. I hope this will be no more than another experience and I'll soon be home. We don't know how long we'll be here. It may be ten days or two months. The population of Malvinas is terrified, but many are well armed. We fear an uprising, but it's a matter of keeping everything under control.

A few days later there were only thirty-nine Marines and a few army soldiers left. Scaglia was one of the few soldiers who stayed for the entire conflict, and his role driving heavy trucks transporting troops, weapons, food and casualties meant he had a broad overview of the fight. He took shipments delivered by air over to Port Stanley and was also part of the team who launched the Exocet missile that hit HMS *Glamorgan* with such devastating results. It is an act that continues to haunt him. He remembered watching the fighting on the beaches, the maelstrom of flares and tracer bullets, and the chilling screams of the dying and wounded.
    Throughout his time, Scaglia found a lifeline in letters. He felt that every letter was a potential farewell and an opportunity to tell loved ones just how much he loved them. In early May he wrote:

I'm missing you so much here. I don't know how long I'll be here, but I think it will be for quite a while . . . I'm desperate to receive a letter from you. Things here haven't changed; everything is just as BAD! But you mustn't worry . . . At least we live in hope. But if it did come to something, don't worry; I'll take great care

Mi querida familia:
        Espero que se encuentren bien.
Yo por estos lados los estoy extrañando muchísimo.
No sé cuanto tiempo voy a estar acá pero me parece que
va para largo. No he tenido noticias de ustedes de-
bido a que escribo una carta e inmediatamen-
te me tengo que ir con el camión con otro batallón.
Pero me parece que esta vez sí voy a estar acá un buen
tiempo. Espero con ansias una carta de ustedes. Por
acá las cosas siguen iguales (MAL). Pero no se pre
ocupen yo tengo fe en que no va a pasar nada.
Por lo menos la esperanza es lo último que se pierde.
Si acá se arma pierden, cuidado que me voy a
cuidar al máximo. Está muy jodida la ma-
no. En las Georgias están a los tiros y nosotros aquí
esperando. Esto no es una carta para preocuparlo
sino que les toca la justa.
En estos momentos quisiera estar con ustedes
pero ya que no puedo quiero con desesperación
recibir una carta de ustedes.
Mi los reclusco bastante bien. Pido lo que
puedo. Quesos, dulces, frutas, etc. etc...

20 Part of the letter from José Scaglia, early May 1982.

of myself. Things are pretty tough here. They're shooting at each other in South Georgia and we're just waiting. I don't mean to worry you with this letter; I just want to be honest.

Letters also became a cathartic statement of how his end goal was simply to get out alive. Letters bestowed a strange inner peace and confidence in his situation: he had no control over whether a bomb would drop and kill him.

I suffer as I write this letter . . . and I can't stop crying. This situation, keeping us apart and not knowing if I'll come back is so painful. To top it all, I'm alone . . . The other day I read that tomorrow is unattainable, no one can know about the future, an unfathomable mystery, so who knows if tomorrow, very soon, this will all come to an end . . . These are dreams, I know, but life is a dream . . . I'll stop writing nonsense now.

Equally, letters from home were vital. 'I learned to value communication and I wrote and wrote,' he recalled. 'I do not know if I was aware what death meant at that time. I was consumed with the pain I was causing my loved ones.'

Soon after arriving on the Falklands, after witnessing horrific bloodshed and losing comrades, Scaglia wrote a farewell letter to his family.

Dear Parents.

Thank God the bombing is over and that I'm alive. It's no use; the Devil looks after his own. Folks, don't worry, I'm taking great care. Things are pretty strained here. Everyone is nervous, very tense and the alarms keep going off. I'm in the city centre. I'm with a group of logistics support for the time being, and so far we've used our 'tricks' to eat well, but we're pretty well looked after on the whole. As I said, I'm in the city centre and I doubt they'll be dropping any bombs here.

They bombed the airport and other places on the island, but not the city. I'm hoping they'll keep their scruples and won't bomb the city.

I really miss you. Mum, Dad, Alex, Morinís, Daniela and Mariano, I miss you so much and I hope to be able to hug you again. I wouldn't want to die in this pathetic war . . .

Here the English resistance shoots at us at night and they harass us by flying over us during the day. We still have faith in God and we are comforted by the memory of our families . . .

All we can do is hope that this will end soon and we will return alive and well.

It is very hard to be stuck here, completely cut off from everyone else. I'm really feeling rotten. I miss everything, my family, the gym, friends, the neighbourhood, everything.

Keep your faith . . . I don't know how this will end. I hope it will all end well. Please write to me and I might be lucky to receive one. You know I'm alone and it's difficult to get any letters, but I never give up hope . . .

I miss you all terribly. This will end one day. Bye, I send my love to Lito, the gym, the bona and a very big kiss to all of you.

Negro.[39]

On 16 June 1982 Scaglia turned twenty; at the time he was imprisoned in the island airport and worried about being killed. He and his comrades were starving and forced to steal tins of peaches and to scrabble on the floor when chocolate was dropped from the helicopters overhead. He left the islands on 21 June, having been held prisoner for a week.

Returning to Argentina, Scaglia hid himself away. The army were branded 'losers' by a culture hell-bent on success. His only relief was that the government, 'a dictatorship', was then toppled and veterans started to be viewed with respect and pity. Scaglia suffered from post-traumatic stress and longed for the adrenalin rush that had become addictive during the conflict. There seemed to be no policy to move the country forward, and no support for the beleaguered soldiers and bereft relatives.

In September 1982 Scaglia was able to leave the navy. He was jobless and broke. He started a career with a telephone company, eventually becoming manager. He married in 1987 and had two sons – John Joseph and Augustine. Today he is separated from his wife but finally feels at peace, working as a diving instructor – a job that he loves: 'That's my passion and it gives me the peaceful silence I have sought since 1982.'

Scaglia's teenage letters still evoke painful and raw memories. Re-reading them reinforces the hell he once endured but also underlines the pain of youth during a conflict whose memories still run deep in Argentina.

~ 8 ~

CONFLICTS IN IRAQ AND AFGHANISTAN

The human race is not made up of super heroes and heroes but people going about their ordinary business. I never saw the limelight or front page news. I proved ordinary people are capable of extraordinary deeds and proved this in times of crisis. Hopefully the courage I have shown makes the pain easier. I have died doing what I loved. Thank you to all the people in my life.[1]

THE DATE 11 SEPTEMBER 2001, or 9/11 is etched in the world's consciousness. The al-Qaeda attack by two planes deliberately smashing into the iconic Twin Towers of New York did not just prompt a retaliatory invasion of Afghanistan. This visceral act of zealous terrorism signalled the beginning of a change in war and politics between the West and what President George W. Bush came to call the 'axis of evil'.[2] Britain and America found themselves 'shoulder to shoulder',[3] locked into a devastating global war on terror that continues to this day.

Unlike most earlier conflicts, this was never going to be a war against one enemy or one ideology. Iraq and Afghanistan would become wars without traditional front lines. Moreover, these conflicts have not ended with the taking of a capital, the toppling of a leader or the imposition of elected governments. Rebuilding, retraining and re-education in the midst of continued insurgency have meant that troops are fighting and facing daily danger, as they seek to win a more esoteric battle for hearts and minds that may one day deliver peace.

9/11 not only gave al-Qaeda a veneer of credibility but galvanised support for it. Bush announced, 'It will not stop until every terrorist group has been found, stopped and defeated.' October 2001 saw the USA, the UK and an alliance of Afghan troops launch Operation Enduring Freedom in search of al-Qaeda's Osama Bin Laden, who was under the protection of the Taliban in Afghanistan. By the end of that 2001 troops had crushed the Taliban government, but so quickly that it left a dangerous political vacuum that developed into an ongoing guerrilla war. British Defence Secretary John Reid's now-infamous speech that troops would leave Afghanistan 'without firing a single shot' has proved woefully short-sighted. By August 2009, British troops alone had fired twelve million bullets.[4] Troops from thirty-seven different nations have now served in Afghanistan under the International Security Assistance Force (ISAF) umbrella, although the timetable for complete combat withdrawal is set for 2015. Ominously, one Taliban Pashtun[5] responded to this by stating, 'The West has all the watches and we have all the time.'[6]

The First Gulf War of the 1990s had failed to oust Saddam Hussein from Iraq, and his regime had intensified. Added to the al-Qaeda threat was a dogged insistence in America and Britain that Hussein was developing weapons of mass destruction. In 2003, the Second Gulf War started. An invasion bound up in continued controversy and debate, it led to a bloody six-year battle. The war became one of the most unpopular in history. It was played out against a backdrop of heavy civilian and troop casualties, questions in the UK and USA over the legality of the invasion,[7] and a growing sectarian battle within Iraq. By August 2010 most combat forces had left the country, leaving a small NATO force to carry out border patrols, mentoring and training.

In the eyes of the insurgent fighters of Iraq and Afghanistan, the rationale for engaging has been simple: these are Western wars waged against Islam. For virtually everyone else, the politics and reasons for these wars will long continue to be argued over and debated. Whether oil, money, megalomania, human rights, regime change or democracy – all have their advocates, apologists and believers. History will make the final judgement on whether either occupation has been worth it.

Casualty figures from Iraq and Afghanistan are a sobering reminder of the human cost. In Iraq 4,759 allied troops were killed, and in Afghanistan the death toll at the time of writing stood at 2,390. Indeed, far from things winding down in Afghanistan, March 2011 saw calls for reinforcements in Helmand, putting complete withdrawal an ever-more distant prospect. It is even harder to gain reliable figures of Afghan and Iraqi dead: estimates range from over twenty thousand in Iraq and over fifteen thousand in Afghanistan.[8] Likewise, civilian casualties from each conflict can only be estimated at over 109,000 in Iraq and approaching 10,000 in Afghanistan; devastating 'collateral damage' that has made any decisive victory all the more difficult. 'I know that because of the nature of war you are going to have civilians killed but, my god, there must be a way that we can limit things . . . I'm starting to lose faith in our government and its policies . . . maybe it is just that my mind is opening up and I'm feeling a loss of innocence,' divulged one US sergeant.[9]

Iraq and Afghanistan have become the most unpopular and controversial conflicts since Vietnam. They have forced inquiries, resignations and searching questions. Politics aside, we should never lose sight of the troops who have gone there regardless; countless individuals who have continued to put their lives on the line in a complex, punishing, often thankless role. As Lance Bombardier Anthony Makin said, 'It's not nice to send our troops out there to die . . . but at the end of the day we do it. It's what we get paid for. It's our job.' Their legacy is still to be understood and fully appreciated – we can only hope it will have been worth it.

The Prospect of War

Virtually all troops when given their deployment details have shared the excitement, anticipation and nerves of their military forebears on the eve of battle. For loved ones left at home, the final drive to the camp to bid goodbye has been agonising. They never want to think about the worst happening, but at the same time, there's a desire to drink in every last word, smell and gesture to keep them going through the months apart. The stoicism of men and women going into conflict is unchanging, as is their reticence in admitting fear to loved ones. Before leaving for Afghanistan, men from the Royal Welsh Regiment decided to make video goodbyes for loved ones and were in jubilant mood, with messages of 'can't wait to be back' and 'make sure you feed the cat!' Even as the conflicts have progressed and soldiers have deployed knowing the perils they face, they still maintain a public stiff upper lip. When Sarah Adams's son James Prosser left for Afghanistan, she recalled how a totally different James sat in the car – quiet, pensive, nervous, but 'totally prepared. He believed in it.'

American Major Brown's succinct summary on arriving in Iraq was simply 'what a shit hole!'[10] Captain Pierre Piché described it as 'like the Wild West. No police, no hospitals, no government.'[11] In Afghanistan, British troops faced the unknown prospect of engaging with 'Terry Taliban', 'without doubt the most demanding tour of my career to date . . . Leaving Alison and the girls gets harder every time and I hate it,' wrote Will Pike in his diary.

No amount of preparation could prepare soldiers for the reality of battle: disorientating and shocking. Many soldiers have talked of being incredibly pumped up and eager to engage with the enemy; a novelty that wears off swiftly, but is paradoxically addictive – an adrenalin rush that can never be matched. 'You put yourself through the most stressful, most intense, most emotionally, mentally and physically draining experience that exists in this universe. You fail, you die,' explained Corporal Stephen Bouzane.[12]

Incredible camaraderie makes leaving friends and family behind a little easier. Fellow soldiers are the only people who truly know what the other is thinking, feeling and seeing in the arena of war. Indeed, one overriding reason for troops wanting to do their duty in the line of fire has been to protect and look out for their friends. 'I would die for these guys before I die for my own blood brother,' revealed Staff Sergeant Robin Johnson in Iraq.[13] These are powerful bonds forged through a hellish shared experience.

CHANGING ATTITUDES TO WAR

The decision to go to war in both Iraq and Afghanistan was divisive, and the human toll has not dampened that controversy. Most soldiers initially deploying to these arenas felt they were doing the right thing and fighting in a just cause. Captain Pierre Piché wrote home from Iraq to affirm, 'I'm not an idealist who thinks I can change the world but I can still be doing some sort of good. I want to be able to believe in what I'm doing.'[14]

As the conflicts continued, many letters revealed a marked change in attitude, particularly among US service personnel. One US sergeant hearing about detainee abuses and witnessing loss of civilian life in Iraq compared it to 'seeing shades of gray where I used to see just black and white . . . I spend lots of time trying to de-conflict my ideas . . . coming here was the right thing to do, but now because of bad leadership it is time to change direction.'[15]

Although it is impossible to generalise, many soldiers found it difficult to reconcile doubts over the reasons for war with being in that country, 'fighting a losing battle,' according to Martyn Compton, who was horrifically burned in Afghanistan. Nevertheless, they all set aside politics to fight. For every soldier who disagreed with the conflicts, another wholeheartedly embraced the mission, and letters home were full of descriptions of good work done in Iraq and Afghanistan. Indeed, for many, the experiences have been – and continue to be – positive and self-affirming, a force for good in a devastated land. 'The more we actually interact with the Afghan people, the more I feel that we are serving a purpose here . . . these people . . . are trying to achieve something we in Canada have long since taken for granted . . . There is nowhere I'd rather be right now,'[16] wrote Captain Nichola Goddard.

Newspaper reports have not helped morale in many cases – focusing on death, danger and destruction, ignoring the positive work being done, and the unbelievable stresses placed on soldiers fighting overseas. One sergeant grappled with his emotions in the arena of war, unburdening himself in a letter to his wife.

It is hard to keep going and then reading what the press say about us like how we're bad and do bad things, they should come here and smell their friend's burning flesh and hear the screaming . . . I ain't no fucking saint but when they hit yours and hurt yours you want to get the fuckers and make them pay . . . To see kids maimed and scared to go out on patrol, lose their mates and still have to go out there, with crap kit too . . . I wanna come home. I wanna hold you in my arms and hear you tell me I don't have to fight no more, tell me I'm safe and most of all I want those dreams to stop, those sounds of screaming and that smell of death I want it all to stop.[17]

War-weariness has also had a massive impact on soldiers' enthusiasm for the conflicts. American soldiers could spend up to fifteen months on operational tour. In Britain the Ministry of Defence Harmony guidelines of a six-month tour with a two-year gap was never going to be sustainable when fighting a war on two fronts. In 2008, the British Chief of Defence Staff warned that the army was severely overstretched and any additional demands would lead it to breaking point.

For Afghan and Iraqi insurgents, the motivation has been unbending. The chilling video wills of suicide bombers are a saddening testament to this. 'Some hypocrites say that we are doing this for money – or because of brainwashing – but we are told by Allah to target these pagans . . . I invite my fellows to sacrifice themselves,' recorded one fifteen-year-old, while another simply stated, 'If I die, do not cry for me. I will be in Heaven waiting for you.'[18]

LIVING CONDITIONS AND MORALE

Although the news reports have inevitably focused on high-adrenalin attacks and patrols, troops in Iraq and Afghanistan have experienced periods of boredom and non-contact action, just as in previous conflicts.

Daily living conditions have varied enormously in both conflict. For example, the main British camp, Camp Bastion, in the 'Desert of Death' of Dasht-i-Margo became a quasi-town, equipped with coffee shops, Pizza Hut and Burger King. There was a gym, air conditioning, bunk beds with duvets and carpets, volleyball courts, even a makeshift polo ground. Finnish soldiers have enjoyed saunas and two beers a night at their base at Kandahar, where Canadian soldiers rigged up a makeshift ice-hockey rink – minus the ice.

Most troops fighting in Iraq and Afghanistan, though, have at some point lived in forward operating bases (FOBs), sometimes built from scratch. Some have been basic mud huts with water-bag showers and a plastic bag as a toilet. 'In case you were wondering, I stink,' wrote Robert Allen Wise.[19]

Operating conditions in both Iraq and Afghanistan would have been alien to most soldiers: calories sweated away in fifty-degree heat. Captain Charlotte Cross described her feet virtually rotting in heavy boots, and troops drinking upwards of ten litres of water a day. These conflicts have seen rifle grips and boots melting in the scorching sun, one officer comparing the heat to a hairdryer. Sand-sickness was on a par with homesickness. 'Something of a dustbowl, very talcum powdery dust which gets everywhere,' described Will

Pike of Bastion, where 'there are sandstorms and whirlwinds like twisters every day – sometimes so bad you can hardly see.' Afghan winters were tough, with temperatures dropping to minus twenty. Then there was the local wildlife with which to contend: scorpions, camel spiders, huge lizards, sand fleas and water snakes were all part of operational tour.

Even in an age of multimedia, the exchange of handwritten letters has touchingly continued, and the impact of letters on morale is as important as it has always been. In areas where telephone coverage[20] or internet access was patchy or power cuts frequent, the old-fashioned bluey has remained a vital lifeline with home. In main camps, post could arrive every few days, often shared with friends who received nothing, whether a letter from home or a macabre gift of a wheelchair catalogue from a mate! A further recent communication development has been the e-bluey: a letter written online that is printed out and delivered by hand, without having been read. The men in Michael Pritchard's base started a competition to see whose mother wrote the most e-blueys! Facebook has become an extended interface with home. In the main camp in Afghanistan, soldiers make regular phone calls, can send text messages from a special phone and pick up voicemails from a dedicated 'paradigm' number. When troops are operating from FOBs, however, they can often be cut off from all forms of communication with loved ones, a situation families have described as 'almost unbearable'. When they return to a well-equipped camp with internet and post, the relief (home and away) has been palpable.

WARFARE AND PEACEKEEPING
A TWENTY-FIRST-CENTURY WAR

The majority of service personnel killed in Iraq and Afghanistan have been men in their twenties. The coalition forces have had the very latest weapons, but they have found themselves in a fight that is tougher than expected, against an enemy who engages in close-quarter fighting and benefits from better knowledge of the land, culture and terrain. Alongside the peacekeeping role of rebuilding and training the indigenous police and army, combat has continued in guerrilla form, sometimes with fixed bayonets. It has been difficult to know who is friend or foe. The Taliban have easily bought allegiance and tip-offs from Afghan police desperate to top up meagre wages. Captain Charlotte Cross in 2006 described how 'they're corrupt and useless. None of the people trust them.'[21] It has made soldiers understandably suspicious and on high alert when on patrol. While the majority of Afghan and Iraqi civilians are simple people wanting a better life, free of tyranny and bloodshed, the feeling that a teenager or female could be a suicide bomber has not been idle paranoia. 'The worst case scenario saw the police (in league with the Taliban) acting as a sort of Trojan Horse followed by a rushed assault by Taliban . . . It is immensely disquieting to have such an enemy within,' noted Will Pike. Likewise Ranger Stuart Devine admitted, 'Every time you kill one he's bound to have a friend, a father, a brother . . . There are millions of them, and the more you kill, the more they'll fight.'[22]

Modern warfare has been a rude awakening for many. Jerry Ryen King described one mission in Iraq: 'I got off the helicopter my night vision broke, I was surrounded by the sound of artillery rounds, people screaming in Arabic, automatic weapons, and the terrain didn't look anything like what we were briefed.'[23]

Missions to clear Iraqi villages have evoked scenes of the First World War, with insurgents buried deep into muddy canal trenches and empty buildings. Troops have operated in swirling clouds of sand churned up by helicopters, tracer bullets spinning overhead, F16 bombers dropping huge bombs, explosions that temporarily winded and deafened, mortars loaded into firing tubes, machine guns on sandbag mounts, suicide bombers, RPGs, grenades and improvised explosive devices (IED) – a terrifying test of troops' nerves. Pressure activated by the wheels of a vehicle, IEDs could be set off by a simple wire tug, or remotely by mobile phones or even garage door openers. Men have spoken of the panic of being immobilised by IEDS if they are not killed outright. 'You're immediately expecting a secondary attack or an ambush,' explained Corporal Simon Flores, who lost his foot in an explosion. Soldiers experience an extreme adrenalin rush in these situations and operate almost on auto-pilot to extricate themselves or fight back. Will Pike recorded in his diary, 'it is strange that the dangers and risks are not really an issue whilst one is deployed. It is before and afterwards when you have time to think and mull things over that you really feel the fears and risks.'

The major difference from previous conflicts has been the sheer unpredictability of the battle in Iraq and Afghanistan. There is no charge 'over the top' and no grand battle to be fought on a specific date; the risks are constant and all surrounding, whether the troops are on patrol or in camp. From the moment troops entered Iraqi or Afghan airspace, the threat of being killed has been present. For many, 'never knowing if this will be my last endeavour'[24] has been an enormous pressure.

Letters and emails home have largely glossed over the grisly details of day-to-day combat. Blood and guts have been confined to diaries or simply internalised. To compound the dread at home with a letter full of the gory descriptions soldiers used to relish is now felt to be insensitive and needless. Sarah Adams could always sense if her son James was 'down in the dumps' and found it excruciatingly difficult, 'because there's nothing I could do'. Moreover, the news of death or injury has been all too quickly relayed and when the communications go down[25] it signals a terrifying period of anxiety for families.

Witnessing death during combat is the shocking by-product of military life. Soldiers have described a lingering stench of death and blood that never evaporates. The wars in Iraq and Afghanistan have been devoid of the grudging respect and admiration for the enemy of historical conflicts – the Taliban are almost dehumanised and so different from Western views culturally that it has been hard to find empathy. Some have admired their tenacity, but with a weariness and sadness. 'It's at times like this that you fully see war to be the utter waste of humanity that it is and you invariably question why. The only answer to me is Plato's adage that only the dead have seen the end of war', recorded Lieutenant Robert Grant in his diary following the death of a friend,[26] while a Danish doctor described seeing marines who had witnessed indescribable slaughter walking 'like zombies. I can't help thinking that they had grown up today. The innocence evaporated as they all had to face their own mortality.'[27]

FAREWELL LETTERS: COMMON THEMES

It has been during these conflicts that for the first time men have been routinely advised to write a farewell letter before deployment. Unlike previous wars, soldiers often know when they will be posted abroad and have time to think about those implications. The trauma of being in these conflict situations is stressful enough, and as in the Falklands, writing a farewell letter is seen as a sensible way to deal emotionally with the risks ahead, before the men and women are in the thick of action.

For some parents, the idea of a last letter has been too much. Sarah Adams, whose son James Prosser was killed in Afghanistan, explained: 'James was really deep. He didn't want to go into that emotional place to write a letter because he knew it would break my heart. The thought of him thinking he wouldn't make it haunts me. There was never any doubt for me that he was always smiling.' His Royal Welsh welfare officer Mo Monaghan advised men to write a farewell letter but estimates only 30 per cent actually did. 'I've seen the pain of families without a letter,' he explained. For Lisa and John Foster, whose son Robbie was killed in a friendly-fire incident in Afghanistan in 2007, his farewell letters were invaluable. His mother rereads his words every month, while his father is just happy to know it's there even though he's not drawn to read it. 'You can have memories of words spoken, but letters are something tangible. I can go and get that letter out when I want to and I know darn well where I stood. If something happened to me, I'd want that letter to go with me. Because it's mine,' Lisa explained. Similarly, Marie Perry, whose son

Michael Pritchard was killed in Afghanistan in another friendly-fire incident in 2009, says, 'Every time I read it I cry my heart out and my heart just breaks for my precious boy. I don't read it often but keep it by my side at all times. It is always with me.'

Many men wrote with specific instructions for their funerals – or 'celebrations'. Chris Briggs wrote a farewell letter on his second tour of Afghanistan. He recalled being in a church service before leaving and the realisation that they would not all come back suddenly hitting home. They received a 'trauma management briefing' and were urged to write a letter so no loose ends would be left undone. Unusually, he talked about it with his friends, and they all included instructions for their funerals. One man would be putting £500 behind the bar for his celebration, while Chris himself chose songs he wanted played and bequeathed his life savings to his parents for an early retirement. 'Lots of the guys said writing a letter was like tempting fate but it was really important for me to do. We were patrolling in no-go areas and the Taliban were closing in at Nad'e Ali.[28] I got upset whilst writing it. My parents were shocked when I told them I'd written it'. They never read it; he returned home safely. Similarly, one squadron leader gave detailed instructions for his funeral in his letter 'and was quite adamant that I didn't want any great fuss. I have always struggled with funerals and made it quite clear that I didn't want people to be judged on whether they came to see me off or not.'

One marked theme of letters from Iraq and Afghanistan has been humour. Many men have spoken of trying to lighten the underlying message of such letters and, above all, trying to impart their own personality into them. Private William Cushley ended his farewell note with the postscript: 'You can keep the $50!'[29] If soldiers imagine their loved one reading it, it is just as important that the recipient imagine them saying it. The use of everyday vernacular has been common throughout history, but farewell letters from Iraq and Afghanistan are significantly lighter in tone and heavier in everyday colloquialism in a way previous letters have not been. The politics and controversy of war in the Middle East must be partly responsible for the tone: few now celebrate the glory of a soldier's death in battle; it has become about pride in the duty of doing a job.

One overriding theme of farewell letters from these conflicts has been their political nature – especially in American letters. US Sergeant Ryan Wood blogged, 'it is walking on that thin line between sanity and insanity. That feeling of total abandonment by a government and a country you used to love because politics are fighting this war . . . and it's a losing battle . . . and we're the ones ultimately paying the price.'[30] One anonymous American soldier used his farewell letter to blast the 'Dont' ask don't tell'[31] policy for gay recruits: 'I am angry at certain senators . . . They hide behind a vitriolic rhetoric fraught with illogical arguments and innuendo . . . gay soldiers who are still serving in silence will continue to put on our rucksacks and do what our country asks of us – and wait.'[32] Despite this, all these letters have been at pains to reinforce the pride of being a soldier and the love they have for the job – regardless of politics. Michael Pritchard wrote how much he loved his job as a military police officer, despite losing three colleagues during his tour of Afghanistan – events that led him to write a farewell letter of his own.

One further theme unique to these conflicts has been the emergence of 'non-traditional' farewell formats. Although most men still write letters, technological advances mean that blogs, video, email and CD messages have all been used to say farewell by those fighting in Iraq and Afghanistan. Master Corporal Raymond Arndt left a CD with the words,

> Should this disk be read then the worst has happened and I have died. I ask only that people try to understand what I was trying to do, and not to be mad or hate the army . . . I'll keep the beer cold till we meet again.
> > And when he gets to the pearly gates,
> > To Saint Peter he will tell,
> > One more soldier reporting sir,
> > I've served my time in hell.[33]

Above all, as in every conflict, farewell letters are heartfelt messages of love and regret. Ben Hyde, killed in Iraq, stated, 'I'm up in the stars looking down on you making sure you are safe. I'm sorry I've been a pain, but I know the good times outweigh the bad tenfold.'[34] Anthony Butterfield, also killed in Iraq, wrote, 'you all mean the world to me. I hope I've made you all proud. I love you with all of my heart.'[35] Army Sergeant Joseph C. Nurre, killed in Iraq, wrote to his parents, 'I know your grief is heavy now, but though you are stricken with sadness, let joy enter your hearts because you can know that I am with God . . .'[36]

Many of the fallen from Iraq and Afghanistan live on in a virtual world. Online memorials and Facebook pages are crammed with messages from those left behind. Grief has become a public affair – from the thousands who lined the streets of Wootton Bassett in silent tribute to the coffins flown back to Britain, to the solemn military repatriation of the American dead; iconic images relayed worldwide. Des Feeley, whose daughter Sarah was the first British woman killed in Afghanistan, described,

> the repatriation cortege of Sarah and her colleagues was one of the most moving experiences of my life. Given the huge numbers of people assembled, the only heart-breaking audible sound to be heard was quite literally that of the hearse's tyres slowly rolling over the road's surface, but with each passing vehicle the most intense grief imaginable . . . etched across each and every face.

The curt and impersonal report of 'another soldier killed in combat. Next of kin have been informed' is in sharp contrast to the real story behind each person killed in conflict. It is through their remarkable and honest farewell letters that mere statistics are transformed into individuals. It is through farewell letters that the personality and motivations of the fallen become a tangible legacy, providing fathomless comfort for those left behind.

The wars in Iraq and Afghanistan have rivalled previous conflicts in terms of letters, but these have also been wars that have been reported more than any other. Emails, blogs, videos and photographs have brought these wars into the public consciousness as never before. Soldiers' blogs have provided an almost running commentary on action, and letters and emails made public have given a heart-pumping perspective from the thick of the action. Rolling news and helmet-mounted cameras have captured close-quarter combat in new ways, and the tragic aftermaths of attacks have been laid bare for the world to see. It is easy in this multimedia world to become desensitised to death and destruction, yet the simplicity of a farewell letter still has the ability to make people stop, contemplate and remind themselves that these are not faceless troops. They are individuals, whose deaths cause infinite ripples through infinite lives.

Gunner Lee Thornton
Killed in Iraq, 7 September 2006

Lee 'Thorny' Thornton was born in Blackpool on 25 November 1983, the oldest of four boys (Plate 28). An avid Blackpool football fan, he was extremely close to his brothers – play-fighting and playing football with them in the park. Like most ordinary young men, he enjoyed socialising with his friends, watching films and bowling. Loving and compassionate, he always saw the best in people and had an enthusiastic, sunny outlook – so much so his catchphrase was 'no worries'.

In August 2000 Lee joined the army, aged just sixteen. Despite the apprehension of family and friends, he was adamant; he craved adventure and meeting new people. Following training, he was posted to the 12th Regiment Royal Artillery. It was a perfect career for a man with an eagerness to serve and a passion for sport. He competed in the Cambrian Patrol competition[37] in 2004 and 2005, and ran a marathon for charity in 2005 too. He was based at Baker

Barracks in Portsmouth and spoke enthusiastically about the tight camaraderie of army life; he was incredibly proud to wear his uniform and fight for his country. He had no qualms about going to Iraq: it was simply his duty as a soldier.

Lee had already decided to leave the army when his tour in Iraq had ended, to start a new adventure of babies and marriage to fiancée Helen. In Helen's eyes, Lee was an emotional and sensitive soul. They had first met through friends when Helen was just sixteen, but feeling too young for a long-distance relationship, they did not start dating until a few years later. Theirs was a simple, old-fashioned love story. The attraction and connection was instant and they considered one another soul mates. While there was no doubt that they wanted to spend the rest of their lives together, Helen, 'the less spontaneous and sensible one', believed they should wait until she had finished her teaching degree and their lives were a little more settled. It is a decision about which she still feels deep regret.

When Lee discovered he would be deployed to Iraq it was the jolt he and Helen needed to get engaged. They exchanged rings, booked a venue for the wedding and Helen bought her dress. Lee was initially in Iraq for five weeks before returning on leave; not a moment too soon for his fiancée. She recounted:

> I never thought of him dying. I know this sounds silly, but we never spoke of it, neither of us thought it would happen to him. We even joked about it, saying, 'keep your head down; you don't want it to get shot off'. It was so rare for anyone to die in comparison to the amount of people out there.

In common with many who deployed to Iraq, Lee had the confidence of youthful invincibility. For this eager character to be anything other than full of life was a prospect nobody wanted to acknowledge. Lee was evidently well aware of the risks of war, though. No doubt he would have been briefed on survivability and knew that since the start of war over two thousand soldiers (largely American) had already been killed in Iraq.

Lee had first gone to Iraq in 2003 on Operation TELIC, one of the largest deployments since the Second World War. It was his first foray into real combat, although he had been on exercise in Germany, Cyprus, Poland and Canada. Serving in Iraq in 2003, 58 Eyre's Battery carried out an air defence role as insurgency broke out in the wake of Hussein's fall. By the time of Lee's second tour in May 2006 the situation was still volatile; Iraq had a new constitution, but suicide bombings, insurgency and sectarian violence were as intense as ever. Public support for the war was at an all-time low and questions were being asked about the effectiveness of personal kit and vehicles in protecting the troops. There were chinks of light: areas were being handed back to provincial governments and British combat fatalities were still comparatively low at seventy-six.

Before returning to operational duties in Iraq, Lee wrote a number of farewell letters to his family and fiancée. Whether he was just covering bases, or had a premonition about dying, nobody knows. It was in his nature to care deeply about others, and the act of writing letters was very much a manifestation of this, as well as a means of coping with a return to the unpredictable arena of war. The five weeks already spent in Iraq had exposed him to roadside bombs during dangerous patrols, and most soldiers would have contemplated the prospect of not returning home, however fleetingly. Lee's role involved protecting armoured units, as well as vehicle patrols and recce-ing gun positions. It was a skilled job in arduous conditions.

Helen remembered Lee being away as a physical ache; it was almost impossible to quantify how much she missed him. Communication both ways became vital and Lee was a prolific correspondent to Helen and his family. Each week Helen sent a box of treats to Lee and wrote to him daily. Likewise Lee would try and phone every other day, as well as sending emails, letters and even video diaries of his experiences in Basra. Lee also kept a written diary where he poured out his thoughts about day-to-day life in this inhospitable land.

On 5 September, Lee volunteered to go on patrol in a 'gesture of defiance' against the perpetrators of an attack that had killed two of the regiment just a few days earlier. Chillingly, their vehicle hit a roadside bomb so powerful it threw the driver twenty metres down the road. Despite the palpable shock of losing colleagues in devastating circumstances, Lee was determined to carry on with the job. Soon after leaving the security of Shaibah Logistics Base, the men came under fire in Al Qurna, north of Basra. Lee suffered a single gun-shot to the neck and was quickly airlifted to hospital in Germany, but the bullet had penetrated his brain and severed his spinal cord, leaving him quadriplegic. Furthermore, on the flight he had suffered a stroke, rendering him brain dead. Lee's parents, Helen and her mother were flown to the hospital where he was on a life-support machine. At the time, Helen was not aware of the seriousness of the situation and recalled that on arrival she wanted to buy Lee a McDonald's, knowing he would hate hospital food. When the family were asked if they wanted a priest, the enormity of the situation started to sink in and they faced the heartbreaking knowledge that they would have to switch off his life support. Until that moment, Helen had not admitted the possibility of Lee dying, and the news was devastating. 'It felt as though I had been punched in the stomach, I was sick and couldn't breathe. I was totally devastated and felt that my world had ended. I was crying so much I nearly collapsed. I was shaking uncontrollably and blabbering irrationally.' The family took turns to spend time with him, and Helen spoke to him softly, cradling his body, trying to imprint his face and smell into her mind. Lee died on Thursday 7 September 2006. He was just twenty-two.

Helen knew that Lee had written a farewell letter, and had left it with her mother with instructions that she should not read it unless the worst happened. Although she opened it a few days after Lee's death, she was still numb and the next six months passed in an emotional fog. 'I felt sad when I read the letter as it was what he had written for me if he had died and he had written it with sadness thinking that he may die.' She found it difficult to articulate the value of that letter, along with four further letters she received in the post following his death. Although re-reading the letter provided inestimable comfort, it was a bittersweet compensation: 'I had thousands [of letters] from the age of sixteen. It made me realize that I would never read his words again.'

Hi babe,

I don't know why I am writing this because I really hope that this letter never gets to you, because if it does that means I am dead. It also means I never had time to show you just how much I really did love you.

You have shown me what love is and what it feels like to be loved. Every time you kissed me and our lips touched so softly I could feel it. I got the same magical feeling as our first kiss. I could feel it when our hearts get so close they are beating as one.

You are the beat of my heart, the soul in my body; you are me because without you I am nothing. I love you Helen, you are my girlfriend, my fiancée and my best friend.

You are the person I know I could turn to when I needed help, you are the person I looked at when I needed to smile and you are the person I went to when I needed a hug.

When I am away it is like I have left my soul by your side.

You have shown me so much while you have been in my life that if I lost you I could not live. You have shown me how to live and you have shown me how to be truly happy.

I want you to know that every time I smile that you have put it there. You make me smile when others can't. You make me feel warm when I am cold.

You have shown me so much love and so much more. I want you to know how much you mean to me. You are my whole world and I love you with all my heart, you are my happiness. There is no sea or ocean that could stop my love for you. It is the biggest thing I have ever had.

When I say I love you I am trying to say . . . that you make me feel warm and great about myself, you make me smile and laugh everyday; you make time to talk to me and listen to what I have to say.

I know God put me and you on this earth to find each other, fall in love and show the rest of the world what true love really is.

I know this is going to sound sad but every night I spent away I had a photo of you on my headboard. Each night I would go to bed, kiss my fingers then touch your face.

I put the photo over my bed so you could look over me as I slept. Well now it is my turn to look over you as you sleep and keep you safe in your dreams. I will always be looking over you to make sure you're safe.

Helen, I want to say something and I mean this more than I ever did before. You were the love of my life, the girl of my dreams.

Just because I have passed away does not mean I am not with you. I'll always be there looking over you, keeping you safe.

So whenever you feel lonely just close your eyes and I'll be there right by your side. I really did love you with all I had, you were everything to me.

Never forget that, and never forget I will always be looking over you. I love you, you are my soul mate.

Love always and forever.

Lee.[38]

As well as the letter to Helen, Lee had written messages for his whole family, including his brothers Ryan, Sean and Jake. In their letter he urged them to follow their dreams and promised always to be looking over them and to be there if they needed to talk. Sean and Jake have since joined the army in their brother's memory, a decision that has been excruciating for their mother Karen: 'It's not what I wanted for them but as Lee says, they have to follow their dreams.' Lee's memory has not diminished. An online memorial continues to attract countless messages, including poems and notes from his mother every few weeks. It is through Lee's final letters, however, that she, Helen and all the family and friends still feel closest to him; his words, his wishes, his personality remain vibrant and alive in the lines of his farewell letters.

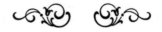

PFC Jesse Givens

Killed in Iraq, 1 May 2003

Born in March 1969 in Springfield, Missouri, Jesse graduated from Glendale High School in 1988 and attended Missouri State Southern University (Plate 29). He met his future wife Melissa while he was working as a security guard at a retail store. The attraction was instant, and their relationship started after her twenty-third birthday, when he went home with her, and never left! A literate, thoughtful bookworm and budding artist, Jesse was the complete opposite of the then party-loving Melissa, who remembers that she 'needed him. He kept me grounded and sane.' They fell deeply in love; Jesse was the first man that Melissa's young son Dakota (whom he nicknamed Toad) had trusted and liked – it was a gut instinct Melissa shared. Today she finds comfort in an unflinching belief that the speed of the relationship was God's will: 'He knew we didn't have much time,' she said.

Jesse found a job as an ironworker, and set about raising Dakota as his own. Watching the appalling aftermath of 9/11 moved a patriotic Jesse to tears, and one week later he came home to inform a shocked Melissa he had joined the army. Ironically, Jesse had been touched by the thought of all the children who would be growing up without parents following the Twin Towers attacks – a position Melissa has found difficult to reconcile with what has happened to her own family.

At Fort Knox, Jesse breezed through basic training. In 2002 the family moved to Fort Carson, an army base near Colorado Springs, and in May they married. By the end of the year, Melissa was pregnant – a baby they touchingly named 'Bean' after seeing him for the first time during the scan. On 14 February 2003 Jesse was given orders to deploy to Iraq as part of the 3rd Armored Cavalry Regiment. As early as November 2002, Jesse had known that deployment to Iraq would be inevitable, and he worked out his conflicting emotions in the pages of his journal. His pride as a soldier struggled with his instincts as a husband and father, but he was determined to do his duty. It is clear that he was keenly aware of the mortal risks of a war zone from the outset:

I am not going to pretend that I understand why we are thinking about going to war with Iraq . . . No matter what the reasons, I will go and fight with all my heart. Not to win a war, but to come home to my wife and my children. I took an oath to protect my country. Not for the sake of saving the world, but for the hopes that my family wouldn't have to live in a world filled with hate, fear and sadness - a world which America was exposed to on Sept. 11, 2001. If we are involved in combat and I fall, who will raise my children? Who will be there for my wife? I sacrifice not only my life, but a husband and a father's life also. Who will see that my wife can support my children through all of their years? Who will provide my family with their basic needs? I didn't ask for your pity or money, I just ask that we do this for the right reasons. I ask that when you send soldiers into battle, that they are not just numbers. I ask that you see our roles as fathers, sons, daughters, wives and husbands – as well as seen as the proud Americans who want to serve our country. When all is said and done, will we, the United States military, shed blood, or pass at the hands of our enemies for a just cause? Will you remember those who we leave behind, and honor them as well as our fallen brothers and sisters?

Before leaving for Iraq Jesse assured his parents he was working with the best platoon and equipment the army had, but was unable to promise Dakota a safe return. 'I can't promise I'll come home,' he admitted. A fearful Melissa raised the topic of 'what ifs' and life insurance, and on the night before he left, they simply lay on the bed, entwined in each other's arms, desperate to remember the touch of one another.

The last time Melissa saw Jesse was 6 April 2003, as she struggled to say goodbye. Her final memory of him was in her rearview mirror as she drove away from the car park, tears streaming down both their faces: 'it was like popping a cork and letting uncontrollable emotion come out.' The guilt at not staying haunts her to this day. 'I could have had three more hours,' she remembers, but at the same time the anguished anticipation of him going was at least over.

Throughout his time in Iraq, as a prolific letter writer, Jesse wrote countless notes home – most often complaining about the flies and it being 'hot as hell!' He also managed to make one phone call, in which he told Melissa that he had written a farewell letter but that she should not open it. He reiterated how much he loved her, and Melissa detected nothing in his voice that revealed he was scared that he might not be coming home. Unbeknown to Melissa, though, Jesse had written a number of farewell letters that would continue to emerge even after his death.

On 1 May Jesse was in an M-1A1[39] tank crew fighting fires set by insurgents when the sandy bank on which they were parked suddenly caved in. The 65-ton vehicle slid into a canal off the Euphrates River. Unable to make it through the escape hatch, Jesse drowned in the tank – the first man from his unit to die.

Among his personal effects were two letters, one of which was practically falling apart and was poignantly stained with the muddy waters that had claimed his life. Heartbreakingly, Melissa cannot touch this letter: the fragile contents are sealed in a plastic casing, marked with 'do not open: hazardous material' stickers. Knowing that these toxic waters claimed her husband's life makes this letter particularly hard to comtemplate. 'I don't know if you will ever understand the light you brought into my life. I want you to know I have every moment we ever spent together in my heart,' were the only sentences still legible.

Another letter in his wallet, containing a pressed Coloradan flower given to him by Dakota, read, 'My angel, my wife, my love, my friend. If you're reading this, I won't be coming home.' Desperately sad and achingly touching, it was small comfort to know that these letters were possibly the last thing he clutched before he died.

In a bitterly ironic twist, Melissa received the news of Jesse's death just one hour after Bush had announced the end of major combat operations in Iraq. That morning she had awoken with a sickening feeling, and refused to leave the house. She remembered two men in uniform and a chaplain asking her to come to the door. Deep down, Melissa knew that a visit in person meant death, but she was unable to accept what they were telling her. In her grief-stricken confusion she could not believe he had drowned, and remembered repeating, 'There's no water, he's in the desert.' The news came as a physical blow, literally knocking the air out of her. 'They took everything from me with that news. All my dreams. Ever since I have been picking up the pieces of a broken life, like a shattered piece of glass.'

Jesse's final farewell letter arrived three weeks after his death, just days after Melissa had given birth to Carson, a son who would never meet his father. It was a complete surprise as Melissa assumed the fragments found on Jesse's body were the farewell letters he had talked about on the telephone. Nevertheless, in the mailbox was one final farewell. 'Thank God because it helped me so much – helped me moved through the grief.' It took Melissa twenty minutes before she could bring herself to read it. She sat alone on the porch, and remembers it was one of the most surreal experiences of her life. She sat in silence for hours, digesting the words he had written.

My family:
   I never thought I would be writing a letter like this, I really don't know where to start. I've been getting bad feelings though and well if you are reading this . . .
   I searched all my life for a dream and I found it in you . . . The happiest moments in my life all deal with my little family. You will never know how complete you have made me. Each and every one of you. You saved me from loneliness and taught me how to think beyond myself. You taught me how to live and to love. You opened my eyes to a world I never even dreamed existed . . .
   Dakota, you are more son than I could ever ask for. I can only hope I was half the dad. You taught me how to care until it hurts, you taught me how to smile again. You taught me that life isn't so serious and sometimes you have to play. You have a big beautiful heart. Through life you need to keep it open and follow it. Never be afraid to be yourself. I will always be there in our park when you dream so we can still play together. I hope someday you will have a son like mine. Make them smile and shine just like you. I hope someday you will understand why I didn't come home. Please be proud of me. Please don't stop loving life. Take in

every breath like it's your first. I will always be there with you. I'll be in the sun, shadows, dreams, and joys of your life.

Bean, I never got to see you but I know in my heart you are beautiful. I will always have with me the feel of the soft nudges on your mom's belly, and the joy I felt when we found out you were on the way. I dream of you every night, and I always will. Don't ever think that since I wasn't around that I didn't love you. You were conceived of love and I came to this terrible place for love. Please understand that I had to be gone so that I could take care of my family. I love you Bean.

I have never been so blessed as the day I met Melissa. You are my angel, soulmate, wife, lover, and my best friend. I am sorry. I did not want to have to write this letter. There is so much more I need to say, so much more I need to share. A million lifetimes' worth. I married you for a million lifetimes. That's how long I will be with you. Please keep our babies safe. Please find it in your heart to forgive me for leaving you alone . . . Do me a favor, after you tuck Toad and Bean in, give them hugs and kisses from me. Go outside look at the stars and count them. Don't forget to smile.

Love Always
Your husband
   Jess

Melissa has determined that her sons will never forget their father. His belongings have been lovingly packed into trunks, his photos adorn her house, the flag from his coffin is framed, and Dakota still sleeps with a raggedy blanket that Jesse braided together. In Carson, Melissa can see Jesse's eyes and facial expressions. Jesse even made a videotape of bedtime stories for Dakota, so he would still hear his voice despite being over seven thousand miles away. At the end of the tape, they discovered yet another message from this man who was consumed with love for his family. He had recorded it just hours before leaving: a haunting message that reanimates Jesse's ghost.

OK, you guys. We did the stories. Now I want to take some time by myself to tell you I love you very much. Melissa, please take care of Dakota, and give him hugs and kisses. Dakota, please take care of your mom. When the Bean gets here, tell him I love him very much. Sorry I wasn't here. Give him hugs and kisses for me. Say your prayers every night . . . Dakota don't let the fuzzy butt-tickling monkey get you, or the toe-eating alligator. Um, I'm not real good at this kind of stuff. Buddy, I'm proud of you. You're the most wonderful boy a guy could have, and I'm going to miss you a lot. Melissa, I'm sorry I'm not going to be home. I'm sorry . . . I love you guys. I'm going to miss you with all my heart, and I'll be thinking about you all the time. I'll be praying for you. I'll be home as soon as I can. I love you guys.[40]

> My family: 22·April·03
>
> I never thought that I would be writing a letter like this, I really don't know where to start. I've been getting bad feelings though and well if you are reading this....
>
> I am forever in debt to you, Dakota, and the bean. I searched all my life for a dream and I found it in you. I would like to think that I made a positive difference in your lives. I will never be able to make up for the bad I am so sorry. The happiest moments in my life all deal with my little family. I will always have with me the small moments we all shared. The moments when you quit taking life so serious and smiled. The sounds of a beautiful boys laughter or the simple nudge of a baby unborn. You will never know how complete you have made me. Each one of you. You saved me from loneliness and taught me how to think beyond myself. You taught me how to live and love. You opened my eyes to a world I never dreamed existed. I am proud of you. Stay on the path you chose. Never lose sight of what is important again, You and our babies.

21 Part of the letter from Jesse Givens, 22 April 2003 (with kind permission of Melissa Givens).

Like virtually all of the military fallen in these most recent conflicts, Jesse's memory has not diminished. Facebook tributes and online memorials continue to inspire condolences from complete strangers, as well as giving Melissa a bittersweet, though cathartic, outlet to write and be connected to her husband. Her pain, she believes, will never subside: 'My heart physically hurts. It's like someone reached their hand inside my chest and pulled it out.'

Jesse's letters and writings are bundled together, and regularly re-read by Melissa. The words have become engraved in her mind, but they are so important, she believes she would not have coped without them. They will be passed onto the boys when they are older, but for the present, Melissa takes them out whenever she wants to feel close to Jesse. 'I wish the letters never stopped, so I could keep having new words to read,' she explained.

KINGSMAN JAMIE HANCOCK
Killed in Iraq, 6 November 2006

BORN ON 30 JANUARY 1987 to mum Lynda and father Eddie, a joiner, Jamie and his older brother Joey were raised by their father when their parents separated in 1996 (Plate 30). Jamie Hancock was a streetwise charmer from the town of Hindley Green near Wigan, a former mining community with a large army contingent. Joey was a corporal at Catterick, North Yorkshire, and Jamie looked up to him, determined to follow in his footsteps. Never mollycoddled, he was very much an outdoors type and hated being stuck in front of the television. He liked walking the fields, was a good target shooter like his father and from an early age proved himself a natural marksman with the air rifle. He was also a keen boxer and had lots of friends, who would fill the house at weekends, regaling one another with stories of girls, drinking and high jinks.

At sixteen Jamie left Hesketh Fletcher Secondary School and went to work in a local biscuit factory. He was itching to apply for the army, though, and signed up at his local recruitment office. In May 2005 he went to the Infantry Training Centre at Catterick and was posted to the 1st Battalion Queen's Lancashire Regiment as a rifleman. He was eager to volunteer for Iraq, which meant changing units to the King's Regiment and undergoing four months of intense training before deploying in October 2006. When his father asked why he wanted to go, Jamie simply stated, 'They wanted people.' With an inherent sense of duty, Jamie identified with the national flag and was incredibly proud to be a soldier. A quick learner, he had mastered driving warrior armoured vehicles and was eager to go out to Iraq to start making a difference to ordinary people; helping them get back to some sense of normality after three years of war. Jamie deployed with notions of painting schools and protecting women and children – the reality on arriving in Basra was an unpleasant shock.

'We can't even open the gate for getting shot at,' he told his father. He described driving warrior tanks down dusty streets, desolate save for the occasional palm tree, and hearing bullets pinging off the side. He was angry at what he perceived as dangerous political correctness at road blocks, where translators read a set text to the people they searched. In Jamie's eyes, the process recklessly slowed things down and endangered troops. There were not enough troops to control a city of 1.3 million people. Infantry numbers were down and there was, according to senior soldiers, a woeful lack of air support and unmanned aerial vehicles (UAVs).

Eddie Hancock, self-educated in Middle East politics, was vehemently opposed to the war from the beginning. He knew that his son wanted to go, though, and did not feel he could prevent him. He recalled an incident that revealed how diametrically opposed he and his son were politically, when they were play-wrestling. His son's wallet fell to the floor and 'amongst the condoms and credit cards was a small picture of the queen.' His son solemnly explained, 'this tells me what I am and who I am.' Eddie remembered, 'I was really surprised for a young man to say that in this day and age – extraordinary.' It was a side of his son he had never before seen and, although he did not share his passion for queen and country, was incredibly proud of him.

Eddie and Jamie drove their van to Catterick the night before he would deploy to Iraq, and he remembered them drinking a flask of coffee and chatting late into the night. Anxieties were starting to creep in as Jamie started a conversation with the words, 'Dad, if I don't come back . . .' Despite his father's protestations, he continued: he was adamant that he wanted to be buried in his Number Twos[41] and that the National Anthem should play at his funeral. Like many soldiers throughout history, Jamie had experienced a premonition that he would not return, and wanted to share this with his father. Eddie warned him that it would be dangerous and impressed on him to be as careful as possible. Not once did he consider that it might be the last time he would see his son.

When Jamie arrived in Iraq, he communicated regularly with his dad through letters and phone calls. Eddie would also send packages of much-craved jelly sweets and athlete's foot cream. The entire time he was there, Jamie carried a crumpled brown note from his brother that read, 'Take care kid. I am so proud of you, and I love you with all my heart', along with a small card inscribed with the values and standards of a Kingsman: pride, humour, loyalty and honesty.

On 6 November 2006 Jamie was shot by machine-gun fire while on sentry duty in a sangar in the Old State Building. This sandbag-fortified watchtower in central Basra was a vulnerable target. Despite body armour and combat helmet, a bullet penetrated Jamie's chest when his attackers gained access to a building opposite and fired directly into the sangar.

Jamie had been in Iraq for less than three weeks when he was killed. Eddie remembered the shattering news in a phone call from his distraught oldest son at six o'clock on a Monday evening. Barely able to speak through his tears, his son kept repeating that there was terrible news. Eddie looked out of his window to see the grim procession of army officer, policeman and priest on the pathway. His legs buckled; he remembered a pain at the back of his throat, and a feeling that his chest would burst. 'I knew then he was dead,' said Eddie, unable to erase that day from memory.

Eddie went to RAF Brize Norton to witness the sombre repatriation of his son, and when he returned home Jamie's last letter had arrived on the mat. Although not a traditional 'in the event of my death' letter, it was a final farewell and final testament to his thoughts about Iraq. It took Eddie a long time to open the envelope, but has become his most treasured letter.

Hi Dad
   I am now in Basrah Palace. I am going to the old state building tomorrow. It's really mad here I got here last nite, the weather is getting cooler. It rains about now to December. I had my first rocket attack about two hours ago. I was up on the roof just looking at the view and I heard a whizzing noise then a big bang 'fuck me I shit myself.' One of the rockets didn't explode it went straight through the toilets. Unlucky ;-) Basrah looks really nice. The Palace is amazing. It's all made of marble. I have taken a picture of it I will show you when I get home.
   Thanks for all the creams and powders they came in handy.
   Ok I love you loads, tell Joey I love him too.
   Jamie xxxx[42]

In accordance with his wishes, Jamie was buried in uniform at St John's Church, accompanied by the regimental band. Since his death, Eddie has thought about him every single day. Each time he passes the war memorial he looks at the picture of his son. He talks to him when alone at work. His father cannot bring himself to unpack Jamie's kit-bag, which remains in his untouched bedroom, and sometimes he likes to go in there, unzip the bag and simply put his head inside, breathing in the scent of his son. Jamie's urn is

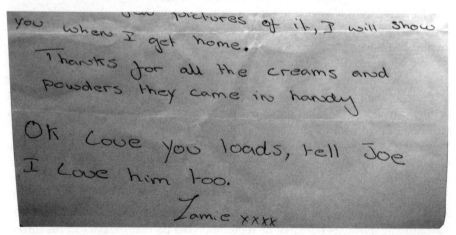

22 Part of the letter from Jamie Hancock, c. 2006 (with kind permission of Eddie Hancock).

also kept in the bedroom, regularly touched and kissed. In spirit, Jamie even returns to Catterick, safe in his father's rucksack, when he visits his eldest son. In fact, it is the vision of Jamie saying goodbye at Catterick that burns brightest for Eddie: 'a big hug and a smiling face'.

Given his vocal distaste for the war in Iraq, Jamie's father has remained bitter about his son's death. 'If he'd died on the beaches, defending his country I would have felt better, but he died for something irrelevant, in a monumental cock-up . . . I miss him.' Eddie has dismissed sympathies offered by then Prime Minister Tony Blair and others as 'sanctimonious hogwash'. Condolences from his army comrades have been warmly received: 'He was a magnet for his peers who were drawn by his infectious sense of fun and all-embracing nature,' wrote his company commander.

Jamie's letters, particularly his last one, have become treasured possessions that Eddie often re-reads: 'Those words are the same as looking at someone in a coffin.' It is when he reads the letters that father once again is touching and talking to his son.

GUARDSMAN NEIL 'TONY' DOWNES
Killed in Afghanistan, 9 June 2007

BORN IN SEPTEMBER 1986, Tony Downes was a fun-loving, compassionate 'brain-box', achieving eighteen GCSEs at Middleton Technology School (Plate 31). Son of publicans Sheryl and Ronnie, he spent his formative years growing up in the King's Head pub in Droylsden, Manchester. His father had been in the navy and from childhood Tony had been in the RAF cadets – a military life seemed to be his destiny. Initially he wanted to join the marines, but a leg injury meant that was impossible. Instead, at the age of eighteen, he joined the army. His mother remembers not being 'overly keen', but would never have considered preventing her son following his dream, and recalled him being 'dead chuffed' when he was accepted into the 1st Battalion Grenadier Guards.

His first active service came in Iraq in 2006; his family were remarkably calm and relaxed about his going. At that time, the British death toll was comparatively low, democracy seemed to be making some headway and Tony was eagerly anticipating the thrill of finally going on operations in a real combat zone. In March 2007 the news that he would be deploying to Afghanistan was an altogether different proposition. His parents were nervous and tried to avoid watching the news, despite their son's insistence that he would be fine.

At this point, Tony was in a relationship with Aldershot travel agent Jane Little. They had met in a local pub when he asked her to dance, and the attraction was instant. Falling in love, they discussed marriage and Tony started looking for rings when he was in Afghanistan. Jane was captivated by his fun-loving disposition and constant laughter. Although he did not admit to any anxiety about deploying, Jane was inconsolable in the few days before he left for Afghanistan.

It was at this time that Tony gave her a farewell letter he had written. Jane handed it to her mother for safekeeping, not really thinking about the enormity of him having written this. It was only when her mother started crying that she realised the implications of what he had done – a chink in his cheerful armour where he had dealt with the horrible possibility of not returning.

If he was nervous, he did not show it, and both Jane and Tony's mother tried to suppress their worries, at least outwardly. Tony had also written a farewell letter to his parents and when he told them, his mother made light of the situation. 'I said get out, I don't want to see that, go away!' Sheryl remembered, but at the same time was deeply touched. 'I think it really was just in case because I had no idea he was having these thoughts.' The letter was kept by her husband and Sheryl soon forgot about it.

While in Afghanistan, Tony wrote home regularly as well as sending texts, emails and chatting online with Jane. He was involved in an operation to widen and deepen irrigation ditches for the locals near Sangin in Helmand Province, working alongside the Afghan National Army. He was also involved in gathering intelligence during patrols of Sangin, Gereshk and Babaji, often manning a weapons-mounted installation kit (WMIK) grenade machine gun. The night before he was killed, he had telephoned his father and texted his mother and Jane. He was in positive, excitable mood, looking forward to coming home in a few weeks and telling them he had lost weight. He never divulged operational information and kept conversations light, well aware that talk of the continual dangers would upset those at home. He was a little more open with his friends and siblings, although generally maintained the cheeky, happy-go-lucky persona and confidence that he would return home. Nerves were heightened two weeks before Tony was killed when another soldier from his unit died. Everyone with ties to the regiment was affected – it made Tony realise that nobody was invincible, and made Jane incredibly worried for him.

On the morning of 9 June 2007 Tony was on patrol with the Afghan National Army, near Sangin. This area, a vital supply route for the Taliban, was one of the deadliest places in Afghanistan. It was an area riddled with mines and Taliban insurgents, with ill-defined tribal loyalties and difficulties in finding trustworthy police to patrol alongside soldiers. Tony was killed when his vehicle was hit by a land-mine explosion.

The dreaded knock at Sheryl's door came on that Saturday evening at 7.30. The bar was filling up, and on seeing the police, she naturally assumed they were there to talk about pub business. When they asked to go somewhere quiet to talk, an unsuspecting Sheryl took them up onto the stage in the pub. The next few minutes passed in the horrific blur of a nightmare. An army card was produced, but Sheryl still has no recollection of what she was told. She simply kept thinking about the fact she had heard from her son merely hours beforehand. Sheryl called Jane shortly afterwards, who was in high spirits dressing up for an evening out. The news was a body blow, and she recalled her anguished screams of 'No, no, no.' Almost immediately, Jane was compelled to find and read his farewell letter. 'I was in so much pain, it physically hurt,' she remembered, and the words swam in front of her eyes.

Tony was killed at 10.30 in the morning and his death was instantaneous. 'It's some consolation to know he wouldn't have felt a thing,' admitted his mother. It took a few days before she was able to read her son's final letter. Feeling raw and ripped apart, she needed the reassurance of her husband that the words were comforting and that she would feel better for reading it. Sheryl recalled reading and reading and reading those words – some of which are so personal to the family that she is unwilling to share them with a wider audience. Tony had also left notes for his brothers and sisters; powerful musings for a twenty year old who must have spent hours thinking through what he would say.

Hi Clampets.[43] Well I guess by now you have heard the good news. I am up in heaven now with grandad and nana – sure they are stopping me pulling the birds. Well don't be mad, don't be sad. I died doing what I had to do and that was serving the British. Mum just think you won't be going in the bottle bin anymore,[44] and dad hope I made you proud. Celebrate my life because I love you and I will see you all again.[45]

The letter Tony had written to Jane remains a treasured object. It brings his personality back to life, and she remembers being struck by the profound thought that these would be his final words to her.

Hey beautiful! I'm sorry I had to put you through all this, darling. I'm truly sorry. Just thought I'll leave you with a last few words.
All I wanna say is how much I loved you and cared for you. You are the apple of my eye and I will be watching over you always.
Mary, Jane, Ian, Tom, Craig, Lee, thank you all for accepting me in to be able to care for your daughter/sister. I will not forget how nice you have been to me! Bet now my bloody lottery numbers will come up, ha ha!

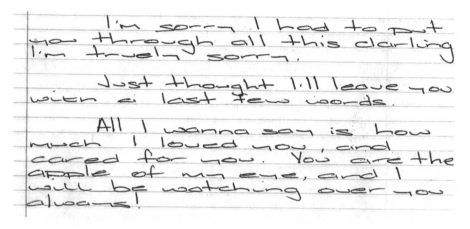

I'm sorry I had to put you through all this darling I'm truely sorry.

Just thought I'll leave you with a last few words.

All I wanna say is how much I loved you, and cared for you. You are the apple of my eye, and I will be watching over you always!

23 Part of the letter from Tony Downes, 2007 (with kind permission of Jane Little).

Jane I hope you have a wonderful and fulfilling life. Get married, have children etc. I will love you forever and will see you again when you are old and wrinkly! I have told my parents to leave you some money out of my insurance, so have fun bbe! OK . . . gonna go now beautiful. Love you forever.

Tony x x x[46]

Tony was hugely popular in the regiment, and his death prompted a flood of condolences from all ranks wanting to pay tribute to his 'energy and enthusiasm . . . huge intellect . . . whether in tunic or bearskin or combats, he was held in the highest regard by all who had the pleasure to serve alongside him.'

Jane keeps his farewell letter in her bedroom, in a chest full of Tony's possessions. Reading and talking about the letter provokes tears and smiles each time. She often reads it if she is feeling sad, and sometimes is simply drawn to open the chest and read it for no particular reason. Her memories of, and love for Tony, are undiminished, and honouring his wishes, she hopes one day to live the wonderful life he wished for her. Tony's mother still reads her son's letter: 'not often, but I can't not read it. It's just Tony all over. I see him writing it. It's witty; it's him.' The words Tony wrote are a cherished reminder of his heroic voice, and offer enduring comfort amid the grief of everyone he touched.

MAJOR ANDREW OLMSTED

Killed in Iraq, 3 January 2008

BORN IN 1972 IN Maine, Andrew Olmsted was educated at St John's High School in Shrewsbury, Massachusetts (Plate 32). He went on to study history and government at Clark University in Worcester. 'He loved this country while recognizing all its flaws over the years,' remembered his father. His parents were Nancy and Wesley, he had a brother Eric, and sister Catherine. Andrew was an Eagle Scout – the highest rank in the Scouts – and was a bookish student who excelled in writing and achieved excellent grades. He had a passion for philosophy, economics, music from the 1980s, movies, Disneyworld and the Boston Red Sox. Andy showed a keen interest in the military from an early age, signing up for the Reserve Officers' Training Corps (ROTC) and National Guard Service in the summer before he attended university. Friends remembered him as a larger than life character with a signature Fedora hat; he was witty, self-effacing, passionate about debating and had just finished a draft of a novel.

In 1992 Andrew served as a platoon leader with the 66th Armored Battalion at Fort Hood in Texas, then went to Camp Casey in Korea. In 1997, he returned to Fort Carson, Colorado, and a year later at Hammond Castle he married Amanda Wilson, whom he had met at university. In May 2007 after training at Fort Riley, he was deployed to Iraq on a mission to train the Iraqi army. A self-described libertarian determined to make a difference, he also blogged for a local newspaper. One post affirmed, 'The sooner the Iraqi government doesn't need U.S. support to provide security for its people, the sooner we will probably be asked to leave.' He was assigned to the Military Transition Team, 1st Brigade, 1st Infantry, working with the Fifth Iraqi Army Division. Tragically, his life was snuffed out in the country he was so desperate to help.

Towards the end of 2007 the situation in Iraq was improving: the monthly death toll for US troops had reached a heartening low, and civilian deaths were decreasing. Militant extremists were still going strong, however, particularly in mixed Sunni–Shiite neighbourhoods. Andy knew that he and the rest of his eleven-man team would be facing the dangers of roadside bombs, continued insurgency and the deadly accuracy of sniper fire. Operating from the Kirkush Military Training Base near an FOB called Caldwell and working throughout the Diyala Province, Andy's work with the Iraqi army took him thousands of miles across this dangerous region and along the Iranian border. Andrew kept a meticulous blog throughout his time in Iraq for the Denver newspaper *Rocky Mountain News*. He wrote about 'Team Nightmare' handing out gifts to children, the ever-present threat of suicide bombers and hunting groups who laid IEDs. Sporadic contacts with the enemy were quickly diffused: 'we established that the Coalition isn't afraid to face the enemy on his own turf.'[47]

He was keenly aware of cultural differences and wrote eloquently about finding caches of enemy weapons and the incredible camaraderie between men working exhausting shifts.

On 3 January 2008 Andrew was carrying out testing duties in As Sadiyah, attempting to persuade three suspected insurgents, who had crashed into a ditch, to surrender. As he reasoned with the men, he was felled by an unseen sniper, as was one of his comrades, Captain Thomas Casey. The rest of Andy's team fought back and killed all those at the ambush site. Andrew was evacuated out of the area by helicopter, but to no avail. The bullet had killed him instantly. Within a fortnight, his body was repatriated to the USA for a full military burial.

His poignantly named 'Final Post' took the form of a public blog – his final words touching a mass audience, in the same way he had blogged his life throughout Iraq. He had asked a fellow blog friend, Professor Hilary Bok, to post the blog in the event of his death. It contains heartfelt words from a man who did not want his death to be in vain, a fitting testament to his humour, compassion and penchant for science fiction. His was not the voice of a journalist, but rather an authentic, logical military voice from the heart of Iraq. Olmsted did not tell any of his family that he had written this final post.

> I am leaving this message for you because it appears I must leave sooner than I intended. I would have preferred to say this in person, but since I cannot, let me say it here.
>
> G'Kar, *Babylon 5* . . .

This is an entry I would have preferred not to have published, but there are limits to what we can control in life, and apparently I have passed one of those limits. And so, like G'Kar, I must say here what I would much prefer to say in person. I want to thank Hilzoy for putting it up for me. It's not easy asking anyone to do something for you in the event of your death, and it is a testament to her quality that she didn't hesitate to accept the charge. As with many bloggers, I have a disgustingly large ego, and so I just couldn't bear the thought of not being able to have the last word if the need arose. Perhaps I take that further than most, I don't know. I hope so. It's frightening to think there are many people as neurotic as I am in the world. In any case, since I won't get another chance to say what I think, I wanted to take advantage of this opportunity. Such as it is . . .

What I don't want this to be is a chance for me, or anyone else, to be maudlin. I'm dead. That sucks, at least for me and my family and friends. But all the tears in the world aren't going to bring me back, so I would prefer that people remember the good things about me rather than mourning my loss. (If it turns out a specific number of tears will, in fact, bring me back to life, then by all means, break out the onions.) I had a pretty good life, as I noted above. Sure, all things being equal I would have preferred to have more time, but I have no business complaining with all the good fortune I've enjoyed in my life. So if you're up for that, put on a little 80s music (preferably vintage 1980–1984), grab a Coke and have a drink with me. If you have it, throw 'Freedom Isn't Free' from the Team America soundtrack in; if you can't laugh at that song, I think you need to lighten up a little. I'm dead, but if you're reading this, you're not, so take a moment to enjoy that happy fact.

'Our thoughts form the universe. They always matter.'

Citizen G'Kar, *Babylon 5*

Believe it or not, one of the things I will miss most is not being able to blog any longer. The ability to put my thoughts on (virtual) paper and put them where people can read and respond to them has been marvelous, even if most people who have read my writings haven't agreed with them. If there is any hope for the long term success of democracy, it will be if people agree to listen to and try to understand their political opponents rather than simply seeking to crush them. While the blogosphere has its share of partisans, there are some awfully smart people making excellent arguments out there as well, and I know I have learned quite a bit since I began blogging. I flatter myself I may have made a good argument or two as well; if I didn't, please don't tell me . . .

Blogging put me in touch with an inordinate number of smart people, an exhilarating if humbling experience. When I was young, I was smart, but the older I got, the more I realized just how dumb I was in comparison to truly smart people. But, to my credit, I think, I was at least smart enough to pay attention to the people with real brains and even occasionally learn something from them. It has been joy and a pleasure having the opportunity to do this.

'It's not fair.'
'No. It's not. Death never is.'

Captain John Sheridan and Dr. Stephen Franklin, *Babylon 5*

'They didn't even dig him a decent grave.'
'Well, it's not how you're buried. It's how you're remembered.'

Cimarron and Wil Andersen, *The Cowboys*

I suppose I should speak to the circumstances of my death. It would be nice to believe that I died leading men in battle, preferably saving their lives at the cost of my own. More likely I was caught by a marksman or an IED. But if there is an afterlife, I'm telling anyone who asks that I went down surrounded by hundreds of insurgents defending a village composed solely of innocent women and children. It'll be our little secret, ok?

I do ask (not that I'm in a position to enforce this) that no one try to use my death to further their political purposes. I went to Iraq and did what I did for my reasons, not yours. My life isn't a chit to be used to bludgeon people to silence on either side. If you think the U.S. should stay in Iraq, don't drag me into it by claiming that somehow my death demands us staying in Iraq. If you think the U.S. ought to get out tomorrow, don't cite my name as an example of someone's life who was wasted by our mission in Iraq. I have my own opinions about what we should do about Iraq, but since I'm not around to expound on them I'd prefer others not try and use me as some kind of moral capital to support a position I probably didn't support. Further, this is tough enough on my family without their having to see my picture being used in some rally or my name being cited for some political purpose. You can fight political battles without hurting my family, and I'd prefer that you did so.

On a similar note, while you're free to think whatever you like about my life and death, if you think I wasted my life, I'll tell you you're wrong. We're all going to die of something. I died doing a job I loved. When your time comes, I hope you are as fortunate as I was . . .

As passionate as I am about personal freedom, I don't buy the claims of anarchists that humanity would be just fine without any government at all. There are too many people in the world who believe that they know best how people should live their lives, and many of them are more than willing to use force to impose those beliefs on others. A world without government simply wouldn't last very long; as soon as it was established, strongmen would immediately spring up to establish their fiefdoms. So there is a need for government to protect the people's rights. And one of the fundamental tools to do that is an army that can prevent outside agencies from imposing their rules on a society. A lot of people will protest that argument by noting that the people we are fighting in Iraq are unlikely to threaten the rights of the average American. That's certainly true; while our enemies would certainly like to wreak great levels of havoc on our society, the fact is they're not likely to succeed. But that doesn't mean there isn't still a need for an army (setting aside debates regarding whether ours is the right size at the moment). Americans are fortunate that we don't have to worry too much about people coming to try and overthrow us, but part of the reason we don't have to worry about that is because we have an army that is stopping anyone who would try.

Soldiers cannot have the option of opting out of missions because they don't agree with them: that violates the social contract. The duly-elected American government decided to go to war in Iraq. (Even if you maintain President Bush was not properly elected, Congress voted for war as well.) As a soldier, I have a duty to obey the orders of the President of the United States as long as they are

Constitutional. I can no more opt out of missions I disagree with than I can ignore laws I think are improper. I do not consider it a violation of my individual rights to have gone to Iraq on orders because I raised my right hand and volunteered to join the army. Whether or not this mission was a good one, my participation in it was an affirmation of something I consider quite necessary to society. So if nothing else, I gave my life for a pretty important principle; I can (if you'll pardon the pun) live with that . . .

I'm afraid I can't really offer any deep secrets or wisdom. I lived my life better than some, worse than others, and I like to think that the world was a little better off for my having been here. Not very much, but then, few of us are destined to make more than a tiny dent in history's Green Monster. I would be lying if I didn't admit I would have liked to have done more, but it's a bit too late for that now, eh? The bottom line, for me, is that I think I can look back at my life and at least see a few areas where I may have made a tiny difference, and massive ego aside, that's probably not too bad.

'The flame also reminds us that life is precious. As each flame is unique; when it goes out, it's gone forever. There will never be another quite like it.'

Ambassador Delenn, *Babylon 5*

I write this in part, admittedly, because I would like to think that there's at least a little something out there to remember me by. Granted, this site will eventually vanish, being ephemeral in a very real sense of the word, but at least for a time it can serve as a tiny record of my contributions to the world. But on a larger scale, for those who knew me well enough to be saddened by my death, especially for those who haven't known anyone else lost to this war, perhaps my death can serve as a small reminder of the costs of war. Regardless of the merits of this war, or of any war, I think that many of us in America have forgotten that war means death and suffering in wholesale lots. A decision that for most of us in America was academic, whether or not to go to war in Iraq, had very real consequences for hundreds of thousands of people. Yet I was as guilty as anyone of minimizing those very real consequences in lieu of a cold discussion of theoretical merits of war and peace. Now I'm facing some very real consequences of that decision; who says life doesn't have a sense of humor?

But for those who knew me and feel this pain, I think it's a good thing to realize that this pain has been felt by thousands and thousands (probably millions, actually) of other people all over the world. That is part of the cost of war, any war, no matter how justified. If everyone who feels this pain keeps that in mind the next time we have to decide whether or not war is a good idea, perhaps it will help us to make a more informed decision. Because it is pretty clear that the average American would not have supported the Iraq War had they known the costs going in. I am far too cynical to believe that any future debate over war will be any less vitriolic or emotional, but perhaps a few more people will realize just what those costs can be the next time.

This may be a contradiction of my above call to keep politics out of my death, but I hope not. Sometimes going to war is the right idea. I think we've drawn that line too far in the direction of war rather than peace, but I'm a soldier and I know that sometimes you have to fight if you're to hold onto what you hold dear. But in making that decision, I believe we understate the costs of war; when we make the decision to fight, we make the decision to kill, and that means lives and families destroyed. Mine now falls into that category; the next time the question of war or peace comes up, if you knew me at least you can understand a bit more just what it is you're deciding to do, and whether or not those costs are worth it.

'This is true love. You think this happens every day?'

Westley, *The Princess Bride*

'Good night, my love, the brightest star in my sky.'

John Sheridan, *Babylon 5*

This is the hardest part. While I certainly have no desire to die, at this point I no longer have any worries. That is not true of the woman who made my life something to enjoy rather than something merely to survive. She put up with all of my faults, and they are myriad, she endured separations again and again . . . I cannot imagine being more fortunate in love than I have been with Amanda. Now she has to go on without me, and while a cynic might observe she's better off, I know that this is a terrible burden I have placed on her, and I would give almost anything if she would not have to bear it. It seems that is not an option. I cannot imagine anything more painful than that, and if there is an afterlife, this is a pain I'll bear forever.

I wasn't the greatest husband. I could have done so much more, a realization that, as it so often does, comes too late to matter. But I cherished every day I was married to Amanda. When everything else in my life seemed dark, she was always there to light the darkness. It is difficult to imagine my life being worth living without her having been in it. I hope and pray that she goes on without me and enjoys her life as much as she deserves. I can think of no one more deserving of happiness than her.

'I will see you again, in the place where no shadows fall.'

Ambassador Delenn, *Babylon 5*

I don't know if there is an afterlife; I tend to doubt it, to be perfectly honest. But if there is any way possible, Amanda, then I will live up to Delenn's words, somehow, some way. I love you.[48]

At pains to ensure his death would not be used as a political banner brandished in favour or against the war, Andrew sought to explain, rationalise and offer a personal point of view with his final blog. He used it not only to say farewell, but to declare publicly his powerful love for Amanda. Within days of it being posted on his blog-site, there were almost half a million hits. His father Wes recalled how he and his wife 'would sit at the computer each night and read the new comments and weep'. They had received the news from two army officers, but even before the men had spoken, Andrew's parents knew the news they were about to deliver. Olmsted's military funeral at Colorado Springs saw him decorated with new medals. The final words from the chaplain were 'now he belongs to the ages' – a quote Olmsted had loved. He was a soldier who enjoyed military life and was passionate about helping others. He genuinely believed he could make the world a better place.

Andrew Olmsted bequeathed remarkable words from beyond the grave, that live on not only in the virtual world of the internet, but in all who knew him. His name has been put to a scholarship at his former high school, and his family have dedicated a corner of their home to Andy – complete with letters, blog comments, his funeral flag and his photographs.

~ ~

PICTURE CREDITS FOR PLATES

1: Courtesy of the Duke of Lancaster's Regiment Museum
2: Courtesy of Mahn und Gedenkstätten Wöbbelin
Background to plates 1 & 2: Staffordshire Record Office
3: With thanks to the Rhode Island Historical Society (J.A. O'Niell, RHi X3)
6: Campbell Collections of the University of KwaZulu-Natal
7: Courtesy of the Handcock family
Background to plates 7 & 8: Australian War Memorial (negative number 3DRL/3834) and with kind permission of the Handcock family
9, 10, 11, 22 and background to plates 10 & 11: Imperial War Museums
12: Canadian Letters and Images Project
13: Australian War Memorial (negative number H16398)
15: Tasmanian Archive and Heritage Office
16: Courtesy of the Binning family
17: Courtesy of the Neufeld family
19 and background to plates 19 & 20: Second World War Experience Centre
20: Courtesy of the Chiran Peace Museum
21: Courtesy of Ted Courtright
23: Courtesy of Christine Mates
24: Courtesy of David Morgan
25: Courtesy of Sara Jones
26: Courtesy of the Howell family
27: Courtesy of José Scaglia
28: Courtesy of Helen O'Pray
29 and background to plates 28 & 29: Courtesy of Melissa Givens
30: Courtesy of Eddie Hancock
31: Courtesy of the Downes family
32: Courtesy of the Olmsted family

~ ~

NOTES

INTRODUCTION

1 Colonel Bob Stewart, Former British Army Officer.
2 87/232, Australian War Memorial.
3 William L. Clements Library, University of Michigan.
4 Barrie Jay, *Early Forces Mail,* Gloucester: The Stuart Rossiter Trust Fund, 1997, p. 5.
5 Mills Lane (ed.), *Dear Mother: Don't Grieve About me. If I Get Killed, I'll Only Be Dead. Letters from Georgia Soldiers in the Civil War,* Savannah, GA, Beehive Press, 1977, p. xii.
6 With kind permission of Judith Wiles.
7 The Papers of Reverend E.V. Tanner, Department of Documents, Imperial War Museums.

1 AT WAR WITH FRANCE

1 8804-32, Captain Philip Wodehouse, National Army Museum.
2 H.F.B Wheeler and A.M. Broadley, *Napoleon and the Invasion of England,* Stroud, Nonsuch Publishing, 2007, p. 7.
3 David A. Bell, *The First Total War,* London, Bloomsbury, 2007, p. 223.
4 Every county had their own militia units, where each man signed up for five years.
5 National Museum of Scotland.
6 Andrew Uffindell, *The National Army Museum Book of Wellington's Armies,* Oxford, Sidgwick & Jackson, 2003, p. 187.
7 Wheeler and Broadley, *Napoleon and the Invasion of England,* p. 76.
8 9/34/46, Wiltshire and Swindon Archives.
9 Wheeler and Broadley, *Napoleon and the Invasion of England,* p. 215.
10 Bell, *The First Total War,* p. 41.
11 RSR MS 1/46, West Sussex Record Office.
12 4479/1-3, Staffordshire Record Office.
13 12571/8, Bristol Record Office.
14 Uffindell, *The National Army Museum Book of Wellington's Armies,* p. 141.
15 1980-09-9, National Army Museum.
16 12571/8, Bristol Record Office.
17 Peter Snow, *To War with Wellington,* London: John Murray, 2010, p. 41.
18 John Goldworth Alger, *Paris in 1789–94: Farewell Letters of Victims of the Guillotine,* London, George Allen, 1902, p. 52.
19 There are references to literate soldiers writing letters for the illiterate.
20 9/34/46/4, Wiltshire and Swindon Archives.
21 Gareth Glover, *Waterloo Archive,* Barnsley, Pen & Sword, 2011, Vol. 4.
22 Ian Fletcher (ed.), *In the Service of the King,* Staplehurst, Spellmount, 1997, p. 29.

23 AMS 6185/6, East Sussex Record Office.
24 23M93/15/1/58, Hampshire Record Office.
25 DD/WD/105/1, Nottinghamshire Archives.
26 RSR MS 1/46, West Sussex Record Office.
27 Thought to be a mixture of typhus, malaria, dysentery and typhoid.
28 Around thirty-five pounds as a modern equivalent.
29 4479/1-3, Staffordshire Record Office.
30 With thanks to Captain Gregory M. Gorsuch, MSC, USN, Ret.
31 DD/798/16, Nottinghamshire Archives.
32 3450/54, Wiltshire and Swindon Archives.
33 Uffindell, *The National Army Museum Book of Wellington's Armies*, p. 21.
34 12571/8, Bristol Record Office.
35 Fletcher, *In the Service of the King*, p. 193.
36 D2375/68/5, Derbyshire Record Office.
37 RSR MS 1/46, West Sussex Record Office.
38 413/382, Wiltshire and Swindon Archives.
39 Uffindell, *The National Army Museum Book of Wellington's Armies*, p. 153.
40 WI/5508, Bedfordshire and Luton Archives.
41 D2375/68/5, Derbyshire Record Office.
42 DD/798/16, Nottinghamshire Archives.
43 540/222, Wiltshire and Swindon Archives.
44 Uffindell, *The National Army Museum Book of Wellington's Armies*, p. 22.
45 Ibid., p. 312.
46 Fletcher, *In the Service of the King*, p. 99.
47 1980-09-9, National Army Museum.
48 451/547, Wiltshire and Swindon Archives.
49 D593/B/1/22/33A, Staffordshire Record Office.
50 http://www.kittybrewster.com/ancestry/obitandbiog_Captain_George_Duff_Memoir.htm.
51 WI/5508, Bedfordshire & Luton Archives.
52 Christopher Lee, *Nelson and Napoleon: The Long Haul to Trafalgar*, London, Headline, 2005, p. 320.
53 4479/1-3, Staffordshire Record Office.
54 Frederick Llewellyn (ed.), *Waterloo Recollections*, Leonaur, 2007, p. 207.
55 Ibid, p. 239.
56 With thanks to Captain Gregory M. Gorsuch, MSC, USN, Ret.
57 Snow, *To War with Wellington*, p. 226.
58 Lee, *Nelson and Napoleon*, p. 349.
59 Uffindell, *The National Army Museum Book of Wellington's Armies*, p. 279.
60 NAM - 6305-112-2, National Army Museum.
61 With thanks to the National Maritime Museum for this and the preceding quotation.
62 *Naval Chronicle*, Vol. XV, p. 289.
63 Gareth Glover (ed.), *It All Culminated at Hougoumont: The Letters of Captain John Lucie Blackman, Coldstream Guards*, Godmanchester, Ken Trotman, 2009.
64 Ibid.
65 Wellesley later became the Duke of Wellington.
66 Glover, *Waterloo Archive*, Vol. 3.
67 Rifle salute.
68 D(W)1778/V/1034 Staffordshire Record Office, with thanks to the Earl of Dartmouth.
69 Lieutenant-General Sir F.W. Hamilton, *The Origin and History of the First or Grenadier Guards*, London, John Murray, 1874, p. 21.

70 Glover, *Waterloo Archive*, Vol. 4.
71 1300/3102, Wiltshire and Swindon Archives.
72 Osnabruck.
73 9/34/46/1024, Wiltshire and Swindon Archives.
74 WO 121/54/35, The National Archives.
75 Christian Gottfreid Körner, Theodor Richardson, George Fleming and Frederich Kind, *The Life of Carl Theödor Körner*, London, Thomas Hurst & Co., 1827, p. 26.
76 Bell, *The First Total War*, Page 298.
77 Ibid., p. 299.
78 Körner et al., *The Life of Carl Theödor Körner*, p. 34.
79 *The Mirror of Literature, Amusement, and Instruction*, Vol. 10, No. 274 (Saturday 22 September 1827).
80 James Sheehan, *German History 1770–1866*, Oxford, Oxford University Press, 1993, p. 384.
81 Bell, *The First Total War*, p. 299.
82 *Army and Navy Chronicle*, Vol. 2 (1 January–30 June 1836), p. 200.
83 The Royal Regiment of Horse Guards, who were known for their blue uniforms.
84 With kind permission of the Queen's Dragoon Guards Collection and Peter Galloway.
85 DD1251/1-3, Nottinghamshire Archives.
86 WO 12/96, The National Archives.

2 The American Civil War

1 University of Washington Libraries, Special Collections, Watson C. Squire Papers, Acc# 4000-001, Box 17.
2 Drew Gilpin Faust, 'The Civil War Soldier and the Art of Dying', *Journal of Southern History*, Vol. 67 (February 2001).
3 The only casualty was a Confederate horse.
4 Historians have argued that Lincoln may have been anti-slavery but was also anti-black, and planned to colonise blacks. The concept of emancipation was less concerned with civil rights, and more a war measure.
5 William Henry Ruse Civil War Collection 1863–5, Ms 89-068, Special Collections, Virginia Polytechnic Institute and State University.
6 Civilian merchants.
7 *Bradford Observer*, 1 May 1862.
8 University of Washington Libraries, Special Collections.
9 Henry A. Bitner Letters 1861-1863, Accession #11395, Albert H. Small Special Collections Library, University of Virginia, Charlottesville, Va.
10 www.civilwarpoetry.org
11 Mills Lane (ed.), *Dear Mother: Don't Grieve About Me. If I Get Killed, I'll Only Be Dead. Letters from Georgia Soldiers in the Civil War*, Savannah, GA, Beehive Press, 1977, p. xii.
12 Valley of the Shadow Project: Two Communities in the American Civil War, University of Virginia Library.
13 Ibid.
14 *Bradford Observer*, 1 May 1862.
15 The Valley of the Shadow Project.
16 Leave of absence.
17 William F. Margraff, *A Civil War Soldier's Last Letters*, New York, Vantage, 1975, p. 14.
18 MS 22421D 29/30, National Library of Wales.
19 Peace democrats.

20 Virginia Adams (ed.), *On the Altar of Freedom: A Black Soldier's Civil War Letters from the Front*, New York, Warner Books, 1991, p. 9.
21 Lane, *Dear Mother*, p. xii.
22 Item 5, Theodorik Wingfield Montford Letters, MS 571, Georgia Historical Society, Savannah, Georgia.
23 Ibid.
24 Lane, *Dear Mother*, p. xxii.
25 Jacob Middower Papers 1864, Pearce Civil War Collection, Navarro College, Corsicana, Texas.
26 Calvin Shedd Civil War Papers, University of South Carolina, South Carolinia Library Manuscripts Division.
27 Lane, *Dear Mother*, Page 124.
28 Ibid., p. 249.
29 The Valley of the Shadow Project.
30 Ibid.
31 MS 22421D 23/24, National Library of Wales.
32 Lane, *Dear Mother*.
33 Aaron Sheehan-Dean (ed.), *Struggle for a Vast Future: The American Civil War*, Oxford, Osprey Publishing, 2006, p. 117.
34 Former slaves.
35 Charles Beardsley, 'Diary of a Contraband', at http://goulddiary.stanford.edu/.
36 Ms 89-068, Virginia Polytechnic Institute and State University.
37 Matthew McCann Papers 1864–5, Pearce Civil War Collection, Navarro College, Corsicana, Texas.
38 Lane, *Dear Mother*, p. 43.
39 John Newton Carnahan Letters 1824–62, Ms 2009-112, Special Collections, Virginia Polytechnic Institute and State University.
40 James M. Stamper Papers 1864, Pearce Civil War Collection, Navarro College, Corsicana, Texas.
41 Papers of the Black, Kent, and Apperson Families 1779–1984, Ms 74-003, Special Collections, Virginia Polytechnic and State University.
42 Georgia Archives, William Stillwell Collection, ac 1940–102m.
43 William Latham Candler Papers 1861–3, Ms 1997-007, Special Collections, Virginia Polytechnic Institute and State University.
44 The Valley of the Shadow Project.
45 Box 3- Folder 10, Dowtin, Tom. MARBL, Emory University, Atlanta, Georgia.
46 Lane, *Dear Mother*, p. 88.
47 Virginia Military Institute.
48 Georgia Archives, Stillwell Collection.
49 Faust, 'The Civil War Soldier and the Art of Dying', p. 16.
50 http://www.brotherswar.com, US National Park Service.
51 The Valley of the Shadow Project.
52 Ms 89-068, Virginia Polytechnic Institute and State University.
53 Faust, 'The Civil War Soldier and the Art of Dying', p. 10.
54 Levi Pennington, http://sunsite.utk.edu/civil-war/levi.html.
55 Ms 2009-112, Virginia Polytechnic Institute and State University.
56 Franklin R. Crawford, *Proud to Say I Am a Union Soldier: The Last Letters Home from Federal Soldiers Written During the Civil War 1861–1865*, Westminster, MD, Heritage Books, 2005, pp. 135 and 165.
57 A rank attained largely though his relationship with the governor rather than through any military training.

58 Robin Young, *For Love and Liberty: The Untold Civil War Story of Major Sullivan Ballou and his Famous Love Letter*, New York, Thunder's Mouth Press, 2006, p. xxiii.
59 Evan C. Jones, 'Sullivan Ballou: The Macabre Fate of an American Civil War Major', *America's Civil War*, November 2004.
60 Crawford, *Proud to Say I Am a Union Soldier*, p. 13.
61 Georgia Archives, Ira P. Woodruff Collection (from a transcribed copy on microfilm).
62 His service record listed him as a mechanic.
63 Also known as Bull Run.
64 Probably an Enfield or Springfield rifle, whose balls were known as miniés.
65 James E. Rearden Civil War Collection 1861–1920, Ms 2007-013, Special Collections, Virginia Polytechnic Institute and State University.
66 Report of Brigadier General Joseph B. Kershaw, C.S. Army.
67 Samuel Cooper, *The First Lines of the Practice of Surgery*, London, Longman, 1813.
68 American Genealogical-Biographical Index, 1999, Godrey Memorial Library, Middletown, Connecticut, www.godfrey.org.
69 Courtesy of the Burton Historical Collection, Detroit Public Library.
70 Ibid.
71 *The Times*, 22 September 1862.
72 fact, on 9 September, Reuters announced Pope's victory.
73 Burton Historical Collection.
74 Of the 317 deaths in the 114th Regiment, 192 were as a result of disease.
75 Special Collections, Colgate University Libraries, Hamilton, New York.
76 Lane, *Dear Mother*, p. 74.
77 Ibid, p. 78.
78 He was allowed to keep the apples!
79 Courtesy of Hargrett Rare Book and Manuscript Library, University of Georgia Libraries.

3 The Anglo-Zulu War

1 Rumoured to be the final words of Captain D.B. Mariarty, killed at Ntombe Drift, recorded in J.P. Mackinnon and S.H. Shadbolt, *The South African Campaign of 1879*, reprinted London, Greenhill Books, 1995.
2 Private John Morgans, *North Wales Express*, 11 April 1879.
3 W.B. Bartlett, *Zulu: Queen Victoria's Most Famous Little War*, Stroud, The History Press, 2010, p. 47.
4 Ibid., p. 48.
5 L.9.48, With kind permission of the Regimental Museum of the Royal Welsh, Brecon.
6 Frank Emery, 'The Anglo-Zulu War as Depicted in Soldiers' Letters', *South African Military History Society Journal*, June 1982.
7 A type of spear.
8 Ian Knight and Ian Castle, *Zulu War*, Oxford, Osprey Publishing, 2004, p. 111.
9 Royal Engineers Museum and Institute.
10 1957-05-22, National Army Museum.
11 Ibid.
12 Frank Emery, *The Red Soldier*, Kent, Hodder and Stoughton, 1977, p. 199.
13 Ian Knight, *The Zulu War*, Basingstoke, Sidgwick & Jackson, 2003, p. 70.
14 *North Wales Express*, 28 February 1879.
15 KCM 89/41/1, Letters from Charlie, Killie-Campbell Africana Library.
16 D1980.135, Regimental Museum of the Royal Welsh, Brecon.

17 1957-05-22, National Army Museum.
18 KCM 89/41/1, Killie-Campbell Africana Library.
19 Royal Engineers Museum and Institute.
20 Bartlett, *Zulu*, p. 195
21 L.9.48, Regimental Museum of the Royal Welsh, Brecon.
22 D1980.135, Regimental Museum of the Royal Welsh, Brecon.
23 Emery, *The Red Soldier*, p. 155.
24 A regiment.
25 Bartlett, *Zulu*, p. 177.
26 James Bancroft, *The Rorke's Drift Men*, Stroud, Spellmount, 2010, p. 147.
27 *Western Mail*, 27 March 1879.
28 Emery, 'The Anglo-Zulu War', p. 97.
29 A spiritual practice that was a mark of respect and allowed the spirit to be released into the afterlife.
30 Bartlett, *Zulu*, p. 224.
31 Emery, *The Red Soldier*, p. 95.
32 A close study of the evidence for this incident suggests that it is probably apocryphal.
33 Donald Morris, *The Washing of the Spears*, London, Sphere, 1973, p. 420.
34 Adrian Greaves, *Rorke's Drift*, London, Cassell, 2002, p. 130.
35 Michael Diamond, 'Popular Entertainment and the Zulu War', *Journal of the Anglo-Zulu War Historical Society*, December 1998.
36 *Aberystwyth Observer*, 26 July 1879.
37 Bartlett, *Zulu*, p. 152
38 Emery, *The Red Soldier*, p. 99.
39 *Western Mail*, 27 March 1879.
40 *North Wales Express*, 19 September 1879.
41 KCM 89/41/1, Killie-Campbell Africana Library.
42 Frank Emery, *Marching over Africa. Letters from Victorian Soldiers*, Kent, Hodder and Stoughton, 1986, p. 80.
43 The regimental banner.
44 L.9.48, Regimental Museum of the Royal Welsh, Brecon.
45 *Western Mail*, 27 March 1879.
46 2010-09-15, National Army Museum.
47 Emery, *The Red Soldier*, p. 108.
48 Ibid., p. 131.
49 *North Wales Express*, 19 September 1879.
50 Emery, *The Red Soldier*, p. 155.
51 Emery, *The Red Soldier*, p. 128.
52 *Daily Telegraph*, 18 August 1879.
53 Greaves, *Rorke's Drift*, p. 155.
54 Saul David, *Zulu*, London, Penguin, 2004, p. 254.
55 Emery, *The Red Soldier*, p. 193.
56 Bartlett, *Zulu*, p. 223.
57 *Otago Daily Times*, 25 February 1879.
58 Letter from Duke of Cambridge to Lord Chelmsford, 25 February 1879.
59 Katherine John, *The Prince Imperial*, London, Putnam, 1939, p. 435.
60 Ibid., pp. 431–3.
61 Ibid., p. 447.
62 Morris, *The Washing of the Spears*, p. 520.
63 Augustin Filon, *The Prince Imperial*, London, William Heinemann, 1913, p. 240.
64 John, *The Prince Imperial*, p. 469.

65 Morris, *The Washing of the Spears*, p. 533.
66 *North Wales Express*, 19 September 1879.
67 1957-05-22, National Army Museum.
68 John, *The Prince Imperial*, p. 500.
69 Augustin Filon, *Recollections of the Empress Eugenie*, London, Cassell, 1920, p. 297.
70 Ibid., p. 302.
71 Ironically, Ward is noted as 'temperate' on his service records.
72 *Aberdare Times*, 29 March 1879.
73 WO97/2131/194, The National Archives.
74 Irving Steyn, 'Soldier's Tale of Zulu Battlefront 100 Years Ago', *Cape Town Argus Supplement*, 10 September 1983.
75 L.22.53, Regimental Museum of the Royal Welsh, Brecon.
76 WO97/3511/55, The National Archives.
77 *Western Mail*, 27 March 1879.
78 Whitworth Porter, *History of the Corps of Royal Engineers*, London, Longmans, Green & Co., 1889, p. 46.
79 Royal Engineers Museum and Institute.

4 The Boer War

1   Robert Percy Rooke, Canadian Letters and Images Project.
2   PRO 2040, Australian War Memorial.
3   Letter from Sydney Marks, Ladysmith History website.
4   8226, National Archives of Scotland.
5   Canadian Letters and Images Project.
6   Effie Karageorgos, 'Loyal to the Empire? An Alternative View of Australian Soldiers in the South African War, 1899–1902', paper presented at the conference, 'Writing the Empire: Scribblings from Below', 24–6 June 2010, University of Bristol.
7   Canadian Letters and Images Project.
8   Denis Judd and Keith Surridge, *The Boer War*, London, John Murray, 2003, p. 126.
9   Frank Emery, *Marching over Africa: Letters from Victorian Soldiers*, Kent, Hodder and Stoughton, 1986, p. 178.
10 Ibid., p. 27.
11 Canadian Letters and Images Project.
12 Graaff-Reinet Museum Archival Repository.
13 Letter from Trooper W.H. Snyder, published in the *Berwick Register*, 3 May 1900.
14 C.R. Prance, 'War Letters from the Veld 1900'.
15 Letter from Arthur McBeth, New Zealand History Online.
16 Pierre du Toit, 'The War Experiences of Mike du Toit', *South African Military History Journal*, Vol. 11, No. 5 (2000).
17 MMK7654/318, McGregor Museum, Kimberly, Letters of Private C. Edwards.
18 19790733-001, George Metcalf Archival Collection, Canadian War Museum.
19 MMK7654/1e, McGregor Museum, Kimberly, Letters of Private Bertram Lang.
20 Thomas Pakenham, *The Boer War*, London, Weidenfeld and Nicolson, 1979, p. 115.
21 MMK7654/246h, McGregor Museum.
22 Literacy in 1900 was estimated to be just 12.2 per cent, but with virtually no illiteracy in the army itself.
23 Anonymous poem.
24 SC70/8/1288/23, National Archives of Scotland.
25 With kind permission of the Museum of the Boer Republics.
26 Craig Wilcox, *Australia's Boer War*, Melbourne, Oxford University Press, 2002, p. 222.
27 SC70/8/1288/7, National Archives of Scotland.

28 Museum of the Boer Republics.
29 National Archives of Scotland.
30 Steve Lunderstedt (ed.), *Summer of 1899: The Siege of Kimberley*, Kimberley, Kimberley Africana Library, 1999.
31 Du Toit, 'The War Experiences of Mike du Toit'.
32 SC70/8/1288/6, National Archives of Scotland.
33 G.R. Witton, *Scapegoats of the Empire*, Clock and Rose Press, 2004.
34 Letter of 2 March 1902.
35 3DRL/3834, Australian War Memorial, with kind permission of the Handcock family.
36 Pakenham, *The Boer War*, p. 539.
37 Wilcox, *Australia's Boer War*, p. 225.
38 Ibid., p. 295.
39 CO 418/25 ff 734-35, The National Archives.
40 W.K. Hancock, *Smuts: The Sanguine Years 1870–1919*, London, Cambridge University Press, 1962, p. 110.
41 Ibid., p. 124.
42 Pakenham, *The Boer War*.
43 Hancock, *Smuts*, p. 131.
44 Ibid., p. 132.
45 Ibid., p. 137.
46 Ibid., p. 137.
47 Ibid., p. 164.
48 Ibid., p. 120.
49 Courtesy of the Archives of the Regimental Headquarters of the Mercian Regiment.
50 12997 05/18/1.33, Department of Documents, Imperial War Museums, with kind permission of R.W. Purser.
51 Roslyn Maddrell, *Letters from the Front: Boer War to WWII through Letters Sent by Servicemen to their Families in Braidwood*, Braidwood, Roslyn Maddrell, 2004.
52 Judd and Surridge, *The Boer War*, p. 127.
53 SC70/8/1288/15, National Archives of Scotland.
54 MS 959, Auckland War Memorial Museum.

5 The Great War

1   1 DRL/42, Australian War Memorial, Major B.B. Leane.
2   Richard Holmes, *Tommy: The British Soldier on the Western Front 1914–1918*, London, Harper Perennial, 2004.
3   Ian Passingham, *All the Kaiser's Men: The Life and Death of the German Army on the Western Front 1914–1918*, Stroud, Sutton Publishing, 2003.
4   MS 8844, National Library of Australia.
5   SC70/8147/25, National Archives of Scotland.
6   Philipp Witkop (ed.), *German Students' War Letters*, London, Methuen, 1929, p. 69.
7   SC70/8/193/1, National Archives of Scotland.
8   SC70/8/250/2, National Archives of Scotland.
9   With kind permission of Cat Whiteaway.
10 With kind permission of Jackie Weaver and the Great War Digital Archive, Oxford University.
11 Witkop, *German Students' War Letters*, p. 15.
12 With kind permission of Mrs D Henderson.
13 SC70/8/140/3, National Archives of Scotland.
14 Witkop, *German Students' War Letters*, p. 155.
15 John Bickersteth (ed.), *The Bickersteth Diaries*, Barnsley: Pen and Sword, 2005.

16 Major Robert Loraine was a famous early aviator and actor who also served in the Boer War.
17 PP/MCR/406, Department of Documents, Imperial War Museums, with kind permission of Lord Eric Avebury.
18 Martin Gilbert, *Somme: The Heroism and Horror of War*, London, John Murray, 2006.
19 The 'Big Push' was initially planned for 29 June, but famously postponed due to heavy rain.
20 H.W. Wallis Grain, *The 16th (Public Schools) Service Battalion (the Duke of Cambridge's Own) Middlesex Regiment and the Great War, 1914–1918: A Short History of the Battalion*, London, 1935.
21 *Daily Telegraph*, 20 January 1932.
22 12701 03/29/1, Department of Documents, Imperial War Museums.
23 War diaries, 49th Canadian Infantry Battalion, Library and Archives Canada.
24 The Canadian Letters and Images Project.
25 Colonel G.W.L. Nicholson, *The Official History of the Canadian Army in the First World War: Canadian Expeditionary Force 1914–1919*, Ottawa, Queen's Printer, 1962, p. 323.
26 B2455/1, National Archives of Australia.
27 AWM 4/23/53/5, Australian War Memorial.
28 *Minenwerfers* or mortars.
29 Heavy German 5.9-inch shells that threw up clouds of black smoke on impact.
30 Verey lights – a flare gun.
31 AWM 4/23/53/8, Australian War Memorial.
32 Witkop , *German Students' War Letters*, pp. 239–40.
33 Ibid., pp. 241–2.
34 Jack Sheldon, *The German Army on the Somme, 1914–1916*, Barnsley, Pen & Sword, 2005, p. 263.
35 The attack actually started a day later, on 21 February.
36 Witkop, *German Students' War Letters*, pp. 242–3.
37 Giosuè Borsi, *A Soldier's Confidences with God: Spiritual Colloquies of Giosuè Borsi*, trans. Rev. Pasquale Maltese, New York, PJ Kenedy & Sons, 1918, pp. 225–26.
38 Ibid., p. 1.
39 Ibid., p. 301.
40 This letter was released to the newspaper by Borsi's mother, and was printed across the world. This abridged version is taken from the *New York Times*, 8 October 1916.
41 John R. Schindler, *Isonzo: The Forgotten Sacrifice of the Great War*, Portsmouth: Greenwood Press, 2001.
42 NS 1827/1/1, Tasmanian Archive and Heritage Office.
43 These were all key battles in which the 2nd Division had fought.
44 B2455/1, National Archives of Australia, Inquest Report 1919.
45 Standard German field-gun fire.
46 WO 95/1722, The National Archives.
47 A London bank
48 A will entirely handwritten and signed by the testator, not witnessed. Incidentally, the family pasted the letter and will into their family bible, which caused huge problems when the War Office was finalising William's effects. The bible was a massive tome – not the sort of thing that could be sent by post.
49 With kind permission of the Binning and Fulton families.

6 The Second World War

1 PR84/091, Flight Officer Colin Flockhart, Australian War Memorial Archives.
2 www.war-letters.com.

3 Ordinary German soldier.
4 Stephen G. Fritz, *Frontsoldaten: The German Soldier in World War II*, Lexington, KT, University Press of Kentucky, 1995, p. 13.
5 ARMY 187/SUTTON, Liddle Collection, University of Leeds.
6 06/76A, Department of Documents, Imperial War Museums, with kind permission of Elizabeth Mattison.
7 5778/2/50, Staffordshire Record Office.
8 The Second World War Experience Centre, Wetherby.
9 93/29/1, Imperial War Museums.
10 9007-107-2, National Army Museum.
11 The Canadian Letters and Images Project.
12 Fritz, *Frontsoldaten*, p. 86.
13 3.2002.0867, Museumsstiftung Post Und Telekommunikation, Berlin.
14 5778/2/65, Staffordshire Record Office.
15 G.D. Bushell, 'A Letter from the Heat of the Battle of Britain', *South African Military History Journal*, Vol. 5, No. 1 (June 1980).
16 ARMY 069/FOLLEY, Liddle Collection.
17 A US infantryman.
18 An American decoration awarded to soldiers wounded or killed while serving with the US military.
19 www.pbs.org/wgbh/amex/dday/sfeature/s.f_letters.html.
20 ARMY 069/FOLLEY, Liddle Collection.
21 Intelligence Bulletin, November 1943.
22 PP/MCR/17, Department of Documents, Imperial War Museums.
23 Fritz, *Frontsoldaten*, p. 2.
24 Ibid.
25 PP/MCR/17, Department of Documents, Imperial War Museums.
26 The Second World War Experience Centre.
27 RAF045/GLOVER, Liddle Collection.
28 RAF052/HAY, Liddle Collection.
29 Fritz, *Frontsoldaten*, p. 31.
30 The Second World War Experience Centre.
31 Average German soldier.
32 ARMY 069/FOLLEY, Liddle Collection.
33 Department of Documents, Imperial War Museums.
34 3.2002.7565, Museumsstiftung Post Und Telekommunikation, Berlin.
35 Jean Larteguy (ed.) and Nora Wydenbruck (trans.), *The Sun Goes Down: Last Letters from Japanese Suicide-Pilots and Soldiers*, London, William Kimber & Co, 1956, p. 109.
36 Chiran Peace Museum, Kagoshima Prefecture.
37 D5994/3/60(i), Derbyshire Record Office.
38 AMERICAN 003, Liddle Collection.
39 Fritz, *Frontsoldaten*, p. 78.
40 PR 00392, Australian War Memorial.
41 Ian Gardner and Roger Day, *Tonight we Die as Men*, Oxford, Osprey, 2009, p. 113.
42 http://fizkid.tripod.com/id92.html.
43 SC70/10/58/2, National Archives of Scotland.
44 92/45/1, Department of Documents, Imperial War Museums, with kind permission of Mrs Catherine Parkes and Mrs C.E. Clissold-Jones.
45 *Northern Star*, 20 April 2010.
46 3.2002.0280, Museumsstiftung Post Und Telekommunikation, Berlin.
47 Chiran Peace Museum.
48 Larteguy, *The Sun Goes Down*, pp. 98–9.

49 93/5/1, Department of Documents, Imperial War Museums, with kind permission of Barbara Cookson.
50 The Second World War Experience Centre.
51 99/64/1, Department of Documents, Imperial War Museums.
52 Fritz, *Frontsoldaten*, p. 80.
53 Annette Tapert, *Despatches from the Heart*, London, Hamish Hamilton, 1984, p. 107.
54 Catherine Reilly, *Chaos of the Night*, London, Virago, 1984, p. 13.
55 3.2002.0826, Museumsstiftung Post Und Telekommunikation, Berlin.
56 A branch of Anabaptism.
57 CWM 20050108-003 George Metcalf Archival Collection, Canadian War Museum, with kind permission of the Neufeld family.
58 Projector infantry anti-tank gun.
59 Although Morrison described having to defecate in a bully-beef tin on occasion!
60 WO 169/4991, The National Archives.
61 This denoted that an attack on the delta was imminent.
62 DS/MISC/63, Department of Documents, Imperial War Museums.
63 WO 169/4991, The National Archives.
64 He won the Nobel Prize for Physiology or Medicine, 1935.
65 3.2002.7135, Museumsstiftung Post Und Telekommunikation, Berlin, with kind permission of the Spemann family.
66 Ibid.
67 Ibid.
68 Ibid.
69 Ibid.
70 Ibid.
71 AIR 27/1005, The National Archives.
72 AIR 27/1000, The National Archives.
73 With kind permission of the Second World War Experience Centre.
74 Justin McCurry, 'We Were Ready to Die for Japan', *Guardian*, 28 February 2006.
75 26 March to July 1945.
76 The Second World War Experience Centre.
77 'Baka' in Japanese means idiot or lunatic.
78 Chiran Peace Museum.
79 The main kamikaze sortie base for Japanese attacks on Allied ships around Okinawa.
80 A traditional wine.
81 Body-crash.
82 Albert Axell, *Kamikaze*, Harlow, Longman, 2002.
83 A simplified alphabet where each symbol represented a syllable.
84 Full of spiritual and godly energy.
85 The Japanese word has a deeper meaning, to strike back against those who have caused harm and oppression in battle.
86 With thanks to Bill Gordon (http://wgordon.web.wesleyan.edu) and the Chiran Peace Museum.
87 Symbolic flowers in Japan, representing the transience of life.
88 With thanks to Bill Gordon.
89 *Evening Standard*, 22 February 1944.
90 *The Times*, 1 March 1944.
91 WO 170/1421, The National Archives.
92 The children's birthday.
93 With kind permission of the Second World War Experience Centre.
94 With kind permission of Ted Courtright.

95 The squadron's original planes were a gift from the Nizam of Hyderabad, hence took his name.
96 AIR 27/862, The National Archives.
97 His brother, who would also be killed in action, lost at sea in 1942.
98 AIR 27/858, The National Archives.
99 74/93/1, Department of Documents, Imperial War Museums, with kind permission of the Scott family.
100 WO 27/858, The National Archives.

7 The Falklands Conflict

1 With kind permission of John and Heather Prime.
2 Two hundred front-line planes to twenty-five Sea Harrier and six Harrier GR3 jets.
3 *Daily Telegraph*, 13 March 2007.
4 Fleet Air Arm Museum Archives.
5 David Tinker, *A Message from the Falklands*, Harmondsworth, Penguin , 1983.
6 David Hart Dyke, *Four Weeks in May: A Captain's Story of War at Sea*, London, Atlantic Books, 2007, p. 20.
7 Hew Pike, *From the Front Line: Family Letters and Diaries 1900 to the Falklands and Afghanistan*, Barnsley, Pen and Sword, 2008, p. 134.
8 *Sun*, 4 May 1982.
9 Hart Dyke, *Four Weeks in May*, p. 71.
10 LIA/38, East Sussex Record Office, with kind permission of the Tucknott family.
11 Fleet Air Arm Museum Archives.
12 LIA/38, East Sussex Record Office, with kind permission of the Tucknott family.
13 Rear Admiral John Lippiett, *War and Peas*, Bosham, Pistol Post Publications, 2007, p. 23.
14 Pike, *From the Front Line*, p. 136–7.
15 An anti-ship missile. Literally translated, the name means flying fish.
16 With kind permission of the Callus family.
17 With thanks to the Falkland Islands Museum and National Trust.
18 *Kirby Times*.
19 LIA/38, East Sussex Record Office, with kind permission of the Tucknott family.
20 Hart Dyke, *Four Weeks in May*, p. 103.
21 Pike, *From the Front Line*, pp. 136–7.
22 Lippiett, *War and Peas*, p. 203.
23 *Daily Telegraph*, 8 June 2007.
24 With kind permission of Pam Boggs.
25 Lippiett, *War and Peas*, p. 22.
26 Tinker, *A Message from the Falklands*.
27 With kind permission of Captain David Hart Dyke.
28 Lippiett, *War and Peas*, p. 165.
29 The US Secretary of State.
30 With kind permission of Christine Mates.
31 With kind permission of David Morgan.
32 The British taskforce landing at San Carlos, 21 May.
33 Actions that contributed to his award of the Distinguished Service Cross.
34 John H. Jones Wilsey, VC, *The Life and Death of an Unusual Hero*, London, Arrow, 2003.
35 Three other men were killed in the incident: Captain David Wood, Captain Chris Dent and Corporal Hardman.
36 Radio title for commander.
37 *The Times*, 31 May 1982.

38 With kind permission of Margaret Howe.
39 With kind permission of José Scaglia.

8 CONFLICTS IN IRAQ AND AFGHANISTAN

1 Rifleman Martin Kingett, killed in Afghanistan, February 2010, with kind permission of Freya Ballatyne.
2 Bush's State of the Union address in January 2002 first used this term, to describe all governments accused of helping and harbouring terrorism and seeking or producing weapons of mass destruction.
3 Former British Prime Minister Tony Blair's description of his relationship with Bush.
4 Peter Darman, *Blood, Sweat and Steel: Frontline Accounts from the Gulf, Afghanistan and Iraq*, London, New Holland, 2010, p. 13.
5 Ethnic Afghan.
6 Nick Allen, *Embed*, Stroud, Spellmount, 2010, p. 266.
7 No weapons of mass destruction were ever found in Iraq.
8 Wikileaks have published these estimates, with no official endorsement of their veracity.
9 *Guardian*, 2 December 2006.
10 Allen, *Embed*, p. 74.
11 *Last Letters Home*, HBO and the New York Times, a film by Bill Couturié (2005).
12 'Last Letters from Kandahar', *Macleans Magazine*, 31 October 2007.
13 *New York Times*, 25 March 2008.
14 *Last Letters Home*.
15 *Guardian*, 2 December 2006.
16 'Last Letters from Kandahar', *Macleans Magazine*, 31 October 2007.
17 *Guardian*, 2 December 2006.
18 http://www.rickross.com/reference/islamic/islamic90.html.
19 *Last Letters Home*.
20 British soldiers would get on average thirty minutes of calls per week.
21 Andy McNab (ed.), *Spoken from the Front: Real Voices from the Battlefields of Afghanistan*, London, Transworld, 2009, p. 103.
22 James Fergusson, *A Million Bullets: The Real Story of the British Army in Afghanistan*, London, Bantam Press, 2008, p. 282.
23 *New York Times*, 25 March 2008.
24 Ibid.
25 Op Minimize: all communication is routinely shut down when an incident has occurred, to prevent news leaking out before the next-of-kin have been informed.
26 Allen, *Embed*, p. 47.
27 Ibid, p. 61.
28 Their former power-base.
29 'Last Letters from Kandahar', *Macleans Magazine*, 31 October 2007
30 *New York Times*, 25 March 2008.
31 An American policy (repealed in December 2010) barring gay military from revealing their sexual orientation.
32 *Huffington Post*, 12 December 2010.
33 'Last Letters from Kandahar', *Macleans Magazine*, 31 October 2007
34 With kind permission of John Hyde.
35 *Newsweek Magazine*, March 2007.
36 With kind permission of Charles and Leigh Nurre.
37 An internationally renowned military exercise over tough terrain, carrying over sixty pounds of kit

38 With kind permission of Helen O'Pray.
39 The main armoured battle-tank.
40 With kind permission of Melissa Givens.
41 Dress uniform.
42 With kind permission of Eddie Hancock.
43 Tony's pet name for his parents.
44 A running gag where Tony would pick up his mum and put her in the pub's bottle bin – regardless of where she was and how she was dressed.
45 With kind permission of Sheryl Downes.
46 With kind permission of Jane Little.
47 Andy Olmsted Blog, *Rocky Mountain News*.
48 http://obsidianwings.blogs.com/obsidian_wings/2008/01/andy-olmsted.html, with kind permission of Wes and Nancy Olmsted.

~ ~

BIBLIOGRAPHY

1 AT WAR WITH FRANCE

Bell, David A., *The First Total War*, London, Bloomsbury Publishing, 2007.

Chuquet, Arthur, *Human Voices from the Russian Campaign of 1812*, London, Andrew Melrose Ltd, 1913.

Fletcher, Ian (ed.), *In the Service of the King*, Staplehurst, Spellmount Ltd, 1997.

Fremont-Barnes, Gregory and Todd Fisher, *The Napoleonic Wars*, Oxford, Osprey Publishing, 2004.

Glover, Gareth, *Letters from the Battle of Waterloo*, London, Greenhill Books, 2004.

Hall, Christopher, *Wellington's Navy: Sea Power and the Peninsular War 1807–1814*, London, Chatham Publishing, 2004.

Hamilton, Lieutenant-General Sir F.W., *The Origin and History of the First or Grenadier Guards*, London, John Murray, 1874.

Hart, B.H. Liddell, *The Letters of Private Wheeler 1809–1828*, Moreton-in-Marsh: Windrush Press, 1951.

Körner, Christian Gottfried, Theodor Körner, George Fleming Richardson and Frederich Kind, *The Life of Carl Theödor Corner*, London, Thomas Hurst & Co., 1827.

Lee, Christopher, *Nelson and Napoleon: The Long Haul to Trafalgar*, London, Headline, 2005.

Llewellyn, Frederick (ed.), *Waterloo Recollections*, Leonaur Ltd, 2007.

Siborne, William, *History of the War in France and Belgium in 1815*, London, British Library, 2010.

Snow, Peter, *To War with Wellington*, London, John Murray, 2010.

Uffindell, Andrew, *The National Army Museum Book of Wellington's Armies*, Oxford, Sidgwick & Jackson, 2003.

Wheeler, H.F.B and A.M. Broadley, *Napoleon and the Invasion of England*, Stroud, Nonsuch Publishing, 2007.

2 THE AMERICAN CIVIL WAR

Adams, Virginia (ed.), *One the Altar of Freedom: A Black Soldier's Civil War Letters from the Front*, New York, Warner Books, 1991.

Crawford, Franklin R., *Proud to Say I Am a Union Soldier: The Last Letters Home from Federal Soldiers Written during the Civil War 1861–1865*, Maryland, Heritage Books, 2005.

Foreman, Amanda, *A World on Fire: An Epic History of Two Nations Divided*, London, Allen Lane, 2010.

Hunter, Jerry, *Sons of Arthur, Children of Lincoln: Welsh Writing from the American Civil War*, Cardiff, University of Wales Press, 2007.

Keegan, John, *The American Civil War*, London, Hutchinson, 2009.

Lane, Mills (ed.), *Dear Mother: Don't Grieve About Me. If I Get Killed, I'll Only Be Dead. Letters from Georgia Soldiers in the Civil War*, Savannah, GA, Beehive Press, 1977.

Margraff, William F., *A Civil War Soldier's Last Letters*, New York, Vantage Press, 1975.

McPherson, James. M., *Battle Cry of Freedom: The Civil War Era*, New York, Oxford University Press, 1988.
Sheehan-Dean, Aaron (ed.), *Struggle for a Vast Future: The American Civil War*, Oxford, Osprey Publishing, 2006.
Smith, Gustavus Woodson, *The Battle of Seven Pines*, New York, C.G. Crawford, 1891.
Young, Robin, *For Love and Liberty: The Untold Civil War Story of Major Sullivan Ballou and his Famous Love Letter*, New York, Thunder's Mouth Press, 2006.

Articles
Faust, Drew Gilpin, 'The Civil War Soldier and the Art of Dying', *Journal of Southern History*, Vol. 67 (February 2001).
Jones, Evan C. 'Sullivan Ballou: The Macabre Fate of an American Civil War Major', *America's Civil War*, November 2004.
Pedley, Brian, 'What Did You Do in the Civil War, Dafydd?', *The Times*, 8 January 2004.

Television
The American Civil War, dir. Ken Burns, 1990.
Abraham Lincoln: Saint or Sinner, BBC4, February 2011.

3 THE ANGLO-ZULU WAR

Bancroft, James, *The Rorke's Drift Men*, Stroud, Spellmount, 2010.
Bartlett, W.B., *Zulu: Queen Victoria's Most Famous Little War*, Stroud, The History Press, 2010.
Curtis, S.J., *History of Education in Great Britain*, London, University Tutorial Press, 1948.
David, Saul, *Zulu*, London, Penguin, 2004.
Emery, Frank, *Marching over Africa: Letters from Victorian Soldiers*, Kent, Hodder and Stoughton, 1986.
Emery, Frank, *The Red Soldier*, Kent, Hodder and Stoughton, 1977.
Filon, Augustin, *Recollections of the Empress Eugenie*, London, Cassell & Co., 1920.
Filon, Augustin, *The Prince Imperial*, London, William Heinemann, 1913.
Greaves, Adrian, *Rorke's Drift*, London, Cassell & Co., 2002.
John, Katherine, *The Prince Imperial*, London, Putnam, 1939.
Knight, Ian, *The Zulu War*, Basingstoke, Sidgwick & Jackson, 2003.
Knight, Ian and Ian Castle, *Zulu War*, Oxford, Osprey Publishing, 2004.
Morris, Donald, *The Washing of the Spears*, London, Sphere, 1973.
Mackinnon, J.P., and S.H. Shadbolt, *The South African Campaign of 1879*, reprinted London, Greenhill Books, 1995.
Porter, Whitworth, *History of the Corps of Royal Engineers*, London, Longmans, Green & Co., 1889.
Seward, Desmond, *Eugénie*, Stroud, Sutton Publishing, 2004.

Articles
David, Saul, 'The Forgotten Battles of the Zulu War', *BBC History Magazine*, February 2009.
Diamond, Michael, 'Popular Entertainment and the Zulu War', *Journal of the Anglo-Zulu War Historical Society*, December 1998.
Emery, Frank, 'The Anglo-Zulu War as Depicted in Soldiers' Letters', *South African Military History Society Journal*, June 1982.
Knight, Ian, 'A Minor Episode of the Campaign', *Journal of the Anglo-Zulu War Historical Society*, June 2004.
Laband, John, 'An Empress in Zululand', *Journal of the Anglo-Zulu War Historical Society*, June 2000.

Television and Radio
The Sun Turned Black, Radio Wales, 1999.
'Zulu: The True Story', *Timewatch*, BBC Television, 2004.

4 THE BOER WAR

Emery, Frank, *Marching Over Africa. Letters from Victorian Soldiers*, Kent, Hodder & Stoughton, 1986.

Fremont-Barnes, Gregory, *The Boer War*, Oxford, Osprey, 2003.

Gilson, Captain Charles J.L., *History of the 1st Batt. Sherwood Foresters in the Boer War*, London, Swan Sonnerschein & Co., 1908.

Hancock, W.K., *Smuts: The Sanguine Years 1870–1919*, London, Cambridge University Press, 1962.

Jackson, Tabitha, *The Boer War*, London, Channel 4 Books, 1999.

Judd, Denis and Keith Surridge, *The Boer War*, London, John Murray, 2003.

Maddrell, Roslyn, *Letters from the Front: Boer War to WWII through Letters Sent by Servicemen to their Families in Braidwood*, Braidwood, Roslyn Maddrell, 2004.

Pakenham, Thomas, *The Boer War*, London, Weidenfeld and Nicolson, 1979.

Reitz, Deneys, *Commando, A Boer Journal of the Boer War*, London, Faber & Faber, 1929.

Wilcox, Craig, *Australia's Boer War*, Melbourne, Oxford University Press, 2002.

Wilkinson, Frank, *Australia at the Front: A Colonial View of the Boer War*, London, John Long, 1901.

Witton, G.R., *Scapegoats of the Empire*, Clock and Rose Press, 2004.

Articles

Du Toit, Pierre, 'The War Experiences of Mike du Toit: Eleven Days in the Anglo-Boer War', *Journal of the South African Military History Society*, Vol. 11, No. 5 (2000).

'Fortune and Valour', *Journal of the 12th/16th Hunter River Lancers*, 1991.

Garson, N.G., 'Smuts, the South African National War Museum and 1967', *Journal of the South African Military History Society*, Vol. 10, No. 6 (1997).

Henry, Adam, 'Australian Nationalism and Lost Lessons of the Boer War', *Journal of the Australian War Memorial*, No. 34 (June 2001).

Hoy, Anthony, 'Breaker Morant: Justice Denied', *The Bulletin*, Article 19.

Karrageorgos, Effie, 'Loyal to the Empire? An Alternative View of Australian Soldiers in the South African War, 1899–1902', paper presented at Bristol University, 19 May 2010.

Pretoriana, Magazine of the Old Pretoria Society, No. 56 and 57 (1968).

Saks, David, 'The Wartime Correspondence of Jeannot Weinberg', *Journal of the South African Military History Society*, Vol. 12, No. 1 (June 2001).

Smart, Andy, 'Boer War Fighter who Never Returned Home', *Nottingham Evening Post*, 6 May 2010.

Smith, R.W., 'Modderfontein 17 September 1901', *Journal of the South African Military History Society*, Vol. 13, No. 1 (2004).

5 THE GREAT WAR

Barton, Peter, *Passchendaele: Unseen Panoramas of the Third Battle of Ypres*, London, Constable, 2007.

Bickersteth, John (ed.), *The Bickersteth Diaries*, Barnsley, Pen and Sword, 2005.

Campbell, P.M., *Letters from Gallipoli*, Edinburgh, privately published, 1916.

Carlyon, Les, *Gallipoli*, Sydney, Pan Macmillan, 2001.

Day-Lewis, C. (ed.), *The Collected Poems of Wilfred Owen*, London, Chatto & Windus, 1963.

Freeman, RR., *Hurcombe's Hungry Half Hundred: A Memorial History of the 50th Battalion A.I.F 1916–1919*, Norwood, South Australia, Peacock Publications, 1991.

Gammage, Bill, *Broken Years: Australian Soldiers in the Great War*, Melbourne, Penguin Books, 1975.

Holmes, Richard, *Tommy: The British Soldier on the Western Front 1914–1918*, London, Harper Perennial, 2004.

Jay, Barrie, *Early Forces Mail*, Bristol, Stuart Rossiter Trust Fund and Robert Johnson, 1997.

Macdonald, Lyn, *They Called it Passchendaele: The Story of the Third Battle of Ypres and the Men who Fought in it*, London, Book Club Associates, 1978.

Moynihan, Michael (ed.), *A Place Called Armageddon, Letters from the Great War*. Newton Abbot, David & Charles, 1975.

Passingham, Ian, *All the Kaiser's Men. The Life and Death of the German Army on the Western Front 1914–1918*, Stroud, Sutton Publishing, 2003.

Pootle, Mark and John Ledingham (eds), *We Hope to Get Word Tomorrow. The Garvin Family Letters 1914–1916*, London, Frontline Books, 2009.

Sheffield, Gary, *The Somme*, London, Cassell, 2003.

Sheldon, Jack, *The German Army on Vimy Ridge 1914–1917*, London, Frontline Books, 2008.

Warner, Philip, *The Battle of Loos*, Oxford, Purnell, 1976.

Witkop, Philipp (ed.), *German Students' War Letters*, London, Methuen & Co., 1929

6 THE SECOND WORLD WAR

Bayly, Christopher and Tim Harper, *Forgotten Armies. Britain's Asian Empire and the War with Japan*, London, Penguin, 2005.

Boegel, Gary, *Boys of the Clouds: An Oral History of the 1st Canadian Parachute Regiment 1942–1945*, Bloomington, IN, Trafford Publishing, 2005.

Day-Lewis, Tamasin (ed.), *Last Letters Home*, London, Macmillan, 1995.

Dring, Colin Martin, *A History of RAF Mildenhall*, Mildenhall, Mildenhall Museum Publishing, 1980.

Fritz, Stephen G., *Frontsoldaten. The German Soldier in World War II*, Lexington, KT, University Press of Kentucky, 1995.

Gardner, Ian and Roger Day, *Tonight We Die as Men*, Oxford: Osprey Publishing, 2009.

Hartigan, Dan, *A Rising of Courage. Canada's Paratroops in the Liberation of Normandy*, Calgary, Drop Zone Publishers, 2000.

Larteguy, Jean(ed.) and Nora Wydenbruck (trans.), *The Sun Goes Down: Last Letters from Japanese Suicide-Pilots and Soldiers*, London, William Kimber & Co. Ltd, 1956.

Peters, Major M.L. and Luuk Buist, *Glider Pilots at Arnhem*, Barnsley, Pen & Sword Aviation, 2008.

Place, Timothy Harrison, *Military Training in the British Army, 1940–1944*, Oxford, Routledge, 2000.

Ross, Tony and Joan Charles, *Dear Joan: Love Letters from the Second World War*, Edinburgh, Mainstream Publishing, 2010.

Seaton, Albert, *German Army: 1933–45*, Worthing, Littlehampton Book Services, 1982.

Shephard, Ben, *A War of Nerves: Soldiers and Psychiatrists in the Twentieth Century*, Cambridge, MA, Harvard University Press, 2001.

Sommerville, Donald, *The Complete Illustrated History of World War Two*, London, Lorenz Books, 2008.

Tapert, Annette, *Despatches from the Heart*, London, Hamish Hamilton, 1984.

Television and Radio
The Battle of Britain, BBC1, 2010.
Battle of Britain Night, BBC4, 2010.
Wellington Bomber, Peter Williams Television for BBC4, 2010.

7 THE FALKLANDS CONFLICT

Eyles-Thomas, Mark, *Sod That for a Game of Soldiers*, Stansted, Kenton Publishing, 2007.

Hart Dyke, David, *Four Weeks in May, A Captain's Story of War at Sea*, London, Atlantic Books, 2007.

Lippiett, Rear Admiral John, *War and Peas*, Bosham: Pistol Post Publications. 2007.

McManners, Hugh, *Forgotten Voices of the Falklands*, London, Ebury Press. 2008.

Morgan, David, *Hostile Skies: The Battle for the Falklands*, London, Phoenix, 2006.

Pike, Hew, *From the Front Line: Family Letters and Diaries 1900 to the Falklands and Afghanistan*, Barnsley, Pen and Sword, 2008.

Tinker, Lieutenant David, *A Message from the Falklands*, Harmondsworth, Penguin Books, 1983.
Wilsey, John H. Jones, VC, *The Life and Death of an Unusual Hero*, London, Arrow, 2003.

Television
Sea of Fire: HMS Coventry at War, BBC, June 2007.
Falklands 25: A Soldier's Story, ITV4, 2007.

Newspapers
Daily Mail
Guardian
Sun

8 CONFLICTS IN IRAQ AND AFGHANISTAN

Allawi, Ali A. *The Occupation of Iraq: Winning the War, Losing the Peace*, New Haven, CT, Yale University Press, 2007.
Allen, Nick, *Embed*, Stroud, Spellmount, 2010.
Blair, Tony, *A Journey*, London, Hutchinson, 2010.
Burden, Matthew Currier, *The Blog of War*, New York, Simon & Schuster, 2006.
Darman, Peter, *Blood, Sweat and Steel: Frontline Accounts from the Gulf, Afghanistan and Iraq*, London, New Holland, 2010.
Fergusson, James, *A Million Bullets: The Real Story of the British Army in Afghanistan*, London, Bantam, 2008.
Keegan, John, *The Iraq War*, London, Hutchinson, 2004.
McNab, Andy (ed.) *Spoken from the Front: Real Voices from the Battlefields of Afghanistan*, London, Transworld, 2009.
Sponek, H.C. von, *A Different Kind of War: The UN Sanctions Regime in Iraq*, Oxford, Berghahn Books, 2006.
Williamson, Murray and Major General Robert H. Scales, *The Iraq War*, Cambridge, Belknap Press of Harvard University Press, 2003.

Newspapers
Daily Mail
Guardian
Observer

Television and Radio
If You're Reading This, Tinderbox for BBC Radio 4, 2008.
Last Letters Home, HBO 2005.
Soldier's Haven, Tinderbox for BBC Radio 4, 2007.
Where Next: A Soldier's Journey, Tinderbox for BBC Radio 4, 2008.
While the Boys are Away, BBC Radio 4, March 2011.

INDEX